Legal Ontology Engineering

Law, Governance and Technology Series

VOLUME 3

Series Editors:

POMPEU CASANOVAS, *UAB Institute of Law and Technology, Bellaterra, Barcelona, Spain*

GIOVANNI SARTOR, *University of Bologna (Faculty of Law-CIRSFID) and European University Institute of Florence, Italy*

Scientific Advisory Board:

For further volumes:
http://www.springer.com/series/8808

Núria Casellas

Legal Ontology Engineering

Methodologies, Modelling Trends, and the Ontology of Professional Judicial Knowledge

Springer

Núria Casellas
Institute of Law and Technology
Universitat Autònoma de Barcelona
Edifici B
08193 Bellaterra
Spain
nuria.Casellas@uab.es

ISBN 978-94-007-3754-9 ISBN 978-94-007-1497-7 (eBook)
DOI 10.1007/978-94-007-1497-7
Springer Dordrecht Heidelberg London New York

Softcover reprint of the hardcover 1st edition 2011

Printed on acid-free paper

Springer is part of Springer Science+Business Media (www.springer.com)

To my mother, Roser,
and all my family.

Foreword

This is the third volume of the Law, Governance and Technology Series. The first one, also devoted to ontologies,[1] stressed the plurality of theoretical approaches and the diversity of applications that Semantic Web technologies have to offer to the legal domain. As Núria Casellas shows in this third one, legal ontologies come to the age as a specific set of related conceptual tools and techniques to assist people to perform better on their everyday tasks.

Short after the Internet and the World Wide Web, lawyers, judges and jurists have begun to realize that the use of technology has rapidly changed the habits of their working life. Sentencing, drafting or contracting are traditional legal tasks. However, they are nowadays performed following steps and internal processes which are already different. The way they are conducted now is not exactly the same as it was before, only 20 years ago.

This means that what we meant by "legal knowledge" has to be changed too. Legal knowledge becomes more complex as technology improves the way to handle it. Jurisprudence is not only a matter of legislation, rulings and doctrine. The way lawyers interact with information and knowledge systems is relevant as well.

In 2001, at the time we started up the Observatory of Judicial Culture in the Spanish Judicial School, only 20% of newly recruited judges had some computer skills. At present, all of them are used to browse over extended legal databases and, as we have had the opportunity to test several times along our Projects, they gather and compile freely information from the Internet–and not only from legislation, precedents and the case records–when ruling.

Here lies the reason why research on human-machine interaction, legal knowledge systems and Artificial Intelligence applications is so important for the law. Regulation will increasingly rely on our capability to convert massive information

[1] See Sartor et al. (2011).

into structured knowledge. And we must figure out tools that help us to properly manage information in concrete contexts and situations.

Núria Casellas shows in this volume that legal core and domain ontologies are crucial to develop such tools. In doing so, she draws a broad landscape. But, beyond that, I think the reader will find an added value, because she has been able to show at the same time the details of the whole ontology lifecycle. She describes knowledge acquisition techniques, ontology building methodologies, and evaluation tests within the realistic environment of Courts and judicial settings.

The Ontology for Professional Judicial Knowledge (OPJK) introduced in the volume is the result of an extended empirical research and many attempts to capture the nuances of practical and judicial knowledge. I remember her surprise coming back from her first fieldwork in several Spanish Courts, after interviewing not only Magistrates but clerks, court experts and attorneys, and thinking of how to proceed with this legal knowledge which is not contained into the legal rules and written procedures. She acknowledged that difficult theoretical problems are always grounded on practical problems and common behavior that have to be well described and understood, first. From this point of view, the ability to share and reuse knowledge is but an extension of what humans naturally do in their social environments. And these complexities gave rise to some questions, such as:

> How may we enable legal information interoperability? How may we foster legal knowledge usability and reuse between information and knowledge systems? How may we go beyond the mere linking of legal documents or the use of keywords or Boolean operators for legal information search? How may we formalize legal concepts and procedures in a machine-understandable form?
>
> In short, how may we handle the complexity of legal knowledge to enhance legal information search and retrieval or knowledge management, taking into account the structure and dynamic character of legal knowledge, its relation with common sense concepts, the distinct theoretical perspectives, the flavor and influence of legal practice in its evolution, and jurisdictional and linguistic differences?[2]

This means a user-centered approach to legal ontology building. I like the questions she raises, and I am glad I could help to raise them.

UAB, February 2011

Pompeu Casanovas
IDT Director

[2]Extracted from the blogpost "Semantic Enhancement of Legal Information. Are We Up for the Challenge?" available at: http://blog.law.cornell.edu/voxpop/2010/02/15/semantic-enhancement-of-legal-information%E2%80%A6-are-we-up-for-the-challenge/

Preface

Current needs for legal information and content management demand better solutions towards legal knowledge representation to enhance legal information search and retrieval or knowledge management. With the introduction not only of syntax but also of meaning in information exchange, information retrieval and information management and organization shall be enhanced and automated reasoning might be implemented. The implementation of technologies for human-machine understanding are the basis for the development of legal semantic applications.

Nowadays, these attempts have been driven by the success of the WWW and, especially, by the Semantic Web Vision. Berners-Lee et al. (2001) described the Semantic Web as an extension of the Web "in which information is given well-defined meaning, better enabling computers and people to work in cooperation." Thus, a shift from the current human-readable Web to the machine-readable Semantic Web, the use of knowledge representation languages and tools (ontologies) will allow semantics to be added to the Web or to semantic applications. Law, Knowledge Management and Artificial Intelligence thus converge in this interdisciplinary area of research.

This publication describes the ontologies as a type of knowledge representation and, specifically focuses on legal ontologies as the form of representation and formalization of legal knowledge, and discusses issues related to knowledge acquisition, knowledge extraction, modelling methodologies, tools for ontology construction, and ontology evaluation. For this, the book is devoted to the analysis of the definitions of 'ontology', and to offer an extensive account of legal ontologies present in the current literature.

From these initial analyses, this book will explore how legal experts or professionals may participate in legal ontology construction. To this end, this publication includes the experience of modeling an particular ontology for the legal domain, the Ontology of Professional Judicial Knowledge, as a case study. This ontology was developed during the participation of the Institute of Law and Technology (directed by Dr. Pompeu Casanovas) together with the software company iSOCO in the nationally funded project Iuriservice, which, in turn, was one of the case studies of the European research project SEKT (Semantically Enabled Knowledge Technologies (EU-IST-2003-506826).

The Ontology of Professional Judicial Knowledge represents practical judicial knowledge (ethnography) for the construction of an *intelligent* software application for information search and retrieval. This application, Iuriservice, is a web-based decision support tool directed to newly incorporated judges and it aims at supporting decision-making during their on-call period (Casanovas et al. 2004, 2005b). The aim of the system is to discover the best semantic match between the user's question or input question (formulated in natural language) and a stored question, so as to offer an answer that satisfies the user (Blázquez et al. 2005). To find the question-answer pair that best matches the input question, the system is enhanced with knowledge representation techniques from the area of artificial intelligence: ontologies.

This publication is based on the Ph.D research "Modelling Legal Knowledge through Ontologies. OPJK: the Ontology of Professional Judicial Knowledge" that was defended at the Law School of the Universitat Autnoma de Barcelona (UAB), in December 2008. In turn, that research was the result of my work in the Iuriservice and SEKT (Semantically Enabled Knowledge) projects, at the Institute of Law and Technology (IDT-UAB).

Therefore, I would like to thank Prof. Pompeu Casanovas for giving me the opportunity to discover and conduct stimulating research in the area of Law and Technology and to participate in such projects. The Iuriservice[1] and the SEKT[2] projects not only provided the framework of my research, but also entailed an outstanding professional opportunity and personal experience. From these two projects, I would like to thank every partner for all their guidance, and fruitful discussions. Especially, I would like to thank John Davies, Frank van Harmelen, Zhisheng Huang, Aleks Jakulin, Michel Klein, Atanas Kiryakov, Stefan Schlobach, York Sure, Christopher Tempich, Ian Thurlow, Johanna Vlker, Denny Vrandecic, for their support and collaboration during the SEKT Project, and to Richard Benjamins, Mercedes Blzquez, Jess Contreras, Jos Manuel Lpez-Cobo, and Ral Pea from the iSOCO company in the Iuriservice project and the SEKT Legal case study. Finally, I would like to thank all the colleagues that worked and helped or contributed somehow to the development of the Iuriservice system and its ontology, including evaluation experts and the judges of Spanish School of the Judiciary.

I would also like to thank Mark Musen (Stanford Center for Biomedical Informatics Research) to allow me to prolong my stay in the United States after the ICAIL International 2007 conference, and to Daniela Tiscornia (Istituto di Teoria e Tecniche dell'Informazione Giuridica, ITTIG) for kindly allowing me to finish my thesis research in Italy.[3]

[1] FIT-150500-2002-562 and MEC SEJ2006-10695.

[2] EU-IST-2003-506826.

[3] This stay in Italy was financially supported by AGAUR (2008-BE-1-00076).

The content of this book has been extended from that initial research in order to include more recent ontology modelling efforts. In this sense, I would like to express my gratitude for all the valuable comments and criticisms received by my thesis tribunal, reviewers and colleagues, which helped make significant improvements to this final publication: Joost Breuker, John Davies, Enrico Franceconi, Giovanni Sartor, Marco Schorlemmer, Daniela Tiscornia, etc. Moreover, I would also like to acknowledge some of the recent projects (such as OntoMedia or NEURONA), where I have participated in the ontology design and development tasks in these last years.[4]

I am also grateful to all my colleagues from the Institute of Law and Technology, and from the Legal Philosophy area, the Political Science and Public Law Department, and, in general, from the UAB Law School, for always supporting me and encouraging me in this and all other tasks. In particular, I would like to thank Josep Maria de Dios and Francesca Puigpelat, for all their help.

Special thanks to Joan-Josep Vallbé for all the unconditional support, fruitful discussions, comments, technical assistance, and version proof-reading. Needless to say that any inaccuracies or errors are but my own.

Last, but not least, I would like to thank my family and friends for their neverending patience and encouragement.

Bellaterra

Núria Casellas
January 2011

[4]ONTOMEDIA: TSI-020501-2008-131, Neurona (AVANZA) Project: TSI-200100-2008-134, SGR 2009SGR-0688, and CSO-2008-05536-SOCI.

Contents

List of Figures

List of Tables

Acronyms

AAAI	Association for the Advancement of Artificial Intelligence
AI	Artificial Intelligence
AKEM	Application Knowledge Engineering Methodology
BATNA	Best Alternative to a Negotiated Agreement
CABALA	Consultazione Assistita di Basi di Dati di Leggi Ambientali
CODeP	Conceptual or Content Design Patterns
CLO	Core Legal Ontology
CContology	Customer Complaint Ontology
DODDLE	Domain Ontology rapiD DeveLopment Environment
DOLCE	Descriptive Ontology for Linguistic and Cognitive Engineering
EU	European Union
FBO	Frame-based Ontology of Law
FOLaw	Functional Ontology of Law
HCOME	Human-Centered Ontology Engineering Methodology
HTML	HyperText Markup Language
IAAIL	International Association for Artificial Intelligence and Law
ICAIL	International Conference on Artificial Intelligence and Law
IJCAI	International Joint Conference on Artificial Intelligence
IPROnto	Intellectual Property Rights Ontology
Jur-IWN	Jur-(Ital)Wordnet
KAON	Karlsruhe Ontology Management Infrastructure
KBS	Knowledge-based Systems
KM	Knowledge Management
KR	Knowledge Representation
KSE	Knowledge Sharing Effort
LKIF	Legal Knowledge Interchange Format
LLD	Language for Legal Discourse
MAS	Multi-Agent System
MTCO	Multi Tier Contract Ontology
NeOn	Networked Ontologies

NLP	Natural Language Processing
OCL.NL	Ontology of Dutch Criminal Law
ONIONS	ONtologic Integration On Nave Sources
OPJK	Ontology of Professional Judicial Knowledge
ORSD	Ontology Requirement Specification Document
OTK	On-To-Knowledge
OWL	Ontology Web Language
PROTON	PROTo ONtology
PSM	Problem-solving Method
RDF	Resource Description Language
SEKT	Semantically Enabled Knowledge Technologies
SKOS	Simple Knowledge Organization System
SPARQL	SPARQL Protocol and RDF Query Language
SUMO	Suggested Upper Merged Ontology
T2K	Text to Knowledge
UPON	Unified Process for ONtology
URI	Uniform Resource Identifier
UCC	US Uniform Commercial Code
W3C	World Wide Web Consortium
WWW	World Wide Web
XML	eXtensible Markup Language

Chapter 1
Introduction

1.1 Legal Knowledge Management

The organization and formalization of legal information for computer processing in order to support decision-making or enhance information search, retrieval and knowledge management is not recent, and neither is the need to represent legal knowledge in a machine-readable form. Since the first ideas of computerization of the law on the late 1940s early 1950s (American School of Jurimetrics[1]) and the appearance of the first legal information systems in the 1950s and the first legal expert systems in the 1970s, paraphrasing Bing (1991), computers have now been used in legal information systems for more than 60 years.[2]

Traditionally, the most important meeting points between Law and Computer Science (Legal Informatics, Legal Information Technology, Legal Knowledge Management, Artificial Intelligence and Law, etc.[3]) have been legal information search and retrieval, legal knowledge representation and management, legal reasoning, argumentation and expert and knowledge-based systems (KBS) design.

In particular, the formalization of legal information and knowledge for computer processing was of interest to the Artificial Intelligence (AI) community since its first steps. Nevertheless, although the American Association for Artificial Intelligence (AAAI, currently the Association for the Advancement of Artificial

[1]See Mulder et al. (2010) for a recent redefinition of *jurimetrics*.

[2]See Bing (1991) for an extensive introduction to legal information retrieval systems until the 1980s (or Bing (2010) for a brief account), and Bench-Capon (1990) for an account of legal knowledge based systems until the 1990s. Also, see Leith (2010) and Susskind (2010) for a critique of expert systems in the legal domain and a personal view on the development of legal informatics, respectively.

[3]This is to be distinguished from Information Technology Law or Computer Law, which refers to the legal implications of the (mis)use of information and communication technologies, computers, intelligent agents and electronic institutions (e.g. surveillance and privacy, cybercrime, intellectual property, robot liability, etc.).

N. Casellas, *Legal Ontology Engineering: Methodologies, Modelling Trends, and the Ontology of Professional Judicial Knowledge*, Law, Governance and Technology Series 3,
DOI 10.1007/978-94-007-1497-7_1, © Springer Science+Business Media B.V. 2011

Intelligence) was founded in 1979 and the International Joint Conference on Artificial Intelligence (IJCAI) is taking place every 2 years since 1969, the AI and Law community began much later. For example, the International Association for Artificial Intelligence and Law (IAAIL) was founded on 1987 and the first meeting of the ICAIL conference (now the biennial official conference of IAAIL) took place in Boston on that same year, and the Foundation for Legal Knowledge Based Systems (JURIX) has held annual international conferences on legal knowledge and information systems since 1988.[4]

A significant panel of the IJCAI 1985 conference entitled *AI and Legal Reasoning*, chaired by Edwina Rissland,[5] discussed the characteristics of the legal domain and its main points of interest for the application of AI techniques. The discussion was directed at pointing out the challenge that the legal domain and its special characteristics offered to AI (Rissland 1985)[6]:

1. "While it is a domain which has established standards for deriving new truths (e.g., *stare decisis* or the doctrine of precedent), it is more of a "scruffy" domain than a "neat" one, despite its orderly, rule-like surface veneer. It is very much an experience-based example-driven field";
2. "Legal reasoning and argumentation take special skills and that learning to think like a lawyer requires considerably more than rote memorization of a large number of cases, a daunting task in itself";
3. The legal domain "has the unique property of being pseudo-formalized, i.e., there exists a large body of formal rules that purport to define and regulate activity in the domain. However, these rules are often deliberately ambiguous, contradictory and incomplete" (D.A. Waterman);
4. "The Law combines many different kinds of reasoning processes" such as rule-based, case-based, analogical, hypothetical (D.A. Waterman);
5. "The Law is in a constant state of change, so expert legal reasoning systems have to be easy to modify and update" (D.A. Waterman);
6. "Law is an area for "expert systems" in the sense of involving professional knowledge but it is unusual in that we have to expect the experts to disagree" (A. Garner);
7. and the idea that, in legal reasoning, natural language and common sense understanding are intertwined (A. Gardner). Moreover, "modelling what a lawyer does is more complex than modelling experts in technical/scientific domains. First, all of these complex conceptualizations are expressed in natural language, so modelling the comprehension ability of the lawyer requires solving the natural language problem" (M.O. Dyer).

[4]JURIX was initially a Dutch conference that took international dimensions later on. See also the workshop DEON (tri-annual workshop on deontic logics), at http://www.defeasible.org/deon2010, retrieved August 18, 2010.

[5]Panel: Kevin D. Ashley, Michael O. Dyer, Ann Gardner, L. Thorne McCarty and Donald A. Waterman.

[6]The synergy between AI and Law is revisited in Rissland et al. (2003).

Some other relevant issues and challenges discussed were:

- The open-textured nature of legal concepts and the implications this has for using AI-techniques, especially knowledge representation;
- The complementarity of rule-based and case-based reasoning – how cases are used, especially when rules "run out";
- The pervasive role of analogy in legal reasoning;
- The special role played by hypotheticals in the legal domain and how hypos help with argumentation and strategic case planning. Hypotheticals "remake experience, create experience, organize and cluster cases and tease out hidden assumptions" (E. Rissland);
- The interleaving of justification, explanation, and argumentation;
- The appropriateness and feasibility of intelligent aids for practicing litigators and other legal experts. Two main categories of intelligent applications for the legal domain were foreseen: conceptual legal retrieval systems and legal analysis and planning systems (L.T. McCarty).[7]

For 40 years now, different artificial intelligence and knowledge engineering[8] techniques have been applied to the legal domain to construct expert and other knowledge-based systems.[9] According to Schreiber et al. (1999) the top three benefits obtained from the use of knowledge systems (in general) are (a) faster decision-making, (b) increased productivity, and (c) increased quality in decision-making.

And from this previous experience, during the 1990s, the knowledge management discipline took off with the widespread of information and communication technologies and the growing interest in knowledge – procedural and

---

[7]It is interesting to note that the panel showed a "cautious optimism that it would eventually be possible to develop a lawyer's workbench which would include tools ranging from standard retrieval tools like the existing WESTLAW and LEXIS full text retrieval systems, document generation aids, scheduling and calendar managers, to tools needing more intelligence like briefing assistants and interpretive analysis programs which could understand cases. This caution is based upon the nearly common experience of how long it takes to develop a program that can handle a few cases or problems, let alone the plethora occurring in real practice" (Rissland 1985).

[8]"Knowledge engineering has evolved from the late 1970s onward, from the art of building expert systems, knowledge-based systems, and knowledge-intensive information systems... Knowledge systems are the single most important industrial and commercial offspring of the discipline called artificial intelligence" (Schreiber et al. 1999).

[9]"Knowledge-based systems (KBS) is a subfield of artificial intelligence concerned with creating programs that embody the reasoning expertise of human experts... The systems are at times referred to as *expert systems* and the terms are informally used interchangeably. 'Expert system' is however better thought of as referring to the level of aspiration for the system. If it can perform as well as an expert, then it can play that role; this has been done, but is relatively rare. More commonly the systems perform as intelligent assistants, making recommendations for a human to review. Speaking of them as expert systems thus sets too narrow a perspective and restricts the utility of the technology" (Davies 1999).

conceptual – [10] as an important asset of government and commercial organizations (van Engers 2001). Therefore, the legal domain, as a (professional) knowledge intensive domain was again considered a rich area for the development of knowledge management applications and for knowledge acquisition, modelling and engineering techniques.

Nevertheless, claims such as "searching a large database is an important and time-consuming part of legal work" (Hafner 1980), "our programming research was initiated by the needs of lawyers for high speed computer assistance in their studies" (Kehl et al. 1961), or "the large volume of legal information and the enormous effort required to manually abstract and index cases for every domain of law call for a system which automates the process" (Gelbart and Smith 1991), which drove the development of legal expert systems during the 1980s and 1990s, have not yet been left behind.[11]

Similar claims may be found nowadays as, on the one hand, the amount of available unstructured (or poorly structured) legal information and documents made available by governments, free access initiatives, or *blawgs* is rapidly growing,[12] and all these legal information and legal portals on the Web will probably keep growing as the Web expands. And, on the other, the increasing quantity of legal data managed by legal publishing companies, law firms, and government agencies, together with the high quality requirements applicable to legal information knowledge search, discovery, and management (e.g., access and privacy issues, copyright, etc.) have renewed the need to develop and implement better content management tools and methods.

Information overload, however important, is not the only concern for the future of legal knowledge management; other and growing demands are increasing the complexity of the requirements that legal information management systems and, in

[10] Knowledge acquisition from experts may not only be procedural but also conceptual (Steels 1990; Milton 2007). See also Gaines and Shaw (1989) for a comparison of expert's conceptual systems.

[11] "It is an interesting matter that since the classic 'Handbook of Legal Information Retrieval' edited by Jon Bing was published in 1984, improvement in legal information retrieval has not seen any major advancement. Quite to the contrary, information overload and increased demand for cross-national and cross-lingual legal information has amplified the basic problems. (…) Legal information retrieval systems still do not represent legal structural knowledge, user friendliness regarding search strategies and input formats is lacking, and information about system functions and information content (completeness) is often not sufficient. Also, continuity, representation of time layers and consolidated versions are inadequate and different user situations and information needs are disregarded. Finally, finding the correct search terms is a game of change, language approximation is minimal and even simple linguistic tools are missing" (Liebwald 2007).

[12] Nowadays, also a growing amount of legal information can be found and extracted from Web portals used by the legal community. For example, legal blogs or *blawgs* focus on discussions of substantive law and court decisions or procedural and professional matters (Conrad and Schilder 2007). See the following blawg portals: *Blawgs* at http://www.blawg.com, and the *Rutgers University Law Library guide to legal blogs* at http://law-library.rutgers.edu/resources/lawblogs.php, retrieved November 10, 2008.

consequence, legal knowledge representation must face in the future. Multilingual search and retrieval of legal information to enable, for example, integrated search between the legislation of several European countries (Ajani et al. 2007b), enhanced laymen understanding and access to e-government and e-administration sites or to online dispute resolution capabilities (e.g., BATNA determination in Uijttenbroek et al. (2007a)), legal training and e-learning support (legal reasoning) (Ashley 2009), e-government applications (Cabinet Office 2006; Adams 2008; Charalabidis and Metaxiotis 2009), the regulatory basis and capabilities of electronic institutions or normative and multi-agent systems or MAS (Drumond et al. 2007; Aldewereld et al. 2006; Vázquez-Salceda et al. 2005; Rodríguez-Aguilar 2001), and multimedia, privacy or digital rights management systems, are just some examples of these demands (Bourcier et al. 2010; Genesereth et al. 2010).

Therefore, with these increasing needs for legal information and content management, there is an urgent need to handle the complexity of legal knowledge to construct conceptual structures for knowledge representation to enhance legal information search and retrieval or knowledge management, making human-machine communication and understanding possible.[13]

McCarty emphasized at that 1985 panel that "successful work in law and AI – both theory and application – requires much better *conceptual models* of the legal domain than the field of AI can currently provide 'off-the-shelf'" (Rissland 1985). Currently, legal knowledge representation and, accordingly, of knowledge acquisition, continues to be of most importance for knowledge management in the legal domain. With the introduction not only of syntax but also of meaning in information exchange, information retrieval and information management and organization shall be enhanced and automated reasoning might be implemented. The implementation of technologies for human-machine understanding are the basis for the development of legal semantic applications. AI and KM attempts have been driven by the success of the WWW and, especially, by the Semantic Web vision.

1.2 Semantic Web Technologies and Applications

Berners-Lee et al. (2001) described the Semantic Web as an extension of the Web "in which information is given well-defined meaning, better enabling computers and people to work in cooperation." Thus, we need to shift from the current human-readable Web to the machine-readable Semantic Web (Berners-Lee and Fischetti 1999; Berners-Lee et al. 2001; Berners-Lee 2003).

[13]A recent referential publication on Semantic Web technologies and applications begins with: "That we need a new approach to managing information is beyond doubt. The technological developments of the last few decades, including the development of the World Wide Web, have provided each of us with access to far more information than we can comprehend or manage effectively" (Warren et al. 2006).

Therefore, the Semantic Web is a prolongation of the current Web, sometimes also referred to as Web 3.0,[14] enriched with semantic metadata, with *meaning*. "This contrasts with the metadata on today's Web, encoded in HTML (HyperText Markup Language), which purely describes the format in which the information should be presented: using HTML, you can specify that a given string should be displayed in bold, red font but you cannot specify that the string denotes a product price, or an author's name, and so on" (Warren et al. 2006). The use of semantic metadata could enhance the storage, search and retrieval of information, together with human-computer interaction. "The aim of the Semantic Web is to allow much more advanced knowledge management systems," and to overcome current limitations regarding searching information, extracting information, maintaining information, uncovering information and viewing information (Antoniou and van Harmelen 2004b, 2008).

These efforts also include the Web of Data (or Linked Data), which relies on the existence of standard formats to allow the access and query of interrelated datasets, which may be granted through SPARQL endpoints (e.g. Govtrack.us, Legislation.gov.uk, etc.). Sharing and connecting data on the Web in compliance with the Linked Data principles enables the exploitation of content from different Web data sources with the development of search, browse, and other mashup applications (see the Linking Open Data cloud diagram in Fig. 1.1).[15]

For example, in the search and retrieval area, nowadays we still perform most legal searches in online or application databases using keywords (that we believe to be contained in the document that we are searching for), maybe together with a combination of Boolean operators, or supported with a set of predefined categories (metadata regarding, for example, date, type of court, etc.), a list of pre-established topics, thesauri (e.g., EuroVoc, Westlaw (2003)), or a synonym-enhanced search.[16]

[14]"There is no widespread agreement on exactly what the semantic web is for or exactly what it is. Some good ideas about what the semantic web will be used for have emerged from the W3C effort to define a standard ontology language" (Uschold 2003). Further, there exist different visions regarding the enhancement of the current web (already an extension of the original that now encompasses collaborative tools and social networks, a social web or web 2.0): folksonomies, social tagging, folktologies, etc. For an insight of some of the discussions see, for example, Uschold (2003), Gruber (2005, 2006) and d'Aquin et al. (2007). Also, the AAAI 2009 Spring Symposia included a symposium entitled "Social Semantic Web: Where Web 2.0 Meets Web 3.0" (http://tw.rpi.edu/sss09, retrieved August 18, 2010), and the International Semantic Web Conference 2010 hold the Third International Workshop on Social Data on the Web (SDoW2010) http://sdow.semanticweb.org/2010

[15]The Linked Open Data diagram may be found at http://richard.cyganiak.de/2007/10/lod/. For more details on Linked Data efforts and community visit http://linkeddata.org and http://www.w3.org/standards/semanticweb/data. Also, this topic was the object of a special issue of the *International Journal On Semantic Web and Information Systems* (see Bizer et al. (2009) and visit http://www.ijswis.org/?q=node/31 for more details).

[16]"Today, search engines for legal information retrieval do not include legal knowledge into their search strategies. These strategies include keyword and metadata search but do not address the semantics of the keywords, which would allow, for instance, conceptual query expansion. In other words, there is no semantic relationship between information needs of the user and the information

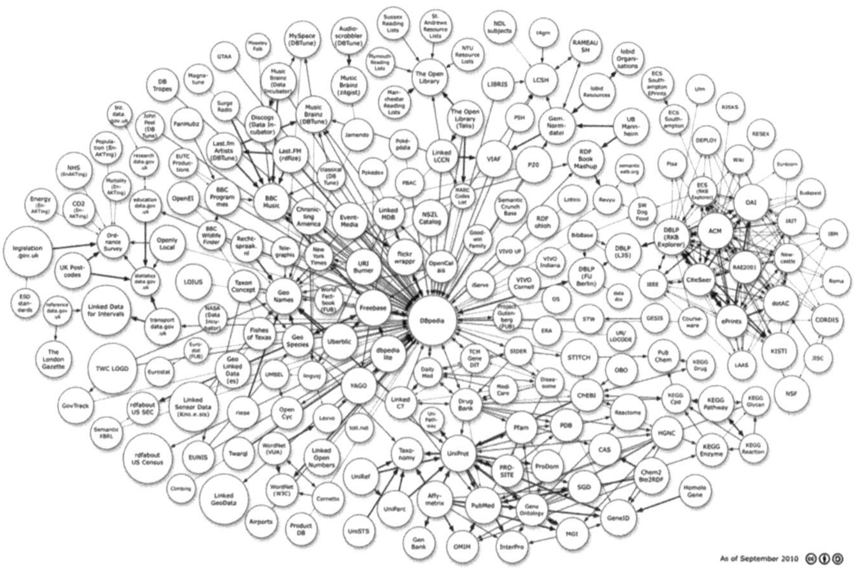

Fig. 1.1 The Linking Open Data cloud diagram by Cyganiak and Jentzsch

These searches rely mainly on syntactic matching, and – with the exception of searches enhanced through the use of categories, synonyms, or thesauri – they will return only documents that contain the exact term searched for. These searches do not offer solutions or help towards the interaction between symbols, terms, and concepts. To perform more complex searches, to go beyond the term, we require that the search engine *understand* the semantic level of legal documents; a shared understanding of the domain of knowledge becomes necessary.[17] The use of semantic metadata and knowledge technologies could improve the results. Also, it could (Warren et al. 2006):

- improve information visualization (result clustering, merging and summarization);
- offer reasoning capabilities and automatic knowledge creation;

---

content of documents apart from text pattern matching" (Peters et al. 2007). Also, different search algorithms have also been developed to aid searches and provide more precision and recall. See, for example, Google technology (http://www.google.com/corporate/tech.html, retrieved August 18, 2010) and Google research (http://research.google.com/about.html, retrieved August 18, 2010) or Yahoo! Research in search sciences (http://labs.yahoo.com/Search_Sciences). Finally, see Jones (2009) for a criticism on legal database interface design.

[17]Although efforts are being made by several legal companies to offer more accurate solutions, e.g., La Ley-Wolters Kluwver offers and expanded synonym search (http://www.atencionclientes.com/FAQ/LALEY/FAQ_Buscar_Sinonimos.htm).

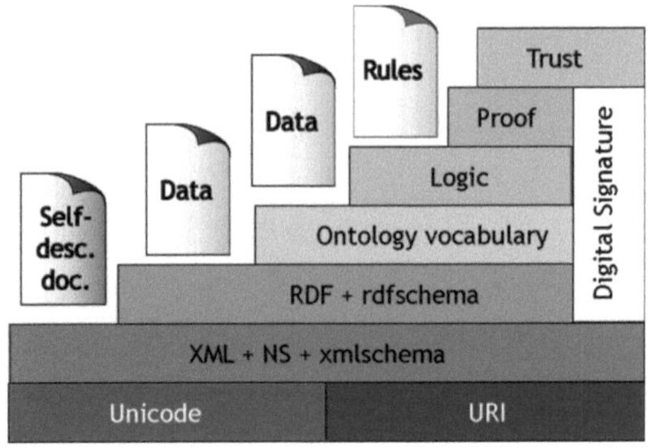

Fig. 1.2 Semantic Web Stack by Berners-Lee (2000)

- integrate information from heterogeneous sources (mappings);
- describe semantically web services functions towards large-scale implementations of service oriented architectures.

Towards that shift, new languages and tools (ontologies) were needed to allow semantics to be added to the current web as its development of the Semantic Web is based on the formal representation of meaning in order to share with computers the flexibility, intuition and capabilities of the conceptual structures of the human natural language. Making information machine-readable is just one step towards the envisaged possibility of global knowledge sharing and reusing (Berners-Lee et al. 2001). And, if meaning was to be *well-defined* and available for reuse, "it absolutely needs the interoperable infrastructure that only global standard protocols can provide" (Berners-Lee 2003).

The task of developing interoperable technologies (languages, guidelines, software and tools) was taken in by the World Wide Web Consortium (W3C).[18] These technologies were arranged in the Semantic Web Stack according to increasing levels of complexity. In this stack, higher layers depend on lower layers (and the latter are inherited from the original Web, see Fig. 1.2). A *layer cake* (Berners-Lee 2000) of technological complexity that has been modified and updated as technological changes and requirements have evolved (see the comparison in Fig. 1.3 or in Horrocks et al. (2005)).

These include URI (Uniform Resource Identifier) and Unicode,[19] which are original from the WWW and provide global identifiers and international character encoding standards. Further languages include XML (eXtensible Markup Language),[20] a superset of HTML (HyperText Markup Language) that offers more expressivity to the Web and is usually used to add structure to documents, and the so-called ontology languages: RDF/RDFS (Resource Description

[18]Tim Berners-Lee is the director of this international consortium: http://www.w3.org

[19]http://www.unicode.org

[20]For details on XML technology visit http://www.w3.org/standards/xml/.

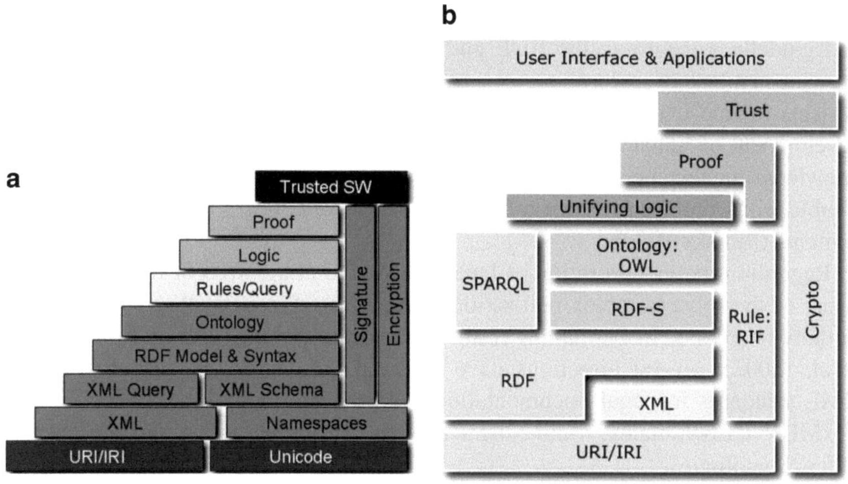

Fig. 1.3 An example of updated Semantic Web Stacks. (**a**) Bratt (2004) (**b**) Bratt (2008)

Framework/Schema), OWL 1, and OWL 2 (Ontology Web Language). While the RDF language offers simple descriptive information about the resources on the Web, encoded in sets of triples of subject (a resource), predicate (a property or relation), and object (a resource or a value), RDFS allows the description of sets.[21] Further, the OWL language (Ontology Web Language) offers a more expressive language to define structured ontologies (e.g. class disjointness, union or equivalence, etc.), that can be used by different systems to improve the accuracy of web searches, to share information, to define terms or to describe and represent a domain (Berners-Lee et al. 2001). Currently OWL may be distinguished between OWL 1 and OWL 2, an extension and revision of the previous version.[22]

Moreover, a specification to support the conversion of existing thesauri, taxonomies or subject headings into RDF triples has recently been published: the SKOS, Simple Knowledge Organization System standard. These specifications may be exploited in Linked Data efforts, such as the New York Times vocabularies. Also, EuroVoc, the multilingual thesaurus for activities of the EU is, for example, now available in this format.

Standardization efforts towards establishing the rule, logic, and proof layers, up to adding trust to the Semantic Web, are still work in progress. However, in the last decade, the efforts towards the construction of the Semantic Web have multiplied.

[21] Triples can be written using XML tags. Visit http://www.w3.org/standards/techs/rdf#w3c_all for more information on RDF.

[22] See Chap. 3 and visit http://www.w3.org/standards/techs/owl#w3c_all, retrieved August 18, 2010, for more information.

The World Wide Web Consortium has published and revised various specifications and guidelines regarding the RDF and OWL languages. On the other, there are growing numbers of research projects and companies (for the example the European projects funded under the VI Framework Programme) dedicated to research and development of semantic web applications, and to foster the use of ontologies for knowledge management in different areas.[23] At last, we may no longer say that "the trouble with computer science today is an obsessive concern with form instead of content" (Minsky 1970).

Regarding the incorporation of legal knowledge in the Web or into IT applications, or the more complex realization of the *Legal Semantic Web* (see Fig. 1.4), initially mentioned in Benjamins et al. (2005a), and recently specified by Biasiotti et al. (2008), several directions have been taken, such as the development of XML standards for legal documentation and drafting (including Akoma Ntoso,[24] LexML,[25] CEN Metalex,[26] and Norme in Rete[27]) or, in particular, the construction of legal ontologies.[28]

1.2.1 Legal Ontologies for Legal Knowledge Representation

"Ontology as a branch of philosophy is the science of what is, of the kinds and structures of objects, properties, events, processes and relations in every area of reality" (Smith 2003). In the subfield of computer science and information science known as Knowledge Representation, the term "ontology" refers to a consensual and reusable vocabulary of identified concepts and their relationships regarding some phenomena of the world, which is made explicit in a machine-readable language.

---

[23] A relevant cluster of projects was the European Semantic Systems Initiative (http://www.essi-cluster.org) that included: Adaptive Services Grid (ASG, http://asg-platform.org), Data, Information, and Process Integration with Semantic Web Services (DIP project, http://dip.semanticweb.org), Knowledge Web (http://knowledgeweb.semanticweb.org), Project Super (Semantics Utilised for Process Management Within and Between Enterprises, http://www.ip-super.org), Tripcom (Triple Space Communication project, http://www.tripcom.org), and SEKT (Semantically Enabled Knowledge Technologies, http://www.sekt-project.com). The ESSI initiative created an Ontology working group to aligns the research and development efforts regarding ontology creation and management between the ESSI projects. See also Benjamins et al. 2005b.

[24] Akoma Ntoso: http://www.akomantoso.org

[25] LexML: http://www.legalxml.org

[26] CEN Metalex: http://www.metalex.eu

[27] Norme in Rete: http://www.ittig.cnr.it/Ricerca/UnitaEng.php?Id=40

[28] The digitalisation of legal information and the availability of legal information on the Web (e.g., the Free Access to Law movement, specified in the Declaration on Free Access to Law at http://www.worldlii.org/worldlii/declaration, retrieved August 18, 2010), the development of legal XML standards (see, for the state of the art, Baglioli et al. (2007) and Biasiotti et al. (2008)), within others, are also important areas of research.

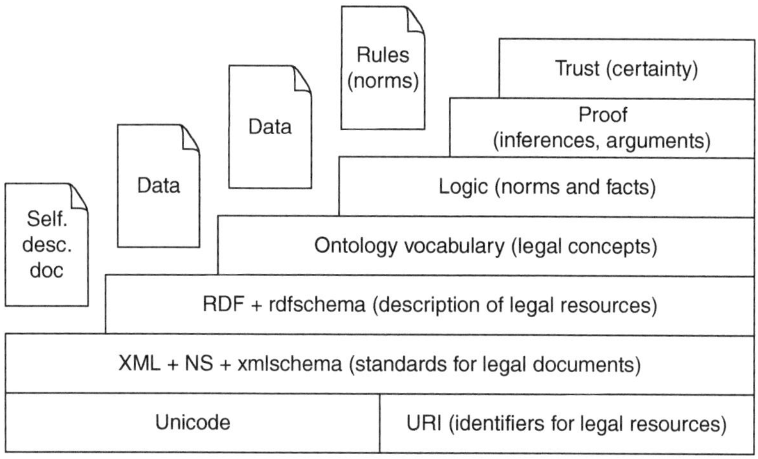

Fig. 1.4 Different levels of the Legal Semantic Web by Biasiotti et al. (2008)

Ontologies may be regarded as advanced taxonomical structures, where concepts formalized as classes (e.g., "Mammal"), are defined with axioms, enriched with the description of attributes or constraints (for example, "cardinality"), and linked to other classes through properties (e.g., "eats" or "is_eated_by"). "[I]n the context of AI systems using human knowledge, we identify the ontology with the set of formal terms with which one represents knowledge, since the representation completely determines what 'exists' for the system" (Gruber 1992).

Thus, the term *ontology* has been borrowed from Philosophy to be used in Computer Science and Artificial Intelligence in more operative sense. The most well-known definition of the AI ontology is Gruber's who defined ontology as an "explicit specification of a conceptualization" (Gruber 1993a, b).[29] A latter more complete (and nowadays most referred to) definition by Studer et al. (1998), based on Gruber's, is "an ontology is a formal, explicit specification of a shared conceptualization." Many other definitions of *ontology* have been offered from the areas of KBS engineering and artificial intelligence. The different definitions offered on the term and the consequences implied by these definitions will be discussed in Chap. 2.

Although there are different views in the literature regarding the scope of the definition or main characteristics of ontologies, the use of ontologies is seen as the key to implement the semantics for human-machine communication. Several ontologies have been built for different purposes and knowledge domains, for example, the common sense knowledge Cyc and OpenCyc ontologies,[30] SUMO

[29]Smith (2003) and others (Schneider 2003) have extensively criticised this subjacent idea of "conceptualization."

[30]Cyc: http://www.cyc.com (OpenCyc: http://www.opencyc.org)

(the Suggested Upper Merged Ontology),[31] the upper ontology PROTON (PROTo ONtology),[32] or the DOLCE foundational ontology (Descriptive Ontology for Linguistic and Cognitive Engineering).[33] Also, WordNet,[34] which offers a large lexical database of English, has been represented in RDF/OWL formats,[35] the FRBRoo Ontology for bibliographic information,[36] or the Gene Ontology,[37] a domain ontology representing genes and gene product attributes.

Therefore, most domains are of interest for ontology modelling, however, the legal domain offers a perfect field for conceptual modelling and for ontology use in different types of intelligent applications and legal reasoning systems, not only for its complexity as a knowledge intensive area, but also for the high amount of data that it generates. In this sense, during the last decade, the use of legal ontologies as a technique to represent legal knowledge has increased and, as a consequence, a very interesting debate about their capacity to represent legal knowledge and its relation to the different existing legal theories has been raised.[38] Moreover, it has been suggested that *ontologies* may be the "missing link" between legal theory and AI (Valente and Breuker 1994c).

The list of existing ontologies built for the legal domain is growing rapidly. Chapter 4 will describe the existing legal ontologies and compare their main design principles, established by the description of ontology definitions and typologies contained in Chap. 2, and the overview of ontology development tools, languages and methodologies offered by Chap. 3.

---

[31] SUMO: http://suo.ieee.org

[32] PROTON: http://proton.semanticweb.org

[33] DOLCE: http://www.loa-cnr.it/DOLCE.html, there are different versions available (Lite, Ultralight), see diagram in Fig. 1.5.

[34] WordNet: http://wordnet.princeton.edu

[35] WordNet 2.0: http://www.w3.org/TR/wordnet-rdf/, Wordnet 3.0 OWL: http://www.ontologyportal.org/WordNet.owl

[36] FRBRoo: http://www.cidoc-crm.org/frbr_inro.html

[37] GO: http://www.geneontology.org

[38] "The 80s experiences in the field of legal knowledge formalization were mainly dedicated (especially in continental civil-law countries) to the choice of the best paradigm of representation (declarative versus deductive approach, rule-based, logic-based), while in the 90s most of the AI&Law community turned its attention to the features of legal reasoning and of the dialectic dimension of law (deontic modalities, defeasible reasoning, argument construction). Investigation on the type of entities of legal knowledge has been understated though. As a consequence, legal expert systems never came out of the level of prototypical applications, since they were lacking a solid methodology for knowledge modelling: formalizing legislative knowledge was a subjective process, time- and cost-consuming, relatively unreliable from the user perspective, and not easily re-usable by different applications. An ontology-based approach offers a solid support in the formalization process, as it permits the explicitation of the underling assumptions, and the formal definition of the components of legal knowledge. Accordingly, the tasks carried out in the past are being faced in a new perspective" (Gangemi et al. 2003a).

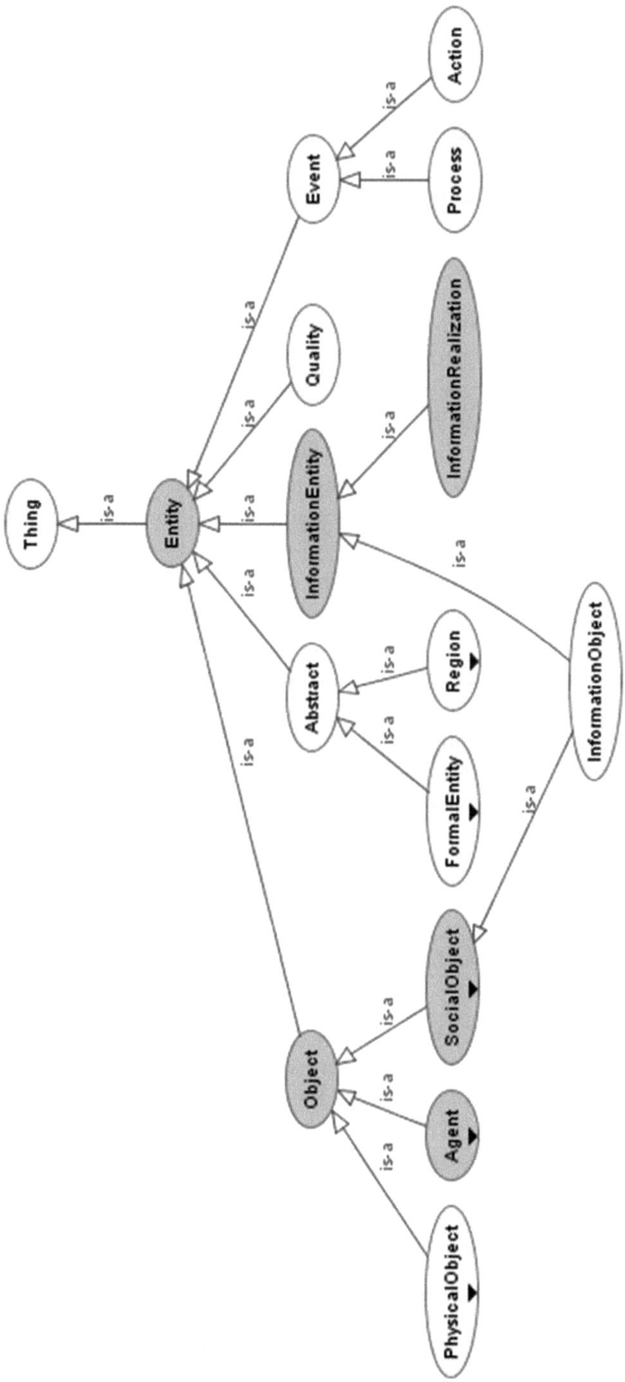

Fig. 1.5 An excerpt of DOLCE-UltraLite top classes

1.2.2 Legal Experts for Legal Ontology Development

Several authors have recognised that legal theory and AI and Law could benefit from interdisciplinary research, so receiving mutual influence (van der Lieth Gardner 1987; Susskind 1987). Gordon (1994), for example, uses AI models to clarify the theories of judicial discretion proposed by German conceptualism (Puchta and Jhering), American realism (Holmes), Hart, Rödig and Alexy. Groendijk and Tragter (1994) describe the legal knowledge base system MILIEU, which supports police officers regarding environmental legislation in the criminal area, and where design choices have been based on "a legal theory about how penal environmental law should be applied." Further examples are supplied by Valente and Breuker (1994c).

Surprisingly, while much effort has been made by computer scientists and AI experts towards the representation of legal knowledge and the formalization of law, there has been less interest by legal experts, academics, and theorists towards contributing to the representation of law, legal knowledge or legal theory in a machine-readable form, or towards bridging the gap between legal thought, legal theory or legal practice and computer programming and knowledge engineering for the legal domain.[39]

In fact, while classical legal theory is being referred to as basis for argumentation and reasoning frameworks developed by computer scientists and information technology experts, while developing models of legal documents, models of legal norms and cases (towards argumentation and reasoning) or models of legal concepts, few legal theorists have made specific contributions to this interdisciplinary field of research. Moreover, several claims regarding the lack of understanding of the legal domain by computer experts may be found in the literature, generally referring to the lack of acceptance of AI tools by legal experts.

> Noticeable is also that several contributions in the field of AI and law appear to be incompatible with respect to the understanding of the law and legal work. (...) It is no secret that very few systems have been accepted by the legal community. The problems, however, are not primarily of a technical nature. With little doubt, the difficulties are more closely related to a too shallow understanding of the requirements of the domain taken as a whole (Wahlgren 1994).

Moreover, at the 2007 ICAIL's closing remarks (Gordon 2007), the IAAIL President at the time, concluded that "lawyers working in AI and Law tend to drift to computer science departments" and that "Law schools courses on legal philosophy, jurisprudence, legal theory, legal methods or legal research and writing are typically not informed by AI and Law results." Furthermore, as "law schools are professional schools and practice-oriented, law is traditionally taught as an art or craft, with little

[39]Noteworthy exceptions in various areas of study are the works of Layman E. Allen, Kevin D. Ashley, Danièle Bourcier, Pompeu Casanovas, Fernando Galindo, Anne von der Lieth Gardner, Thomas F. Gordon, Pamela N. Gray, Graham Greenleaf, Marc Lauritsen, Philip Leith, Arno Lodder, Peter W. Martin, L. Thorne McCarty, Laurens Mommers, Henry Prakken, Giovanni Sartor, Richard Susskind, and Daniela Tiscornia, among others.

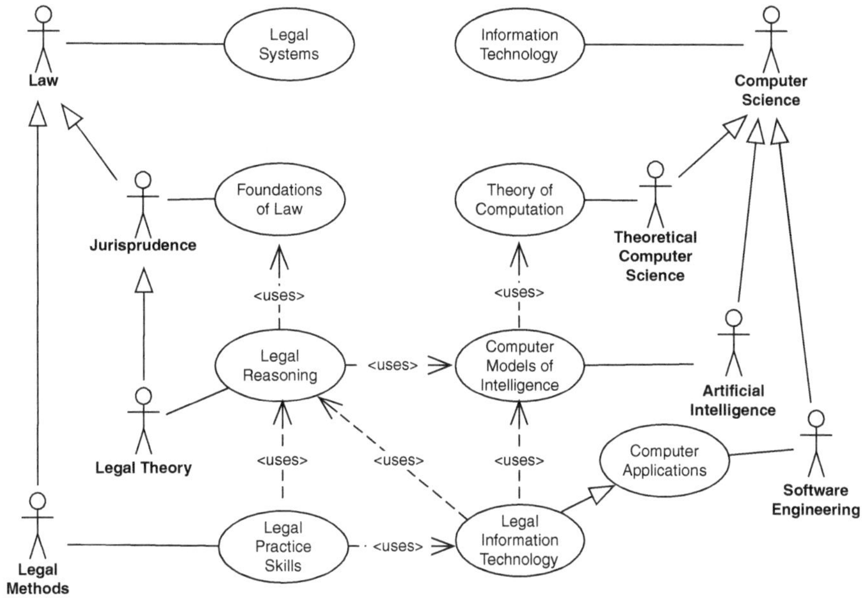

Fig. 1.6 Collaboration model for Law and Computer Science departments proposed by Gordon (2007)

attention to theoretical or methodological foundations. Legal philosophy, theory and methods are not part of the core curriculum. Course offerings on legal theory and related topics are sporadic and unsystematic. The courses are optional and very few students elect to take them." This author demands, thus, more collaboration between Law and Computer Science departments in order to join efforts and to create synergies (see Fig. 1.6).

Law, Knowledge Management and Artificial Intelligence thus converge in an interdisciplinary area or research on the representation of legal (professional or expert) knowledge.[40] In particular, this convergence is relevant for the development of legal ontologies to represent legal knowledge for search and retrieval or reasoning applications for legal professionals, governmental organizations and the public at large.

---

[40]"Professional knowledge is developed as a product of professional action, and it establishes itself through work and performance in the profession, not merely through accumulation of theoretical knowledge, but thorough the integration, tuning and restructuring of theoretical knowledge to the demands of practical situations and constraints" (Bromme and Tillema 1995). Professional and expert knowledge (experts and professionals) are necessarily and closely related: "Current expert research, however, often overlooks the fact that expert activity is mostly professional activity, and that the information processed in its course belongs mainly to the culture of the respective profession. The application of expertise is thus also linked to enculteration within a profession" (Bromme and Tillema 1995).

1.3 Purpose and Contents of this Book

This book describes the ontologies as a type of knowledge representation and, specifically focuses on legal ontologies as the form of representation and formalization of legal knowledge, and discusses issues related to knowledge acquisition, knowledge extraction, modelling methodologies, tools for ontology construction and ontology evaluation, in order to explore the following questions:

1. How are existing legal ontologies modelled?
   (a) Which knowledge acquisition techniques and development methodologies are used?
   (b) How does legal theory and legal thought influence ontology construction?
   (c) How is the acquired knowledge or the resulting ontology evaluated?
2. What is the role of legal experts and legal expertise in legal ontology construction?

To be able to explore and answer these questions, therefore, Chap. 2, **On Ontologies**, will offer an in-depth introduction to ontologies and its design principles. Some of the features that will be taken into account will be (1) purpose or subject of conceptualization, (2) level of conceptualization, (3) richness of conceptualization, (4) level of granularity, etc. Further, the description of **Methodologies, Languages and Tools for Ontology Design**, in Chap. 3, will include a list and a discussion of relevant methodological approaches and useful tools (editors, ontology learning tools, etc.) for the construction of ontologies. A brief overview of ontology languages will also be provided.

Then, Chap. 4, **Legal Ontologies: A State of the Art**, will explore the above-mentioned questions with the analysis and comparison of the most relevant legal ontologies. This chapter will focus in establishing the current trends in legal ontology construction with regards to the methodologies and language used for formalisation, their level of generality, evaluation activities performed, and, in particular, towards the involvement of experts.

To explore how legal experts or professionals may participate in legal ontology construction, as proof of concept, Chap. 5 will describe the development process of the **Ontology of Professional Judicial Knowledge**. The purpose of this ontology is to semantically enhance the search and retrieval capabilities of IURISERVICE, a web-based application that supports legal decision making during the on-call period of Spanish newly recruited judges. This chapter will outline an approach to the construction of legal professional ontologies grounded on empirical data, together with presenting an experimental approach for legal ontology validation based on usability tests from software engineering, the acquisition of the knowledge to be modelled, the corpus of questions regarding practical on-call problems, the assessment of upper ontologies towards reuse, the preparation of the material towards ontology modelling, and the initial grouping of the extracted terms.

Finally, **Some Final Remarks and Issues for Discussion**, in Sect. 5.3, will summarize the work presented in this book and open several issues for future discussion and research.

Chapter 2
On Ontologies

2.1 Introduction

The use of ontologies has been regarded as key to implement the semantics for human-machine communication. And, although initially ontologies were mainly exploited to enable knowledge sharing and reuse in the construction of knowledge-based systems (KBS), nowadays ontologies are a powerful tool to also implement the Semantic Web vision. Therefore, the definition of ontology, its purpose and also main characteristics have had different views and has shifted slightly over time.

The purpose of this chapter is to offer an in-depth introduction to ontologies in order to extract some general ideas about ontology modelling. Therefore, this chapter outlines, first, the scope of the different definitions of ontology, some of the established sets of typologies and other characterizing design criteria. Also, several general guidelines drawn more specifically from legal ontology modelling will be introduced.

The insight in ontology definitions, types and design criteria will support the review of existing legal ontologies in Chap. 4.

2.2 Understanding *Ontology*

Defining *ontology*, its meaning, its essential characteristics, or specifying its possible different types or purposes has not been a peaceful issue, since the term first appeared in knowledge representation and knowledge engineering. Neither has been the description of the typology of ontologies.

2.2.1 What Is an Ontology?

The term *ontology* was borrowed from Philosophy to be used in Computer Science and Artificial Intelligence in a similar but more operative sense. "In philosophy, one

N. Casellas, *Legal Ontology Engineering: Methodologies, Modelling Trends, and the Ontology of Professional Judicial Knowledge*, Law, Governance and Technology Series 3, DOI 10.1007/978-94-007-1497-7_2, © Springer Science+Business Media B.V. 2011

speaks of ontologies as systematic theories about what exists. In the context of AI systems using human knowledge, we identify the ontology with the set of formal terms with which one represents knowledge, since the representation completely determines what "exists" for the system" (Gruber 1992). Moreover, distinctions between terminology, conceptualization, ontology and epistemology and have filled many papers and discussions towards clarifying the meaning of an *AI ontology*. Here, we will summarise 13 of the most well-known ontology definitions and made some of their interrelations explicit. (See Table 2.1 for a quick reference list.)

Definition 1. Initially, within the DARPA Knowledge Sharing Effort (KSE), Neches et al. (1991) understood ontologies as a kind of "top-level declarative abstraction hierarchies" "represented with enough information to lay down the ground rules for modeling a domain. An ontology defines the basic terms and relations comprising the vocabulary of a topic area as well as the rules for combining terms and relations to define extensions to the vocabulary." An ontology would include also terms that could be inferred using rules and not only the explicitly defined terms (Gómez-Pérez 1999). The authors envisioned the possibility to share these "hierarchies" among different knowledge systems, enabling the reuse of knowledge bases and reducing their building costs. The KSE tackled different areas of research: the Interlingua working group (in charge of the specification of a format to interchange knowledge between computers); the Knowledge Representation System Specifications working group; the External Interfaces working group; and the Shared, Reusable Knowledge Bases group (involved directly in the research and development of ontologies).

Definition 2. Gruber, in charge (together with M. Tenenbaum) of the Reusable, Knowledge Bases group of the same KSE, was looking for an answer to "what can be done to enable the accumulation, sharing and reuse of knowledge bases?" He proposed, together with all the existing techniques, the need to specify a *canonical form* for declarative knowledge (taken into account by Genesereth and Fikes (1992) from the KSE in the Interlingua group), and the definition of *common ontologies*. In this case, ontologies were defined as "vocabularies of representational *terms* – classes, relations, functions, object constants – with agreed-upon *definitions* in the form of human readable text and machine-enforceable, declarative constraints on their well-formed use" Gruber (1991).[1] Definitions could then include domain and range restrictions, hierarchical subsumptions, axioms, etc.

Definition 3. Musen (1992), interested in promoting the reuse of knowledge-level[2] problem-solving methods, task models, and domain ontologies in medical informatics, stated that "[c]omputer scientists have co-opted from their colleagues in metaphysics the term ontology to describe formal descriptions of objects in

[1] A similar definition may be found in Gruber (1992).

[2] "The Knowledge Level Hypothesis: There exists a distinct computer systems level, lying immediately above the symbol level, which is characterized by knowledge as the medium and the principle of rationality as the law of behavior" (Newell 1981).

the world, the properties of those objects, and the relationships among them. An ontology thus has at its root a standardized lexicon, but includes additional information that defines how objects can be classified and related to one another."

Definition 4. Wielinga and Schreiber (1993), interested in setting some methodological principles for designing sharable knowledge bases, defined an AI ontology as "a theory of what entities can exist in the mind of a knowledgeable agent." Ontologies, as meta-models which described the structure of a knowledge base, made explicit the commitments taken in the modelling process, thus enabling knowledge sharing and reuse.

Definition 5. Alberts (1994) developed YMIR, an ontology for engineering design, to be shared and reused by humans and computer programs involved in the design process of a domain. The author described that "[o]ne of the major problems in modeling design knowledge is finding a useful set of concepts that the knowledge should refer to, or, in more fashionable terms, an *ontology*. These concepts should be general enough for describing different types of design knowledge in different design domains, but specific enough to do justice to the particular nature of the task at hand: the design of technical systems. This ontology should serve as the basis for a formal description of the knowledge involved in such a task" (Alberts 1994).

Definition 6. However, the most well-known definition of AI ontology is one by Gruber, given also in the framework of the DARPA Knowledge Sharing Effort as was **Definition 2**, but after the presentation of ONTOLINGUA. He defined ontology as an "explicit specification of a conceptualization. The term is borrowed from philosophy, where an ontology is a systematic account of Existence. For knowledge-based systems, what 'exists' is exactly that which can be represented" (Gruber 1993a, b).[3]

Definition 6.1. Gruber's *conceptualization* was however challenged and redefined by Guarino and Giaretta (1995).[4] These authors tried to refine the meaning of ontology, taking into account 7 possible senses of the term used in the literature:

1. Ontology as a philosophical discipline[5];
2. Ontology as a an informal conceptual system;

---

[3]Hoekstra (2001) notes that "according to this definition there is no requirement for an ontology to be formally grounded."

[4]N. Guarino is perhaps one of the authors that has dedicated most effort into the clarification of the meaning of the terms *ontology*, *formal ontology* and *ontological commitment*, together with the relation to its philosophical counterpart and its distinction with epistemology. See (Guarino et al. 1994a, b; Guarino and Giaretta 1995; Guarino 1995; 1997a, b, 1998). Also the works of Sowa (1995, 2000) have been largely influenced by philosophical contributions, especially from C.S. Peirce and A.N. Whitehead (although he also takes into account I. Kant, E. Husserl, or M. Heidegger). This author is well-known for his contribution to the development of conceptual graphs (see, for example, Sowa (1976, 1980) for further insight into his earlier research.

[5]Guarino and Giaretta (1995) proposed to use *Ontology*, with capital "O" to refer to the philosophical discipline. A distinction that has become generally accepted by the AI community.

3. Ontology as a formal semantic account;
4. Ontology as a specification of a conceptualization;
5. Ontology as a representation of a conceptual system via a logical theory;
6. Ontology as the vocabulary used by a logical theory;
7. Ontology as a (meta-level) specification of a logical theory.

Guarino and Giaretta, focusing directly on senses 2–7 and taking special account of sense 4 which they find especially problematic (Gruber's),[6] describe *AI ontology* as being used ambiguously in the literature and, therefore, as having two senses (Guarino and Giaretta 1995):

- **Sense 1** *ontology* is a logical theory that gives an explicit, partial account of a conceptualization. An *ontological theory* is a "designed artifact, a knowledge base of a special kind which can be read, sold or physically shared."
- **Sense 2** *ontology* is a synonym of *conceptualization*. A *conceptualization* is defined as "an intensional semantic structure which encodes the implicit rules constraining the structure of a piece of reality."

Therefore, as a conceptualization is the semantical counterpart of an ontological theory, the same ontological theory may commit to different conceptualizations and the same conceptualization may underlie different ontological theories (Guarino and Giaretta 1995).

Definition 6.1.1. Initially, Uschold and King (1995) ascribed themselves to the two senses of **Definition 6.1**. Later, however, the authors adopted an adapted definition: "an *explicit* account or representation of some part of a conceptualisation" (Uschold 1996) and understood that it may take different forms but it should include at least a vocabulary of terms and some specification of the meaning of those terms. Moreover, "an ontology is virtually always the manifestation of a shared understanding of a domain that is agreed between a number of parties." Their definition is strongly influenced by their work in providing a methodology for ontology building, and it is important to note that these authors also introduced the idea that it was necessary to pay attention to the "different kinds of ontologies that exist and purposes that they serve because this will impact heavily in how to build one" (see Fig. 2.1 for possible purposes). The authors added that "the way to build ontologies depends very heavily on the particular circumstances under which an ontology is desired" (Uschold and King 1995; Uschold and Grüninger 1996b; Uschold 1996).

[6]"The problem with Gruber's definition, however, is that it relies on an extensional notion of conceptualization which, while being compatible with the preliminary characterization given in the previous section, does not fit our purposes of defining what an ontology is. We have already pointed to this problem in Guarino et al. (1994b); we shall discuss it here in detail, proposing an alternative, intensional definition of conceptualization which satisfies our needs" (Guarino and Giaretta 1995).

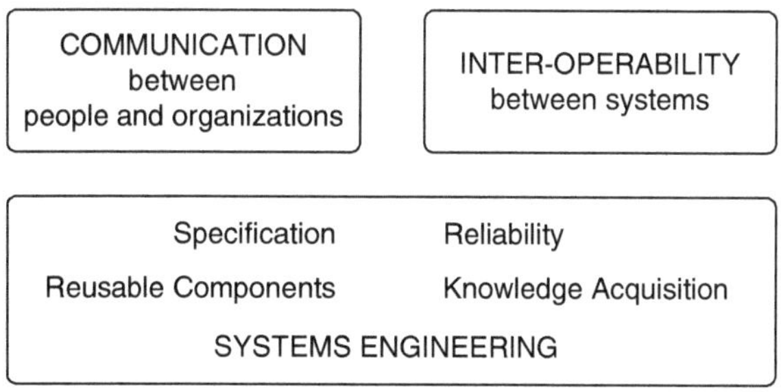

Fig. 2.1 Different uses of *ontologies* (Uschold and Grüninger 1996a; Uschold 1996)

Definition 6.1.2. Later on, Uschold and Jasper (1999) took a "lowest common denominator view" on defining ontologies and state that: "an ontology may take a variety of forms, but necessarily it will include a vocabulary of terms, and some specification of their meaning. This includes definitions and an indication of how concepts are inter-related which collectively impose a structure on the domain and constrain the possible interpretations of terms."

Definition 6.2. van Heijst (1995) took into account the previous definitions by Wielinga and Schreiber (1993), Alberts (1994), Gruber (1993b) and, without specific reference into Guarino's clarification, understood that:

- an ontology was a meta-level description of a knowledge representation, the ontology is not part of the representation itself (from Gruber (1993b));
- an ontology was applicable to all knowledgeable agents, which might have different symbol level representations, ontologies ought to be formulated at the knowledge level (from Wielinga and Schreiber (1993)). Then, ontologies could be used as *mediators* between domain experts and the knowledge represented in a computer system;
- an ontology was often used as a synonym for terminology it is important to bear in mind that is the semantic interpretation of terms and not the terminology itself what constitutes the ontology. Also, the domain and the task to be represented may affect the ontology (from Alberts (1994));

And, thus, defined ontology as "an explicit knowledge-level specification of a conceptualization, i.e. the set of distinctions that are meaningful to an agent. The conceptualization – and therefore the ontology – may be affected by the particular domain and the particular task it is intended for." This latter idea was already present as the *interaction problem* in the work of Chandrasekaran (1986) and Bylander and Chandrasekaran (1987), and reflected an on-going discussion about whether knowledge about the domain and knowledge about reasoning on the domain could be represented independently. For example, Clancey (1981) suggested that the separation of both types of knowledge would better enable their sharing and reuse.[7]

[7] An extensive discussion on the subject may be found in Guarino (1995).

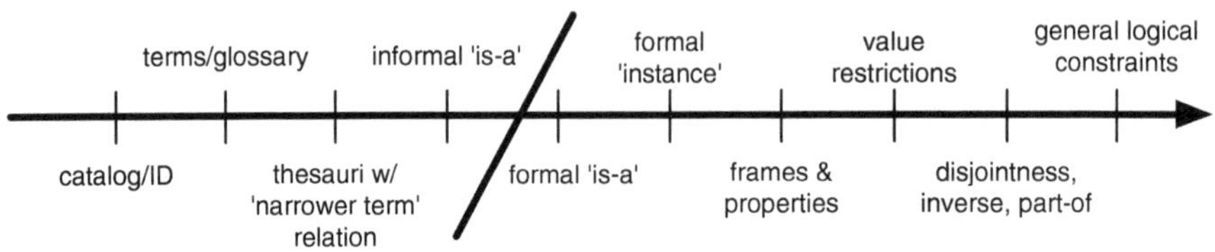

Fig. 2.2 The ontology spectrum by Lassila and McGuinness (2001)

Definition 6.3 Also using Gruber's definition as a starting point, Borst (1997) defined ontology as a "*formal* specification of a *shared* conceptualization." From the idea that most researchers agree with Gruber's definition but "find it too broad" he reduces the scope of the definition by specifying that explicitness is, in fact, achieved through formalization. Moreover, Borst (1997) considers important to emphasize the fact that an agreement on the conceptualization is needed for the ontology to have the ability to be reused. The ontology (the conceptualization that the ontology specifies) has then to be generally accepted. These modifications of **Definition 6** stream from his awareness of the fact that (1) many ontologies have not been *used* to develop a real-life application, (2) many ontologies have not been *reused* for different applications in different domains and, (3) many ontologies are merely taxonomies of domain concepts and fail to capture meta-level and tacit background knowledge. In order to clarify the definition towards constructing *useful* ontologies, Borst (1997) understands conceptualization as "a structured interpretation of a part of the world that people use to think and communicate about the world."

Definition 6.4. Studer et al. (1998), concerned with the role of ontologies in knowledge engineering, took both **Definition 6** and **Definition 6.3** as the input for defining *ontology* as "a formal, explicit specification of a shared conceptualisation." The authors, also concerned with the fact that, in practical ontological engineering research, taxonomies had been considered ontologies, stated that taxonomies neither shared the internal richness of ontologies nor their consensual background. For these authors, *explicitness* refers to the explicit definition of type of concepts used in the ontology and the corresponding constraints on their use; *formality* drives the exclusion of natural language as a representation language for ontologies and expresses the need of this representation language to be machine-readable; and *sharedness* demands consensus on the knowledge represented. Under this definition, it is clear that an informal explicit specification of a shared conceptualization would not account for an ontology, as noted by Gómez-Pérez et al. (2003).

Definition 6.5. Finally, Lassila and McGuinness (2001), within the context of building ontologies for the Semantic Web, considered that from **Definition 6** alone a broad spectrum of interpretations could be derived: not only taxonomies, but also glossaries, thesauri and informal taxonomies had been included in the definition (see Fig. 2.2).

Therefore, the authors required the three following properties to hold in order to consider an explicit specification of a conceptualization to be an ontology (thus, typical and mandatory):

1. finite controlled vocabulary;
2. unambiguous interpretation of classes and term relationships;
3. strict hierarchical subclass relationships between classes.

With these specifications, the authors allowed for a wider definition of ontology with respect to **Definition 6.4** and, therefore, formal is-a hierarchies would be included in the list of ontologies (e.g., taxonomies). Nevertheless, the authors also considered two further sets of properties that ontologies could have: *typical but not mandatory* properties (property specification on a per-class basis, individual inclusion in the ontology, value restriction specification on a per-class basis); and *desirable but not mandatory nor typical* properties (specification of disjoint classes, inverse relationships, part-whole relationships; specification of arbitrary logical relationships between terms).

The definitions described in Sect. 2.2 above are some of the most cited and referred to in the literature, a quick reference list is contained in Table 2.1. There are many other definitions of *ontology*, as many as there might be different approaches towards their purpose and use (Gómez-Pérez 1999). Borst (1997), for example, states that he gives a definition of ontologies that suits him the best. However, most times, the purpose of the ontology lies implicit in the definition.[8] Mainly, each definition allows for the inclusion and exclusion of some conceptual representations on the basis of its purpose and level of formality.

Initially, most definitions were related to application and domain independent ontologies towards knowledge sharing and reuse for KBS, mainly as knowledge interchange formats, which represented both static and dynamic knowledge. Nevertheless, most current approaches agree to the use of ontologies for different purposes, including application and domain dependency of ontologies (see e.g., **Definitions 1, 3, 6.1.1, 6.5**). Also, the conceptualization modelled in the ontology ought to be representative of some kind of *agreement* or *consensual view* of reality (or part of it). Therefore, nowadays

- most ontologies are concerned with modelling *static domain knowledge*, as opposed to *dynamic reasoning knowledge* (Studer et al. 1998)[9];
- ontologies may be used in different ways to support intelligent applications: to provide controlled vocabularies, to be used as site organization and navigation

[8] See (Guarino and Giaretta 1995; Uschold and King 1995) for further comments on this point.

[9] "Ontologies are concerned with static domain knowledge while PSMs deal with modeling reasoning processes. A PSM defines a way of achieving the goal of a task. It has inputs and outputs and may decompose a task into subtasks, and tasks into methods. In addition, a PSM specifies the data flow between its subtasks. An important PSM component is its method ontology because it describes the concepts used by the method on the reasoning process as well as the relationships between such concepts" (Gómez-Pérez et al. 2003).

Table 2.1 List of ontology definitions

Quick reference list of ontologies		
Def.	Author	Definition of *ontology*
1	Neches et al. (1991)	"Top-level declarative abstraction hierarchies" "represented with enough information to lay down the ground rules for modeling a domain. An ontology defines the basic terms and relations comprising the vocabulary of a topic area as well as the rules for combining terms and relations to define extensions to the vocabulary."
2	Gruber (1991)	"Vocabularies of representational *terms*–classes, relations, functions, object constants–with agreed-upon *definitions* in the form of human readable text and machine-enforceable, declarative constraints on their well-formed use."
3	Musen (1992)	"Computer scientists have co-opted from their colleagues in metaphysics the term ontology to describe formal descriptions of objects in the world, the properties of those objects, and the relationships among them. An ontology thus has at its root a standardized lexicon, but includes additional information that defines how objects can be classified and related to one another."
4	Wielinga and Schreiber (1993)	"A theory of what entities can exist in the mind of a knowledgeable agent".
5	Alberts (1994)	"One of the major problems in modeling design knowledge is finding a useful set of concepts that the knowledge should refer to, or, in more fashionable terms, an *ontology*. These concepts should be general enough for describing different types of design knowledge in different design domains, but specific enough to do justice to the particular nature of the task at hand: the design of technical systems. This ontology should serve as the basis for a formal involved in such a task."
6	Gruber 1993a, b	An "explicit specification of a conceptualization. The term is borrowed from philosophy, where an ontology is a systematic account of Existence. For knowledge-based systems, what 'exists' is exactly that which can be represented."
6.1	Guarino (1995)	**Sense 1** *Ontology* is a logical theory that gives an explicit, partial account of a conceptualization. An *ontological theory* is a "designed artifact, a knowledge base of a special kind which can be read, sold or physically shared. **Sense 2** *Ontology* is a synonym of *conceptualization.* A *conceptualization* is defined as "an intensional semantic structure which encodes the implicit rules constraining the structure of a piece of reality."
6.1.1	Uschold (1996)	"An *explicit* account or representation of some part of a conceptualisation."
6.1.2	Uschold and Jasper (1999)	"An ontology may take a variety of forms, but necessarily it will include a vocabulary of terms, and some specification of their meaning. This includes definitions and an indication of how concepts are inter-related which collectively impose a structure on the domain and constrain the possible interpretations of terms."

(continued)

Table 2.1 (continued)

Quick reference list of ontologies

Def.	Author	Definition of *ontology*
6.2	van Heijst (1995)	"An explicit knowledge-level specification of a conceptualization, i.e. the set of distinctions that are meaningful to an agent. The conceptualization – and therefore the ontology – may be affected by the particular domain and the particular task it is intended for."
6.3	Borst (1997)	A "*formal* specification of a *shared* conceptualization."
6.4	Studer et al. (1998)	"A formal, explicit specification of a shared conceptualisation."
6.5	Lassila and McGuinness (2001)	An explicit specification of a conceptualization an ontology that has the following properties: (1) a finite controlled vocabulary, (2) an unambiguous interpretation of classes and term relationships and, (3) a strict hierarchical subclass relationships between classes.

support, to be used as structures from which to extend content, to provide browsing or search support, to be used as sense disambiguation support, to be used towards consistency checking, to provide interoperability support, to support validation and verification testing of data, to provide the foundation for configuration support, and to exploit generalisation/specialisation information, within others (McGuinness 2003).

Ontologies, now, are not only used in the area of knowledge engineering (building KBS) but also in natural language applications, in database and information retrieval areas, and to facilitate communication (Studer et al. 1998). In particular, ontologies are used now to implement semantic content in different types of applications. In fact, most of the above-mentioned list of uses relate to ontologies which emerge on the WWW (McGuinness 2003). The Semantic Web vision has influenced the definition of *ontology* and broadened its scope:

> Ontologies will play a pivotal role in the Semantic Web by providing a source of shared and precisely defined terms that can be used in meta-data. The degree of formality employed in capturing these descriptions can be quite variable, ranging from natural language to logical formalisms, but increased formality and regularity clearly facilitates machine understanding (Horrocks and Patel-Schneider 2003).

Moreover, nowadays, ontologies are also used in the area of multi-agent systems to enable agent communication: "if two agents are to communicate about some domain, then it is necessary for them to agree on the *terminology* that they use to describe the domain" (Wooldridge 1966).[10]

[10]See the work of Rodríguez-Aguilar (2001), Schneider and Cunningham (2003), Boella and van der Torre (2004a, b), Boella et al. (2005), Vázquez-Salceda et al. (2005) and Aldewereld et al. (2006).

Nevertheless, the specific level of formality required (see e.g., **Definitions 6.1.1, 6.4**), together with the relationship between the representation of problem solving (task, method, etc.) knowledge and domain knowledge (see **Definitions 1, 6.2** and **6.3**) have been issues undergoing discussion.

2.3 Types of Ontologies and Design Criteria

The literature has suggested different strategies for ontology classification, analysis and comparison. Several classifications of ontologies have been established based on the purpose, the level of formality, the complexity, etc. These classifications have been influenced by the definitions of ontology given by their authors and the purposes envisioned for the ontologies being built. Here we are interested in describing some of the most relevant typologies and to take into account other design criteria that has been considered interesting towards ontology design and modelling. First general literature and later specific legal literature will be revised.

2.3.1 Typology of Ontologies

Our interest in these several classifications is to outline some of the criteria used for the different typologies and to clarify the similarities and differences of these criteria, together with clarifying the terminology being used to refer to the different types of ontologies. See Table 2.2 for a quick reference guide to the ontology typologies described below.

Typology 1. Initially, Gruber (1993b) attempted a first and early distinction between *representation* ontologies and *content* ontologies. He understood representation ontologies as the ones that provide a framework, but do not offer guidance about how to represent the world. This job was for the content ontologies, which established "claims about how the world (or a conceptualization of it) should be described." Content ontologies are, in turn, intended to be comprehensive (such as CyC), "to be 'conceptual coat rack' on which to 'hang' more specific ontologies and domain knowledge" (Gruber 1993b).

Typology 2. Wielinga and Shreiber Wielinga and Schreiber (1993) distinguished ontologies regarding their *level of complexity* or *ontological commitment*. From the lowest level to the highest, they established five types of ontologies:

1. *Application domain* terminology is of the lowest level of complexity and defines the vocabulary of a knowledge base.
2. *Domain* ontology represents the above-mentioned vocabulary together with a set of types and basic relations.
3. *Domain-model oriented* ontology is a consensus domain ontology that represents general theories within a domain.

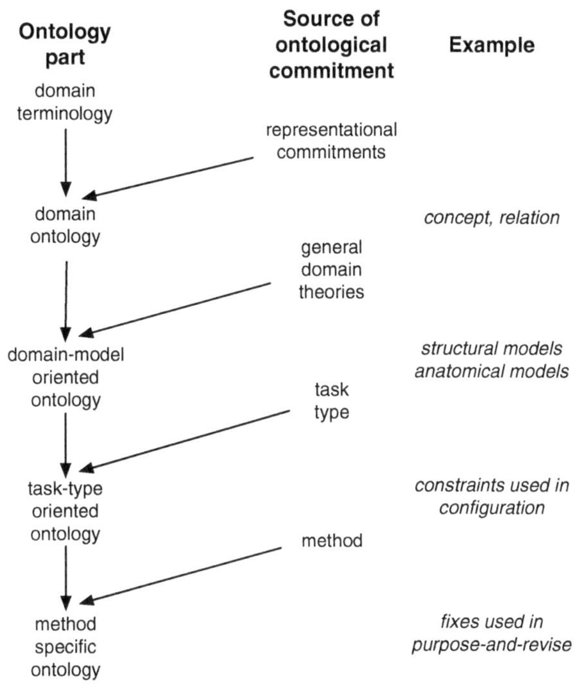

Fig. 2.3 Ontologies and ontological commitments by Wielinga and Schreiber (1993)

4. *Task-type oriented* ontology is a type of ontology which also commits to a certain class of tasks.
5. *Method specific* ontology, which similarly the task-type oriented ontology is committed to the application of a particular problem-solving method.

In addition, the authors also established *meta-ontologies*, which they believed similar to Gruber (1993b) representation ontologies from **Typology 1**, as the fixed set of types and basic relations with standard meaning – the ones used in the domain ontology – (Wielinga and Schreiber 1993) (Fig. 2.3).

Typology 3. Mizoguchi et al. (1995), taking into account **Typology 2** but interested in the development of KBS, established a typology of ontologies based on the idea that "from knowledge base technology perspective, knowledge should be considered in some context, that is, in problem solving situation." For the authors, a KB is always application-specific.[11] From these perspective, they elaborate the following typology:

[11]The authors take a definition of ontology from a knowledge base perspective "as a system of concepts/vocabularies used as primitives for building artificial systems", because they are interested in knowledge for problem solving, "rather than knowledge in general" (Mizoguchi et al. 1995).

- *Content* ontologies or ontologies for knowledge reuse.
- *Communication* ontologies or knowledge sharing ontologies.
- *Indexing* ontologies or ontologies for text retrieval.

Content ontologies include also task ontologies, workplace and general/common ontologies. A *task* ontology describes a problem solving structure in a domain-independent manner and its goal is to provide a necessary and sufficient vocabulary to build a model of problem solving processes (Mizoguchi et al. 1995). In Ikeda et al. (1997) task ontology is further subdivided into three complementary partitions or layers: *core task*, *task domain*, and *task type specific* ontologies. A *workplace* (or domain) ontology is a system of vocabulary for describing a domain, which is further subdivided in *object*, *activity* and *field* ontologies. *General* (or common) ontologies represent common sense knowledge about the world (time, space, function, behavior, etc.).

Finally, and without any relation to the initial distinction, the authors also considered *meta-ontology* as a fourth main type (together with content, communication and indexing ontologies), to refer to representation ontologies (such as Gruber (1993b) and Mizoguchi et al. (1995)).

1. Content ontology
   - Task ontology
   - Generic noun
   - Generic verb
   - Generic adjective
   - Others
2. Workplace ontology
   - Domain ontology
   - Object ontology
   - Activity ontology
   - Field ontology
3. General/Common ontology
   - Things
   - Event
   - Time
   - Space
   - Causality
   - Behavior
   - Function
   - etc.
4. Tell&Ask ontology
5. Indexing ontology
6. Meta-ontology

Typology 4. Uschold and several colleagues explained, in different publications, their experiences in ontology modelling and established a methodology for ontology construction (Uschold and King 1995; Uschold and Grüninger 1996b), the key dimensions that give raise to many different types of ontologies (Uschold 1996) and a framework for understanding and classifying ontology applications (Uschold and Jasper 1999). Here we will only detail their extensive ontology typology.

Uschold (1996) tried to generalise and merge two ontology developments (Enterprise Ontology and Tove presented in Uschold and King (1995) and Grüninger and Fox (1995)) towards the establishment of a methodology (a coherent unified framework), "which would provide useful guidance for anyone wishing to build an ontology." This framework had to take into account the fact that the way to build an ontology depended "on the particular circumstances under which an ontology is desired" (Uschold 1996). Therefore, the authors established three key dimensions that gave raise to many different types of ontologies: formality, purpose and subject matter.

Formality refers to the degree[12] of formal representation of the vocabulary used for meaning specification (the authors ascribed to a wide definition of ontology – **Definition 6.1.1** –). An ontology could be represented in the following degrees of formality (Uschold and Grüninger 1996b; Uschold 1996; Uschold and Jasper 1999):

- *Highly informal* (expressed loosely in natural language e.g., glossaries).
- *Structured informal* (expressed in a restricted and structured form of natural language).
- *Semi-formal* (expressed in an artificially formally defined language).
- *Rigorously formal* (formal semantics, theorems and proofs).

Purpose or intended use of the ontology. The authors considered that at a high level, most ontologies were intended for some reuse, however, "the best method for building an ontology will depend on the degree of formality required, which in turn depends a great deal on the intended *purpose* of the ontology" Uschold and Grüninger 1996b). The authors identified three main categories of uses[13]:

- *Communication* between human agents;
  - Construct a normative model of a system.
  - Create a network of relationships.
  - Provide consistency and lack of ambiguity.
  - Integrate different user perspectives.

[12] Later, Uschold and Jasper (1999) also added that ontologies could not only be distinguished for the *degree* of formality but also for their *amount* of formality (restriction of possible interpretations and reduction of ambiguity), resulting in ontologies rich in meaning or *hi-fat ontologies* and *low-fat ontologies* or ontologies less rich in meaning.

[13] See Uschold and King (1995), Uschold and Grüninger (1996b), Uschold (1996) and Uschold and Jasper (1999) for further details.

- *Interoperability* among computer systems (where ontologies are used as an interchange format);
  - Internal interoperability.
  - External interoperability.
  - Integrated ontologies among domains.
  - Integrating ontologies among tools.
- Systems engineering benefits[14];
  - *Reusability* ("the ontology is the basis for a formal encoding of the important entities, attributes, processes and their inter-relationships in the domain of interest" (Uschold and Grüninger 1996b; Uschold and Jasper 1999)).
  - *Knowledge acquisition* ("speed and reliability may be increased by using an existing ontology as the starting point and basis for guiding knowledge acquisition when building knowledge-based systems" (Uschold 1996; Uschold and Jasper 1999)).
  - *Reliability* ("A formal representation also makes possible the automation of consistency checking resulting in more reliable software" (Uschold and Grüninger 1996b; Uschold and Jasper 1999)).
  - *Specification* ("the ontology can assist the process of identifying requirements and defining a specification for an IT system" (Uschold and Grüninger 1996b; Uschold and Jasper 1999)).
  - *Search* ("an ontology may be used as meta-data serving as an index into a repository of information" (Uschold and Jasper 1999));
  - Ease *maintenance*.

Subject-matter. Finally, the nature of the subject that the ontology is characterising is referred to as the subject-matter, which has also three subcategories.

- *Domain* ontologies: ontologies that represent subjects such as medicine, geology or finance (considering them separately from the problems or tasks);
- *Task, method or problem solving* ontologies: ontologies that represent the subject matter of problem solving are;
- *Representation ontologies or meta-ontologies*: ontologies which represent the subject matter of knowledge representation languages.

Related to the purpose Uschold (1996) identified the notion of **genericity**, which represented the extent to which an ontology can be reused for several situations. In this sense, very generic ontologies were referred to as *upper-level ontologies* and less generic ontologies for particular applications are referred to as *application ontologies*.

[14]In Uschold and Grüninger (1996b) *knowledge acquisition* did not appear in the category of *systems engineering* benefits and *search* and *maintenance* were added by Uschold and Jasper (1999).

Later, Uschold and Jasper (1999) also established a framework for understanding and classifying ontology applications, in fact "scenarios to apply ontologies to achieve one or more purposes." Towards that framework, they specified three main categories for ontology applications: (1) neutral authoring, (2) common access to information (data access or shared services) and, (3) indexing (concept-based search). Although they do not explore this last scenario further, they indicated that this last area is becoming a field of its own that may need a separate framework. They also did not approach the role of large scale general purpose ontologies[15] or of natural language ontologies.[16] However, in the overview of the framework they established different key dimensions for comparison: intended purpose, role of the ontology, actors required, supporting technologies and maturity level. *Maturity level* refers to the degree to which the application has been implemented.

Typology 5. van Heijst and colleagues (van Heijst 1995; van Heijst et al. 1995, 1997a) established also a typology by distinguishing ontologies according to two different dimensions: the *amount and type of structure* of the conceptualization and the *subject* of the conceptualization. It is important to note that van Heijst (1995) incorporated in his typology the *interaction problem*, defined by Bylander and Chandrasekaran (1987) as "representing knowledge for the purpose of solving some problem is strongly affected by the nature of the problem and the inference strategy to be applied to the problem." For the author, this interaction problem caused the ontology in a KBS to be affected by the task and methods that the KBS uses in a way that, "the task at hand determines to a large extent which kinds of knowledge should be encoded" and "the knowledge must be encoded in such a way that the inference strategy used can reach appropriate conclusions efficiently" (van Heijst 1995).

- ***Amount and type of structure***
  - *terminological* ontologies: "specify terms that are used to represent knowledge in a domain of discourse" (e.g., lexicons) (van Heijst 1995; van Heijst et al. 1995, 1997a);
  - *information* ontologies: "specify the record structure of databases" (e.g., database schemata) (van Heijst 1995; van Heijst et al. 1995, 1997a);
  - *knowledge modeling* ontologies: "specify conceptualizations of the knowledge." This type of ontologies have a richer internal structure than information ontologies and are tuned to their particular use. For van Heijst (1995) and van Heijst et al. (1995, 1997a) this type of ontologies is the most interesting, within the context of KBS development.

- ***Subject***
  - *Generic* ontologies are similar to domain ontologies, but the concepts that they define are considered to be generic across many fields, in consequence,

[15] For instance, Cyc, see Lenat et al. (1985), Lenat and Guha (1990) and Lenat (1995).

[16] For example, WordNet, see Miller (1995) or visit http://wordnet.princeton.edu, retrieved November 10, 2008.

they can be reused across domains (e.g., state, event, process, action, etc.). van Heijst (1995) and van Heijst et al. (1995, 1997a) believe that a vague line of separation exists between the two, "however the distinction is intuitively meaningful and is useful for building libraries."
- *Domain* ontologies: "express conceptualizations that are specific for particular domains," and are able to be reused (van Heijst 1995; van Heijst et al. 1995, 1997a)[17];
- *Application* ontologies: are not necessarily reusable and contain all the definitions needed to "model the knowledge required for a particular application" (van Heijst 1995; van Heijst et al. 1995, 1997a). They may include concepts from generic and domain ontologies and may contain method and task-specific extensions;
- *Representation* ontologies clarify the conceptualizations that underly knowledge representation formalisms. They share some similarity to Gruber's "representation ontologies" as they "provide a representational framework without making claims about the world" and the primitives provided by these are used to describe domain and generic ontologies van Heijst (1995) and van Heijst et al. (1995, 1997a).

Van Heijst and colleagues were interested in organizing libraries of ontologies to enable ontology reuse in the medical domain. The classification of ontologies was a first step towards establishing an indexing scheme for that library. However, in order to allow a more fine-grained classification, they also understood that there were some general categories of medical knowledge that are fundamental to all medical reasoning, that there are some domain specific ontological distinctions and that some method specific ontological distinctions may also be needed when specific reasoning methods are used. On these principles, the authors organized the library in two regions: a *core* and *peripheral* library of ontologies. The core library contained definitions of generic concepts and generic categories of a domain and the peripheral library contained definitions of domain and method specific extensions (van Heijst 1995; van Heijst et al. 1997b).

Typology 5.1. Valente and Breuker (1996) understood that "different purposes of (re)use of ontologies also put different requirements on the ontologies." Thus, the authors listed several roles that ontologies could play:

- To be used as repositories for organizing knowledge and information (corporate knowledge, standardised terminologies for professional communities, etc.);
- To be used towards knowledge acquisition;
- To offer documentation (justification) regarding explicit commitments of the KB;
- To enable reuse of knowledge for building new applications;
- To be used as a basis for a knowledge representation language.

[17]It is important to note that the authors make an explicit distinction between domain ontologies and domain knowledge. The latter describes factual situations in a certain domain.

Occupied with the role of enabling reuse, the authors acknowledged **Definitions 1** and **6** and the idea that core ontologies could be useful in order to organize ontology libraries of some domain (**Typology 5**). Taking mainly van Heijst (1995) and van Heijst et al. (1997b) into account, and although they considered that core ontologies were useful towards ontology reuse, they offer a new approach: "[g]ood engineering and pragmatism are of course important for building ontologies, but core ontologies require more than that. They should be based on a clear theoretical view of the elements of the domain, that can provide *principles* for their definition" (Valente and Breuker 1996). And they proposed that core ontologies should: (a) be built parsimoniously, (b) have a clear theoretical basis, (c) attempt to define basic categories of domain knowledge instead of terms, and (d) be coherent (consistent and complete). They referred to these ontologies as *principled core ontologies*.

Typology 6. Guarino (1997b) takes into account the distinctions from van Heijst et al. (1997b) and at the same time criticizes them. On one hand, the author does not share the *interaction problem* statement ("I will defend here the thesis of the independence of domain knowledge" (Guarino 1997b) and, on the other, he finds the first dimension *amount and type of structure* of the classification as "far from being clear". In this sense, first, the author considers that information ontologies are not ontologies "at all." Second, he understands that the distinction between terminological and knowledge modelling ontologies is misleading and, therefore, it should not be hypothesized. And, finally, the authors criticise that no reference has been made to *method ontologies* (Guarino 1997b). However, Guarino (1997b) considered useful the distinction regarding the *subject* of the conceptualization, together with some clarifications.

Later, Guarino (1997a) established also two possible classifications along two different dimensions: the level of detail and the level of dependence. Regarding the level of detail, ontologies could be described as either *reference* or *off-line* ontologies (used to establish consensus on a conceptualization) or *implemented* (shareable) or *on-line* ontologies (used to share an already agreed conceptualization).[18] However, in Guarino (1998), the author refines the description of the level of detail or accuracy and describes the second dimension as level of generality or dependence.

- ***Accuracy***
  - *Fine-grained, reference* or *off-line* ontologies: may be used to establish consensus about sharing a vocabulary (Guarino 1997a, b, 1998);
  - *Coarse* or *implemented (shareable)* or *on-line* ontologies: a minimal set of axioms, in a language of minimal expressivity, to support limited services, in order to be shared among users that already agree on a conceptualization (Guarino 1997a, b, 1998).

[18] Already present in Guarino (1997b).

- ***Generality***
  - *Top-level* ontologies, which describe very general concepts like space, time, matter, object, event, action, etc. and are independent of a particular problem or domain (they could be used by large communities of users).
  - *Domain* ontologies, which describe the vocabulary related to a generic domain;
  - *Task* ontologies, which describe a generic task or activity (e.g., diagnosing or selling);
  - *Application* ontologies, which describe concepts depending both on a particular domain and task (usually specializing domain and task ontologies).

Later, Gangemi et al. (2002) and Masolo et al. (2002, 2003), within the framework of the Wonderweb Project, introduce the concept of *foundational* ontologies as opposed to *lightweight* ontologies, for the development of a library of ontologies towards knowledge sharing and reuse.[19] In these publications, DOLCE (Descriptive Ontology for Linguistic and Cognitive Engineering) is presented as the first module of this library of foundational ontologies.

Typology 7. Borst (1997), from the starting point of engineering ontologies for knowledge sharing and reuse,[20] understood ontologies as being formed by building blocks that conformed different bodies of knowledge. These *modules* of knowledge could be used to construct large ontologies and, thus, be easily reused. These different pieces or *ontological building blocks* were:

- *Domain viewpoints* or *viewpoint* ontologies are concepts organized around base categories of a domain (for example, zoology and botany are viewpoints for the domain of biology). "They define compact and coherent pieces of knowledge in a domain" and are candidates for reusability.
- *Domain* ontologies define domain knowledge and combines viewpoint ontologies (for example the domain ontology of biology would combine the zoology and botany ontologies and provide a taxonomy of all organisms on top). They have the ability to be reused by a large group of applications and problem solving methods. The author also considers that domain knowledge that can be shared by several applications should be part of separate **core** ontology.
- *Abstract* ontologies are the ontologies most suited for reuse because define abstract concepts (that can be used to define more specific concepts in several domains). As an example of abstract concepts, the author offers *taxonomies* (structured overview of classes, subclasses and instances), mereology and topology.

[19] "In contrast with 'lightweight' ontologies, which focus on a minimal terminological structure (often just a taxonomy) fitting the needs of a specific community, the main purpose of foundational ontologies is to negotiate meaning, either for enabling effective cooperation among multiple artificial agents, or for establishing consensus in a mixed society where artificial agents cooperate with human beings" (Gangemi et al. 2002).

[20] Took into account previous work of several authors, Chandrasekaran and colleagues (Bylander and Chandrasekaran 1987; Chandrasekaran 1986) and Fensel et al. (1996).

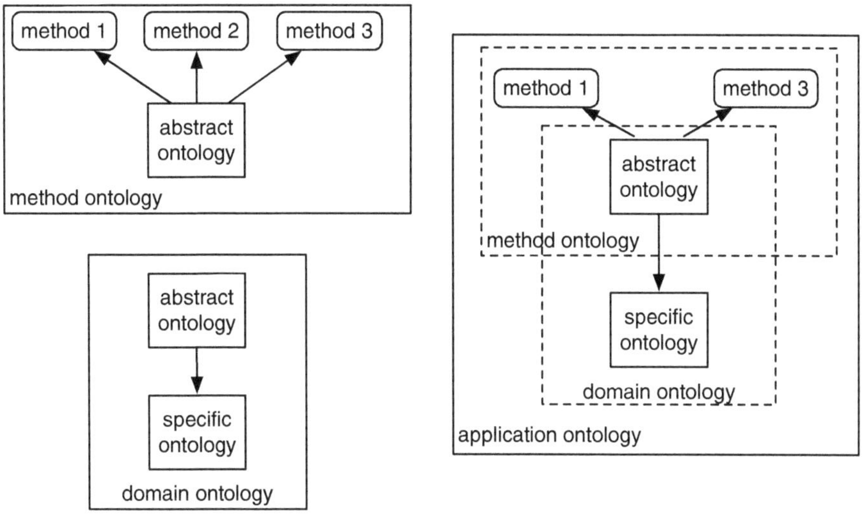

Fig. 2.4 Role of abstract ontologies in domain, method and application ontologies by Borst (1997)

- *Method* ontologies define generic problem solving methods (the way a domain knowledge is to be used in order to perform certain tasks) and may also be reused.
- *Application* ontologies: ontologies used for the design of an application, that usually consist of a domain ontology and methods from a method ontology. Less suitable for reuse.

Finally, it is noteworthy that Borst (1997) considers that "with this modularization, the boundary between abstract ontologies, domain, method and application ontologies becomes vague because of the context in which an abstract ontology is used determines its characterization". See Fig. 2.4 above.

Typology 8. Noy and Hafner (1997) established a framework for the comparison of 10 projects. The comparison was based on goals for ontology research at the time (shareability, design issues and reusability) and some of the criteria relate to ontology typologies. For example, the purpose of the ontology as "many of the features of an ontology depend on the purpose it was created for." The authors considered: natural language understanding (knowledge acquisition from text), information retrieval, theoretical investigation (do not have as an objective to build a working system), knowledge sharing and reuse, simulation and modelling. Also, they made reference to general or domain specific ontologies or criteria regarding their internal richness. Furthermore, the authors recognized the disagreement around considering axioms central to ontology design, and started their comparison with the existence of taxonomies, understanding that "the least it can have [an ontology] is a set of properties and components that are meaningful for each category," which is the internal concept structure.

Typology 9. Studer et al. (1998) were interested in the role of ontologies in knowledge engineering (to facilitate the construction of KBS), although they recognized that ontologies were also valuable for other research areas such as natural language applications (natural language processing or knowledge extraction), database and information systems (e.g., interoperability for data and information retrieval) and to facilitate communication between people in organizations (e.g., knowledge management). The authors are clear about the different types of knowledge that a KBS requires: "at the knowledge level there must be a description of the domain knowledge and the problem-solving method which is required by an agent to solve the problem effectively and efficiently" (Studer et al. 1998). Therefore, the authors distinguished between capturing static knowledge and capturing problem-solving (or dynamic knowledge). Further, they also distinguished between them with regard to their level of generality.[21]

- ***Static knowledge.*** Ontologies that take part in the process of building a domain model, in a problem-solving independent way:
  - *Domain* ontologies (which captured the knowledge valid for a particular type of domain);
  - *Generic* ontologies (that were valid across several domains, such as the Mereology Ontology, taking into account core ontologies from van Heijst et al. (1997b));
  - *Application* ontologies (which included necessary knowledge to model a particular domain, usually a combination of domain and method ontologies);
  - *Representational* ontologies, which do not commit to any particular domain but provide representational entities.
- ***Dynamic knowledge.*** The following ontologies provide a reasoning point of view on domain knowledge and are characteristic for capturing problem solving knowledge:
  - *Method* ontologies, that capture problem solving methods knowledge.
  - *Task* ontologies, which capture terms for specific tasks.

This classification is also a response to Chandrasekaran (1986), Bylander and Chandrasekaran (1987), van Heijst (1995) and van Heijst et al. (1997a), because the authors believe that "[i]n this way, these ontologies help to solve the 'interaction problem', which states that domain knowledge cannot be independently represented from how it will be used in problem solving, and vice versa. Method and task ontologies enable to make explicit the interaction between problem-solving and domain knowledge through assumptions" (Studer et al. 1998).

Regarding the level of formality and internal richness, ontologies should consist in a taxonomy (an is-a hierarchy) of concepts with their attributes, values and relations together with axioms capturing information about the classes, their relations

[21] For Studer et al. (1998), the different levels of generality of an ontology (for KE) correspond to different levels of reusability.

to each other, and their constraints and attribute values. Finally, and according to their **Definition 6.4**, the model should reflect consensus, a common agreement to be considered an "ontology." "The question is then of course, consensus between whom? In practice, this question does not have one unique answer; it depends on the context" (Studer et al. 1998).

Typology 10. Chandrasekaran et al. (1998, 1999) indicated that ontologies played different roles in information systems, natural language understanding and knowledge-based systems. The authors understood ontologies as content theories, which might be further understood as either a representation vocabulary (a set of terms with which to describe a set of facts of a domain) or as a body of knowledge that described some domain through a representation vocabulary (a set of facts about the domain). Moreover, ontologies could be distinguished between the knowledge that is being modelled *domain factual* knowledge or *problem-solving* knowledge (the knowledge of how to achieve certain goals), which are also referred to as *method* ontologies in (Chandrasekaran et al. 1999).[22] However, and keeping in line with the interaction problem presented in Bylander and Chandrasekaran (1987) and Chandrasekaran (1986), the authors stated that "exactly what aspects of reality in some domain get identified and written down in a particular ontology depends on what tasks the ontology is being built for" (Chandrasekaran et al. 1998). Finally, the authors also acknowledged the fact that "ontologies range in abstraction, from very general terms that form the foundation for knowledge representation in all domains, to terms that are restricted to specific knowledge domains. For example, space, time, parts, and subparts, are terms that apply to all domains; malfunction applies to engineering or biological domains; and hepatitis applies only to medicine" (Chandrasekaran et al. 1999). This general level of abstraction is referred to as upper ontology or top-level ontology. However, the authors remind that there is no sharp distinction between this domain independent upper level ontologies and ontologies that are domain specific.

Typology 11. Lassila and McGuinness (2001), more recently and according to **Definition 6.5**, classified ontologies according to the richness of their internal structure. From an initial list including (from less rich to more rich): controlled vocabularies, glossary of terms, thesauri, informal is-a hierarchies, formal is-a hierarchies, formal instance relationships, frames, value restrictions, arbitrary logical statements and, finally, first order constraints, the authors only consider *ontologies* the ones that contained more than formal is-a hierarchies (included) (Lassila and McGuinness 2001; McGuinness 2003). Therefore, formality is a requirement for the construction of ontologies. Furthermore, regarding their internal structure, ontologies which contained at least formal is-a hierarchies are considered *simple* ontologies and ontologies that include further formalisms, frames, restrictions and

[22]This distinction is similar to Studer et al. (1998)'s *static domain* knowledge and *dynamic reasoning* knowledge.

constraints are referred to as *structured* ontologies (McGuinness 2003). A possible representation of their classification could be:

- ***Simple ontologies***
  1. that include formal is-a hierarchies;
  2. that include 1 and formal instance relationships;
  3. that include 2 and frames (property information);
  4. that include 3 and value restrictions;
- ***Structured ontologies***
  5. that include 4 and specification of disjoint classes, inverse and part-whole relationships;
  6. that include 5 and general logical constraints.

Typology 12. However, the most recent and thorough analysis has been provided by Gómez-Pérez, Corcho and Fernández-López. These authors, in several publications, have not only analysed typologies of ontologies, but also the evolution of the definition and their design criteria and methodology for construction. In Gómez-Pérez (1999), Corcho et al. (2001) and Gómez-Pérez et al. (2003) they have given an extensive account of the most commonly used types of ontologies according to their *subject* of conceptualization.[23] Their latest account, classifies the most commonly types of ontologies within:

- *Knowledge representation* ontologies capture the representation primitives used to formalise knowledge in KR paradigms (Gómez-Pérez 1999; Corcho et al. 2001; Gómez-Pérez et al. 2003). The authors refer to van Heijst et al. (1997a) and give as an example the Frame Ontology from Gruber (1993b).
- *General or common* ontologies are also inspired in van Heijst et al. (1997b) but also in Mizoguchi et al. (1995) and are used to represent common sense knowledge that is to be reusable across domains. The Mereology Ontology from Borst (1997) is cited as an example (Gómez-Pérez et al. 2003).[24]
- *Top-level or upper-level* ontologies "describe very general concepts and provide general notions under which all root terms in existing ontologies should be linked," in similar terms as Guarino (1998).

[23]They also provided a typology of ontologies regarding their *richness of internal structure*, inspired by Lassila and McGuinness (2001) and McGuinness (2003). However, the list presented by Gómez-Pérez et al. (2003) included also informal representations of knowledge (e.g., glossaries and thesauri).

[24]At first, *general* and *meta-ontologies* (also referred to as core or generic ontologies) were first considered to be differentiated types of ontologies. However, in later publications, meta-ontologies disappeared as a class and general ontologies took the content of meta-ontologies. Therefore, originally, general ontologies included "a vocabulary related to things, events, time, space, causality, behavior, function, etc." and were based on only on Mizoguchi et al. (1995). So, the Mereology ontology was an example of a meta-ontology, based only on van Heijst et al. (1997b) (Gómez-Pérez 1999; Corcho et al. 2001).

- *Linguistic* ontologies describe semantic constructs rather than model specific domains. Their main characteristic is to be bound to the semantics of grammatical units (Gómez-Pérez et al. 2003): WordNet, Generalized Upper Model (GUM) and SENSUS.
- *Domain* ontologies (again inspired by van Heijst et al. (1997b) and Mizoguchi et al. (1995)) provide vocabularies about concepts and their relationships within a domain and the activities that take place in it. Gómez Pérez and colleagues state that there is a clean boundary between domain and upper-level ontologies (Gómez-Pérez et al. 2003).
- *Task* ontologies (such described by Mizoguchi et al. (1995) and Guarino (1998) describe the vocabulary related to a generic task or activity by specializing the terms in the top ontologies, providing a vocabulary to solve problems associated with tasks that may or may not belong to the same domain.
- *Domain-task* ontologies are task ontologies reusable in a given domain, but not across domains (application-independent).
- *Method* ontologies give definitions of the relevant concepts and relations applied to specify a reasoning process so as to achieve a particular task.
- *Application* ontologies (van Heijst et al. 1997b) are application-dependent and contain all the definitions needed to model the knowledge required for a particular application (specialize the vocabulary of task and domain ontologies for the envisioned application).

Although this last classification contains most of the relevant types of ontologies cited in the literature to that time it is vague and confusing. First, although the authors used to cite a list of typologies in their papers, when they defined them later on they used to add some more types and not refer to some others. As an example, *index ontologies* and *tell and ask ontologies* are cited but not defined in Gómez-Pérez (1999) and Corcho et al. (2001). Also, top-level ontologies and linguistic ontologies are not included in their initial listings of most well-known ontologies, although they are further explained later on in the same papers (Gómez-Pérez 1999; Gómez-Pérez et al. 2003). Finally, also, *method ontologies* were not regarded as a type to be mentioned until much later (see Gómez-Pérez (1999) and Gómez-Pérez et al. (2003) for comparison). Second, these different types of ontologies not only differ on their *subject* of conceptualization but they also on their *level* of conceptualization or the *purpose* of its use.

These confusions and redefinitions may be explained from the fact that they did not seek to give an "exhaustive typology" but only to "present the most commonly used types of ontologies." Although this approach is appealing because it allows to outline a wide variety of typologies for reference, it might be misleading as the criteria that defines the typology is not clear or, furthermore, it seems to include several criteria at the same time.

However, the authors also present a further and interesting distinction between *light-weight* ontologies (ontologies that "include concepts, concept taxonomies, relationships between concepts, and properties that describe the concepts"), in contrast with *heavy-weight* ontologies, which "add axioms and constraints to clarify the intended meaning of the terms gathered on the ontology" and allow reasoning) (Corcho et al. 2001; Gómez-Pérez et al. 2003).[25]

Typology 13. Finally, Ding and colleagues (Ding et al. 2005, 2007), more recently, classified existing Semantic Web ontologies into four major categories: (1) *meta-ontologies* (the main ontology languages, RDF, RDFS, DAML+OIL and OWL, which offer a small vocabulary and corresponding axioms); (2) *comprehensive upper* ontologies, which provide a high level model about the world using the ontology constructs provided by meta-ontologies and require agreement across multiple domains (Cyc, Wordnet, SUO, etc.); (3) *domain specific* ontologies (built a systematic vocabulary for certain domains, e.g. legal ontologies) and (4) *simple specialized* ontologies (solve usability problems from comprehensive and specific ontologies, concentrating on a set of basic and commonly-used concepts and are often used in interchange languages in knowledge sharing (e.g. Dublin Core, FOAF ontology and Creative Commons ontology).

From all the above typologies, we may draw several conclusions. First, in general, as reusability has been seen as the main objective for the development of ontologies (or as a main characteristic in its definition), most typologies are, in fact, organized in levels of reusability, understood as levels of generality. It is generally believed that the more general the ontology is the less commitments offers to a domain and, therefore, the more reusable it becomes across domains and applications.[26] Therefore, the point of view (the area and purpose of the research) of the authors underlies many of the previous classifications, as it also happened with the definitions of ontology.

Second, although at first the purpose of most ontologies was to aid the development of knowledge-based systems or offer interchange formats, currently ontologies may play several roles in many different areas. Third, it is generally accepted that ontologies require some level of formality, although several authors demand *heavy* formalizations. Fourth, nowadays, most authors draw clear lines between (a) knowledge that may be shared across domains vs. domain specific knowledge, and (b) between dynamic vs. static knowledge.

Finally, it is also necessary to bear in mind that although, for classification or practical purposes, it is useful to draw clear lines between purpose and subject-matter, general and domain knowledge or dynamic and static knowledge, it is not so easy to draw a clear cut line between them. In this sense Chandrasekaran et al. (1998) already noted that "there is no sharp line of abstraction separating the general

[25]In this sense categorizations can be made in reference not on the subject of their conceptualization but on the richness of their internal structure. The more expressive ontologies are the ones that express general logical constraints (Lassila and McGuinness 2001; Gómez-Pérez et al. 2003).

[26]This leads to the so-called *reusability-usability trade-off*: the more reusable an ontology is, the less usable it becomes. It is, in fact, obvious, that a top level ontology regarding `Time`, `Space` and `Objects` is far more reusable across different domains than an ontology regarding `Wine`. Generality increases reusability, but it should be noted that *clear* ontological commitments and clear distinctions between PSM and domain knowledge may do as well.

Table 2.2 Quick reference list of ontology typologies

Author/s	Purpose	Subject-matter	Generality	Formality	Richness
Gruber (1993b)	Development of KBS	Representation ont. (RF) Content ontologies			
Wielinga and Schreiber (1993)	Development of KBS	Meta-ontologies (RF) Application-domain terminology (SK) Domain ontology (SK) Domain-model ontology (SK) Task-type ontology (DK) Method-specific ont. (DK)	1. Method-specific 2. Task type 3. Domain-model 4. Domain 5. Application domain		
Mizoguchi et al. (1995)	Content Communication Indexing	Meta -ontologies (RF) General ontologies (SK) Domain ontologies(SK) Task ontologies (DK)	1. General 2. Domain/task		
Uschold and Grüninger (1996b), Uschold (1996) and Uschold and Jasper (1999)	Communication Interoperability Engineering software systems (ESS): – reusability – knowledge acquisition – reliability – specification – search – maintenance	Knowledge representation languages (RF) Domain ontology (SK) Task, method and problem solving ontologies (DK)	1. Upper-level 2. Application l.	1. Highly formal 2. Semi-formal 3. Structured informal 4. Highly informal	1. Hi-fat 2. Low-fat

(continued)

Table 2.2 (continued)

Author/s	Purpose	Subject-matter	Generality	Formality	Richness
van Heijst (1995) and van Heijst et al. (1995, 1997a)	Specify – terms – record structure – conceptualizations	Representation ont. (RF) Generic ontologies (SK) Domain ontologies (S&DK) Application ont. (S&DK)	1. Generic 2. Domain 3. Application		a. Terminological ont. b. Information ont. c. Knowledge modeling ont.
Valente and Breuker (1996)	Repository Knowledge acquisition Documentation Reuse Knowledge representation language		1. Core 2. Domain		
Guarino (1997a, 1998)	Development of KBS	Top-level ontologies (SK) Domain ontologies (SK) Task ontologies (DK) Application ont. (S&DK)	1. Top-level 2. Domain/task 3. Application		1. Fine-grained 2. Coarse
Borst (1997)	Development of KBS	Abstract ontologies (SK) Method ontologies (DK) Domain ontologies (SK) Domain viewpoints or viewpoint ontologies (SK) Application ont. (S&DK)	1. Abstract 2. Core 3. Domain/method 4. Domain viewpoints		
Noy and Hafner (1997)	Natural language understanding Information retrieval Theoretical investigation		1. General 2. Domain specific	Formal (taxonomy)	a. Taxonomy b. Properties and roles – other concept relations – part-whole relations c. Axioms

(continued)

Table 2.2 (continued)

Author/s	Purpose	Subject-matter	Generality	Formality	Richness
Studer et al. (1998)	Development of KBS (mainly) Natural language understanding Information systems Ease communication (KM)	Static knowledge – generic ontologies – application ont. – representational ont. (RF) – domain ontologies Dynamic knowledge – method ontologies – task ontologies	1. General 2. Domain independ. 3. Domain-specific	Formal	a. Is-a hierarchies b. Axioms
Chandrasekaran et al. (1999)	Information systems Natural language understanding Development of KBS	Representation vocabulary Knowledge representation – domain factual knowledge – problem solving knowledge	1. Upper or top 2. Domain-specific		
Lassila and McGuinness (2001) and McGuinness (2003)	Semantic Web			Formal	Structured (1. arbitrary logical constraints, 2. disjoint classes and others) Simple (3. value restrictions, 4. frames, 5. formal instance relationships, 6. formal is a hierarchies)

(continued)

Table 2.2 (continued)

Author/s	Purpose	Subject-matter	Generality	Formality	Richness
Gómez-Pérez (1999), Corcho et al. (2001) and Gómez-Pérez et al. (2003)		Knowledge rep. ont. (RF) General or common ont. (SK) Top-level ontologies (SK) Linguistic ontologies (SK) Task ontologies (DK) Domain-task ontologies (S&DK) Method (S&DK) Method ontologies (DK) Application ontologies (S&DK)	1. Top/upper-level 2. General and common 3. Domain, task and method 4. Application		1. Heavy-weight 2. Light-weight
Ding et al. (2005, 2007)	Semantic Web	Meta-ontologies (RF) Comprehensive upper ont. (SK) Domain specific ont. (SK) Simple specialized ont. (SK)	1. Comprehensive upper 2. Domain-specific	Formal	

from the domain-specific. Domains come in different degrees of generality." Also, while it may be possible to differentiate dynamic and static knowledge (Studer et al. 1998), the aspects of reality that are encoded in ontologies might be still influenced by the purpose of the tool and the task or problem that the system would like to resolve (Bylander and Chandrasekaran 1987; van Heijst 1995).

2.3.2 *Other Design Criteria*

Gruber (1993a) stated that, as ontologies are designed "in order to guide and evaluate our designs, we need objective criteria that are founded on the purpose of the resulting artifact." Therefore, he proposed a set of criteria for the design of ontologies based on the purpose of knowledge sharing and interoperation among programs. The criteria were: (1) Clarity: an ontology should effectively communicate the intended meaning of defined terms (definitions should be objective and all definitions should be documented in natural language); (2) Coherence; (3) Extendibility; (4) Minimal encoding bias (avoid representational choices based on implementation benefits), and (5) minimal ontological commitment (define only necessary domain terms). These design criteria have been broadly accepted and taken into account by most authors.

For example, Uschold and colleagues (Uschold and Grüninger 1996b; Uschold 1996) listed and defined the same general criteria based on Gruber (1993a) to help building the ontology: (1) clarity, (2) consistency and coherence, and (3) extensibility and reusability (maximize subsequent reuse and extensibility, which could be achieved by a minimal ontological commitment and a minimal encoding bias). In this sense, "making too many ontological commitments can limit extensibility, while making too few can result in the ontology being consistent with incorrect or unintended worlds" (Uschold 1996). Uschold (1996) also included other guidelines mainly directed at the identification of terms and the production of definitions: go middle-out and handling ambiguity.

Furthermore, Gómez-Pérez (1999) and Gómez-Pérez and Benjamins (1999) also established later a list of design criteria "that have been proved useful in the development of ontologies" based on the previous authors and other contributions:

- **Clarity and Objectivity**: "which means that the ontology should provide the meaning of defined terms by providing objective definitions and also natural language documentation";
- **Completeness**: "which means that a definition expressed by a necessary and sufficient conditions is preferred over a partial definition (defined only by a necessary or sufficient condition)";
- **Coherence**: "to permit inferences that are consistent with the definitions";
- **Maximum monotonic extendibility**: "it means that new general or specialized terms should be included in the ontology in such a way that is does not require the revision of existing definitions";

- **Minimal ontological commitments**: "which means to make as few claims as possible about the world being modeled (...) giving the parties committed to the ontology freedom to specialize and instantiate the ontology as required";
- **Ontological distinction principle**: "which means that classes in an ontology must be disjoint";
- **Minimization of the semantic distance between sibling concepts**;
- **Modularity**;
- **Diversification of hierarchies** to increase the power provided by multiple inheritance mechanisms;
- **Standardization of names** whenever is possible.

From the above, minimal ontological commitment has gathered much attention and discussion from the literature. See, for example, Guarino (1995), Guarino and Giaretta (1995), van Heijst et al. (1997b) and Borst (1997). Ontological commitments constraint the semantic interpretation of natural language terms in the ontology and also might include choices regarding the structure of time, space, etc. (Gómez-Pérez et al. 2003). *Minimal ontological commitment* is interested in guaranteeing extensibility and reusability of the ontology. Guaranteeing usability is a matter for maximum (or high) ontological commitment. Surely a trade-off exists, therefore, between high and low commitments. As follows from the analysis of ontology definitions, on the one hand, the type and the purpose of the ontology (and hence, reusability or usability) influence the level of ontological commitment that has to be made. And this is not a decision which might be easily verified or evaluated.

2.3.3 On Legal Ontologies

In the field of legal ontology design few interest has been payed at establishing specific frameworks for general legal ontology analysis, comparison or classification or offer specific design criteria. Nonetheless, some authors have provided some relevant contributions.

Bench-Capon and Visser (1997) discussed the role of ontologies in legal information systems. The authors took into account that although initially the main motivation for using ontologies had been *knowledge sharing* ("Gruber's motivation for using ontologies is knowledge sharing"), there were others such as *verification* of a knowledge base, *software engineering* considerations (e.g., standards for documenting knowledge systems), *knowledge acquisition*, *knowledge reuse*, and *domain-theory development* (ontologies would make explicit fundamental assumptions about the nature of legal knowledge). The authors considered that all these motivations were relevant for the legal domain.

These authors analysed two legal ontologies at the time and took into account several aspects: whether the conceptualization was "resource intensive," the level of genericity of the ontology and, its relation to legal theory. Also, they took into account if the ontology was being developed as a precursor to building a knowledge base for a particular application. As conclusions, they offered several findings:

- (legal) ontologies are designed for particular purposes;
- "There is no agreement on what exactly should be specified in a(n) (legal) ontology, nor on the level of detail an ontology should be specified at."
- "Different authors create substantially different conceptualisations of the legal domain even when their aims are rather similar."
- "Ontologies provide a useful basis for comparison and analysis of different approaches in AI and Law research."
- "There is a trade-off between domain reusability and epistemological completeness."
- "The distinction between a statute-specific and a generic legal ontology is useful and necessary."

Still, although the authors accepted that legal ontologies could present substantial differences and that "[t]he important thing is to be clear as what the ontology is for, and to avoid using one for the purpose for which it was not intended", at the same time they also endorsed the views that "[a]t the lower level of detail the ontology must make commitments to a particular task and the information available to those performing that task" and the distinction between statute-specific and generic legal ontology was based on the view of describing legal knowledge as only a system of norms (general or specific).[27]

Later, Visser and Bench-Capon (1997) compared again the same ontologies but offered several criteria for ontology comparison (although they stated that only fruitful comparisons of ontologies could be made if they were developed for the same purpose). Towards establishing these criteria they took into account Gruber (1993a), Uschold and Grüninger (1996b) and others. The adopted criteria were:

1. Epistemological adequacy: degree to which the ontology resembles the cognitive framework of the human problem solver.
    - Epistemological clarity;
    - Epistemological intuitiveness;
    - Epistemological relevance;
    - Epistemological completeness;
    - Discriminative power.
2. Operationality: effort required to implement the ontological concepts and relations in a representational language.

[27] Bench-Capon (2001) emphasises that "I content that task neutrality is a chimera: the most that can be achieved is an ontology which is even-handed between several, *identified* tasks." (Emphasis in the original) Also, "[w]hat ontologies cannot do is make the knowledge available for effort-free reuse. Nor in my view, can ontologies be sensibly developed except in the context of a particular task." "So, let us build ontologies for particular systems as part of our development methodology. But let us not build ontologies not driven by any task, in the hope that they may one day prove to be the answer to every problem that may in a domain."

- Encoding bias;
- Coherence;
- Computationality.

3. Reusability: degree in which the ontology can be reused to conceptualize new legal tasks, methods and subdomains.

 - Task-and-method reusability;
 - Domain reusability.

The authors considered that "[h]ence, an abstract ontology will have a greater reusability than an ontology with a high level of detail (at the cost of discriminative power)" (Visser and Bench-Capon 1997). So, "there is a trade off between domain reusability (can we use the ontology for different legal subdomains) and epistemological completeness (do we cover all relevant terms) (Visser and Bench-Capon 1997). And that as long as "an ontology is meant to be generic, it is important to establish (...) where it can and cannot be effectively applied" (Visser and Bench-Capon 1997).

Later, the authors compared four ontologies in Visser and Bench-Capon (1998b). Two of these ontologies had already been compared in Visser and Bench-Capon (1997) and Bench-Capon and Visser (1997).[28] In this contribution, the authors introduce as a comparison criteria the distinction of different types of *ontological commitments*, understood as "the assumptions underlying an ontology, independent of the existence of an agreement between communicating agents." The authors distinguished between task, method and domain commitments.

- Task commitments: the ontology defines entities and relations that express a task-specific perspective on the domain knowledge.
- Method commitments: the ontology defines entities and relations that express a method-specific (how a task can be performed) perspective on the domain knowledge.
- Domain commitments: the ontology defines entities and relations that relate to a particular domain (the world modelled). A *generic domain ontology* would consist on "an ontology that makes commitments towards a particular domain but is generic in that it can be refined for many subdomains" (Visser and Bench-Capon 1998b).

[28]McCarty's Language for Legal Discourse, Stamper's NORMA formalism, Valente's Functional Ontology of Law and Van Kralingen and Visser's Frame-Based Ontology, although only Valente's and Van Kralingen and Visser's had been proposed as *ontologies* of the legal domain. "As far as our list is concerned, at the time of this research only two of the four ontologies were actually proposed as ontologies and are described in a dedicated ontology language (viz. LFU and FBO). The other two proposals (viz LLD and NOR) are representational formalisms from which we (viz. the authors) have derived some of their underlying ontological assumptions" (Visser and Bench-Capon 1998b).

The authors considered further that ontologies could contribute to five different areas:

1. Domain-theory development;
2. Knowledge acquisition;
3. System design;
4. System documentation;
5. Knowledge exchange.

Finally, the authors concluded that all four conceptualizations had been developed as basis for the design of legal knowledge systems and make several commitments to the legal domain, although all four ontologies "are meant to take very few task and method commitments" (Visser and Bench-Capon 1998b). Towards criteria for ontology comparison, the authors established the same criteria already used in Visser and Bench-Capon (1997) and Bench-Capon and Visser (1997).

These conclusions led the authors towards establishing the need for the creation of an *ontology library* for the legal domain, and they proposed the development of legal ontology libraries (Visser and Bench-Capon 1998a), taking into account several features for legal ontology indexing: Intra Ontology Features and Inter Ontology Features. Ontology authors, relevant publications, tools used for design, purpose of the ontology, task-method or subdomain commitments, language used and fundamental distinctions were some of the Intra Features, while the Inter Ontology Features focused on the relationships with other legal ontologies included within the library. Their analysis of the above-mentioned four legal ontologies at the time allowed the authors to offer an overview of their situation with respect to method and domain specificities, together with their core-level development (see Fig. 2.5).

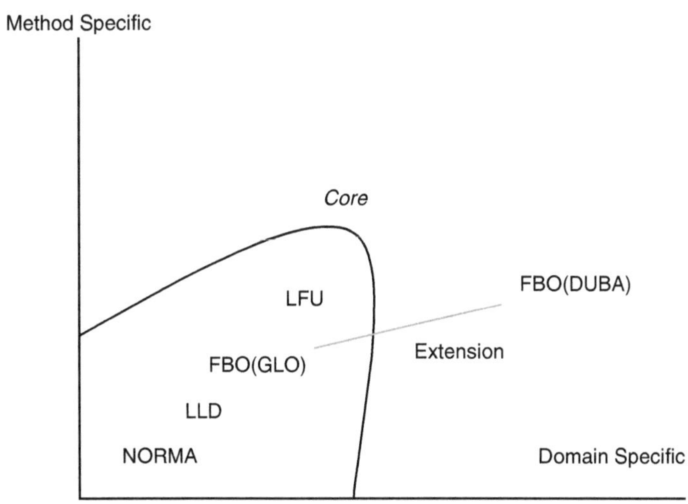

Fig. 2.5 Method and domain specificity by Visser and Bench-Capon (1998a)

Furthermore, an important contribution towards the categorization of ontologies is found in Valente (2005). The author proposes a set of types and roles of ontologies in order to analyse several legal domain ontologies developed at the time. The author acknowledged that "different authors mean different things by the term 'ontology'" and that "ontologies are used in very different ways".[29] Ontologies could play five different roles [30]:

(a) Organize and structure information;
(b) Reasoning and problem solving;
(c) Semantic indexing and search;
(d) Semantic integration/interoperation;
(e) Understand a domain.

The author provided a list of thirteen legal ontologies classified according to their role, their formalization and particular application. Later, this classification was further developed by van Laarschot (2005), who added the analysis of the level of generality (core or domain) and by Casanovas et al. (2006) and Breuker et al. (2008), who added further comments and ontologies to the list, respectively.

In addition to the previous views, the development of core ontologies in the legal domain has been quite popular. However they have been understood in a rather different manner with respect to the **Typologies 5** (van Heijst 1995) and **7** (Borst 1997). In particular, Breuker (2003) established that:

> (...) it appears that law does not have its own ontological foundation. When legal philosophers discuss the ontological assumptions in law and legal reasoning, it is invariably about normative knowledge. This is different from other knowledge based fields of practice like medicine (...) or engineering (...), which have abstract ontological foundations in notions about physics, mathematics, etc. Jurisprudence and legal philosophy are primarily concerned with the *justification* of law and legal systems, rather than the *explanation* of the working of law and its relation to social reality. (...) Therefore, it is no surprise to see that 'core ontologies' about law are rather epistemic frameworks (...), who make the same classical philosophical distinction between epistemology and ontology, construct 'ontologies' that mix both ontological and epistemological entities.

This same argument may be found in Breuker et al. (2002a), Breuker and Hoekstra (2004a, b) and Breuker et al. (2005).

Finally, some critical points in the design of legal ontologies were isolated by (Liebwald 2007). Note that the above argument is also present:

1. Legal ontologies need to be flexible and dynamic and must describe processes instead of models;
2. The formalization of implicit legal knowledge has proved to be difficult;
3. Application-oriented, specific domain ontologies are at the moment the most feasible option;

[29]This author also considers that the term 'ontology' should not be used when referring to domain-independent knowledge representations – representation languages – (Valente 2005). Also, although the origins of ontologies were related to knowledge sharing and reuse, most ontologies are built "with some application in mind."

[30]This view is also taken by Breuker et al. (2007).

4. The cross-linking of different domains and the connection between legal concepts and world concepts is still problematic;
5. modelling ontologies "is extremely cost and labor-intensive; they demand expert knowledge and a high level of consistency. The quality of the conceptualizations and their relationships are of utmost importance and cannot merely be replaced by a high number of low-quality concepts" (Liebwald 2007).
6. "[o]ntology developers should always consider the specific needs of the intended application area(s) and user group(s)" (Liebwald 2007).
7. "When dealing with European legal texts, merely reducing languages, legal systems and legal traditions to the highest common denominator will not contribute to a better mutual understanding. It is of highest importance to factor in national differences in legal language, concepts and structure. Contrary to e.g. a biological taxonomy, a legal ontology is not language and country independent" (Liebwald 2007).

As a conclusion, legal ontologies may be constructed, as any other ontology, towards several purposes and they may have different levels of generality (generally referred to as generic or core and statute-specific or domain). Nevertheless, some authors ascertain that the fact that, different from the construction of ontologies in other domains, "law does not have its own ontological foundation" (Breuker et al. 2005), which leads to assume that ontology and epistemology are tangled in the conceptualization of legal core ontologies. From this point of view, law is a dynamic, normative field and its conceptualization would necessarily include those aspects, together with the representation of world knowledge or common sense knowledge (see, for example, Lame (2002) and Breuker and Hoekstra (2004a)).

2.4 Some Conclusions: A Set of Types

For the analysis of legal ontologies (Chap. 4), we would like to ascribe to a working definition that allows the inclusion of most of purposes and uses, by ascribing to the use of a broad definition of ontology taking the "lowest common denominator view" as proposed by Uschold and Jasper (1999) in **Definition 6.1.1** (also by Noy and Hafner (1997)), but taking into account the need for some shared view of the particular world of part of the world being modelled.

> An ontology may take a variety of forms, but necessarily it will include a *shared* vocabulary of terms, and some specification of their meaning. This includes definitions and an indication of how concepts are inter-related which collectively impose a structure on the domain and constrain the possible interpretations of terms.

We believe that this view enables a purpose and application independent definition of *ontology*.[31] Consensual agreement should be ensured during the knowledge acquisition process. Our interest in legal ontology analysis will be mainly directed

[31] As does the generic definition by (Haase et al. 2006) "[o]ntologies are artefacts that are designed for a specific purpose to satisfy certain requirements and needs emerging in the real world."

at legal machine-readable ontologies, but formalization is to be taken as a matter of degree. Similarly, Gómez-Pérez et al. (2003), recently, as did Uschold and colleagues, have acknowledged the variety of purposes of ontologies and the plurality of communities that model them and so, have expressed that "ontologies aim to capture *consensual* knowledge in a generic way, and they may be reused and shared across software applications and by groups of people" (Gómez-Pérez et al. 2003).

Furthermore, most criteria revised in Sects. 2.3.2 and 2.3.3 might be useful towards the design process of an ontology: clarity, completeness, coherence, maximum monotonic extendibility, minimal ontological commitments, modularity, standardization of names, etc. However, in general, they are difficult to consider or to evaluate *ex post*, from an external point of view, or without access to the complete ontology documentation. Moreover, also some of the specific criteria set for legal ontology comparison by Visser and Bench-Capon (1997) (e.g., epistemological adequacy) is too complex to be assessed,[32] and also is mainly directed to generic or core ontologies. Nevertheless, when possible, *clarity* (all definitions are reported to be documented in natural language), standardization of names, *coherence* (internal logical consistence has been reported) and reusability will be considered.

At the same time, from all the typologies of ontologies offered by the literature, a set of classification criteria may be set aside to clarify the revision of legal ontologies (see Fig. 2.6). These criteria is focused on the purpose of the ontology, its subject-matter, the generality of the ontology and, finally, on its formalization or richness of internal structure. Generally, the purpose or use of the ontology influences, the subject-matter, the level of generality, and the level of formality of the ontology.

- **Purpose**. What is the aim of the construction or of the use of a particular ontology? This dimension may include both the general area of application and the specific intention of the ontology constructed. Taking into account the work of Uschold and King (1995), Uschold and Grüninger (1996b), Uschold (1996), Noy and Hafner (1997), Studer et al. (1998), Visser and Bench-Capon (1998b), Chandrasekaran et al. (1999) and Valente (2005), ontologies may:

  1. Enable interoperability between systems;
  2. Provide benefits for KB or information systems engineering;

     - Aid the process of knowledge acquisition;
     - Offer reusability;
     - Allow reasoning and problem solving;
     - Perform semantic annotation, indexing, search and retrieval;
     - Provide system documentation, within others.

[32] For example, "[a]ssessing the epistemological completeness of an ontology is problematic because in order to determine whether an ontology facilitates the modelling of some piece of legal knowledge we need to identify this piece of knowledge first. This requires at least some commonly accepted theory about legal knowledge that tells us what pieces of knowledge exist in the legal domain. The problem is that we do not have such a theory. Briefly stated, there is no golden standard for the comparison" (Visser and Bench-Capon 1997).

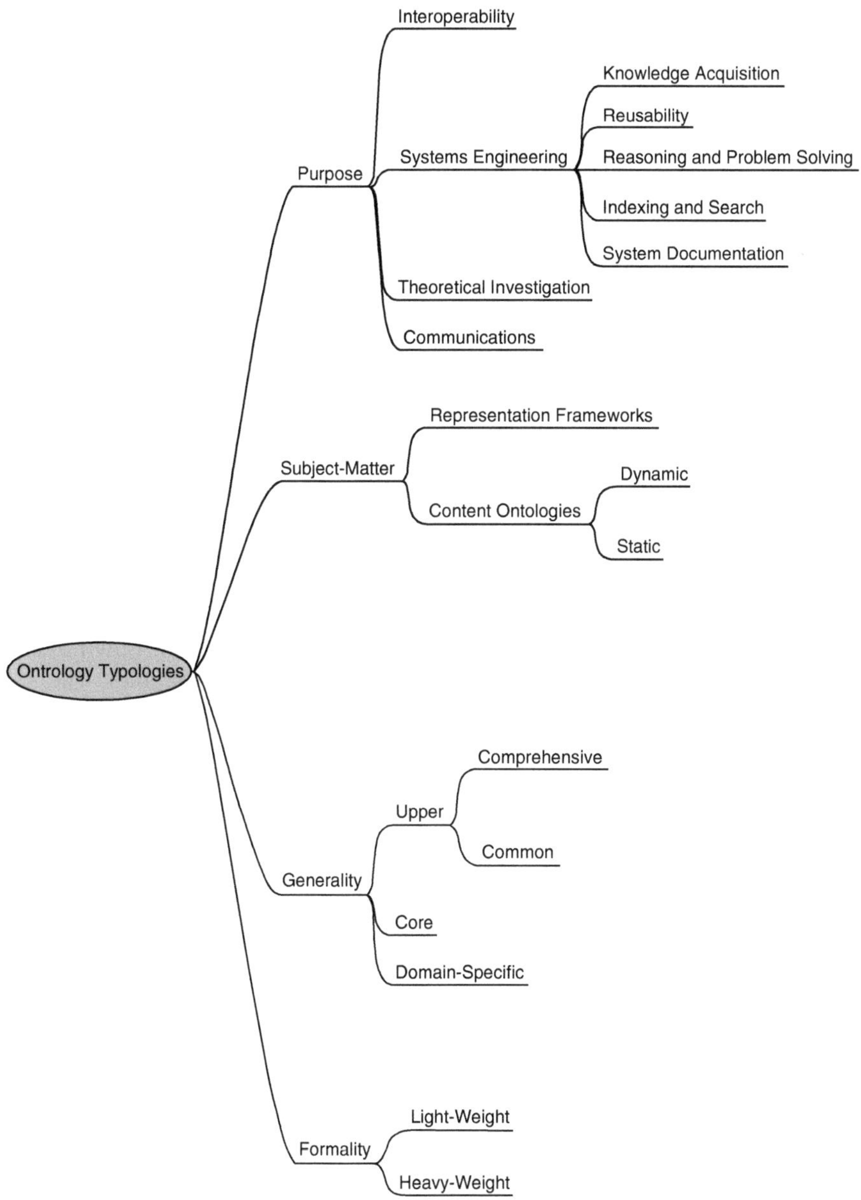

Fig. 2.6 Typology of ontologies

3. Conform a theoretical investigation;
4. Enable communication (between human agents) through the organization and structuring of knowledge;

- **Subject-matter**. What is the type of knowledge that the ontology aims at representing? Here it could be useful to make first a distinction between *representation frameworks* or languages and *content* ontologies (understood, in general, as including claims regarding some world).[33] Taking into account Studer et al. (1998) and Chandrasekaran et al. (1999), content ontologies could be further divided into *dynamic knowledge* ontologies and *static knowledge* ontologies.
- **Generality**. The level of generality, usually related to reusability issues, would include several levels ranging from more abstract, general and independent ontologies towards dependent and specific ontologies (Guarino 1997a, 1998; Borst 1997). Nevertheless, some issues need to be clarified. First, some authors refer to *domain ontologies* to describe a level of generality and to describe static knowledge representation regarding a specific domain, at the same time. Therefore, a clear distinction (or a clear terminology) between levels of generality and types of subject-matter is required. Second, and as a consequence, the level of generality and the subject-matter combine towards the distinction of domain, task and method ontologies. Domain, task and method ontologies refer to two different types of knowledge (domain and problem-solving) and may have, therefore, several levels of generality (core or specific). The so-called application ontologies are then specific ontologies which combine static and dynamic knowledge for a specific knowledge area and might become the less reusable of all (Uschold 1996; Guarino 1998). Finally, some ontologies might include several levels of generality at the same time. The levels might be distinct and modularized, even reused. A special type of these are "large scale general purpose ontologies" (Uschold and Jasper 1999) or *universal* ontologies, that aim at modelling all existing common-sense or natural language knowledge (some linguistic ontologies, such as WordNet, could be considered *universal*). Therefore, several levels of generality may be established:
  - *top or upper-level* ontologies (Guarino 1997a, 1998). These ontologies might, in turn, be considered either *upper comprehensive* ontologies (in the sense of describing "very general concepts and provide general notions under which all root terms in existing ontologies should be linked"), or *upper common* ontologies (providing descriptions of some general notions that may be shared across domains, e.g., the Mereology ontology) (Mizoguchi et al. 1995; van Heijst 1995);
  - *core* ontologies include top-level concepts of a domain, which allows reusability when formalizing knowledge of that part of the world (van Heijst 1995; Valente and Breuker 1996; Borst 1997; Studer et al. 1998; Breuker 2003);

[33] Most authors refer to representation frameworks as also representation ontologies or meta-ontologies. Towards this division we take especially into account the works of Gruber (1993b), Uschold and King (1995), Uschold and Grüninger (1996b), and Uschold (1996).

  - *domain-specific* ontologies (also understood as *subdomain* ontologies, as the knowledge they capture is specific of some part of a domain, e.g., Criminal Law).

- **Formality and richness of internal structure**. Which is the level of formality (or machine-readability) of the constructed ontology? Here we could include the list by Uschold and Grüninger (1996b), Uschold (1996) and Uschold and Jasper (1999) regarding highly formal, semi-formal, structured informal and highly informal. The revision of existing legal ontologies of Chap. 4, mostly considers ontologies that include, at least, some formalization. Therefore, our classification will mostly include semi-formal ontologies and highly formal ontologies, which could also be referred to as light-weight ontologies and heavy-weight ontologies, respectively, according to Gómez-Pérez et al. (2003).

Chapter 4 will revise the most relevant existing legal ontologies with respect to the above-mentioned criteria and aspects. Nevertheless other aspects may be also taken into account when possible such as the size of the ontology, its publication or availability, or its use in applications, etc. as suggested by Noy and Hafner (1997).

Nevertheless, some further design criteria may be taken into account: has the process followed a particular methodological approach for ontology construction? How was the knowledge acquisition process performed? Which tools have been used to support the ontology learning and developing process? In which representation language has the ontology been formalized (implemented)? A brief introduction to methodologies, tools and languages is presented in the following chapter.

Chapter 3
Methodologies, Tools and Languages for Ontology Design

3.1 Introduction

Ontologies may be characterized by their purpose, subject-matter and level of formality, hence by their typology, and also by the design criteria followed. Nonetheless, other decisions during the development and design of an ontology may also characterize them.

The use of a methodological approach to knowledge-based construction, and thus, to ontology construction, may offer support to "successfully reach their goals in time" (Sure et al. 2006). An ontology engineering methodology considers, generally, several management (e.g., scheduling), development (e.g., conceptualization and formalization), and support activities (e.g., knowledge acquisition and evaluation) (Gómez-Pérez et al. 2003; Sure et al. 2006). These activities may conform a methodological life-cycle to support the construction of ontologies, from their specification to their implementation and maintenance.

Further, the use of specific tool support and decisions regarding the encoding language towards formalization also describes the resulting ontology constructed.

In this chapter we revise the literature to offer a brief account of some of the most relevant methodologies, formal representation languages and tools in order to give an overview of the methodological steps for the construction of legal ontologies and to offer further criteria for the analysis of other existing legal ontologies (Chap. 4).

3.2 Methodologies and Methods for Ontology Design

A methodology may be understood as an organized set of procedures and guidelines for, in this case, aiding and guiding the development of an ontology during its life-cycle or some parts of it. IEEE (1990) defines *methodology* as "a comprehensive integrated series of techniques or methods creating a general systems theory of how a class of thought-intensive work ought to be performed".

N. Casellas, *Legal Ontology Engineering: Methodologies, Modelling Trends, and the Ontology of Professional Judicial Knowledge*, Law, Governance and Technology Series 3, DOI 10.1007/978-94-007-1497-7_3,

Current ontology methodologies are mostly adapted from existing software and knowledge system engineering methodologies. Therefore, most ontology methodologies share a number of elements with software and knowledge systems engineering methodologies, although tailored to the more specific task at hand.[1]

Thus, a methodology is composed of methods, techniques, processes and activities (Gómez-Pérez et al. 2003), and may follow several approaches to develop an ontology: bottom-up, top-down and middle-out. "[T]he choice of whether to go top-down, middle-out or bottom-up has a number of effects (...) A bottom-up approach results in a very high *level of detail*. This, in turn (1) increases overall *effort*, (2) makes it difficult to spot *commonality* between related concepts and (3) increases risk of *inconsistencies* which leads in turn to (4) *re-work* and yet more effort. A top-down approach results in better control of the level of detail, however starting at the top can result in choosing and imposing arbitrary high-level categories" (Uschold and Grüninger 1996b). Current ontology methodologies offer guidance towards knowledge acquisition, ontology development (design and conceptualization), formalization, evaluation, evolution and maintenance. Many onto-methodological proposals have been reported and thorough accounts may be found in Fernández-López and Gómez-Pérez (2002) and Gómez-Pérez et al. (2003).

3.2.1 Current Ontology Methodologies

In this section we will briefly describe several of the most relevant existing ontology methods and methodologies for ontology development.

Methodology 1. Initially, Lenat and Guha (1990) described the process followed in order to model Cyc, an ontology originally conceived to capture shared knowledge about the world. The methodology consisted of several steps: (1) manual extraction of common sense knowledge, (2) computer aided extraction of common sense knowledge, and (3) computer managed extraction of common sense knowledge (by using the knowledge already stored in the Cyc database obtained in previous steps).

Methodology 2. Later, Grüninger and Fox established several steps towards a methodological construction and evaluation of ontologies (based on their experience building the TOVE project ontologies): (1) to specify an scenario that motivates the ontology and its applications, (2) to define the requirements of the ontology as a

[1] Fernández-López (1999) discussed the question "Why and how can the IEEE Standard be applied to Ontology Development", and argued that as the definition of software included in the IEEE Standard Glossary of Software Engineering Terminology (IEEE 610.12-1990) was "computer programs, procedures, and possibly associated documentation and data pertaining to the operation of a computer system", concluded that as "ontologies are part (sometimes only potentially) of software products", (...) "ontologies should be developed according to the standards proposed for software generally, which should be adapted to the special characteristics of ontologies".

set of competency questions that the ontology must be able to answer, (3) to define the terminology of the ontology – its objects, attributes, relations –, (4) to specify the definitions and constraints on the terminology and (5) to evaluate the ontology testing the competency questions against completeness theorems (Grüninger and Fox 1995).

Methodology 3. Also, Uschold and colleagues (Uschold and King 1995; Uschold and Grüninger 1996b; Uschold 1996) offered a set of guidelines towards ontology construction and merging. "Explicit tool support is given by the Ontolingua Server but actually these principles heavily influenced the design of most of the more advanced ontology editors" (Sure 2003). Their proposal identified several parts in the ontology building process (Fig. 3.1).

1. Identifying the purpose, which includes:
   - The identification of the range of intended users;
   - An assessment of the range of purposes and compare to one's circumstances;
   - The selection of motivating scenarios and competency questions;
   - Producing a user requirements document for the target software system (in relation to the ontology).
2. Deciding on the level of formality.
3. Building the ontology in several stages:
   - Ontology capture: This process might take different steps:
     - Scoping: identification of the key concepts and relationships in the domain of interest. Brainstorming and grouping might be useful methods, as well as using a middle-out approach (instead of top-down or bottom-up);
     - Producing definitions: to establish precise, unambiguous text definitions for such concepts and relations;
     - To agree on all the above (and on a *meta-ontology*, terms regarding the representation framework).
   - Ontology coding (committing to the meta-ontology to be used, choosing a representation language, writing the code);
   - Integrating existing ontologies.
4. Evaluation/Revision Cycle: Uschold indicates the clarity, consistency and coherence criteria, the checking against the purpose or the competency questions and uses some specific ideas from Gómez-Pérez (1994a, b, 1995).

Methodology 4. The KAKTUS methodology (Bernaras et al. 1996) is mainly focused on the development of ontologies for particular applications and takes a bottom-up approach. Their design process takes into account the possibility of reusing (refined and extended) ontologies already developed for the use of different applications in the domain. First, the application is specified and lists of relevant

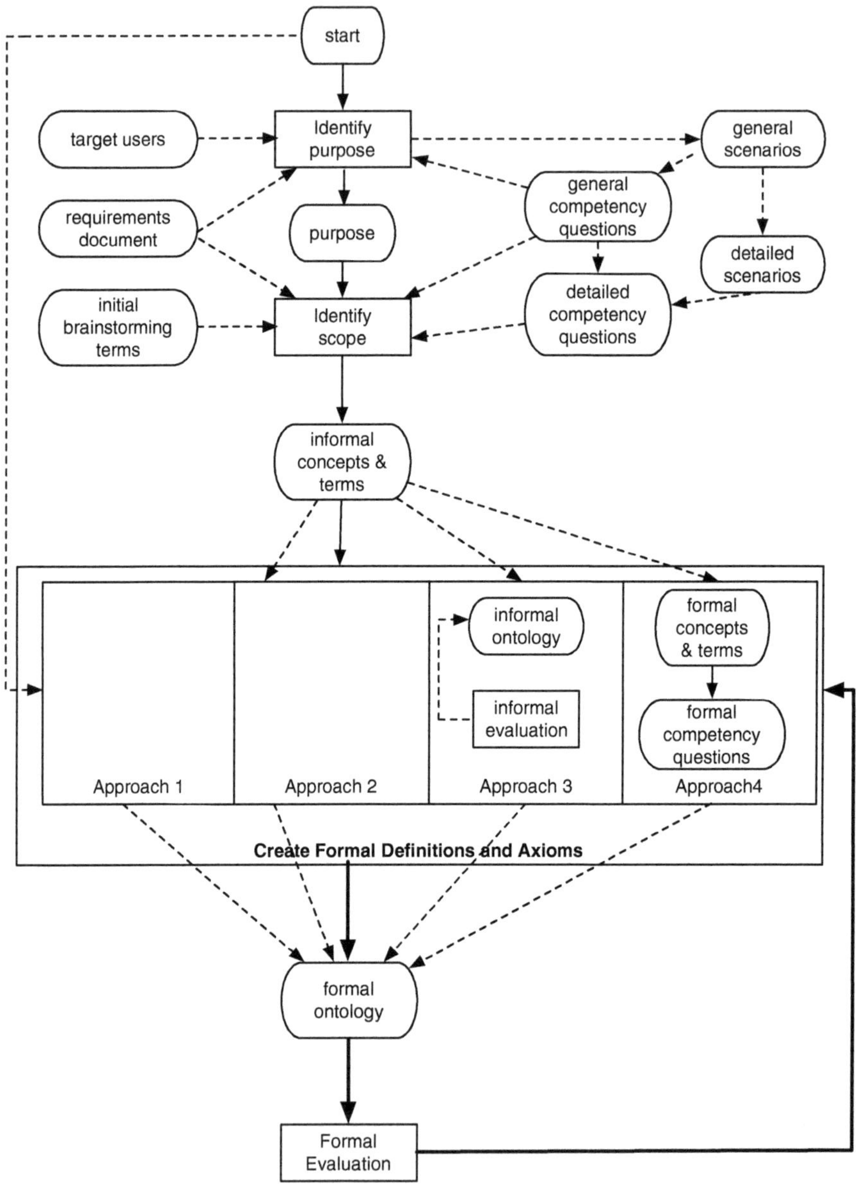

Fig. 3.1 A view on methodological steps by Uschold (1996)

terms and tasks are provided. Second, a preliminary design is made according to the previous lists and specifications, which may include searching for already developed ontologies. Finally, the ontology is refined towards the final design of the application. No specific tools supported this methodology.

Methodology 5. The CommonKADS[2] methodology is mainly directed at the development of KBS (was developed from KADS and is also referred to as KADS II). Nevertheless, it offers useful features also for ontology engineering (Sure et al. 2004). This methodology for the construction of a knowledge model includes activities which could be relevant towards ontology construction, and the identification of different roles in knowledge-system development (see Fig. 3.2). First, a previous task and organization analysis is to be conducted, which includes a feasibility study (problems and opportunities, organizational context and solutions) and impact and improvements study. Once the requirements and needs are identified, the construction of the knowledge model begins:

1. Knowledge identification
   - Domain familiarization (information sources, glossary, scenarios);
   - List of potential model components for reuse (task- and domain-related components).
2. Knowledge specification
   - Choose task template (provides initial task decomposition, e.g., diagnosis, assessment, etc.);
   - Construct initial domain conceptualization (main domain information types):
     - Domain-specific conceptualizations: "the domain structures that we recognize directly in a domain, ant that are likely to be present in any application independent of the way in which it is being used" (Schreiber et al. 1999).
     - Method-specific conceptualizations
   - Complete knowledge-model specification (knowledge model with partial knowledge bases).
3. Knowledge refinement
   - Validate knowledge model (paper simulation, prototype of reasoning system);
   - Knowledge-base refinement (complete the knowledge bases).

Moreover, Schreiber et al. (1999) includes the description of some knowledge elicitation techniques which could be used to gather the data needed for knowledge modelling: interviewing, protocol analysis, laddering, concept sorting and repertory grids. Interviewing is considered the most commonly used techniques and may have different forms: structured, unstructured, etc. Furthermore, the authors recommend them for the identification and specification stages where they may be used to gather information about key concepts and relations, especially, if interviews are taped and

[2]See: Schreiber et al. (1999) and http://www.commonkads.uva.nl/frameset-commonkads.html, retrieved August 18, 2010.

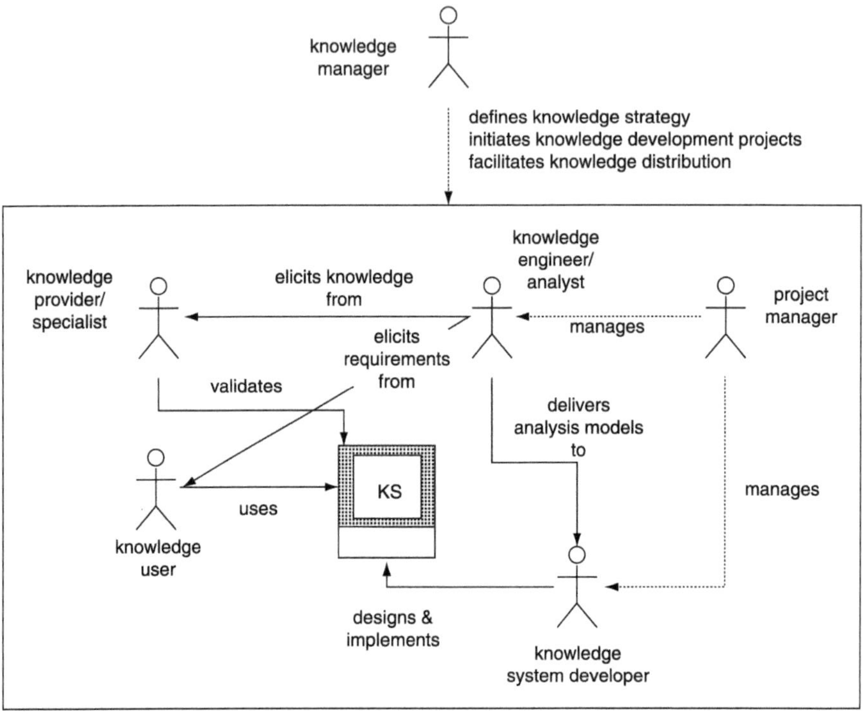

Fig. 3.2 View of roles in CommonKADS knowledge-system development (Schreiber et al. 1999)

transcripts created. "The transcript can be used in knowledge-analysis tools (…) to create markups in order to identify potential concepts, properties, and relations" (Schreiber et al. 1999).

The CommonKADS method was tailored for legal knowledge-system development based on four major design steps: analysis, conceptual modelling, formal modelling, and implementation (Visser et al. 1997; Visser 1998). The method offered guidance towards the design of legal knowledge systems, not to the design of ontologies. However, they may be regarded as ontology modelling methodological steps. During the analysis phase, the domain knowledge, the sources (cases, articles, statutes, etc.) are identified and the tasks that the LKS has to perform using that domain knowledge have to be identified. During the conceptual modelling phase, the method (task performing) needs to be described, the domain ontology selected and adapted and knowledge acquired and modelled. These two steps conform the *expertise model*, where domain knowledge and control knowledge (problem solving knowledge) need to be separated. "This step is necessary because legal sources, intuitively modelled as domain knowledge, often contain procedural aspects (which suggests to model them as control knowledge)" (Visser et al. 1997). An ontology for the legal domain (FBO) and the domain analysis method KANT gave support towards the construction of legal knowledge systems (Visser 1998). Methodology for the development of LKBS (Visser et al. 1997; Visser 1998; van Kralingen et al. 1999):

1. Analysis phase:
   (a) Task identification
   (b) Domain identification
2. Conceptual modelling phase:
   (a) Method description
   (b) Domain ontology selection and adaptation
   (c) Knowledge acquisition and modelling
3. Formal modelling phase:
   (a) Determine boundaries of control and domain knowledge
   (b) Define control knowledge
   (c) Create statute-specific ontology (involves the KANT method (Visser et al. 1997; van Kralingen et al. 1999))
      (i) Creation of a TOO (Test-On-Objects) structure
      (ii) Creation of a EAV (Entity-Attribute-Value) structure
      (iii) Creation of a class hierarchy
      (iv) Selection of predicate names to model the class hierarchy
   (d) formalize domain knowledge
   (e) Define inferences
4. Implementation phase
   (a) Select language and platform
   (b) Implementation

Methodology 6. METHONTOLOGY is an extensive methodology, described in Fernández-López et al. (1997), Fernández-López (1999), Fernández-López and Gómez-Pérez (2002) and Gómez-Pérez et al. (2003). The methodology describes the different steps to be taken not only in the conceptualization process (see Fig. 3.3) of an ontology but also during the ontology development life cycle, represented in Fig. 3.4.[3]

The methodology takes into account development activities as well as management and support activities (control and quality assurance together with knowledge acquisition (from experts or semi-automatic ontology extraction), integration,

[3]A detailed methodology to build legal ontologies based on METHONTOLOGY has been presented in Corcho et al. (2005).

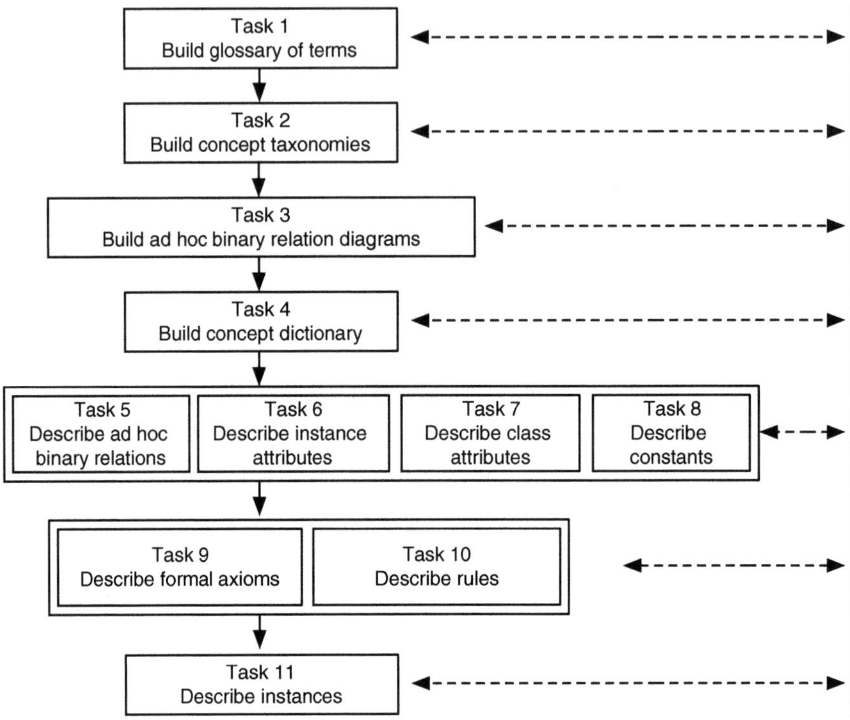

Fig. 3.3 Tasks of the conceptualization activity according to METHONTOLOGY from Corcho et al. (2005)

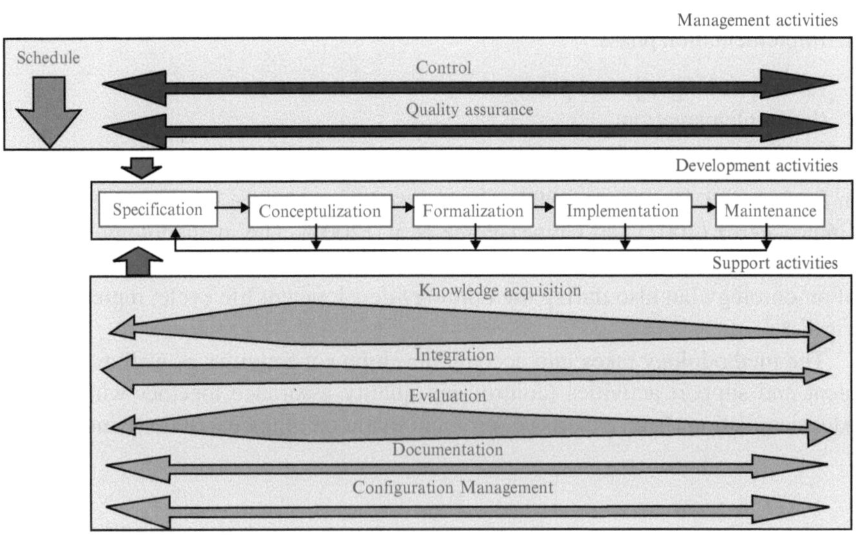

Fig. 3.4 METHONTOLOGY overview Corcho et al. (2005)

evaluation (ontology verification, validation, and assessment), documentation and configuration management). Regarding development, the activities are:

- Specification: establishes informally or formally (competency questions) the purpose and scope of the ontology (why, what use, who are the end users).
- Conceptualization: organize the knowledge acquired.
  - Build a glossary of terms (with definitions, synonyms and acronyms) following a middle-out strategy;
  - Classify terms into one or more taxonomies of concepts (understood as abstractions of one or more terms);
  - Define binary relations between the concepts;
  - Built the concept dictionary (class attributes);
  - Detail the concept dictionary (cardinality, inverse relations, properties, etc.)
  - Define axioms and rules.
- formalization.
- Implementation.
- Maintenance.

Ontology evaluation is understood by Gómez-Pérez et al. (2003) as a "technical judgment of the content of the ontology with respect to a frame of reference [competency questions, specifications] during every phase and between phases of their lifecycle". Gómez-Pérez (2001) and Gómez-Pérez et al. (2003) recommend a taxonomical evaluation to discard circularity, inconsistency, partition or redundancy errors, within others.

Finally, several tools (ODE and WebODE) were built to give technological support to this methodology, although several other existing tools may also be used – Protégé, OntoEdit and KAON, within others – (Gómez-Pérez et al. 2003; Corcho et al. 2005).

Methodology 7. Noy and McGuinness (2001) offered **Ontology Development 101** a simple knowledge-engineering methodology in 7 steps. It is presented just as a set of ideas to aid ontology construction: "there is no single correct ontology-design methodology and we did not attempt to define one. The ideas that we present here are the ones that we found useful in our own ontology-development experience" (Noy and McGuinness 2001). They acknowledged Protégé-2000 as the ontology-development environment used to present their examples.

- Determine the domain and the scope of the ontology:
  - What is the domain that the ontology will cover?
  - For what we are going to use the ontology?
  - For what types of questions (competency questions) the information in the ontology should provide answers?
  - Who will use and maintain the ontology?

- Consider reusing existing ontologies
- Enumerate important terms in the ontology[4]
- Define the classes and the class hierarchy. Several approaches:
  - Top-down
  - Bottom-up
  - Combination
- Define the properties of classes-slots, such as:
  - "intrinsic" or essential properties
  - "extrinsic" properties
  - parts, if structured
  - relationships to other individuals
- Define the facets of the slots, such as:
  - Slot value-type: string, number, boolean slots, enumerated slots, instance-type slots.
  - Domain and range.
- Create individual instances of classes in the hierarchy.

This guide is referenced at the Protégé ontology editor webpage and it is also available in French, Spanish, Russian and Portuguese.[5]

Methodology 8. The ON-TO-KNOWLEDGE (OTK) methodology is extensively described in Sure and Studer (2002), Sure (2003, 1993), and Sure and Studer (2003), and was influenced by the methodological proposes from Uschold and colleagues, CommonKADS and METHONTOLOGY. The methodological process is divided into five steps (Fig. 3.5):

1. Feasibility study: identify stakeholders (users and supporters of the system), identify uses cases describing usage scenarios and their supporting uses cases.
2. Ontology Kickoff: initiates the development of the ontology,
   - Description of an Ontology Requirements Specification Document (ORSD), which includes:
     - Goal, domain and scope of the ontology;
     - Design guidelines;
     - Knowledge sources;
     - (Potential) users and usage scenarios;

[4] "It is useful to write down a list of all terms we would like either to make statements about or to explain to a user. What are the terms we would like to talk about? What properties do those terms have? What would we like to say about terms?" (Noy and McGuinness 2001).

[5] Visit http://protege.stanford.edu/publications/ontology_development/ontology101.html, retrieved August 18, 2010, for more information.

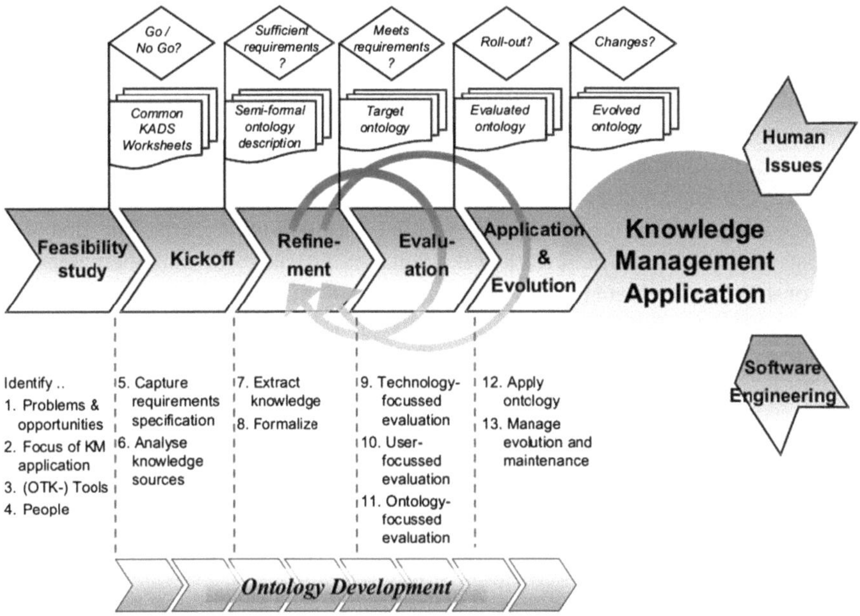

Fig. 3.5 Steps of OTK methodology or knowledge meta-process (Sure and Studer 2002)

  - Competency questions;
  - Supported applications.

- Analysis of knowledge sources (build initial lexicon);
- Create a semi-formal description of ontology (draft).

3. Refinement: Knowledge is acquired and formalized in a cyclic approach.

- Knowledge elicitation process with domain experts (based on input from kickoff phase), modification or extension of draft ontology;
- formalization of target ontology.

4. Evaluation:

- Technology-focused evaluation: mainly consistency and language conformity checking.
- User-focused evaluation: assessment of the requirements specified and the competency questions established in the resulting ontology, and testing results from prototype application.
- Ontology-focused evaluation: formal analysis of ontologies (e.g., OntoClean evaluation methodology).

5. Application.

Methodology 9. Termontography[6] is a method for compiling multilingual termbases which can be integrated in ontological architectures (Geentjens et al. 2006), developed by the Department of Applied Linguistics (Centrum voor Vaktaal en Communicatie, Belgium). "Termontography is a multidisciplinary approach in which theories and methods for multilingual terminological analysis of the sociocognitive approach are combined with methods and guidelines for ontological analysis" (Temmerman and Kerremans 2003). An approach that dedicates effort into acquiring user requirements and working with domain experts. The first step consists in obtaining a "framework of domain specific categories and intercategorial relationships" to facilitate the "manual and semi-automatic extraction of knowledge from a textual corpus" (Kerremans et al. 2003). Therefore, the authors define the method to work middle-out, as it combines top-down and bottom-up approaches. The Termontography workflow (see Fig. 3.6) consists of:

1. Analysis Phase: "from a general ontology user requirements report, the termontographer defines his Termontology Specification Report (TSR)", where purpose, scope of the domain and user requirements are described.
2. Information Gathering Phase: search of relevant textual material in cooperation with domain experts.
3. Search Phase: Term extraction and elaboration of first version.

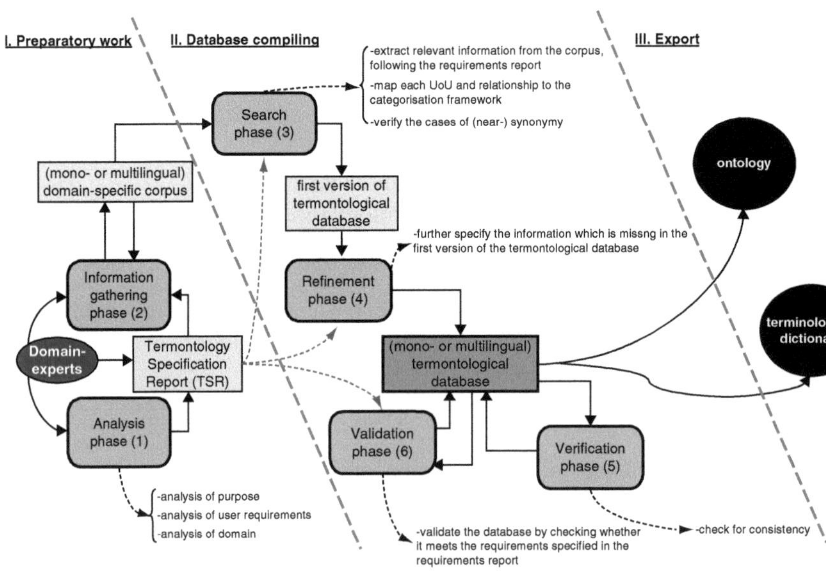

Fig. 3.6 The Termontography workflow (Temmerman and Kerremans 2003)

[6]For more information visit the Wiki Termontography at http://c2.com/cgi/wiki?WikiTermontography and the CVC webpage at http://taalkunde.ehb.be/cvc, and for more references on the method consult Temmerman and Kerremans (2003) and Kerremans et al. (2004).

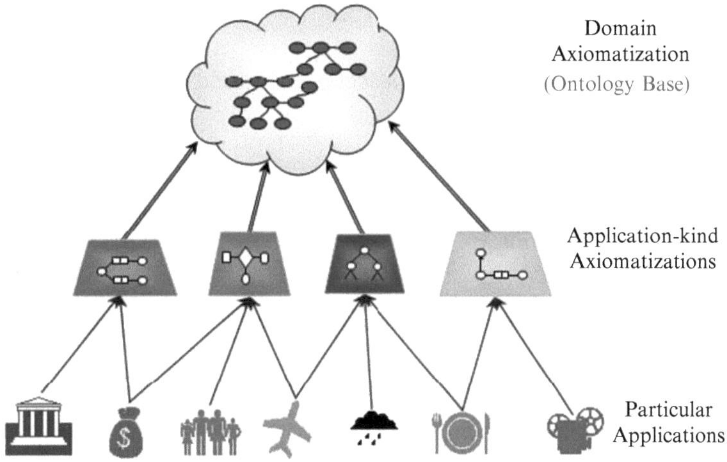

Fig. 3.7 The DOGMA framework by Jarrar and Meersman (2007)

4. Refinement Phase: completion of first version.
5. Verification Phase: consistency and correctness checking.
6. Validation Phase: validation against the initial requirements established.

The Termontography Workbench offers tool support towards the compilation of multilingual terminological resources (Baer et al. 2006) and the Multilingual Categorisation Framework Editor (CFEditor) supports the creation of linguistic ontologies (Baer et al. 2008; Kerremans et al. 2007). Finally, this methodology has been combined with DOGMA, discussed below (e.g. see Baer et al. (2009)).

Methodology 10. The DOGMA approach (Jarrar and Meersman 2002; Spyns et al. 2002, 2008; Jarrar 2005; Jarrar and Meersman 2007; Leenheer et al. 2007) to ontology modelling is database inspired and is aimed at guiding "ontology builders towards building ontologies that are both highly reusable and usable, easier to build, and smoother to maintain" (Jarrar and Meersman 2007). The framework is founded on the relationship (formal, double-articulation) between *domain axiomatizations* and *application axiomatizations* (see Fig. 3.7). While domain axiomatizations are captured at the ontology base as the intended meaning of the domain vocabularies, application axiomatizations are interested with how and why the domain concepts will be used. In Spyns et al. (2008) the main steps of the methodology are established:

1. Preparatory stage:
   (a) Definition of overall purpose
   (b) Feasibility study
   (c) Preparation and scoping
      (i) Define user requirements
      (ii) Define purpose

   (iii) Identify domain experts
   (iv) Compile knowledge sources
   (v) Scope knowledge sources (select passages and define scenarios)

2. Domain conceptualization stage:
   - Knowledge elicitation
   - Knowledge breakdown (verbalization and lexon engineering)
   - Knowledge negotiation
   - Knowledge discovery
3. Application specification stage:
   (a) Structuring
   (b) Definition of competency questions
   (c) Definition of semantic constraints
   (d) Answering competency questions

Also, *AKEM* (Application Knowledge Engineering Methodology) took the DOGMA approach towards ontology modelling and adopted the Rational Unified Process (RUP) for software engineering as its lifecycle model. "Five activities, Problem Determination, Scoping, Analysis, Development and Deployment, are iterated through depending on the phase of the development. Three activities, namely, Test & Validation, Documentation and Control are tasks in every of the five iterative activities" (Zhao and Leary 2005a). The most relevant DOGMA principles are listed in Spyns et al. (2008):

- The meaning of data is separated from the data itself.
- An ontology contains context-independent facts, which can later be grouped by contexts.
- It allows multiple views of a conceptualisation.
- The ontologies are language-neutral.
- Founded on ORM (Object Role Modelling).
- Focus on intensional semantics (instances are not represented in the ontology).
- Meaning is negotiated between stakeholders (see DOGMA-MESS, in the DOGMA Studio Workbench described below).

Several tools have been developed which support this methodological approach, for example, the DOGMAModeler and the more recent DOGMA Studio Workbench.

Methodology 11. The DILIGENT (DIstributed Loosely-controlled evolvInG Engineering of oNTologies) is a methodology focused on a specific modelling scenario.

> In *distributed* development there are several experts, with different and complementary skills, involved in collaboratively building the same ontology. (...) An initial ontology is made available and users are free to use it and modify it locally for their own purposes. There is a central board that maintains and assures the quality of the shared ontology. This central board is also responsible for deciding updates (...), therefore the board *loosely*

controls the process. It is expected that the change rate of the ontology made available should be higher than the usual due to maintenance, therefore this is a more *evolving* process (Sure et al. 2004).

The DILIGENT process includes five activities: (1) build, (2) local adaptation, (3) analysis, (4) revision, (5) local update. In each of these activities of the process, domain experts, users, knowledge engineers and ontology engineers are assigned different roles (Pinto et al. 2004; Sure et al. 2004).[7]

Methodology 12. The TERMINAE method (Biébow and Szulman 1999; Aussenac-Gilles et al. 2000b; Després and Szulman 2004, 2007)[8] for the development of ontologies is divided into four steps, and it is assumed that: "(1) the ontology builder should have a comprehensive knowledge of the domain, so that she/he will be able to decide which terms (nouns, phrases, verbs or adjectives) are domain terms and which concepts and relations are labelled with these domain terms; (2) the ontology builder knows well how the ontology will be used. The alignment process takes place during the construction" (Després and Szulman 2004). Terminae modelling steps:

1. Constitution corpus: corpus selection and organization;
2. Linguistic study: linguistic analysis using several natural language processing tools;
3. Normalization according to some structuring principles and criteria;
4. formalization: formalization and validation with a variant language of description logics.

Methodology 13. The *47-step guide to knowledge acquisition* by Milton (2007) is focused on the knowledge acquisition process, and although it declares to have many similarities with CommonKADS, it also declares that "[t]he main difference between the 47-step procedure and other methodologies is its generality, i.e. the 47-step procedure can be used on any knowledge acquisition project whether it is on bee keeping, aircraft design, corporate law or military planning; whether the end-product is a website, an ontology or an intelligent software system" (Milton 2007). The following are the main stages and some of the most relevant steps:

- Start, scope and plan the project (steps 1–13) which includes, within others:
  - To identify a project idea, to gather opinions on it and to make and agree on a proposal;
  - Rating and selection o f knowledge areas, agreement the scope, identification of sources of knowledge;
  - Creation of a project schedule.

[7] The Cicero tool, developed for the NeOn Toolkit builds upon the DILIGENT methodology (Dellschaft et al. 2008).

[8] More information may be found at http://www-lipn.univ-paris13.fr/~szulman/TERMINAE.html, retrieved August 18, 2010.

- Initial capture and modelling (steps 14–29) which includes, within others:
  - To prepare and conduct semi-structured interviews and to transcribe them;
  - To perform an analysis of the transcription, create a concept tree and validate it;
  - Creation of a glossary, a meta-model, model relationships, attributes and values;
  - To model process knowledge;
  - Validation of the models with experts.
- Detailed capture and modelling (steps 30–39) which includes, within others:
  - To perform further interviews and finalize models;
  - To create and assess a prototype end-product;
  - To capture and model detailed procedural and conceptual knowledge from experts (different techniques from interviewing);
  - To perform cross-validation, solve differences of opinion and ensure that all knowledge is validated;
  - To finalize the knowledge-models and the knowledge-base.
- Sharing the stored knowledge (steps 40–47) which includes, within others:
  - Creating and assessing provisional end-product;
  - Creating, releasing and publicising end-product;
  - To document the lessons learned.

Methodology 14. UPON (Unified Process for ONtology) builds on the experience of the methodological development of OntoLearn. The Ontolearn tool and method, offered methodological support towards ontology learning and automatic population of domain ontologies (Navigli et al. 2004; Velardi et al. 2005). The OntoLearn methodology had four steps: discovery of new terms, extraction of definitions, extraction of taxonomic information, and ontology update, and included experts as per-concept evaluators (definitions).

The UPON methodology is based on the Unified Process for software development and takes a use-case driven, iterative and incremental nature (de Nicola et al. 2005). The development process is organized in a workflow cycle of: requirements, analysis, design, implementation, and test. Each of this steps of the workflow has several phases (inception, elaboration,construction, and transition), and iterations (see Fig. 3.8), and supports the participation of domain experts as ontology engineers, especially in the initial stages of development.

The evaluation of the quality of the ontology includes four activities: (a) syntactic quality (formal), (b) semantic quality (consistency), (c) pragmatic quality (fidelity, relevance and completeness),[9] and (d) social quality (usability, reuse, etc. – after publication –) (de Nicola et al. 2009; Barbagallo et al. 2010).

[9]Fidelity can be achieved with the verification of references to the sources used in the description of the terms modelled in the ontology, while Relevance and completeness involve the verification of the correct implementation of the initial requirements (e.g., competency questions).

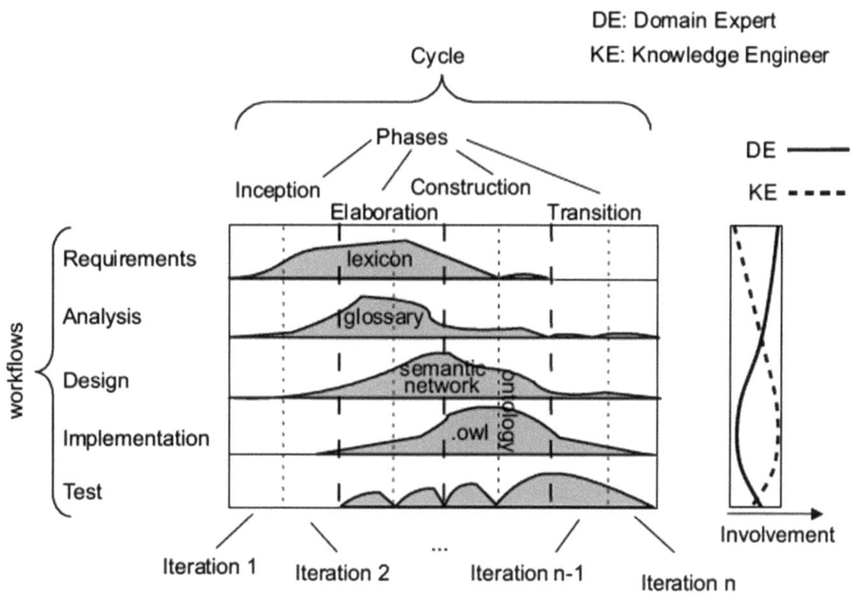

Fig. 3.8 UPON methodological steps and ontology engineers' involvement (de Nicola et al. 2009)

Methodology 15. Finally, the NeOn Methodology offers guidance towards the complex development of ontology networks as different from the development of single ontologies: ontology network development process (identification of activities that are carried out when an ontology network is developed), ontology network life cycle models (framework on which the identified activities are mapped), and ontology network life cycle (the project-specific sequence of activities once mapped) (Suárez-Figueroa et al. 2007).[10]

> A Network of Ontologies is a collection of ontologies related together via a variety of different relationships such as mapping, modularization, version, and dependency relationships. We call the elements of this collection Networked Ontologies (Haase et al. 2006).

Hence, this methodological approach builds upon the experiences of METHONTOLOGY, On-To-Knowledge and DILIGENT, although it is focused on the development of large ontologies, and supports the reuse and re-engineering of previously existing knowledge sources, ontology alignment, ontology network management,

[10]More information on the NeOn European Project (Lifecycle Support for Networked Ontologies IST-2005-027595 6th Framework) may be found at http://www.neon-project.org/web-content. For a quick reference to ontology networks and ontology network life cycle models visit *NeOn Methodology in a Nutshell* at http://www.neon-project.org/web-content/index.php?option=com_content&view=article&id=153, retrieved August 18, 2010. For further reading, you may find the project deliverables at the NeOn Project website, in particular, Suárez-Figueroa et al. (2007, 2008a, b, 2009b, b)

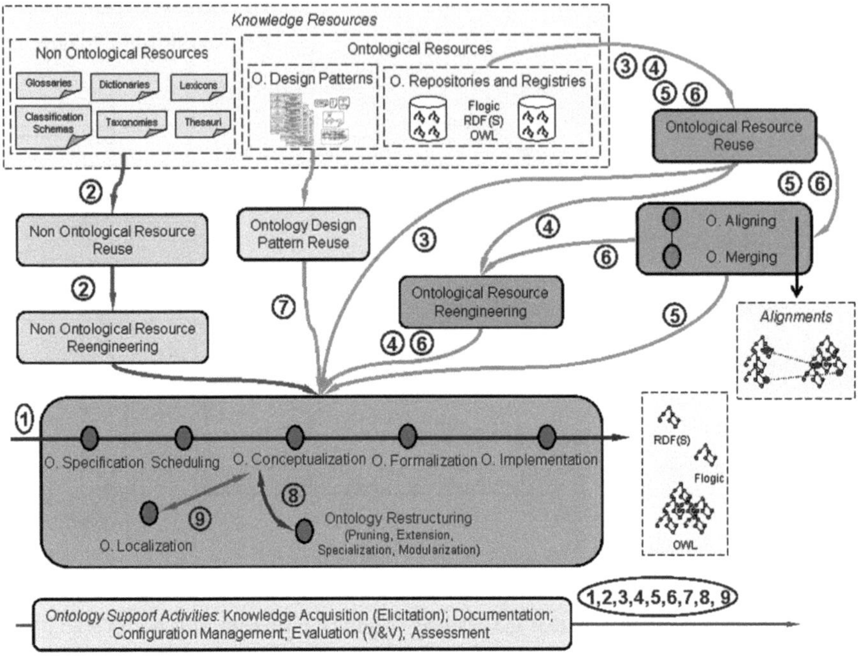

Fig. 3.9 NeOn outline of scenarios for the development of ontology networks (Suárez-Figueroa et al. 2007, 2008b; Gómez-Pérez and Suárez-Figueroa 2009)

ontology evolution, and the collaborative construction of ontologies.[11] Therefore, the NeOn methodological description offers guidelines towards the specification of ontology requirements, ontology search, reuse and re-engineering, ontology development scheduling, conceptualization through the use of ontology design patterns (ODPs, see Sect. 4.2.2.8 in Chap. 4 and Suárez-Figueroa et al. (2008a) and Presutti et al. (2008)), ontology evaluation, modularization, alignment and evolution. To cope with the of the complexity of ontology engineering, nine different scenarios for building ontologies and ontology networks are described (see Fig. 3.9).

In particular, the methodological approach for the definition of ontology requirements (Gómez-Pérez et al. 2008) consists on the definition of the following:

1. Purpose, Scope and Level of Formality
2. Users
3. Uses

[11]"METHONTOLOGY does not consider the reuse and reengineering of non ontological resources, neither the reuse of ontology design patterns. Taking into account the important dimensions considered in the NeOn project, we can say that METHONTOLOGY does not mention anything about collaboration and context. Although some mention about the dynamic dimension is made, no detailed guidelines about how to manage different versions are given" (Suárez-Figueroa et al. 2008a).

4. Requirements (Competency Questions)
5. Group Requirements (categorization of CQs)
6. Validate Requirements
7. Prioritize Requirements
8. Extract Terms

This methodological approach to the elaboration of a document for the specification of ontology requirements (ORSD) is based, within others, on the guidelines offered by Grüninger and Fox (1995), Sure and Studer (2002) and Sure (2003). Nevertheless, the more extensive guidelines offered in Suárez-Figueroa et al. (2008a, 2009b) are mainly directed towards ontology reuse. A ORSD template is included in the NeON Toolkit.

Many other methodologies have been reported. Above we have briefly described some of those which include have been historically relevant or provide extensive set of guidelines for a complete process. Gómez-Pérez and colleagues devoted much research into comparing different ontology building methodologies towards the definition of METHONTOLOGY, their methodological proposal. These authors analysed and compared the above-mentioned Cyc, Grüninger and Fox (1995) and Uschold and King (1995), within others. Detailed comparisons between all these methodologies may be found in Corcho et al. (2003) and Gómez-Pérez et al. (2003). Their analysis are a reference in the knowledge engineering community, see Sure et al. (2004).

Nevertheless, many other methodologies focused on offering specific support towards ontology learning, integration, reuse, evaluation, evolution or cooperative construction of ontologies may be found in the literature. For example, OntoClean, ONIONS, HCOME, IDEF5 or OntoEng. OntoClean is a methodological approach towards formal-based ontology evaluation, which focuses on the notions of essence, rigidity, unity, identity and dependency (Guarino and Welty 2002, 2004).[12] ONIONS (ONtological Integration Of Naive Sources) proposes a methodology for ontology integration, implemented in the medical domain (Gangemi et al. 1996, 1999; Steve et al. 1997).

HCOME (Human-Centered Ontology Engineering Methodology) supports the development of ontologies directly by 'knowledge workers', based on day-to-day active participation and interaction (Kotis et al. 2005; Kotis and Vouros 2006). "In particular, they must be enabled to develop, evaluate and further evolve ontologies individually and conversationally with their co-workers, according to their cognitive abilities, skills, knowledge base and context of work. Ideally, this must happen in the background of the day-to-day knowledge intensive activities of workers, in a seamless way to their working practices, and so that the semantic validity of

[12]The OntoClean ontology (OWL DL and OWL Full versions) may be found at: http://www.ontoclean.org. The Protégé ontology editor offers the possibility of implementing the OntoClean ontology towards evaluation. Moreover, AEON is proposed as a tool which automatically tags concepts with appropriate OntoClean meta-properties (Völker et al. 2005) (http://ontoware.org/projects/aeon, retrieved August 18, 2010).

Ontology life-cycle phases	Goals	Tasks
Specification	Define aim / scope / requirements / teams	- discuss requrements (S) - produce documents (S) - identify collaborators (S) specify the scope, aim of the ontology (S)
Conceptualisation	Acquire knowledge	- import from ontology libraries (P) - consult generic top ontology (P) - consult domain experts by discussion (S)
	Develop & Maintain Ontology	- improvise (P) - manage conceptualisations (P) - merge versions (P) - compare own versions (P) - generalize / specialize versions (P) - add documentation (P)
Exploitation	Use ontology	- browse ontology (P) - exploit in applications
	Evaluate ontology	- initiate arguments and criticism (S) - compare others' versions (S) - browse / exploit agreed ontologies (S) - manage the recorded discussions upon an ontology (S) - propose new ontology versions by incorporating suggested changes (S)

Fig. 3.10 HCOME life cycle (Kotis 2004)

specifications is assured" (Kotis and Vouros 2006). See Fig. 3.10 for an overview of the methodological HCOME life cycle. Furthermore, IDEF5 Ontology Description Capture Method belongs to the set of IDEF methods for business modelling and enterprise engineering (Perakath et al. 1994).[13]

Finally, OntoEng is a recent methodological approach, which takes into account previous developments, such as METHONTOLOGY, Ontology Development 101, etc. It is an iterative design method to develop ontologies which includes five phases (Planning, Analysis and Design, Development, Evaluation and Maintenance) with a total of twelve different design activities (e.g., knowledge acquisition, formalization, implementation, validation, documentation, maintenance, etc.). The methodology is inspired from the development of the V4 Telecoms Business Model Ontology (Al-Debei and Fitzgerald 2009, 2010).

[13]Involves five activities: (1) organizing and scoping (purpose); (2) data collection; (3) data analysis; (4) initial ontology development, and (5) ontology refinement and validation. IDEF5 includes ontology languages. For more information regarding IDEF methods and commercial tools, visit: http://www.idef.com

From the analysis of the above-mentioned methodological descriptions, especially CommonKADS, METHONTOLOGY, On-To-Knowledge, NeOn and UPON ontology building methodologies follow generally a cyclic modelling approach,[14] conformed by several stages which, in turn, include several management, development and support activities. These steps are, in general, a preparatory phase, a development phase and an application phase. The preparatory phase includes activities such as the initial feasibility study and the specification of requirements. The development stage comprehends knowledge acquisition activities, together with ontology conceptualization, formalization, evaluation and refinement. Development activities depend on the criteria established in the preparatory stages and these activities may need to be performed in iterative and *incremental* cycles, thus the need for ontology refinement. Finally, the application phase includes implementation and maintenance activities. The following Table (Table 3.1) includes a comparison of the activities taken into account by the revised methodologies during their development processes.

These methodologies may be also distinguished by the approach taken towards knowledge acquisition for ontology development. For example, Termontography and TERMINAE are bottom-up approaches which focus on the acquisition of low level domain classes or instances through a list of terms extracted by linguistic analysis techniques (e.g. natural language processing or NLP). None of the described methodologies focuses solely in the development of ontologies from a top-down approach, although the use of competency questions and the decision to reuse available top or upper ontologies can be seen as a top-down in ontology design. Nevertheless, most methodologies that include the establishment of competency questions (e.g. METHONTOLOGY, ON-TO-KNOWLEDGE), the analysis of available ontologies towards reuse, and ontology refinement steps, also suggest the extraction of lists of domain terms from texts. Sure and Studer (2003) comments during the description of ON-TO-KNOWLEDGE that, "[t]he usage scenario/competency question method usually follows a *top-down* approach in modelling the domain. One starts by modelling concepts in a very generic level. Subsequently they are refined. This approach is typically done manually and leads to a high-quality engineered ontology. Available top-level ontologies may be reused here and serve as a starting point to develop new ontologies. In practice this seems to be more a middle-out approach, that is, to identify the most important concepts which will then be used to obtain the remainder of the hierarchy by generalization and specialization. However, with the support of automatic document analysis, a typical *bottom-up* approach may be applied. There, relevant lexical entries are extracted semi-automatically from available documents. Based on the assumption that most concepts and conceptual structures of the domain as well the company terminology are described in documents, applying knowledge

[14] In general, they all offer a iterative life-cycle model. CommonKADS "follows a spiral approach that enables structured learning" (Schreiber et al. 1999). METHONTOLOGY is based in the development of evolving prototypes (Fernández-López et al. 1997).

Table 3.1 Comparison of methodological activities

	Preparatory step	Development step	Evaluation step	Tool support
Uschold and Grüninger (1996b)	Purpose	Ontology building: – Capture (brainstorming, grouping, define) – Coding – Integrating	Ontology evaluation	Ontolingua Server and most editors
CommonKADS	Feasibility study (problems, context, solutions)	Identification – domain familiarisation (sources, glossary) – reuse components Specification – task template – initial domain – conceptualization – complete KM Refinement – validate – refine	Knowledge refinement	PCPACK
METHONTOLOGY	Specification	Conceptualization – glossary – taxonomies – relations – concept dictionaries – axioms and rules Formalization	Evaluation	ODE and WebODE (also Protégé, OntoEdit, KAON, etc.)
OD 101	1. Domain and scope 2. Reuse	3. Term list 4. Classes 5. Class properties 6. Slot facets 7. Instantiate		Protégé and others

(continued)

Table 3.1 (continued)

	Preparatory step	Development step	Evaluation step	Tool support
OTK	Feasibility study Kickoff (ORSD)	Kickoff – source analysis – create draft ont. Refinement – KA experts – draft modification – formalization	Evaluation	KAON and KAON2 (OntoEdit)
DOGMA	Overall definition Feasibility Preparation and scoping – user req. – purpose – domain experts – knowledge sources	Domain Conceptualization – elicitation – breakdown – negotiation – discovery Application spec. – structuring – compet. questions – semantic constraints – answering compet. questions	Competency questions	DOGMA Modeler, DOGMA studio workbench
47-step guide	Start, scope and plan	Initial capture and modelling – interviewing – transcription – concept tree – modelization Detail capture and modelling – further KA	Validation of model with experts (initial capture) and various assessments (detailed capture and end-product)	PCPACK
UPON	Requirements W. – domain – purpose – scope – CQs	Analysis W. – reuse – term extraction – concept definition – relations – UML Implementation	Test – consistency – relevance – completeness	

acquisition from text for ontology design seems to be promising" (see also Sure et al. 2004). Therefore, most lifecycle ontology methodologies offer an open approach with various concurrent possibilities (top-down, middle-out, bottom-up), depending on the type and availability of domain sources, the specific domain, the set of requirements, etc.

3.3 Languages and Tools for Ontology Modelling

In order to revise existing legal ontologies it is also important to take into account not only if a specific methodology has been followed but also if any tools for ontology learning or editing were used in the process, together with the languages used in modelling the ontology. Again, extensive revisions regarding both, ontology languages (Gómez-Pérez and óscar Corcho 2002; Gómez-Pérez et al. 2003) and tools (Corcho et al. 2001, 2003; Gómez-Pérez et al. 2003) were performed by Gómez-Pórez and colleagues.

3.3.1 Representation Languages

During the 1990s, several ontology implementation languages were created. For example, KIF was based on first order logic, Ontolingua (from the DARPA Knowledge Sharing Effort) and FLogic on frames in combination with first order logic, and Loom (based on description logics (DL) (Corcho et al. 2003; Gómez-Pérez et al. 2003).[15]

Nevertheless, and with the Internet era, as mentioned in Chap. 1, current ontology languages adapted in order to exploit the possibilities and characteristics of the Web: SHOE (*simple HTML ontology extension*), XML[16] (*Extensible Markup Language*), XOL (*XML-based ontology language*), and RDF[17] (*Resource Description Framework*). The RDF (Resource Description Framework) language offers simple descriptive information about the resources on the Web, encoded in sets of triples: subject (an resource), predicate (a property or relation), object (a resource or a value). "RDF is a language for expressing data models using statements expressed as triples" (Segaran et al. 2009).[18] Although RDF allows the description

[15]For particular information on some of these languages see, for example, Genesereth and Fikes (1992) and Gruber (1992).

[16]W3C recommendation (16 August 2006, edited in place 29 September 2006): http://www.w3.org/TR/xml11, retrieved August 18, 2010.

[17]W3C recommendation (10 February 2004): http://www.w3.org/TR/rdf-primer, retrieved August 18, 2010.

[18]Triples can be written using XML tags. Visit http://www.w3.org/standards/techs/rdf#w3c_all for more information on RDF.

of relationships among resources and the establishment of lists it focuses on resource instantiation. `rdf:type` describes that a resource is an instance of another resource. RDF Schema (RDFS) is the language that allows the description of class systems. "RDFS is about sets. (...) RDFS provides some guidelines about how to use this graph structure [RDF] in a disciplined way. It provides a way to talk about the vocabulary that will be used in an RDF graph. Which individuals are related to one another, and how? How are the properties we use to define our individuals related to other sets of individuals and, indeed, to one another?" Allemang and Hendler (2008). These are the RDFS elements[19]:

More recently, the development of the SKOS (Simple Knowledge Organization System) specification allows the representation in RDF of thesauri, classification schemes, subject heading lists and taxonomies.[20]

As Antoniou and van Harmelen (2004b) and Antoniou and van Harmelen (2004a) describe it, the expressivity of RDF/S was very limited and, at the same time, a number of research groups in America and Europe and the Web Ontology Working Group of W3C identified the need for more expressiveness, for an ontology language with more expressive power. Similarly,

> [th]e Semantic Web will build on XML's ability to define customized tagging schemes and RDF's flexible approach to representing data. The first level above RDF required for the Semantic Web is an ontology language what can formally describe the meaning of terminology used in Web documents. If machines are expected to perform useful reasoning tasks on these documents, the language must go beyond the basic semantics of RDF Schema (McGuinness and van Harmelen 2003).

From the American and the European efforts DAML+OIL[21] (Connolly et al. 2001) appeared, and was taken as the starting point for the development of the Ontology Web Language (OWL) by W3C (Dean et al. 2004; McGuinness and van Harmelen 2003; Smith et al. 2004). See Fig. 3.11 for a graphical representation.

These include URI (Uniform Resource Identifier) and Unicode,[22] which are original from the WWW and provide global identifiers and international character encoding standards. Further languages include XML (eXtensible Markup Language),[23] a superset of HTML (HyperText Markup Language) that offers more expressivity to the Web and is usually used to add structure

---

[19]For the RDF Vocabulary Description Language 1.0: RDF Schema, visit: http://www.w3.org/TR/rdf-schema/, retrieved August 18, 2010.

[20]The relationship between RDF, OWL and SKOS is complex, read more details in the SKOS Simple Knowledge Organization System, Reference W3C Recommendation 18 August 2009 http://www.w3.org/TR/skos-reference, the SKOS Primer, W3C Working Group Note 18 August 2009 at http://www.w3.org/TR/skos-primerSKOS, retrieved August 18, 2010. More information may be found at the W3C SKOS webpage: http://www.w3.org/2004/02/skos, retrieved August 18, 2010.

[21]DAML (DARPA Agent Markup Language, see http://www.daml.org) and OIL (ontology inference layer, see http://www.ontoknowledge.org/oil).

[22]http://www.unicode.org

[23]For details on XML technology visit http://www.w3.org/standards/xml/

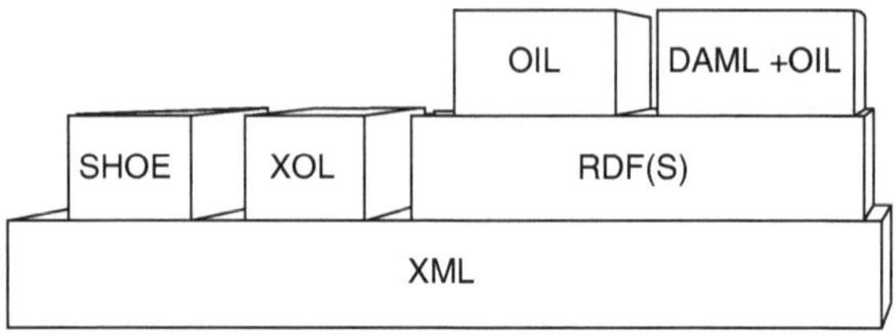

Fig. 3.11 Initial stack of ontology markup languages by Benjamins et al. (2002), a similar but more detailed one, at the time, may be found in Corcho et al. (2003)

to documents, and the so-called ontology languages: RDF/RDFS (Resource Description Framework/Schema), OWL 1, and OWL2 (Ontology Web Language). While the RDF language offers simple descriptive information about the resources on the Web, encoded in sets of triples of subject (a resource), predicate (a property or relation), and object (a resource or a value), RDFS allows the description of sets.[24] Further, the OWL language (Ontology Web Language) offers a more expressive language to define structured ontologies (e.g. class disjointness, union or equivalence, etc.), that can be used by different systems to improve the accuracy of web searches, to share information, to define terms or to describe and represent a domain (Berners-Lee et al. 2001). Currently OWL may be distinguished between OWL 1 and OWL 2, an extension and revision of the previous version.[25]

Currently OWL may be distinguished between OWL 1 and OWL 2, an extension and revision of the previous version. OWL 1 has three species: OWL Full, DL and Lite. OWL Full offers maximum expressiveness and no computational guarantees. OWL Lite offers the possibility to represent simple constraints (cardinality constraints) and hierarchies. OWL DL offers further expressive support, although retains computational guarantees (McGuinness and van Harmelen 2003). The revision of OWL 1 resulted in the OWL 2 standard, because "practical experience with OWL 1 has shown that OWL 1 DL (the most expressive but still decidable language of the OWL 1 family) lacks several constructs that are often necessary for modeling complex domains" Grau et al. (2008). OWL 2 maintains a Full and DL subspecies.[26]

OWL 2 adds new functionalities with respect to OWL 1, such as keys, property chains; richer datatypes, qualified cardinality restrictions, asymmetric, reflexive, and disjoint properties, and enhanced annotation capabilities.Moreover, different

---

[24]Triples can be written using XML tags. Visit http://www.w3.org/standards/techs/rdf#w3c_all for more information on RDF.

[25]See Chap. 3 and visit http://www.w3.org/standards/techs/owl#w3c_all, retrieved August 18, 2010, for more information.

[26]For a succinct and description of the OWL language, including OWL 2 profiles, see Hoekstra (2009b).

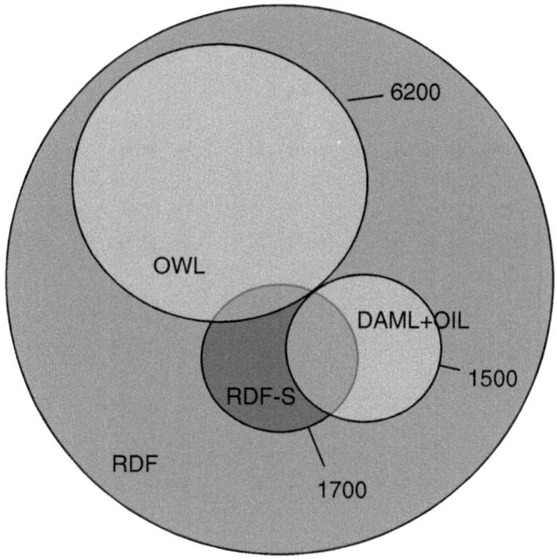

Fig. 3.12 Usage of ontology representation languages (d'Aquin et al. 2007)

profiles are defined for OWL 2, each one of them more restricted than OWL 2 DL: OWL 2 EL, OWL 2 QL, and OWL 2 RL.[27] Ontology web languages are constantly evolving.[28]

Nowadays, most ontologies built towards Semantic Web enhancement are built either using RDF or OWL (d'Aquin et al. 2007), although other languages offer perhaps more expressivity at the moment (e.g., LOOM), as suggested by Corcho et al. (2003) and Gómez-Pérez et al. (2003). d'Aquin et al. (2007) analysed 25,500 semantic documents and ontologies available on the Web and detected that the languages mostly used were RDF, OWL and DAML+OIL (see Fig. 3.12).

Table 3.2 below (reproduced from the research by Gómez-Pérez et al. (2003)) compares some features of the most widely used ontology languages. '+' indicates that the language supports that particular feature and '–' indicates that it does not support it. 'w' are non supported features that are available after some effort (workaround). More detailed descriptions regarding some of ontology web languages may be found also in Antoniou and van Harmelen (2004a, b), Antoniou et al. (2005) and Antoniou and van Harmelen (2008).[29]

[27]All OWL 1 ontologies remain valid OWL 2 ontologies. For further details consult Hitzler et al. (2009) and http://www.w3.org/TR/2009/REC-owl2-overview-20091027/, retrieved August 18, 2010. For more details on OWL profiles read Motik et al. (2009) and Golbreich et al. (2009).

[28]See, for example, the discussions regarding OWL-S. An overview may be found in Antoniou and van Harmelen (2008). See also: http://www.daml.org/services/owl-s, retrieved August 18, 2010.

[29]Also, visit the World Wide Web Consortium (W3C) website for further developments on language specifications (http://www.w3.org).

Table 3.2 Comparative list of ontology languages (Updated from Gómez-Pérez et al. (2003))

	Ontolingua	LOOM	FLogic	SHOE	XOL	RDF(S)	OIL	DAML+OIL	OWL	OWL 2
Concepts										
Instance attributes	+	+	+	+	+	+	+	+	+	+
Class attributes	+	−	+	−	+	w	−	w	w	+
Type constraints	+	+	+	+	+	+	+	+	+	+
Cardinality constraints	+	+	w	−	+	−	+	+	+	+
CONCEPT TAXONOMIES										
Subclass-of	+	+	+	+	+	+	+	+	+	+
Disjoint-decomposition	+	+	w	−	−	−	+	+	+	+
Partition-decomposition	+	+	w	−	−	−	+	+	w	+
Relations										
Binary relations	+	+	+	+	+	+	+	+	+	+
n-ary relations	+	+	w	+	w	w	w	w	w	+
Relation hierarchies	+	+	w	−	−	+	+	+	+	+
Other										
Formal axioms	+	+	+	−	−	−	−	−	−	w
Instances	+	+	+	+	+	+	+	+	+	+
Rules	−	+	−	+	−	−	−	−	−	−

3.3.2 *Ontology Modelling Tools and Environments*

Although the building process is generally manual, several tools have been built in order to support and automate certain aspects of the construction processes of ontologies, especially knowledge acquisition and formalization.

"Like KBS development, ontology development faces the knowledge acquisition bottleneck problem" (Blázquez et al. 1998).[30] Knowledge acquisition has been identified as a *central concern* for the development of knowledge bases for expert systems for nearly 50 years. Knowledge acquisition is again a central concern for the development of ontologies, especially when dealing with modelling expert knowledge, either static or dynamic.

The literature reports many different knowledge acquisition (elicitation or capture) techniques used for KBS construction that may be also taken into account towards modelling (tacit or explicit) procedural and conceptual expert knowledge for ontology construction (summarised in Fig. 3.13).[31]

Moreover, the acquisition of "explicit knowledge implicitly contained in (textual) data" (Buitelaar et al. 2005b) for the construction of ontologies has given rise to the emergence of multiple ontology learning tools.[32] Also knowledge may be acquired by the use of ontology editors. "For example, linguistic tools can analyze the content of domain documents in order to synthesize ontology terms themselves, or to extract content corresponding to a domain ontology as individuals forming a knowledge base. Building complex ontologies today usually relies on the manual composition of the ontology using an ontology editor for the chosen ontology languages(s)" (Denny 2004). Therefore, most ontology building tools are directed towards ontology learning, editing, merging, mapping, and evaluating.

In the following sections we will describe briefly, first some of the most relevant ontology editors and, later, some of the most relevant ontology learning tools, according to the information provided in their documentation.

3.3.2.1 Ontology Development Environments and Editors

- **DOGMAModeler.**[33] The DOGMAModeler is an ontology modelling tool based on the Object Role modelling graphical notation. "The philosophy of

[30] "Developers of expert systems have spoken so much of the knowledge-acquisition 'bottleneck' that the expression has become a chiché. Nevertheless, knowledge acquisition remains the major difficulty in the creation of most practical knowledge bases" (Musen 1993).

[31] See, for example, Steels (1990), Musen (1993), Hoffman et al. (1995), Marcus (1999), Schreiber et al. (1999), Burge (1998) and Milton (2007).

[32] "Although the aims of knowledge acquisition and ontology learning (from text) are certainly overlapping – in essence the acquisition of explicit knowledge implicitly contained in (textual) data – there are, however, also a number of novel and innovative aspects to ontology learning that sets it apart from much of the previous work in knowledge acquisition" (Buitelaar et al. 2005b).

[33] More information & download: http://www.jarrar.info/Dogmamodeler, retrieved August 18, 2010.

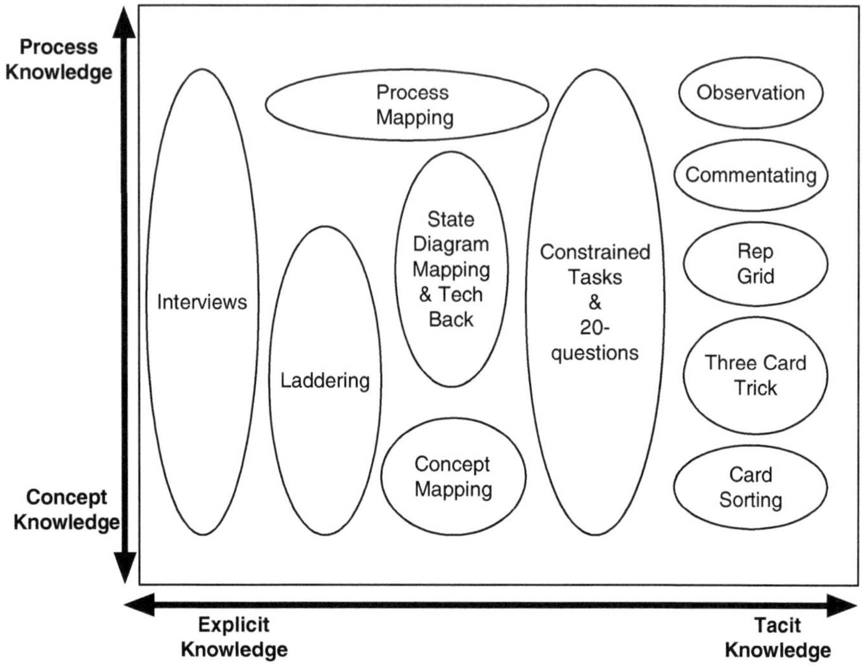

Fig. 3.13 Knowledge acquisition techniques and type of knowledge to be acquired by Epistemics (2003)

DogmaModeler is to enable non-IT experts to model ontologies with a little or no involvement of an ontology engineer" (Spyns and Lisovoy 2003). ORM diagrams may be verbalized in pseudo natural language (including English, Dutch, German, French, Catalan, Spanish, Arabic, Russian, etc. (Jarrar et al. 2006)). The tool itself is offered in English. See Fig. 3.14 for a view of the tool's interface.

- Developers: STAR Lab, Vrije Universiteit Brussel (Mustafa Jarrar)
- Current release: 27/10/2006 (see DOGMA Studio Workbench below)
- Standard formats supported: ORM
- Methodological support: DOGMA methodology and ORM methodology
- Inference and reasoning services: Automatic mapping of ORM diagrams into the DIG description logic interface and reasoning using Racer
- Usability issues:

  Graph view: Yes
  Multi-user or collaborative support: No

- Availability: Free and open source

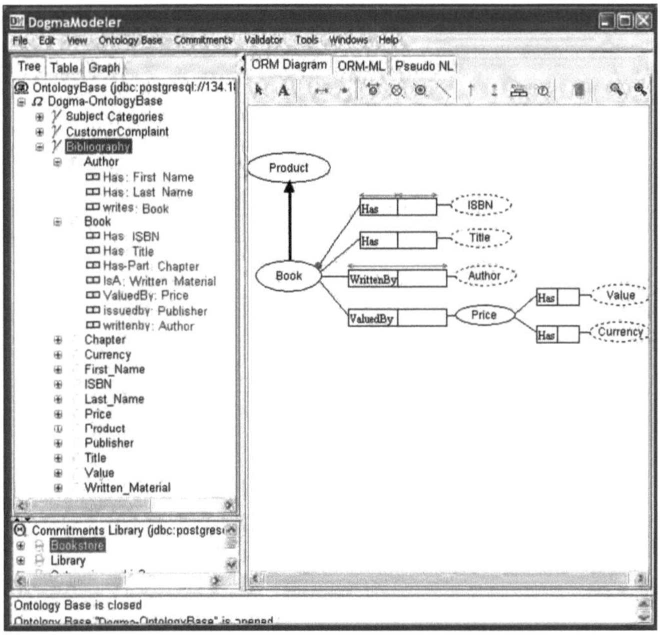

Fig. 3.14 A general screenshot of DogmaModeler

- **DOGMA Studio Workbench.**[34] The DOGMA Studio Workbench, see Fig. 3.14,[35] is the current toolsuite that supports the DOGMA ontology engineering approach. This toolsuite contains a workbench (Eclipse) and a server, with various plug-ins. The DOGMA-MESS (see de Moor et al. (2006) and De Leenheer and Debruyne (2010)) community layer offers an elicitation method based on the use of conceptual graphs (CG) for the distributed negotiation of meaning between stakeholders and consensus building (Fig 3.15).
  - Developers: STAR Lab, Vrije Universiteit Brussel
  - Current release: Not reported
  - Standard formats supported: ORM (an alternative commitment language – Ω-RIDL (Trog et al. 2007) – and the mapping of ORM into OWL-DL is being developed (Spyns et al. 2008; Bach et al. 2010))
  - Methodological support: DOGMA methodology and ORM methodology

[34]More information consult Debruyne et al. (2009) and De Leenheer and Debruyne (2010) and visit: http://starlab.vub.ac.be/website/dogmastudio, retrieved August 18, 2010.

[35]DOGMA pipeline (see Fig. 3.15) from http://starlab.vub.ac.be/website/node/360, retrieved August 18, 2010.

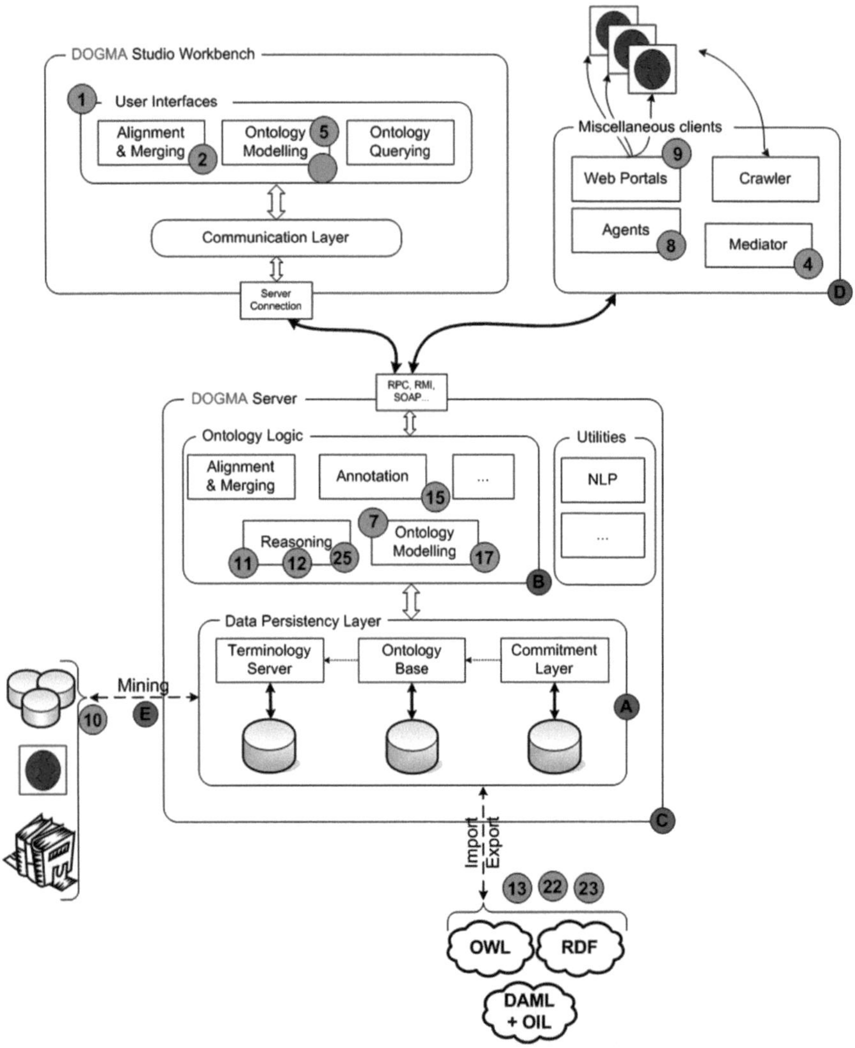

Fig. 3.15 An overview of the DOGMA Studio Workbench and Server

– Inference and reasoning services: DOGMA-MESS has a Prolog+CG implementation[36]
– Usability issues:

Graph view: Yes (research with regards to T-Lex is described in Trog et al. (2006) and Tang and Trog (2010)).

[36]Visit http://prologpluscg.sourceforge.net/index.html, retrieved August 18, 2010, for more information.

Multi-user or collaborative support: Yes

– Availability: The toolsuite is not free and available under demand, although a free trial version is under development.

- **DODDLE & DODDLE-OWL.**[37] "DODDLE-OWL (a Domain Ontology rapiD DeveLopment Environment – OWL extension –) is a domain ontology development tool for the Semantic Web. DODDLE-OWL makes reuse of existing ontologies and supports the semi-automatic construction of taxonomic and other relationships in domain ontologies from documents". DODDLE-OWL has six different modules: Ontology Selection Module, Input Module, Construction Module, Refinement Module, Visualization Module, and Translation Module. See Fig. 5.7 for a view of the architecture (modules). For recent descriptions of the environment see Morita et al. (2006, 2008).

  – Developers: Takeshi Morita (Visiting Researcher, Keio University, Japan/JSPS Research Fellow (PD)), Naoki Fukuta (Faculty of Information, Shizuoka University, Japan), Noriaki Izumi (National Institute of Advanced Industrial Science and Technology, Japan), and Takahira Yamaguchi (Faculty of Science and Technology, Keio University, Japan).
  – Current release: 2005-04-26 (DODDLE-OWL version 0.2). 2009-06-15 (DODDLE-OWL Beta7 version released).
  – Standard formats supported: OWL
  – Methodological support: DODDLE offers a step-by-step process for the construction of domain ontologies from machine readable dictionaries (e.g., WordNet)
  – Inference and reasoning services: Jena 2 is used to export the constructed ontologies into OWL format.[38]
  – Usability issues:

  Graph view: Yes. (Visualization Module (MR3)[39] is connected with DODDLE-OWL and works as a graphical editor for RDF contents and RDFS classes, which allows consistency checking.)
  Multi-user or collaborative support: Not reported

  – Availability: Free (under GNU General Public License)

[37]See also (Sugiura et al. 2004). More information and download from http://doddle-owl.sourceforge.net, retrieved August 18, 2010.

[38]Jena: http://jena.sourceforge.net (For more information on Jena 2 inference support, visit http://jena.sourceforge.net/inference, retrieved August 18, 2010.

[39]http://mr3.sourceforge.net, retrieved August 18, 2010.

- **Hozo**[40] is an environment for ontology development. "The features of Hozo include (1) Supporting to role concepts, (2) Visualization of ontologies in well considered format, and (3) Distributed development based on management of dependencies between ontologies" (Kozaki et al. 2005). All versions are offered in Japanese, the latest version is also offered in English (with Italian menu options).
  - Developers: Mizoguchi Lab., Institute of Scientific and Industrial Research, Osaka University
  - Current release: English version v5.2.30 (13/07/2010), Japanese version v5.2.30 (13/07/2010)
  - Standard formats supported: Ontologies and models may be translated into different formats (hierarchical text, XML/DTD, DAML+OIL, RDF(S), and OWL)
  - Methodological support: "based on both of a fundamental consideration of an ontological theory and a methodology of building an ontology" (Kozaki et al. 2005).
  - Inference and reasoning services: Hozo offers "effective support for avoidance of inconsistency between component ontologies during their construction process" (Kozaki et al. 2005), although no inference engine is reported.
  - Usability issues:

    Graph view: Yes (map generation tool for ontology exploration)

    Multi-user or collaborative support: Hozo supports the distributed development of ontologies "We assume a situation where a target ontology is divided into several component ontologies and they are constructed individually in a distributed environment (and sometimes in parallel by different developers)" (Kozaki et al. 2005).

  - Availability: Free. Also, the Hozo developers offer the Hozo API (or Hozo Core) which allows data created by the Hozo Ontology Editor to be used by a Java application.

- **KAON2 & OWL Tools.**[41] "KAON2 is a successor to the KAON project (often referred to as KAON1, although not backward compatible) and provides a complete is an infrastructure for ontology management.[42] The main difference

[40]More information is available in Kozaki et al. (2005) and Kumazawa et al. (2009). Hozo may be downloaded from http://www.ei.sanken.osaka-u.ac.jp/hozo, retrieved August 18, 2010. A discussion on the representation and formalization of roles in Hozo may be found in Kozaki et al. (2008).

[41]KAON2 and tools may be downloaded from: http://kaon2.semanticweb.org and http://owltools.ontoware.org

[42]"KAON is an open-source ontology management infrastructure targeted for business applications. It includes a comprehensive tool suite allowing easy ontology creation and management and provides a framework for building ontology-based applications". The **KAON IO modeler** was developed by FZY and AIFB and is current release its 1.2.7 (April 2004). It is distributed under

to KAON1 is the supported ontology language: KAON1 used a proprietary extension of RDFS, whereas KAON2 is based on OWL-DL". It includes, a module for extracting ontology instances from relational databases and a DIG interface, allowing access from tools such as Protégé.

- Developers: Information Process Engineering (IPE) at the Research Center for Information Technologies (FZI), Institute of Applied Informatics and Formal Description Methods (AIFB) at the University of Karlsruhe and Information Management Group (IMG) at the University of Manchester.
- Current release: 07/2006 (v.0.27) OntoBroker is a commercial inference engine based originally on KAON2.[43] See below the NeOn Toolkit.
- Standard formats supported: OWL-DL, SWRL, and F-Logic. (The main difference with the previous version of the KAON ontology infrastructure is that it used a proprietary extension of RDFS)
- Methodological support: Not reported
- Inference and reasoning services: Built-in inference engine for answering conjunctive queries (expressed using SPARQL syntax)
- Usability issues:

  Graph view: Not reported
  Multi-user or collaborative support: No

- Availability: Free of charge for universities for non-commercial academic usage.

• **NeOn Toolkit**.[44] The NeOn Toolkit, an extensible Ontology Engineering Environment, is developed within the framework of the NeOn European Project for "improving the capability to handle multiple networked ontologies that exist in a particular context, are created collaboratively, and might be highly dynamic and constantly evolving". This toolkit extends many existing ontology technologies, such as KAON or WebODE (Gómez et al. 2006), and it currently provides 45 plug-ins for a variety of ontology engineering activities: Annotation and Documentation, Development, Human-Ontology Interaction, Knowledge Acquisition, Management, Modularization and Customization, Ontology Dynamics, Ontology Evaluation, Ontology Matching, Reasoning and Inference, and Reuse (Fig. 3.16).[45]

  - Developers: NeOn Project partners: "The consortium is formed by fourteen institutions with extensive experience in research and development from

GNU Lesser General Public License and may be downloaded from http://sourceforge.net/projects/kaon, retrieved November 10, 2008.

[43]OntoBroker: http://www.ontoprise.de/en/home/products/ontobroker.

[44]NeOn IST-2005-027595, http://www.neon-project.org. More information and downloads may be found at http://neon-toolkit.org, retrieved August 18, 2010.

[45]All previous versions plug-ins might not be available for the latest NeOn Toolkit version. The NeOn plug-ins may be found at http://neon-toolkit.org/wiki/Neon_Plugins

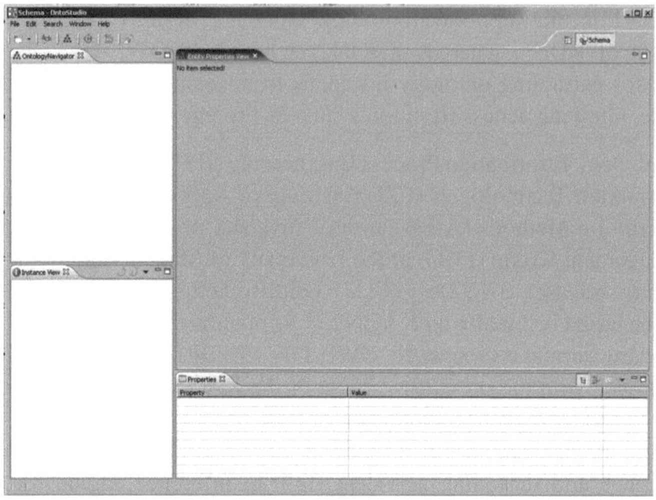

Fig. 3.16 Screenshot of NeOn Toolkit

United Kingdom, Germany, Spain, Italy, Slovenia and France" (Knowledge Media Institute (The Open University, UK), Institut AIFB (Universitaet Karlsruhe, Germany), Ontology Engineering Group (Universidad Politecnica de Madrid, Spain), Software AG (Germany), Intelligent Software Components (iSOCO S.A., Spain), Jozef Stefan Institute (Slovenia), Institut National de Recherche en Informatique et en Automatique (INRIA, France), Natural Language Processing Group (University of Sheffield, UK), ISWeb Group (Universitaet Koblenz-Landau, Germany), Laboratory for Applied Ontology (Italian National Research Council, ISTC-CNR, Italy), Ontoprise GmbH (Germany), Laboratorios KIN, S.A. (Spain), GILW, Food & Agriculture Organization of the United Nations (FAO, Italy), and ATOS Origin (Spain).

- Current release: 20-05-2010, v2.3.1 (Linux 32 and 64 bit, Windows, MacOS)
- Standard formats supported: F-Logic, (subsets of) RDF(S) and OWL1 and OWL2[46]
- Methodological support: Neon Methodology (see Gómez-Pérez et al. 2008; Suárez-Figueroa et al. 2008a)
- Inference and reasoning services: rule and query commercial plugins available
- Usability issues:

Graph view: Yes
Multi-user or collaborative support: Yes (main interest)

[46]For a list of supported OWL2 features see the available documentation http://neon-toolkit.org/wiki/Documentation_and_Support

- Availability: NeOn core is free and open source (commercial plugins are also available).

- **Ontolingua & Chimaera.**[47] The Ontolingua Ontology Editor is a web-based distributed collaborative environment to browse, create, edit, modify, and use ontologies. "The tools in Ontolingua are oriented toward authoring of ontologies by assembling and extending ontologies obtained from the library" (Farquhar et al. 1997). "Chimaera is a merging and diagnostic web-based browser ontology environment" (McGuinness et al. 2000), which was build on top of Ontolingua.

  - Developers: Knowledge Systems, AI Laboratory (KSL), Stanford University
  - Current release: Ontolingua ontology editor 1.0.650 (14/10/2002).
  - Standard formats supported: Ontolingua implements KIF and LOOM. Chimaera may load and export files in OWL and DAML formats.
  - Methodological support: Not reported
  - Inference and reasoning services: Not reported
  - Usability issues:

    Graph view: Not provided.
    Multi-user or collaborative support: Ontolingua supports multiple simultaneous users

  - Availability: Available over WWW, offered by Stanford KSL Network Services (anonymous user is allowed, registration is recommended).

- **Protégé.**[48] "Protégé is an extensible, platform-independent environment for creating and editing ontologies and knowledge bases". This tool offers an intuitive and easy-to-use graphical user interface and can be easily extended with tailored plug-ins. The tool is offered in English although entries may be input in any language or character. Also, "the Protégé-OWL editor is bundled with the 'full' installation of Protégé" (Fig. 3.17).

  - Developers: Stanford Medical Informatics, Stanford University.
  - Current release: v3.4.4 / v4.02 / v4.1 beta
  - Standard formats supported: Version 3 (RDFS, N3, ClIPS and OWL), version 4 (RDF, OWL1 and OWL2– full support in version 4.1–).
  - Methodological support: Not specified (Ontology Development 101, suggested).
  - Inference and reasoning services: DIG reasoning available in version 3. Fact++ and Pellet are embedded in version 4.
  - Usability issues:

---

[47] Information and downloads may be found at http://ksl.stanford.edu/software/ontolingua and http://www-ksl.stanford.edu/software/chimaera/, respectively.

[48] More information and download from: http://protege.stanford.edu

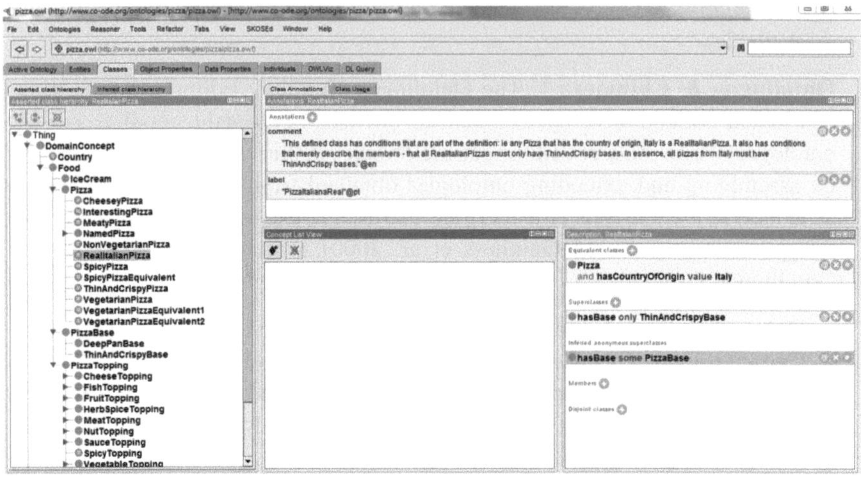

Fig. 3.17 Protégé screenshot

Graph view: Yes, plug-in support. OWL Viz plug-in (GraphViz), and OntoGraph (v 4.1).

Multi-user or collaborative support: Yes. The client-server mode allows the simultaneous edition of a shared ontology stored on a Protégé server. Further, collaborative development of ontologies is supported by Collaborative Protégé, which provides multi-user mode and support towards collaborative ontology development (Tudorache et al. 2010),[49] and by WebProtégé, a web-based ontology editor. [50]

– Availability: Free and open source software (registration recommended).

• **WebODE.**[51] As it is described in the Ontological Engineering Group webpage, "WebODE was built as a scalable, extensible, integrated workbench that covers and gave support to most of the activities involved in the ontology development process (conceptualization, reasoning, exchange, etc.) and supplied a comprehensive set of ontology related services that permit interoperation with other information systems". The WebODE platform was built using a three-tier model, using an application server basis, which provides both high extensibility (easy addition of new services) and usability (easy use of existing services). WebODE

[49]Collaborative Protégé: http://protegewiki.stanford.edu/wiki/Collaborative_Protege, retrieved August 18, 2010.

[50]WebProtégé: http://protegewiki.stanford.edu/wiki/WebProtege, retrieved August 18, 2010.

[51]For more information consult (Vega 2003) and visit http://www.oeg-upm.net

was the web counterpart for ODE (Ontology Design Environment). The NeOn toolkit described above took WebODE into account (Gómez et al. 2006).

- Developers: Ontological Engineering Group, Technical University of Madrid (UPM)
- Current release: 01/11/2003 (v.2.0.9)
- Standard formats supported: WebODE exports to WebODE's XML, Prolog, RDF(S), X-CARIN, OIL, Java/Jess, DAML+OIL, UML and OWL, and imports from WebODE's XML, RDF(S), DAML+OIL, UML and OWL
- Methodological support: METHONTOLOGY
- Inference and reasoning services: WebODE has a built-in inference engine and offers consistency checking regarding type constraints, numerical values constraints, cardinality constraints, and taxonomic consistency verification (common instances of disjoint classes, loops, etc.)
- Usability issues:

  Graph view: integrated graphical taxonomy and views
  Multi-user or collaborative support: It supports groups of users (access to ontologies) and synchronization mechanisms to allow several users to edit the same ontology without errors.

- Availability: In 2006 support was discontinued.

Other commercial editors may also be found in the market, such as, TopBraid Composer, an ontology development environment part of the TopBraid Suit (an integrated toolsuit for the development and implementation of semantically-based solutions). TopBraid Composer's free edition of this product supports the RDF Schema, the OWL Web Ontology Language, and the SPARQL Query Language standards.[52] Further ontology editors are Altova's SemanticWorks 2010,[53] or OntoStudio.[54] To support the HCOME methodology, the HCONE2 Ontology Engineering Environment has been developed.[55] Finally, we may find also the DaFOE editor (Differential and formal ontology editor),[56] and the SWOOP ontology

[52]More information is available at TopQuadrant: http://www.topquadrant.com

[53]A free trial version of this product is available at http://www.altova.com/semanticworks.html, retrieved August 18, 2010.

[54]More information regarding OntoStudio may be found at Weiten (2009) and http://www.ontoprise.de/en/home/products/ontostudio/, retrieved August 18, 2010.

[55]The HCONE2 tool integrates support for the collaborative engineering of ontologies, HCOME-3O (Kotis 2010). More information on HCONE2 may be found at http://icsd-ai.aegean.gr/hcone/index.php, retrieved August 18, 2010.

[56]DaFOE: http://dafoe4app.fr

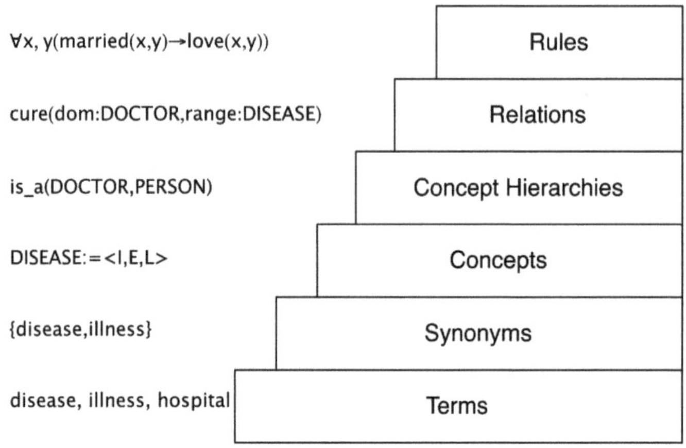

Fig. 3.18 Ontology learning from texts as a layer cake by Buitelaar et al. (2005a)

editor.[57,58] For an extensive revisions of ontology editors consult Mizoguchi and Kozaki (2009), Denny (2004)[59] and Gómez-Pérez et al. 2003.

3.3.2.2 Ontology Learning Tools and Textual Analysis Tools

Ontology learning tools may be used towards obtaining a first input to inform the discussion at the first stages of development, mostly from textual data analysis.[60] Buitelaar et al. (2005b) offered a layered view regarding ontology learning tools from text (see Fig. 3.18). Ontology learning from text is interested in obtaining concept and concept relationships (`subclassOf`, and others) from the terms present in the textual corpus.

> Ontology development is primarily concerned with the definition of concepts and relations between them, but connected to this also knowledge about the symbols that are used to refer to them. In our case this implies the acquisition of linguistic knowledge about the terms that are used to refer to a specific concept in text and possible synonyms of these

---

[57]SWOOP: http://code.google.com/p/swoop, retrieved August 18, 2010.

[58]Further ontology editors such as OILed and OntoEdit are now no longer supported or maintained in their previous websites. OILed: http://oiled.man.ac.uk. OntoEdit: http://ontoserver.aifb.uni-karlsruhe.de/ontoedit

[59]Denny (2004) offers a comparative table including 94 ontology editors, updated during 2004.

[60]Maedche and Staab (2001) distinguished several approaches to ontology learning according to their input: free text, dictionary, knowledge base, semistructured schemata, and relational schemata.

terms. An ontology further consists of a taxonomy backbone (is-a relation) and other, non-hierarchical relations. Finally, in order to derive also facts that are not explicitly encoded by the ontology but could be derived from it, also rules should be defined (and if possible acquired) that allow for such derivations.

Most ontology learning methods are based on natural language analysis on a corpus of text and use WordNet (a lexical database of English nouns, verbs, adjectives and adverbs grouped into synsets),[61] Also, most methods take a semi-automatic approach (human participation in evaluation) to ontology extraction. For this, other textual data analysis tools other than ontology learning tools may also provide useful inputs for ontology development.[62] While *terms* may be generally understood as "linguistic realizations of domain-specific concepts", "[t]he extraction of concepts from text is controversial" (Buitelaar et al. 2005b).[63] Therefore, "[m]ost of the research in concept extraction addressed the question from linguistic or textual perspective, regarding concepts as clusters of related terms" (Buitelaar et al. 2005b). Extensive accounts and comparisons between several ontology learning and textual analysis tools may be found in Buitelaar et al. (2005b), Gómez-Pérez and Manzano-Macho (2003, 2004), Cimiano et al. (2006), Sánchez-Ruenes (2007) and Vallbé (2009). Some of the ontology engineering environments and editors discussed in the previous section may incorporate ontology learning features (e.g. Doddle and Hozo) or ontology learning plug-ins (e.g. Protégé and the NeOn Toolkit). Here we will provide a short overview of some specific tools: Alceste, AntConc, GATE, OntoGen, OntoLearn, OntoLT, TERMINAE, TextOntoEx, Text to Knowledge (T2K), Text2Onto, and Yoshikoder.[64]

Alceste[65] is a software for textual data analysis developed by Reinert (2003), which quantifies the corpus of text for the extraction of its most significant structures (discourse analysis). The corpus is split in chunks, and most significant words (lemmas) are extracted for each segment.

---

[61] Wordnet: http://wordnet.princeton.edu

[62] "A simple technique for extracting relevant lexical entries that may indicate concepts is counting frequencies of terms in a given set of (linguistically preprocessed) documents, the corpus *D*. In general this approach is based on the assumption that a frequent term in a set of domain-specific texts indicates occurrence of a relevant concept" (Maedche and Staab 2004).

[63] For example, Buitelaar et al. (2005b) states that "concept induction or formation should provide: an intensional definition of the concept, a set of concept instances (...), and a set of linguistic realisations". Aussenac-Gilles et al. (2000a) proposes the following method to get from text to concepts. "Terms and lexical relations are syntagms existing in the corpus and regarded as important in the domain. Lexical clustering puts together syntagms which occur in some similar contexts. The syntagms may be interpreted in a local context (sentence or paragraph) then in a global one (text or whole corpus). If they are considered as terms, they give rise to concepts and semantic relations that they label".

[64] DOODLE (Domain Ontology rapiD DeveLopment Environment) includes a module which analyses and extracts terms from an input English or Japanese textual corpus and reuses WordNet or other OWL ontologies to construct taxonomic and other relationships.

[65] Alceste contains dictionaries for French, English, Spanish, Portuguese, Italian and German. And may be purchased from http://www.image-zafar.com/index_alceste.htm, retrieved August 18, 2010, (although a free, registration required, student version is available online).

AntConc[66] is a corpus analysis program, developed by Anthony (2005) which includes a "concordancer, word and keyword frequency generators, tools for cluster and lexical bundle analysis, and a word distribution plot".

GATE[67] (General Architecture for Text Engineering) is developed by the Natural Language Processing Group at the University of Sheffield (UK), and offers several language processing activities, including information extraction (Cunningham et al. 2002; Li et al. 2005). It has been integrated and used in many ontology development environments (e.g. the NeOn Toolkit, TERMINAE, T2K, ...).

OntoGen[68] "is a semi-automatic and data-driven ontology editor focusing on editing of topic ontologies (a set of topics connected with different types of relations)" (Fortuna et al. 2007). The system, developed by researchers at the Jožef Stefan Institute (Slovenia), the uses text-mining techniques to suggest concepts and relations, and the instances of those concepts are documents themselves.

OntoLearn, offers not only a method but also an ontology learning tool from documents and web sites (Missikof et al. 2002; Navigli and Velardi 2004; Velardi et al. 2005). Recently, the developers at the Linguistic Computing Laboratory (Computer Science Department, University of Roma "La Sapienza", Italy) "started to develop web applications to make freely available each of the steps of the OntoLearn methodology" (Sclano and Velardi 2007). TermExtractor (extraction of terms from a corpus of documents in English based on entropy measures) and TAV (TAxonomy Validator, for the visualization of OWL ontologies for validation) may be accessed and used online.[69]

indexOntoLT[70] is a plug-in for Protégé "with which concepts (Protégé classes) and relations (Protégé slots) can be extracted automatically from a linguistically annotated text collection" (Buitelaar et al. 2004).

`R` offers a variety of methods and functions for the extraction of relevant information from a text corpus or a collection of texts (Gries 2009).[71] `R` packages allow the creation of a frequency list from text corpus, Gries (2009) offers a complete range of operations using `R` devoted to quantitative corpus linguistics, a text statistics approach may be found in Baayen (2008), and the `tm` `R` package by Feinerer (2008), offers sets of words according to an occurrence threshold set by the user and produces term-document matrices directly from text collections.

[66]This system works with most languages. AntConc is freely available and may be downloaded from http://www.antlab.sci.waseda.ac.jp/software.html, retrieved August 18, 2010.

[67]It supports several languages and it may be freely downloaded from http://gate.ac.uk

[68]May be downloaded from http://ontogen.ijs.si, retrieved August 18, 2010.

[69]Other tools such as GlossExtractor, are also available. Visit: http://lcl2.uniroma1.it/tools.jsp, retrieved August 18, 2010.

[70]OntoLT has been developed at DFKI GmbH (Germany). Version 2.0 works with Protégé 3.x and it may be downloaded from http://olp.dfki.de/OntoLT/OntoLT.htm, retrieved August 18, 2010.

[71]http://cran.r-project.org, retrieved August 18, 2010.

TERMINAE[72] method and tool aim at guiding knowledge acquisition from texts to build terminological and ontological models. The method suggests a supervised modelling process. Text analysis is supported by several NLP tools (such as term extractor and relation extractor with lexico-semantic patterns) whereas the TERMINAE modelling workbench keeps track of the various status of the knowledge represented in the model, from text fragments to lexical structures (terminological forms) and then conceptual and formal structures (Després and Szulman 2006).

TextOntoEx[73] "constructs ontology from natural domain text using semantic pattern-based approach" (Yehia-Dahab et al. 2008) and supports the construction not only of ontological relations such as taxonomy or equivalence but also domain relations and non-taxonomic conceptual relations (causes, caused by, has member, contain, etc.). The semantic pattern developed to represent text expressions in a generic format contains a combination of abstract ontological classes obtained from top-level ontologies, verb group extracted from a semantic lexicon such as WordNet, and text constant expressions and other optional elements.

Text to Knowledge (T2K) "T2K is a hybrid ontology learning system combining linguistic technologies and statistical techniques" (Lenci et al. 2007).[74]

Text2Onto[75] Text2Onto, a tool for ontology learning from text, is the successor of TextToOnto. TextToOnto was a tool suite built initially upon KAON, in order to support the ontology engineering process by text mining techniques, for the automatic (and semiautomatic) extraction of ontologies for texts in English, Italian and German. Later, Text2Onto incorporated "new strategies for data-driven change discovery" (Cimiano and Völker 2005), within other new features. A Text2Onto plugin is currently available for the NeOn Toolkit ontology engineering environment.[76]

Finally, **Yoshikoder**[77] is "an open-source desktop tool for performing classical computer-aided content analysis in multiple languages" (Lowe 2006). The tool allows obtaining word frequency listings, viewing keywords-in-context, and writing and applying content analysis dictionaries.

---

[72]Logiciel Terminae, developed at CNRS-LIPN and CNRS-IRIT, (version 12-4-2010) may be downloaded from http://www-lipn.univ-paris13.fr/~szulman/TERMINAE.html, retrieved August 18, 2010.

[73]Developed at the Central Laboratory of Agriculture Expert Systems (Egypt) and Faculty of Computers and Information, Cairo University (Egypt).

[74]See Lenci et al. (2009) and Spinosa et al. (2009).

[75]Developed at the Institute of Applied Informatics and Formal Description Methods (AIFB, Universitaet Karlsruhe, Germany) is available from: http://code.google.com/p/text2onto, retrieved August 18, 2010.

[76]NeOn Toolkit Text2Onto plugin is available from: http://www.neon-toolkit.org/wiki/1.x/Text2Onto, retrieved August 18, 2010.

[77]Developed by Will Lowe at Harvard as part of the Identity Project at Harvard's Center for International Affairs, it may be downloaded from http://www.yoshikoder.org

3.3.2.3 Other Ontology Engineering Tools

Many other tools have been developed towards supporting specific features for ontology development (evaluation, collaborative support, etc.).[78] As an example, the OWL ontology browser OwlSight,[79] the Attempto Controlled English ontology editor ACE View,[80] the ONTOMO instance recommendation web-based system (Shin et al. 2009), ImageNotion (for semantic annotation of images) (Walter and Nagypál 2010), the WATSON Semantic Web explorer tool [81] (d'Aquin et al. 2007) or EVOLVA (for ontology evolution support)[82] (Zablith 2009; Zablith et al. 2009). Nevertheless, most of these tools have been developed as ontology environment plug-ins and integrated in ontology editors such as Protégé or the NeOn Toolkit.[83]

3.4 Conclusions and Some Thoughts on Expert Participation in Ontology Development

As stated in the preceding chapter, ontologies may be analysed according to different aspects. Their purpose, subject-matter, level of generality, and level of formality or richness of internal structure. However, the methodologies followed for the construction, the tools used and the language may be established also important development decisions and relevant items for analysis.

Regarding ontology languages, the use of RDF and OWL languages could be recommended as they are currently widely used in ontology development and may offer grounds for reuse and extensibility. Moreover, OWL is in current evolution and proposals for enrichment are being evaluated, and most up-to-date ontology editors include this output format (Protégé and the NeOn Toolkit already support the OWL 2 language). The choice between RDF/S and OWL (including OWL 1 sublanguages and OWL 2 profiles) would depend on the required expressive power and its computational and/or implementational needs. While advanced reasoning applications might require the expressivity of OWL, basic semantic search and navigation support tools might perform adequately with RDF/S representations.

---

[78]Lists of ontology and semantic web related tools may be found at http://semanticweb.org/wiki/Tools, retrieved August 18, 2010

[79]http://pellet.owldl.com/ontology-browser, retrieved August 18, 2010.

[80]ACE View is a Protégé (version 4) plug-in: http://attempto.ifi.uzh.ch/aceview, retrieved August 18, 2010.

[81]Watson: http://kmi-web05.open.ac.uk/WatsonWUI/, retrieved August 18, 2010.

[82]EVOLVA: http://www.neon-toolkit.org/wiki/Evolva, retrieved August 18, 2010.

[83]A complete list of plug-ins for Protégé may be found at: http://protegewiki.stanford.edu/wiki/Protege_Plugin_Library, retrieved August 18, 2010. The list of plug-ins for the NeOn Toolkit may be found at http://www.neon-toolkit.org/wiki/Neon_Plugins, retrieved August 18, 2010.

From current and up-to-date ontology editors and environments, Protégé offers an easy-to-use interface (with graphical visualisation capabilities), consistency checking support, language and domain independence, and a long history of development, together with free availability. Also the NeOn Toolkit offers a complete set of features, although it is mostly directed towards collaborative ontology development. Other ontology editors and ontology have more complex interfaces, are directed towards specific ontology building methodologies (e.g. collaborative and distributed development), support few language textual analysis, or do not offer reasoning or visualization support. For example, DODDLE's and Hozo's textual functionalities may not be available for some languages (e.g. Spanish) and have complex interfaces, Ontolingua's interface lacks graphical visualization, and the DOGMA Studio Workbench requires familiarity with the ORM format and supports the DOGMA approach.

Regarding ontology methodologies, there are several methodological approaches towards ontology engineering, and some useful insights may be obtained from other evaluation or knowledge acquisition techniques and methodologies, although most of their very authors acknowledge the fact that" [the process of model construction] is a difficult area, because no single 'good' solution exists. The best any modelling methodology can do is provide a number of guidelines that have proved to have worked well in practice" (Schreiber et al. 1999).[84] More recently, Hoekstra (2009b) stated that "[o]ntology development remains an art, and no a priori guidelines exist that can ensure the quality of the result".

Exiting methodologies generally follow a cyclic modelling approach, an iterative and incremental cycle of steps. The preparatory step includes activities such as the initial feasibility study and the specification of requirements. The development step comprehends knowledge acquisition activities, together with ontology conceptualization, formalization, evaluation and refinement, and the application step, which includes ontology implementation and maintenance activities. In this sense, as mentioned in Sect. 3.2 ontology building methodologies share a number of elements with software and knowledge systems engineering methodologies. Milton (2007), for example, offers a knowledge acquisition methodology "whether the end-product is a website, an ontology or an intelligent software system". Zhao and Leary (2005a) adopted the Rational Unified Process (RUP)[85] for software engineering as its development model, and similarly de Nicola et al. (2005) adopted the Unified Process. NeOn, METHONTOLOGY and ON-TO-KNOWLEDGE are also influenced by other existing software engineering and systems engineering methodologies and life-cycle models.[86]

[84] A similar comment may be found in Noy and McGuinness (2001).

[85] Rational Unified Process (RUP) is divided within six core engineering workflows: (1) business modelling workflow, (2) requirements workflow, (3) analysis and design workflow, (4) implementation workflow, (5) test workflow, and (6) deployment workflow Rational (2001).

[86] "(...) CommonKADS has been influenced by other methodologies, including structured systems analysis and design, object orientation, organization theory, process reengineering, and quality management" (Schreiber et al. 1999). For an extensive description of software and knowledge engineering development and life-cycle processes see Suárez-Figueroa et al. (2007, 2008b).

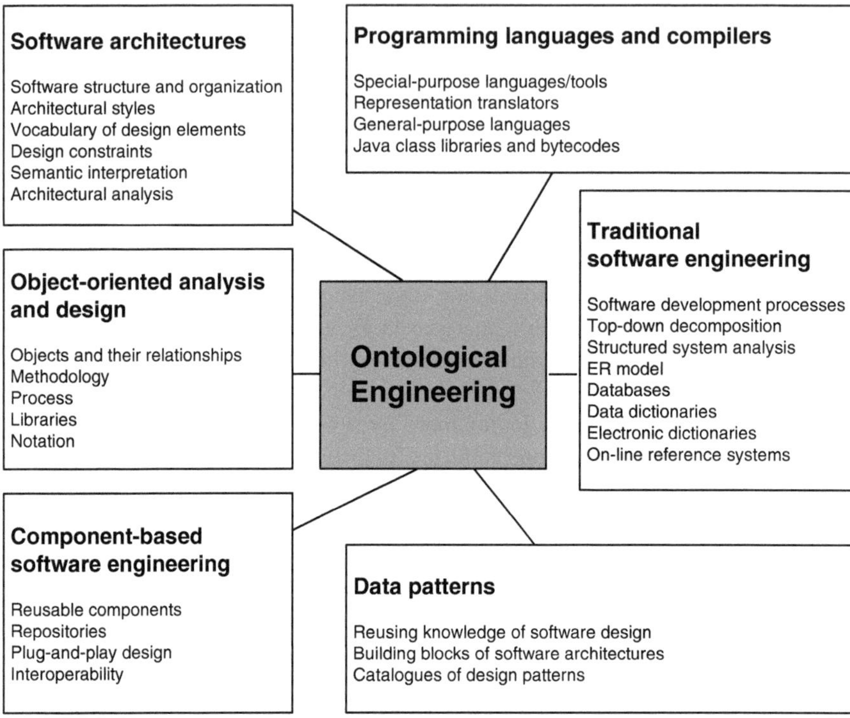

Fig. 3.19 Useful software engineering disciplines for ontology engineering by Devedzić (2002)

Devedzić (2002), in Fig. 3.19, describes the relationship between ontology engineering and other software engineering disciplines that might be inspiring towards the development of ontologies and ontology-based systems.

Moreover, software and systems development processes have undergone since the 1990s a deep standardization process, which indirectly, has influenced ontology methodology development. For example, METHONTOLOGY has its roots in the IDEAL methodology for developing Knowledge-Based Systems and "the skeleton of METHONTOLOGY was developed taking this document [IEEE Standard 1074 for Developing a Software Project Life Cycle Process] as a starting point" (Fernández-López 1999).

Different organizations such the International Organization for Standardization (ISO)[87] and the IEEE Standards Association[88] offer sets of guidelines towards de the construction, evaluation and maintenance of software products and systems.[89]

---

[87]ISO: http://www.iso.org/iso/home.htm

[88]IEEE was originally an acronym for Institute of Electrical and Electronics Engineers, Inc. Visit IEEE at http://www.ieee.org and http://standards.ieee.org

[89]ISO/IEC-9126 product quality metrics (internal and external) Standard (2001, 2003a, b, 2004c), IEEE-1074:2006 development of software project life-cycle process (IEEE 2006), ISO/IEC-25000

Nevertheless, although most ontology methodologies have been highly influenced by the existing standards and methodologies regarding software and systems design, few of the revised methodologies have been deeply influenced by the standards and methods set towards a human-centred perspective to systems (ontology) design, domain expert-centred design. Although, most ontology methodologies may involve domain experts and users at some stages of the development process (mainly knowledge acquisition and evaluation), few of the above-mentioned methodologies describe a complete expert-centred perspective towards ontology engineering and most rely on the existence of previous documentation (e.g. text-based knowledge sources, reusable ontologies, etc.).

Uschold and colleagues (Uschold and King 1995; Uschold and Grüninger 1996b; Uschold 1996) refer to the need of domain expertise to be sufficiently present for the brainstorming sessions (or other corpus of knowledge would need to be consulted). The On-To-Knowledge methodology takes into account a possible user-centred knowledge acquisition process in the basic conception of the Ontology Requirements Specification Document, although it does not acknowledge the possibility of a user-centred evaluation of the outcome of the ontology conceptualization process. User-focused evaluation is directed to assess the satisfaction of users with the knowledge management application, "whether an ontology-based application is at least as good as already existing applications that solve similar tasks" (Sure et al. 2002). CommonKADS loosely includes the participation of experts. The methodology acknowledges several expert-based knowledge acquisition techniques for knowledge elicitation towards knowledge-based systems engineering, and experts may be involved in several validation steps (e.g., communication model validation, user-interface development). METHONTOLOGY involves domain experts for the evaluation of existing ontologies towards reuse (Gómez-Pérez et al. 2003), and Gómez-Pérez (1994b) also regards end-users as possible evaluators of the actual utility of an ontology within a company, without offering further details. Finally, DOGMA, UPON and the NeOn methodologies include the participation of domain experts mainly in the initial stages and in the validation phase. Finally, OntoLearn includes domain experts within the validation cycle of ontology learning and extraction (Velardi et al. 2005; Sclano and Velardi 2007).

series for the establishment of Software product Quality Requirements and Evaluation (SQuaRE) (Standard 2005, 2007a, b), IEEE-830-1998 recommended practice for software requirements specifications, ISO/IEC-18019:2004 guidelines for the design and preparation of user documentation for application software (Standard 2004b), IEEE-1012-2004 software verification and validation (IEEE 2004), ISO/IEC-15288:2008 system life cycle processes (Standard 2008b), ISO/IEC-12207:2008 (Standard 2008a), ISO/IEC-15504 series for process assessment for information technologies (Standard 2004a), ISO/IEC-14598 series for software product evaluation (Standard 1999c), IEEE-1061-1998 quality metrics methodology (IEEE 1998), ISO/IEC-14756-1999 measurement and rating of performance of computer-based software systems (Standard 1999b), ISO/IEC-14764:2006 software maintenance (Standard 2006b), and ISO/IEC-15289:2006 for the management of documentation (Standard 2006c), within others.

UPON, ON-TO-KNOWLEDGE, METHONTOLOGY and NeOn offer interesting and useful approaches to ontology modelling based on systems design, and they could benefit from the application of further human-centred software and knowledge design and validation standard techniques. Human-centred software and knowledge design and user validation are also highly standardised processes which include participation in and evaluation of the general development of software, systems and products, the analysis of their usability, the documentation provided and the quality of their use.[90] Moreover, usability engineering may take into account the effectiveness, efficiency and satisfaction offered by the use of a product (in a certain context (Standard 1998), the user interface development process, and the validation of the activities performed during the development process of a product.

The definition offered by the Usability Professionals' Association is "usability is an approach to product development that incorporates direct user feedback throughout the development cycle in order to reduce costs and create products and tools that meet user needs".[91] This field has been in active development since early 1990s (Nielsen 1994a, b), and has recently characterized several European funded projects.[92] Many particular methods have been developed to cover human-centred design and usability evaluation through the development process of a product, inspired by social science investigation methods (e.g., interviews, observation, etc.).[93] Figure 3.20, includes a table of usability methods organized according to their product development stages.[94]

Ontology engineering could benefit from the inclusion of several human-centred (usability) methods in the ontology development life-cycle, especially towards the construction of domain and core ontologies for specific areas of expert knowledge, especially those which include the modelling of tacit knowledge. Knowledge acquisition for ontology modelling, evaluation of ontologies and the production of documentation (for reuse and assessment[95]) would directly benefit from the application of a similar approach. In particular, the use of tailored *usability* methods for

[90]Human and user-centred design for life cycle of interactive computer-based systems (Standard 1999a), usability methods (Standard 2002), and particular standards for the production of documentation, and the evaluation of quality in use (Standard 1998, 2004b, c, 2006a).

[91]Visit the Usability Professionals' Association website: http://www.usabilityprofessionals.org

[92]The TRUMP, Trial Application Usability Maturity Project, ESPIRIT Project (IST-1999-28015) was also partly funded by the European Commission. The UsabilityNet Project was funded under the 5th Framework Programme (IST-1999-29067), http://www.usabilitynet.org. Finally, the VNET5 Network was funded by the European Commission (IST-2000-25465) from January 2001–2003 (http://www.vnet5.org).

[93]For example, relevant research has focused on the role of ethnography in systems design. See Sommerville et al. (1993), Hughes et al. (1994), Hughes et al. (1995), Blythin et al. (1997) and Sommerville (2004).

[94]This table and other method information is available from: http://www.usabilitynet.org/tools/methods.htm

[95]Some authors refer to this step also as *ontology evaluation* (Gómez-Pérez et al. 2003; Hartmann et al. 2005; Brank et al. 2005).

Planning & Feasibility	Requirements	Design	Implementation	Test & Measure	Post Release
Getting started	User Surveys	Design guidelines	Style guidelines	Diagnostic evaluation	Post release testing
Stakeholder meeting	Interviews	Paper prototyping	Rapid prototyping	Performance testing	Subjective assessment
Analyse context	Contextual inquiry	Heuristic evaluation		Subjective evaluation	User surveys
ISO 13407	User Observation	Parallel design		Heuristic evaluation	Remote evaluation
Planning	Context	Storyboarding		Critical Incidence Technique	
Competitor Analysis	Focus Groups	Evaluate prototype		Pleasure	
	Brainstorming	Wizard of Oz			
	Evaluating existing systems	Interface design patterns			
	Card Sorting				
	Affinity diagramming				
	Scenarios of use				
	Task Analysis				
	Requirements meeting				

Fig. 3.20 Table of usability methods (and related product development stages) by UsabilityNet

ontology evaluation could offer the establishment of certain quality measurements and aid the evaluation of modelling decisions, prior ontology implementation. Thus, as requirement specification, testing and producing end-user documentation are central to enhance the quality and usability of the resulting product, these human-centred steps may enhance the *quality* and *sharedness* of the resulting ontology.[96]

We understand that many ontology building methodologies only intend to "address the very basics of ontology development" (Noy and McGuinness 2001) and thus avoid reference to guiding knowledge acquisition for specific practical needs. Nevertheless, the notion of *shared* knowledge, so much present in the definitions, becomes thus hardly addressed in the methodologies regarding ontology modelling. In general, no reference is made towards acquiring knowledge aside from suggestions towards automatic extraction of lists of terms from textual documents or existing ontology reuse, in order to ensure the sharedness of the knowledge besides (consensual collaborative development). Moreover, some methodologies seem to *assume*, or (unwillingly) give the idea, that the knowledge is either *there* to be gathered, or that, in general, ontology engineers may *understand* the area of knowledge modelled with little effort.

[96]For example, the ontology requirements specification documents provided by On-To-Knowledge and NeOn.

For example, Noy and McGuinness (2001) require "a list of terms", with no reference to how this list is to be obtained. The NeOn Methodology, in order to initiate the development of an ontology with the non ontological resource reengineering approach, suggests that "[t]he goal of this task is to search and compile all the available documentation about the non ontological resource including purpose, components; data model and implementation details. Domain experts and the ontology development team carry out this activity, taking as input the non ontological resource, searching in the non ontological resource web site and in general purpose search engines, or requesting the documentation directly to the non ontological resource author" (Suárez-Figueroa et al. 2008a). Uschold and Grüninger (1996b) recognized that "[b]rainstorming worked well for us; however if collectively those involved possess insufficient domain expertise, another corpus of knowledge may need to be consulted to ensure adequate coverage." They also included more formal "competency questions" for knowledge acquisition, although the questions regarding the domain would normally need to be acquired as well. Gómez-Pérez et al. (2003), in turn, indicates that the objective of the conceptualization activity is "to organize and structure the knowledge acquired during the knowledge acquisition activity, (...) [c]consequently, the conceptualization activity has a strong relationship with the knowledge acquisition activity", although very few attention is payed to the latter during the description of the methodology.

A careful selection of knowledge sources, the use of adequate knowledge acquisition techniques, and life-cycle human-centred design and usability evaluation what may support sharedness and may give overall assistance to the development of ontologies. Certainly, not all ontologies might require the participation of experts in the life-cycle development nor require the extraction of expert knowledge, although in all cases the choice of information sources for knowledge extraction is key.[97]

CommonKADS, 47-step Guide and On-To-Knowledge recognise the importance of this step in the development of both knowledge bases and ontologies. In particular, the Ontology Requirements Specification Document (ORSD) suggested by the On-To-Knowledge methodology *documents* a specification of the knowledge sources to be used or explored and the list of tools to aid the process, if needed. The authors give a list of knowledge sources as an example, including: domain experts (interviews, competency questionnaires), (re-usable) ontologies, dictionaries, internal documents, regulations, telephone indices, organization charts, etc. In accordance to these methodologies, we believe that documenting the knowledge sources chosen for information (knowledge) extraction and validating the conceptualization obtained from them supports the notion of sharedness and aids the final evaluation process. Moreover, documentation of information sources and expert validation might even increase reusability of the ontology produced.

For these reasons, we would like to take into account the recommendations from Schreiber et al. (1999), Sure (2003), Milton (2007) and Suárez-Figueroa et al.

[97]The use of collaborative ontology modelling tools or methodologies could offer support towards sharedness in particular ontology development scenarios.

(2007) towards general ontology development and knowledge acquisition, complete them with the detailed modelling guidelines from Noy and McGuinness (2001), Gómez-Pérez et al. (2003), Spyns et al. (2008), and include several expert-centred and empirically-oriented methods towards professional legal knowledge acquisition, and usability (shareability) evaluation. The methodological steps will follow the general cyclic iterative and incremental approach: specification of requirements, knowledge acquisition, conceptualization, formalization, evaluation and refinement, and take a middle-out approach with regards to conceptualization (Uschold and King 1995; Hoekstra 2009b).

Chapter 4
Legal Ontologies

4.1 A Review

As stated in the preceding chapters, ontologies may be characterized by different aspects: their purpose, subject-matter, level of generality, and level of formality or richness of internal structure, together with the methodologies followed for their development, the tools used, and the ontology language encoded.

Most of the ontologies revised in this chapter have been chosen for their relevance in the history of legal ontology development or their presence in the literature (well-documented). Moreover, we have basically focused as well on revising (semi) formal legal ontologies, at least ontologies which take into account or consider their computational use.

Therefore, from all the previous criteria analysed in Chap. 2 and the review of methodologies, tools and languages contained in Chap. 3, we will consider the following items for the analysis of the existing legal ontologies:

1. What is the purpose and use of the ontology.
2. What is the subject-matter of the ontology.
3. What is the level of generality.
4. What is the level of formality or richness of internal structure.
5. How was the ontology built? Construction approach, methodology followed (knowledge acquisition, evaluation, and participation of legal experts).
6. Tools used for support.
7. Application envisioned and maturity level.
8. Other characteristics: size, availability, clarity, standardization of names, coherence, reusability, etc.

The next section contains a thorough, although not complete, state of the art account of existing legal ontologies, revised according to the preceding criteria (when possible) and the information available in their documentation. In the final section some issues for discussion are brought about.

N. Casellas, *Legal Ontology Engineering: Methodologies, Modelling Trends, and the Ontology of Professional Judicial Knowledge*, Law, Governance and Technology Series 3,
DOI 10.1007/978-94-007-1497-7_4, © Springer Science+Business Media B.V. 2011

4.2 Existing Legal Ontologies

The list of existing ontologies built for the legal domain is growing rapidly. First, we will briefly describe some of these legal ontologies in detail. Later, a further list of relevant legal ontologies will be provided.

4.2.1 Early Conceptualizations of the Legal Domain

At first, some authors offered several early conceptualizations of the legal domain either based on semantic networks or frames, or formalized as a representation languages for the legal domain. Hafner's semantic network of legal concepts, the Language for Legal Discourse (LLD) by McCarty, Stamper's NORMA, and CABALA by (Mariani et al. 1992) are some of them.

Some of these (NORMA and LLD) have been included in many legal ontology comparisons (as conceptualizations of the legal domain) such as in Bench-Capon and Visser (1996) and Visser and Bench-Capon (1998b). "For example, McCarty's Language of Legal Discourse can be seen as an ontology of Law, where his 'modalities' play the role of knowledge categories and are linked together with a formal (logical) presentation" (Valente and Breuker 1994b). Also, "McCarty's work is considered an early attempt to conceptualise the legal domain using a (semi-) formal language" and "Stamper's discussion of NORMA is regarded as a discussion of ontological assumptions specified in a semi-formal language" (Visser and Bench-Capon 1998b). Finally, the Language for Legal Discourse is considered, for example, a (proto) core ontology by Valente and Breuker (1999).[1]

4.2.1.1 Hafner's Semantic Network of Legal Concepts

Hafner (1980) describes four different types of knowledge about legal concepts and relations which were represented in her Legal Research System (LRS, a knowledge-based computer retrieval system): functional knowledge, structural knowledge, semantic knowledge and factual knowledge.

Semantic knowledge is described as a semantic network model of Negotiable Instruments Law used to make inferences about the meanings of queries.

[1] The A-Hohfeld Language for Legal Analysis by Allen and Saxon (1994, 1995) and Allen (1996) was not included in those early discussions by Valente and Breuker (1994b), Bench-Capon and Visser (1996), Visser and Bench-Capon (1998b) and Valente and Breuker (1999). It was at the time introduced as a representational language (used in the MINT – Multiple INTerpretation – system), based on the fundamental legal concepts – right, privilege, power, immunity, etc. – of Wesley N. Hohfeld.

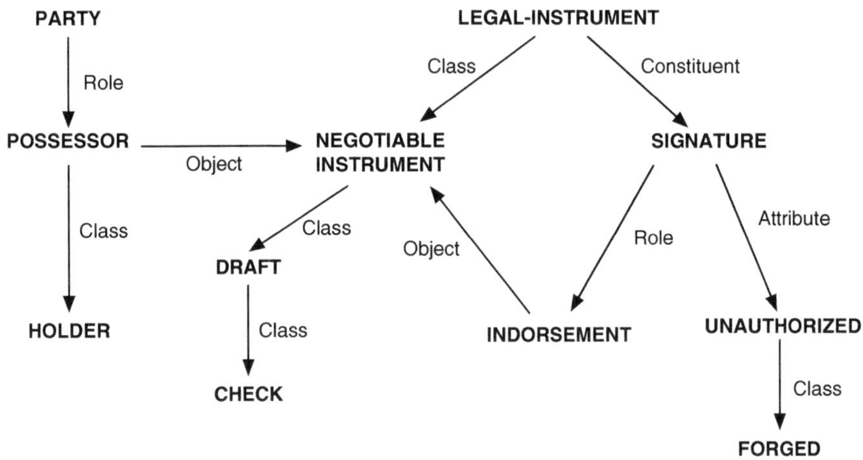

Fig. 4.1 A portion of the LRS semantic network by Hafner (1980)

"A collection of *nodes* defining subject area concepts, such as 'holder', 'forged' and 'endorsement', connected by *links* representing a small set of semantic structures, such as classification and attribution."

The network contains six link types and six basic concepts: PARTY, LEGAL-INSTRUMENT, LIABILITY, LEGAL-ACTION (case), ACCOUNT and AMOUNT OF MONEY. Other 200 legal concepts are defined in terms of these 6 using one or more link connections. (See a portion of the LRS semantic network in Fig. 4.1.) Link types correspond to:

- Set/member links (connects sets to their individual members i.e., concept-instance)
- constituent links (links concepts to their component concepts i.e., part_of)
- super-class/sub-class links (concepts that are sets are linked to concepts that are subsets i.e., sub_class / super_class relationships)
- attribute links (define attributes of concepts and their values)
- role links ("defines a concept such as 'author', which is a role taken by a person with respect to some book or paper.")
- event conditions (defines concepts that change a person's status or condition).

Factual knowledge is defined by rules that are not included within the semantic network model because "they may vary from time to time, from place to place and case to case. Even for legal rules that are firmly established, there may be occasional exceptions" (Hafner 1980).

4.2.1.2 McCarty's Language for Legal Discourse

"Another example of an ontology for the legal domain is McCarty's work on a Language for Legal Discourse (LLD)" (Valente and Breuker 1992). The author advocated the development of "deep conceptual models" of the legal domain, and proposed the development of a *knowledge representation language* that would represent a selected set of common sense categories for a particular legal application, as there are "many common sense categories underlying the representation of a legal problem domain: space, time, mass, action, permission, obligation, causation, purpose, intention, knowledge, belief, and so on" (McCarty 1989). The proposed language is the Language for Legal Discourse, a formal language, with compositional syntax and a well-defined inference mechanism.[2]

The Language for Legal Discourse (LLD) consists of three basic knowledge categories: atomic formula (which are "predicate relations used to express factual assertions" Visser and Bench-Capon (1998b)), rules (which are "formed by connecting atomic formulae with logical connectives" (Visser and Bench-Capon 1998b)) and modalities.[3] The modalities incorporated in LLD are:

- Time, based on a reified temporal logic.
- Events and Actions, based on intuitionistic logic.
- Deontic operators: permitted, forbidden, obligatory and enabled. "Deontic statements are formed by the combination of a name, a (possibly negated) modal operator, a condition, and an action" (Visser and Bench-Capon 1998b).[4]

As Valente and Breuker (1992) exposed, the question is whether this constitutes a typical *legal* ontology, as most of those terms do not specifically belong to the legal domain.

4.2.1.3 NORMA

Stamper (1977) aimed initially at producing a formalism "sufficiently general to encompass any legislation." LEGOL (Legal Oriented Language) was the proposed formalism to express complex rules and regulations (Stamper 1976, 1977; Jones et al. 1979). Later, the LEGOL project evolved into another research project, NORMA (NORMs and Affordances) (Stamper 1994).[5] "Stamper's discussion of NORMA is regarded as a discussion of ontological assumptions specified in a semi-formal language" (Visser and Bench-Capon 1998b). NORMA, the logic of norms and affordances, was based on two assumptions, that there was no knowledge without a knower, and that the knowledge of a knower depended on his behaviour (see the comments by Visser and Bench-Capon (1998b) and Moles (2008)). "Stamper in

[2]This language was used in the TAXMAN Project to write TAXMAN I and II systems (McCarty 1980, 1989, 1991).

[3]Visser and Bench-Capon (1998b) includes LLD representational categories as knowledge categories for ontology comparison, although LLD is not considered by its author as an ontology.

[4]In McCarty (1989) only permissions and obligations were defined.

[5]With the same approach he later participated in the development of the MEASUR methodology for the establishment of requirements (Stamper 1994), which led to the creation of a 'normbase'. This work is still ongoing in the research by Liu (2000).

this project places a great deal of emphasis on norms, which he sees as a field of force that governs the behaviour of individuals and organizations" (Gazendam and Liu 2005).

The main ontological[6] concepts are (a) *agents* (organisms standing in the center of reality), (b) *behavioural invariants* ("description of a situation whose features remain invariant"), and (c) *realizations* (a realization of a situation, an agent performing actions or the combination of an agent and a behavioural invariant) (Visser and Bench-Capon 1998b).

The work of R. Stamper made an essential contribution to the birth and development of the field organizational Semiotics (Gazendam and Liu 2005), and the work initiated by the author has influenced the research of Liu (2000), Liu and Sun (2000) and Moor (2002), within others.

4.2.1.4 CABALA Semantic Network

The CABALA (Consultazione Assistita di Basi di Dati di Leggi Ambientali) semantic network was created by extracting a series of significant terms from legal text, representing nodes of the network and defining two kinds of relations between nodes. BT (*Broader Term*) relation was considered to be transitive and laid down hierarchies among terms. As an example, in the field of noise pollution they identified the BT hierarchies: *Sources of emission*, *Types of noise*, *Ambits for safeguarding*, *Prevention and control*, *Bodies*, *Normative sources*, *Sanctions* and *Pertinent facts*. The nodes of the network were linked by oriented arcs (identifying the relations existing between them). That enabled the system to capture the semantic of the user's queries (Mariani et al. 1992). They used *Related Term* (RT) to identify the specific meaning of the relations as far as their features concern (directionality, transitivity, symmetry, etc.). When developing SEDAM (Sistema Esperto in Diritto dell'AMbiente) the decision was made to use frames for representing technical knowledge instead of the semantic network used in CABALA. However, the authors stated that semantic networks and frames, although different representation formalisms, "allowed taxonomic relationships and inheritance between the concepts to be expressed easily" (Mariani et al. 1992).

4.2.2 Legal Ontologies

Below we will describe some of the most relevant ontologies (proposed as ontologies of the legal domain by their authors), which will be revised taking into account

[6] "The norm based approach aims at developing a semantic database, which takes an ontology model as the conceptual schema. A conceptual schema contains affordances and their dependencies. The schema in principle describes the existence and dependencies of the existence of the affordances, which justifies why it is called an 'ontology model' " (Liu and Sun 2000).

the criteria suggested by the analysis of ontology typologies, methodologies, tools, languages and other relevant design principles. The information provided in this section has been extracted, when possible, from the information contained in relevant publications.[7] See Table 4.4 for a quick overview.

4.2.2.1 The Frame-Based Ontology of Law (FBO)

van Kralingen et al. (1993) adopted an indirect modelling perspective and, based on the works of Hart (1961), Kelsen (1991), Ross (1958, 1968), von Wright (1963) and von Wright (1983) and others, proposed the use of models of "complete" norms, as "[n]orms are the most important elements of legal systems" van Kralingen (1997).[8] Based on these legal theory literature, the author describes several types of norms:

- Norms of conduct
  - Duty imposing norms vs. permissive norms
  - *Sein-sollen* norms vs. *tun-sollen* norms (regarding the regulated object)
  - Individual norms vs. general norms (regarding the norm subject)
  - Hypothetical norms vs. categorical norms (regarding the conditions of application of the norm)
- Norms of competence
  - Power conferring norms vs. duty-imposing and permissive norms
  - Individual norms and general norms (regarding the norm subject)
  - Hypothetical norms vs. categorical norms (regarding the conditions of application of the norm)

The authors considered that the legal system not only comprised norms but also other elements such as legal institutions and legal definitions, defined as "institutional facts" (van Kralingen 1997; Visser et al. 1997). "This brings us to a classification of elements of legal systems with at the top institutional facts, and at the lower levels norms, definitions, subtypes of norms and definitions, *etc.*" (van Kralingen 1997).

The authors believed that "isomorphic" approaches to modelling legal language only take into account some "part" the norms, their *norm formulation* or the *written* part of the norm. However, these approaches did not place normative sentences in their context and did not bridge the gap between the norm and its norm

[7] Information gathering was as thorough as possible, although we apologize if any relevant publication has been overlooked.

[8] A complete norm is a norm that answers five questions: (1) Who is obligated or permitted to do something? (2) Is there an obligation or permission to do something or to leave something undone? (3) What must be done or forborne? (4) Where must something be done or forborne? (5) When must something be done or forborne? The first question is related to the norm subject, the second to the legal modality of the norm and the final three questions relate to the description of the act in different ways (van Kralingen 1997).

formulation. Therefore, *Norm Frames* (van Kralingen et al. 1993) were presented as an "intermediate language for the conceptual representation of legal knowledge," and defined as "theoretical models of a "complete norm".[9] The authors placed special interest in the legal drafting process as it led to norm formulation.

The Frame-based ontology[10] (FBO) consists mainly of three frame structures: the norm frame, the act frame and the concept frame and its main purpose is knowledge acquisition and reuse towards the construction of legal knowledge based systems.[11]

The concept of a complete norm contains a set of elements that constitute its core: norm subject, legal modality (also referred to as deontic operator, norm character, function of a norm), description of the act (content of the norm or object of the norm) and its conditions of application. These elements of a norm, together with other auxiliary elements are placed in a structure, the norm-frame, "a template to represent norms" (van Kralingen 1997). (See Table 4.1). The norm frame comprises:

1. Norm identifier (used as a point of reference for the norm) – auxiliary –;
2. Norm type (norm of conduct or norm of competence) – kernel –;
3. Promulgation (the source of the norm) – auxiliary –;
4. Scope (the range of application of the norm) – auxiliary –;
5. Conditions of application (circumstances under which a norm is applicable) – kernel –;
6. Subject (the person or persons to whom the norm is addressed) – kernel –;
7. Legal modality (ought, ought not, may, or can) – kernel –;

[9] "Frame-based systems are knowledge representation systems that use frames, a notion originally introduced by Marvin Minsky, as their primary means to represent domain knowledge. A frame is a structure for representing a concept or situation such as 'living room' or 'being in a living room'. Attached to a frame are several kinds of information, for instance, definitional and descriptive information and how to use the frame (...) Collections of such frames are to be organized in *frame systems* in which the frames are interconnected" (Nebel 1999). Also, some common features in frame-based systems are (1) frames are organized in (tangled) hierarchies, (2) frames are composed out of slots (attributes) from which fillers have to be specified or computed and (3) properties (fillers, etc.) are inherited from superframes to subframes in the hierarchy according to some inheritance strategy (Nebel 1999).

[10] modellers: Legal Informatics at Liverpool, Department of Computer Science, University of Liverpool (UK) and Center for Law, Public Administration and Informatization, Tilburg University (The Netherlands). Also, Department of Law and Computer Science of the University of Leiden (ONTOLINGUA specification). Consult: van Kralingen et al. (1993), van Kralingen (1997), Visser and Bench-Capon (1996a, b) and Visser et al. (1997).

[11] Moreover, "[t]he ontology contains two separate ontologies, the *generic legal ontology* and the *statute-specific ontology*" (Visser and Bench-Capon 1996a). The generic ontology distinguishes: norms, acts and concept descriptions. In the ONTOLINGUA formalization, the authors discussed the trade-off between formalizing a detailed ontology (useful for domain knowledge acquisition) or a more reusable abstract ontology. Visser and Bench-Capon (1996a) opted for the latter specification.

Table 4.1 Elements of norm frame by van Kralingen et al. (1993)

Norm type (norm of conduct or norm of competence)		
	Element	Typification
1	Catch word	Term used as a point of reference for the norm, preferably a legal-technical term
2	Promulgation	Source of the norm-kernel and the norm authority.
3	Norm goal	State or effect desired by the norm authority (wish of the norm authority).
4	Conditions of application	Uncertain circumstances under which the norm is applicable; they do not form an integral part of the description of the act.
5	Subject	Addressee of the norm.
6	Legal modality	*Ought, ought not, may*, or *can*
7	Object	Typification of the act which falls under the scope of the legal modality. Used as a point of reference for the connection with the sub-frame for the description of an action.

8. Act identifier (used as a reference to a separate act description, represented in a separate frame, the act frame) – kernel –;
   (a) Identifier
   (b) Promulgation
   (c) Scope
   (d) Agent
   (e) Type
   (f) Modality of means
   (g) Modality of manner
   (h) Temporal aspects
   (i) Spatial aspects
   (j) Circumstantial aspects
   (k) Cause of the action
   (l) Aim of the action
   (m) Intentionality of the action
   (n) Final state

The concept frame is used towards the description of the meaning of legal terms ("deal with the meanings of the concepts in the domain" (Visser and Bench-Capon 1996a)) and includes the following elements:

1. Concept to be described
2. Concept type
3. Priority

4. Promulgation
5. Scope
6. Conditions
7. Enumeration of instances

Initially FBO was an informal or "conceptual" ontology (van Kralingen et al. 1993; van Kralingen 1995, 1997), but later it was specified by Visser and Bench-Capon (1996a) in ONTOLINGUA. The methodology followed by the ONTOLINGUA specification is not specifically reported (Visser and Bench-Capon 1996a), although the authors admit that the process was "accompanied by a considerable amount of freedom." This latter formalization consisted of 18 classes, 2 relations and 1 function and there were no instances or axioms (takes only into account the generic legal ontology).[12] FBO was used in FRAMER, an assessment and planning system on the Dutch Unemployment Benefits Act (Visser 1995), and used towards knowledge acquisition in the proposal of a tailored CommonKADS method for legal knowledge-system development based on four major design steps: analysis, conceptual modelling, formal modelling, and implementation. Other implementations of the ontology are reported by Visser and Bench-Capon (1996a), for example in the LEDA system.

4.2.2.2 Functional Ontology of Law (FOLaw)

The FOLaw ontology[13] adopts a functional perspective, based on the assumption that the "legal system as a whole exists to accomplish a certain function" (Valente and Breuker 1996), and that the main function is to "react to social behavior" (Valente and Breuker 1996). Further assumptions are that *legal sources* are the knowledge which specifies how the legal system works, and that the different roles that these legal sources may take conform the different functions that legal knowledge may perform.[14] See Fig. 4.2 for a composition of the main functions envisioned.

Its main purpose was to enable knowledge reuse for building new applications, in particular, enabling the reuse of a library of ontologies. However, authors also included the idea that it could be used for the study of legal knowledge (Valente and Breuker 1996). In designing the ON-LINE[15] architecture for legal problem solving,

[12]The ONTOLINGUA specification is published as an appendix in Visser and Bench-Capon (1996a).

[13]modellers: Valente and Breuker (1994b), Valente and Breuker (1995), Valente and Breuker (1996), and Valente and Breuker (1999).

[14]"Like a knowledge-based system, the legal system executes a number of *tasks*, for which it uses extensive *knowledge*. Consequently, each piece of knowledge used by the legal system has a specific *role* distinguished by the legal system in the operationalization of its functions and tasks" (Valente and Breuker 1996).

[15]ON-LINE Valente and Breuker (1995, 1999) used FOLaw to define specialized representations for objects in each of the categories of the ontology (Valente and Breuker 1995, 1999) for information retrieval and problem solving (legal analysis). PROSA, a training system for solving

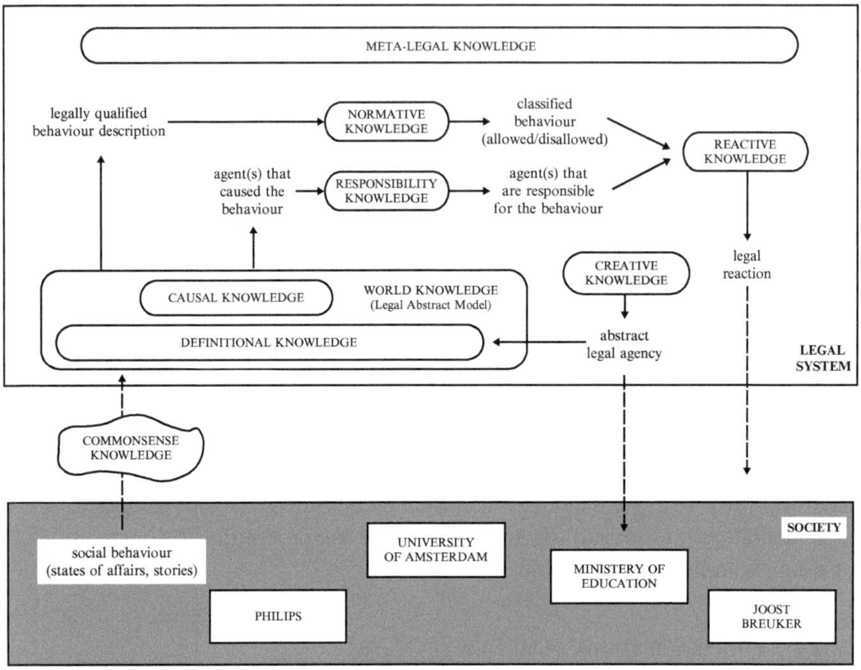

Fig. 4.2 Composition of the main functions of the legal system by Valente and Breuker (1996)

FOLaw was taken into account to distinguish the various types of knowledge in legal reasoning, to explain the dependencies between types of legal knowledge, to organize and index libraries of domain ontologies and to support knowledge acquisition towards the construction of new ontologies (Breuker et al. 2005).

The authors defined a list of primitive categories[16] These were: normative knowledge, world knowledge, responsibility knowledge, reactive knowledge, creative knowledge, and meta-level knowledge (as all non-primitive categories could be defined based on primitive categories).

- Normative knowledge had two related functions: (1) to prescribe behavior and (2) to define a standard of comparison for the social reality. The authors adopted this second function as the central characteristic of normative knowledge although they accepted that there was an on-going debate in legal theory regarding that matter. Therefore, the prescription of behavior is considered an effect of standardization. Furthermore, Valente and Breuker (1996) adopted a conception

legal cases. When applied to ontology based management of legal information systems FOLaw did not provide appropriate support (Breuker et al. 2005).

[16]"Consequently, we propose that core ontologies should attempt to define *basic categories* of domain knowledge. Categories are meant in an Aristotelian/Kantian sense" (Valente and Breuker 1996).

of *norm* derived from Kelsen (1991): norms expressed an ideal world and could be either observed or violated.[17]

- Meta-level knowledge was the knowledge required to solve conflicts between norms.
- World knowledge was composed of two related types of knowledge: definitional knowledge[18] (used by normative knowledge) and causal knowledge (used by responsibility knowledge).
- Responsibility knowledge had the function of assigning or limiting the responsibility of an agent over certain state of affairs. Acts as an intermediary concept between normative and reactive knowledge.[19]
- Reactive knowledge specified which action ought to be taken and how. The authors understood that the criminal codes "contain basically responsibility and reactive knowledge only" (Valente and Breuker 1996).
- Creative knowledge was considered an exceptional function, as it was defined as the creation of entities that did not exist before in the world.[20]

FOLaw had a theoretical basis founded in the literature on legal theory. "The ontology has been elaborated using several ontological distinctions from Legal Theory, particularly from Kelsen, Hart and Bentham" (Valente and Breuker 1994b). As referred in Chap. 1, ontologies have been suggested as the "missing link" between Artificial Intelligence and Law and Legal Theory (Valente and Breuker 1994b). The authors described the primitive concepts that several legal theorists (Kelsen, Hart, Bentham, Hohfeld) had proposed to represent legal knowledge, which they thought could be translated directly into an ontology (Valente and Breuker 1994b). The ontology was formalized in ONTOLINGUA and had six primitive categories (few subconcepts each at most). Some comments are provided regarding evaluation, "some of the comments received so far point to a mismatch between the way these experts reason and the framework provided by the ontology: the ontology, they say, is not 'intuitive'" (Valente 1995).[21]

---

[17]In Valente and Breuker (1994b), the authors distinguished between commanding, derogative (which included permitting) and empowering norms, also inspired by Kelsen (1991).

[18]Referred to as *terminological* in Valente and Breuker (1994b).

[19]In Valente and Breuker (1994b), it contains causal responsibility, related to causal knowledge and legal responsibility.

[20]The authors considered both reactive and creative knowledge "to have a relatively minor character, insofar as they are not part of the core of legal reasoning" (Valente and Breuker 1994b).

[21]"The modelling effort necessary for representing a single regulation (...) is rather large. Furthermore, even if some help is provided by browsers and editing tools, most of this work needs to be done or at least checked by a specialist. It may be necessary to read books or commentaries about the specific regulation being modelled in order to come up with a well-structured model (...) While it is expected that the ontology is able to represent adequately legal knowledge in several types of legislation and legal systems, this issue was not yet tested in practice. Further, in order to model legal knowledge with ON-LINE the user or knowledge engineer must understand the ontology and analyse the legislation in the terms it defines. This may or may not cause problems, depending on the specific knowledge engineer or user in question, but some of the comments

Finally, Breuker and Hoekstra (2004b) described FOLaw as an epistemological framework, rather than a core ontology as it "lacked the abstract, core concepts that make up law," although the authors recognized that it had provided insight into legal reasoning.

4.2.2.3 Ontology of Law as a Dynamic Interconnected System of States of Affairs

Hage and Verheij (1999) presented a "top ontology of the law"[22] based on two characteristics: the law as a dynamic system of states of affairs and the law as an interconnected system of states of affairs: law evolves over time and its elements are not independent of each other. "Our motivation to the development of an ontology is to provide an explicit view of the legal domain with the aim to find heuristic guidelines for legal knowledge representation" (Hage and Verheij 1999). Thus, the model uses three primitives: *states of affairs*, *events* and *rules*.[23] However, the authors also introduce two types of connections between states of affairs: *causation* (horizontal relation between states of affairs, through events) and *constitution* (vertical relation between states of affairs, through rules), "this distinction corresponds to a similar distinction between types of rules" (Hage and Verheij 1999).

- States of affairs ("a possible part of the world as expressed by a (descriptive) sentence").
  - Facts ("states of affairs that obtain"): expressed by true sentences.
  - Non-facts ("states of affairs that do not obtain"): expressed by false sentences.
  - Temporary ("can stop or start obtaining")

    Momentary ("temporary states of affairs that only obtain for a moment")
    States ("temporary states of affairs that deal with the present").
  - Durable ("states of affairs that deal with the past are always durable, because the past does not change")
  - Anankastic (a modal states of affairs that deals with the possible and the impossible. "A specific anankastic states of affairs in the law has to do with competence" (Hage and Verheij 1999)).

---

received so far point to a mismatch between the way these experts reason and the framework provided by the ontology: the ontology, they say, is not 'intuitive'" (Valente 1995).

[22]modellers: Jaap Hage and Bart Verheij, Department of Metajuridica, Universiteit Maastricht, The Netherlands. See Verheij and Hage (1997) and Hage and Verheij (1999).

[23]The notion of states of affairs and events was inspired by von Wright (1963).

  - Deontic (a modal states of affairs that has to do with the obligated, the forbidden and the permitted).

    Ought-to-do type
    Ought-to-be type

  - Probabilistic (a modal states of affairs that has to do with the probable, the certain and the uncertain)

- Events (cause changes). Acts are a special kind of events and consist of the intentional behaviour of an individual (juristic acts and factual acts are special categories of acts).
- Rules (direct connections between states of affairs). "Rules in our sense include many divergent phenomena, such as physical laws, rules of evidence, power conferring rules and legal norms" (Hage and Verheij 1999). In a power conferring rule "the legislator attributes some legal body with the competence to perform a particular juristic act" and the body can therefore perform that act (Hage and Verheij 1999). Rules consist of a condition part (one or more states of affairs) and a conclusion part (one single generic state of affairs). And legal rules and principles are both instances of rules.

  - Constitutive rules: one state of affairs constitutes another.
  - Causal rules: a state of affairs is brought about by an event: "rules that govern the relation between an event and the effects that result from it are called causal rules" (Hage and Verheij 1999).
  - Weak rules or defeasible rules. The application of rules may be blocked or rules may have incompatible conclusions (they cannot lead to all their conclusions).
  - Strong rules: "a rule that guarantees that its conclusion obtains if its conditions obtain" (Hage and Verheij 1999)

Other relevant ideas are: (1) supervenience (it is a common phenomenon that states of affairs supervene others and that events supervene other events) and (2) goals (they play an important role in law and give rise to connections between states of affairs and are considered undetermined rules.[24]

The authors analysed different legal topics from the model of abstract law presented above, for example, (a) rights[25] (the authors discussed three kinds of rights in their abstract model: claims against some concrete person, property rights and human rights and "[i]t turns out that the three kinds of rights are states – momentary states of affairs –), (b) proof ("rules of proof are constitutive rules for facts of the

[24]"[G]oals underlie reasons for deontic states of affairs. Their functioning is related to that of principles, in that they generate reasons which pleased for or against a particular (deontic) conclusion" (Hage and Verheij 1999).

[25]The notion of rights and principles was inspired by the works of Ross (1957) and Dworkin (1978).

kind that something counts as proven" (Hage and Verheij 1999)), (c) juristic acts,[26] or (d) validity[27] (this notion is used for acts, products and rules).

This ontology was aimed at knowledge acquisition, offering heuristic guidelines for legal knowledge representation: (1) identification of types of states of affairs, events and rules occurring in the domain, (2) determining for each state of affairs whether it supervenes on another state of affairs, (3) identifying which states of affairs are states, (4) checking for every event whether the rules which govern its effects have already been identified, (5) checking for all rules in the broad sense whether they are rules in the strict sense, principles or goals, (6) checking for all rules whether their application is defeasible or not, (7) checking for every state of affairs it must be proven. A formalism (first-order language) is provided in the appendix of Hage and Verheij (1999).

4.2.2.4 CLIME Ontology

The CLIME project[28] was aimed at "improving the access and understanding of large bodies of legal information through the Internet" (Winkels et al. 2002), "for the work of those associated with ship classification within the Bureau Veritas organisation" (Boer et al. 2001). Within the project the tool MILE was developed, a legal information server regarding the rules for safety and environmental care at sea and the rules for ship classification (a total of 15,000 different articles).[29]

This system has two modes of operation. The first mode is an information retrieval system, keywords are matched against terms contained in the rules (the system offers conceptual retrieval and normative assessment regarding ship classification rules and regulations). The CLIME ontology (ONtology-based Legal INformation Environment) is used in this part of the system. The other mode, the question answering application, uses the FOLaw framework (Winkels et al. 1998).[30]

---

[26]"Juristic acts are acts to which the law assigns consequences because of the intention to invoke these consequences by means of the act (...) A juristic act supervenes on another act which legally counts as juristic act. To count as a juristic act, the underlying act must satisfy a number of conditions, such as the condition that the actor is competent to perform the juristic act in question" (Hage and Verheij 1999).

[27]Inspired by the work of Kelsen (1991), in a German 1979 edition.

[28]CLIME, Computerized Legal Information Management and Explanation,(EC ESPIRIT programme P25.414), project duration 1998–2001. The CLIME partners were: British Maritime Technologies (UK), University of Brighton (UK); Bureau Veritas (France); TXT (Italy), and University of Amsterdam (Netherlands). Relevant publications are: Winkels et al. (1998, 1999, 2000), Boer et al. (2001) and Winkels et al. (2002). Visit also: http://www.lri.jur.uva.nl/~winkels/clime.html, retrieved August 18, 2010.

[29]From Bureau Veritas ship classification documentation and International Convention for the Prevention of Pollution from Ships, 1973, as modified by the Protocol of 1978 relating thereto (MARPOL 73/78).

[30]The ON-LINE architecture, is used as the basis for the commercial applications developed in the CLIME project, and the representations of the legal knowledge in ON-LINE are based upon FOLaw (Valente and Breuker 1999).

Table 4.2 Top 10 CLIME concepts (Winkels et al. 2000)

Concept	No. of relations
Action	60
System	48
State	40
Entity	36
Examination	34
Metric	31
Ship	30
Documentation	29
Additional-Class-Notation	28
Survey	26

The CLIME ontology, a domain ontology regarding the design, construction, maintenance, repair, operation and inspection of ships, was used towards conceptual indexing and retrieval of information or documents and knowledge acquisition for the construction of legal knowledge bases. "The MILE information server uses the domain ontology to match the user's case description to the case descriptions stored in the norms database" (Boer et al. 2001).[31]

Knowledge acquisition for the CLIME ontology was developed in two stages. At first, knowledge acquisition towards conceptual retrieval was obtained (concepts and relations were identified, created and defined). Later, knowledge acquisition for normative assessment tasks was identified. "This incremental modelling, using a conceptual representation as the basis for a more demanding normative representation, was very successful" (Boer et al. 2001). The domain ontology was built without reuse of any external knowledge representations (Boer et al. 2001), and incorporated a "small, abstract top ontology distinguishing things like artifacts, substances, agents and functions" (Winkels et al. 2002).

Regarding the language used towards formalization, "[t]he CLIME domain ontology uses a restricted and inexpressive language with a fixed number of labeled binary relations between terms. The data model of the ontology can be conceived of as a labeled, directed graph. This model can be trivially translated to RDF format, which depends on a very similar data model. The CLIME representation format has no equivalent for the notion of reification in RDF, and does not allow relation labels to be treated as term nodes" (Boer et al. 2001). In Boer et al. (2001) and Winkels et al. (2002) the ontology was conformed by 3,377 concepts and 11,897 relations (including `is_a` relations). Table 4.2 lists the top ten concepts and their relations of the CLIME ontology.

For the use in the KDE project, the domain ontology was translated to a Protégé-2000 knowledge base Winkels et al. (2002).[32] In this project, the ontology "was

[31]The MILE system was partially evaluated in Winkels et al. (2000).

[32]The Legal Encoding Tools (LET, java and applet versions), the modelling tool for the ontology was developed parallel to the building of the ontology (Winkels et al. 2002). KDE Project (IST 28678-1999).

Table 4.3 Basic categories in Mommers (2002)

Type	Legally-relevant	Legal
Entities	Sentences	Legal rules
	Statements	Legal principles
	Propositions	Legal norms
	Beliefs	Legal decisions
	Artefacts	Legal systematisations
	Rules	Judicial interpretations
	Concepts	Judicial classifications
		Legal concepts
Ontological Status layers	Existence	Legal efficacy
	Constitution	Legal validity
	Recognition	Legal recognition
Epistemic Roles	Reasons	Factual legal knowledge
	Defeaters	Practical legal knowledge
	Factual knowledge	
	Practical knowledge	

used to enhance search in arbitrary technical and legal documents used in business tasks associated with ship classification and survey" (Winkels et al. 2002).

Finally, the CLIME ontology was not made publicly available due to privacy requirements.[33]

4.2.2.5 Mommer's Knowledge-based Model of Law

The author investigated the philosophical and the knowledge representation viewpoints of legal concepts and represented them using *situation semantics*. "In the framework developed concepts are formed by constitutive relationships, relating application conditions to concept names" (Mommers 1998). The author took into account existing ontological claims in different theories of law (Natural Law, Legal Positivism – mainly Hart (1961) and Kelsen (1991), in a German 1979 edition –, Institutional Theories of Law, Hermeneutic Theories, etc.), together with existing modelling proposals from the field of AI and Law (Valente and Breuker 1994b; van Kralingen 1995; Visser and Bench-Capon 1996a; Hage and Verheij 1999). As stated by Valente (2005), its purpose was to offer a theoretical investigation of a domain to promote understanding (Table 4.3).

The author used "situation semantics as a representation language" (Mommers 1998):

> "Whereas computers cannot make inferences directly on natural language yet, we can apply automatic inferencing techniques on represented natural language. Thus, we have

[33]"Bureau Veritas is the owner of most of the CLIME ontology (because Rinke Hoekstra was employed by Bureau Veritas at the time it was made) it cannot be freely distributed for reuse in other projects. It was reused in KDE because in that project Bureau Veritas was a partner" (Boer et al. 2001).

to represent the meaning of natural language, which can be regarded as a representation language itself, in a formal language. I discuss one of these representation languages, viz. situation semantics, because the underlying ontological theory (situation theory) has contributed to the elements of the knowledge-based model of the law presented in this thesis" (Mommers 2002).

The ontology consists of six basic types (entities, ontological status layers, epistemic roles, relations, acts and facts) and each of them has *legally relevant and legal representatives* (Mommers 2001, 2002). The framework is applied to Dutch Penal Law (Mommers 2002).[34]

4.2.2.6 LRI-Core

The development of this core ontology was pushed by the interest to overcome the *epistemological promiscuity* of the FOLaw ontology, and to offer "the development of a 'real' core-ontology for law based upon notions of common sense" (Breuker and Hoekstra 2004a). "The purpose of developing our 'LRI-Core' is not to propose yet-another-upper-ontology, but to provide a broad, rather than 'deep' conceptual structure for the typical *legal*, or legally relevant, 'upper' notions" (Breuker et al. 2002a). The authors understood that many legal concepts were not typical for law, rather, they were specializations of common sense concepts. LRI-Core aims at supporting knowledge acquisition for legal domain ontologies Breuker (2004).[35]

LRI-Core consists at the top level of five portions or worlds: physical concepts (object and process), mental concepts, abstract concepts, roles and occurrences. Although the ontology was not grounded in any existing foundational or top ontology, "(...) LRI-core, is constructed that includes FOLaw, but also knows about legal roles, procedures, documentation, communication and legal sources" (Breuker et al. 2002b). The upper or foundational part of LRI-Core had 5 major *worlds*: physical world (Energy, Matter, Physical_Object, Substance, Physical_Change, Time, Space), mental world (Emotion, Mental_Process, Mental_Object), roles (Case_Role, Social_role, Communication_Role, Function, Social_Organisation), abstractions (Set, Formula, Geometrical_Entity, Number) and occurrences (Situation, History, Spatial_Temporal_Reference, Event, Causation, State).

The ontology was build from scratch Breuker (2004), although "[f]or the construction of LRI-Core (Fig. 4.3) we have been inspired by results from studies in cognitive science: in particular evolutionary, neural and developmental psychology" (Breuker et al. 2005). Details of the literature reviewed may be found in Breuker (2004). The authors considered the reuse of existing top ontologies, nevertheless it was not finally performed due to several reasons: most top ontologies at the time

[34]The author gave also an example of its potential application in a collaborative workspace environment (Mommers 2003).

[35]modellers: Leibniz Center for Law, The Netherlands. Consult relevant publications: Breuker and Hoekstra (2004b), Breuker (2004) and Breuker et al. (2005).

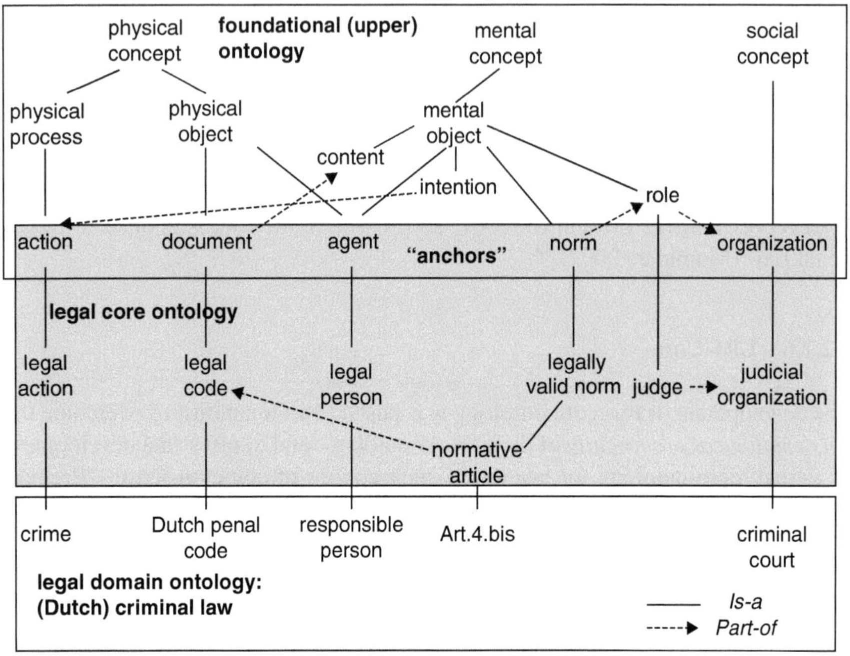

Fig. 4.3 LRI-Core (Breuker and Winkels 2003)

did not cover well the typical legal concepts and were focused on representing "scientific and formal insights as a point of departure, which is divergent from 'naive' or 'folk' theories that make up common-sense" (Breuker et al. 2005). Specifically, the authors considered that the existing upper ontologies at the time covered the *physical and formal-mathematical world* instead of the *social/communicative word*, more typical of the legal domain (Breuker 2004).[36]

The ontology was finally formalized in OWL-DL using Protégé (although in Breuker et al. (2002a) was represented in DAML+OIL/RDF and tested with the FACT reasoner towards consistency,[37] and in Breuker et al. (2002b) LRI-Core

[36]In general, the developers argued that they made a number of different design choices and reuse was not possible: (a) "We do not make the distinction between 'perdurant' and 'endurant' entities as in Sowa's ontology and in DOLCE. In principle all concepts are endurants, i.e., all concepts are 'timeless'; all instances are perdurants (occurrences)". (b) "Mental concepts are not 'non-physical' concepts (DOLCE); the mental world is an analogon of the physical world with an intentional perspective". (c) "Energy is virtually absent in other ontologies. In LRI-Core it plays an important role in defining mental and physical processes". (d) "The notion of role covers in LRI-Core most social concepts, where in other ontologies role is rather a relationship (Sowa)" Breuker et al. (2005).

[37]Other evaluation methodologies were taken into account. "LRI-Core is written in OWL which enables us to do verification of the specifications (consistency checking). However, the question of how we can assess its validity is also actual, but not easy to resolve and certainly not in a very near

was formalized in RDF(S) with Protégé-2000). The size of the ontology was predicted to have around 200 concepts, not more than 300 (Breuker et al. 2002a). In Breuker (2004) LRI-Core (version 2) had about 100 concepts. On the OWL version, consistency checking was performed.

LRI-Core was used to aid the development of ontologies in the e-Court project (directed towards information retrieval and metadata generation and specification) (Breuker et al. 2002b), specifically, used by the Dutch criminal law ontology of the e-Court project to support knowledge acquisition. Also, the idea was to ground or *anchor* the concepts of these criminal law domain ontology regarding Dutch law to LRI-Core, to ease the process of construction of other criminal law domain ontologies (Polish law and Italian law), a solution to the possible divergences between criminal law concepts in different legal systems (Breuker et al. 2002a). The DIRECT (DIscovery of REsponsibility and CausaliTy) Project was based on LRI-Core (although the authors suggested that "this study is to be viewed as an exercise in computational jurisprudence, rather than in legal knowledge engineering" (Breuker and Hoekstra 2004a).

The ontology was in the past available online. However, the development effort initiated in 2000, was discontinued in 2007 towards the development of the LKIF-Core ontology, which took inspiration from the development of LRI-Core. Nevertheless, Breuker et al. (2007) concluded that "the number of legal concepts in LRI-Core was rather small; it was rather a top ontology covering abstract concepts of common-sense rather than the field of law."

4.2.2.7 OCL.NL Ontology of Dutch Criminal Law

This ontology[38] was developed within the e-Court project,[39] a project aimed at semi-automated information management of transcriptions of criminal trial hearings ("the project aims at developing an integrated system for the acquisition of audio/video depositions within courtrooms, the archiving of legal documents, information retrieval and synchronized audio/video/text consultation" (Breuker et al. 2002a).

The ontology was directed at supporting information retrieval contained in hearing session documents and, also, was "intended to work as a reference for the development of similar ontologies of Italian and Polish criminal law.[40]

The core of OCL.NL is conformed by actions, in fact, by *offences* and *punishments*. The role of ontologies in indexing the e-Court hearing documents was

future. Up till now, some 'face-validity' has been established by comparing it with other core or foundational ontologies – in particular: DOLCE – by arguments. That was thusfar the methodology also used through the centuries by philosophers" (Breuker and Hoekstra 2004b).

[38]modellers: Leibniz Center for Law, The Netherlands. For relevant publications see: Breuker et al. (2002a, 2005) and Breuker (2004). The ontology is referred to as CRIME.NL in Breuker et al. (2007).

[39]e-COURT European Project IST-2000-28199, project duration 2000–2003.

[40]"However, due to the translation problems and a limited budget, this part of the project was never really executed" (Breuker 2004).

threefold: (1) they provided a structured vocabulary for meta-data descriptions and maintained consistent use and semantic distinctions, (2) the ontology browser supported the hand tagging of the hearings, and (3) the concepts contained in the ontology were used to index documents (Breuker et al. 2005).

The ontology was initially formalized in RDF/OWL (DAML+OIL) in Protégé to be used by the e-Court System, which ought to be accessible via de web (Breuker et al. 2002a). This formalization decision was due to the fact that at that time, LRI-Core, which was to be reused as upper ontology, was formalized in DAML+OIL. OCL.NL concepts were "anchored" in LRI-Core concepts. The list below (Breuker et al. 2002a) describes the anchoring of the OCL.NL concepts into `agent` LRI-Core concepts (boldface terms).

- agent
    - role
    - person
        - natural-person
        - juristic-person
            - company
            - association
    - collection-of-agents
        - group
        - organization
            - public-organization
                - Ministry-of-Justice
                - court-by-jurisdiction
                    - criminal-court
                    - administrative-court
                - court-by-level
                    - cantonal-court
                    - court-of-appeal

4.2.2.8 Jur-(Ital)Wordnet (Jur-IWN) and Core Legal Ontology (CLO)

Jur-(Ital)Wordnet (Jur-IWN) is an ontology-based extension to the legal domain of the Italian version of EuroWordNet.[41]

[41]The EuroWordNet project aimed at interrelate European languages to the lexical/semantic network developed at Princeton University (Miller 1995). "ItalWordNet (IWN) is the Italian section

Jur-IWN is a semantic lexicon, which could be considered a type of lightweight ontology or lexical ontology (Tiscornia 2007). In these legal ‘lexical ontologies’ synsets[42] are related to each other by several semantic relations such as hyperonymy, hyponymy, meronymy, thematic role or instance-of.[43]

The Jur-IWN ontology could provide a “lexical basis in the construction of specific domain ontologies” Gangemi et al. (2003a), support towards content management, and supply a source of *metadata for content description*, usable for semantic tagging of legislative texts. “Furthermore, the database can be a support tool for information retrieval systems, in order to facilitate access to heterogeneous and multilingual data, and a conceptual source for information extraction, automatic tagging, knowledge sharing, norm comparison, etc.” (Gangemi et al. 2003c). Specifically, “[t]he aim of the Jur-IWN is providing the NormeInRete system[44] with a knowledge base for semantic tagging at the level of articles or even dispositions; that is, recognizing normative entities (the dispositions) inside the text, which is not necessarily the same as the structural entities, and assuming a double view on the text, both as a document and as a collection of dispositions” (Gangemi et al. 2003c). Furthermore, the Jur-IWN approach was also to be tested in the E-Psinet Project, aimed at comparing the regulatory environment of Public Sector Information within Europe (Gangemi et al. 2003c).

Concepts in Jur-IWN are classified as entities of a Core Legal Ontology, CLO: “CLO is a so-called constructive ontology, since it allows to reason over the contextual constraints that can be intentionally adopted by a cognitive agent when recognizing or classifying a state of affairs. Three kinds of legal tasks in the Civil Law countries are supposed to be supported by CLO: conformity checking, legal advice, and norm comparison.” (Gangemi et al. 2005). CLO took into account the DOLCE[45] foundational ontology in order to define its classes,[46] and methodological

---

of the EuroWordnet, developed at the Institute for Computational Linguistic of the CNR of Pisa” (Gangemi et al. 2003c).

[42]“A synset is a set of one or more uninflected word forms (lemmas) with the same part-of-speech (noun, verb, adjective, and adverb) that can be interchanged in a certain context. For example, action, trial, proceedings, law suit form a noun synset because they can be used to refer to the same concept” (Tiscornia 2007).

[43]“Compared to formal ontologies, semantic lexicons, also called lightweight ontologies, are generic and based on a weak abstraction model, since the elements (classes, properties, and individuals) of the ontology depend primarily on the acceptance of existing lexical entries” (Tiscornia 2007).

[44]The NormeInRete portal is no longer available at: www.normeinrete.it

[45]“DOLCE is essentially a top-level FO, while DOLCE+ is an extension of DOLCE containing some modules dedicated to core ontologies of contexts, time, space, plans, etc. The current implementation of DOLCE+ is DOLCE-Lite-Plus” (Gangemi et al. 2005). Visit: http://www.loa-cnr.it/DOLCE.html, retrieved August 18, 2010.

[46]“The current version of CLO is based on the DOLCE+ distinction between descriptions (in this domain legal descriptions), which encompass laws, norms, regulations, crime types, etc., and situations (legal facts or cases in this domain), which encompass legal states of affairs, non-legal

Fig. 4.4 Jur-IWN structure (Gangemi et al. 2003b)

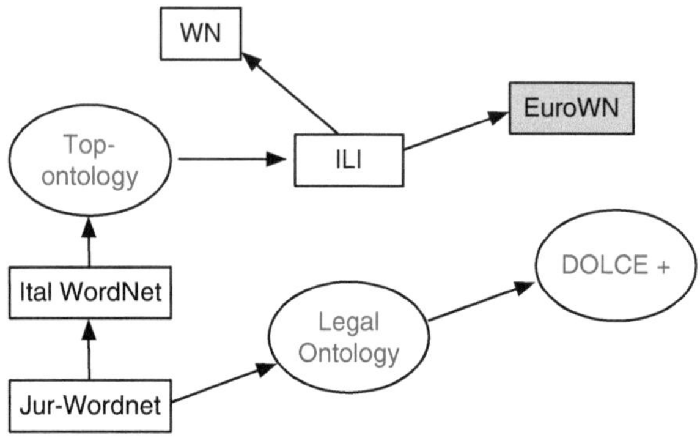

choices were based upon legal theory and philosophy of law.[47] CLO consisted of about 40 to 50 concepts (Sagri et al. 2004) and is currently available in OWL, build using Protégé.[48] For an overview of the Jur-IWN structure, see Fig. 4.4.

Jur-IWN and CLO were modeled from the same knowledge acquisition effort.[49] At first, concepts were extracted from a corpus of stored queries made to legal information systems, the Norme In Rete system and the Italigure/Find system. This extraction produced (a) the Semi database (11,000 keywords and lemmas, conceptually connected), (b) list of terms that are commonly included in AND searches (syntagms, a list of 13,000 two-word expressions, (c) list of terms that are commonly included in OR searches (syntagms of interchangeable terms). "[F]rom syntagms, the taxonomy was automatically created by using head and modifier terms, aided by a parsing of a corpus of dictionary glosses. A consolidated corpus of about 2,000 synsets will be almost automatically augmented through the link with thesauri and keywords for juridical databases" (Gangemi et al. 2005). For concept definitions, handbooks, dictionaries, legal encyclopedias, etc. were used (Sagri et al. 2004).

For the development of the CLO ontology, "[i]n line with the 'bottom-up' approach, the base of the ontology is the higher level of concepts obtained through

---

states of affairs that are relevant to the right, and purely juridical states of affairs" (Gangemi et al. 2003a).

[47]"The methodological choices, as well as the exploitation of properties suitable for the legal domain are based upon the approach of legal theory and of the philosophy of law. Legal world is conceived as *a representation, or a description of the reality*, an *ideal* view of the behaviour of a social group, according to a system of rules that are commonly accepted and acknowledged" (Gangemi et al. 2003c).

[48]The Core Legal Ontology is available at: http://www.loa-cnr.it/ontologies/CLO/CoreLegal.owl, retrieved August 18, 2010.

[49]Laboratory of Applied Ontology (Institute for Cognitive Sciences and Technology, ISTC, Rome, Italy), Institute for Theory and Techniques for Legal Information (ITTIG, Florence, Italy), and Istituto di Linguistica Coputazionale (ILC-NRC, Pisa, Italy) took part in the development of CLO and Jur-IWN. See Gangemi et al. (2003a, c, 2005), Sagri et al. (2004), Dini et al. (2005) and Peters (2004).

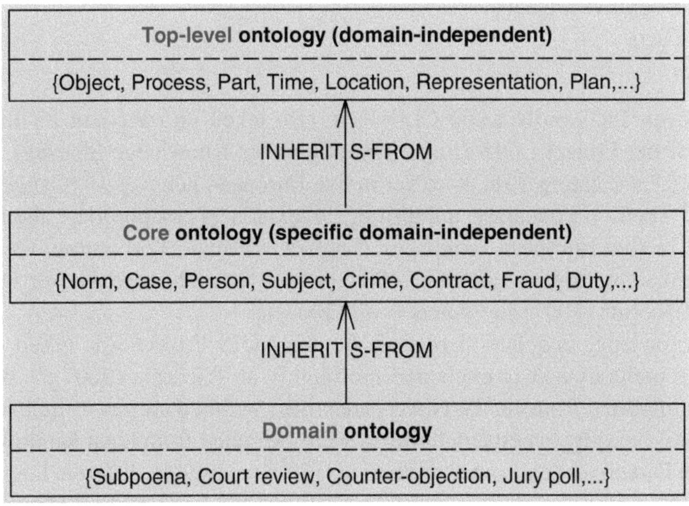

Fig. 4.5 Legal ontology library strata (Gangemi et al. 2005)

the conceptualisation of the terminology: from the 1,500 synsets structured so far, (we expect to reach a satisfactory coverage when about 3,000 synsets will be defined) about 40 concept[s] have been organised into the ontology" (Gangemi et al. 2003c). The CLO ontology is tested through norm comparison (EC directives (Gangemi et al. 2005). See Fig. 4.5 for a graphical representation of the conceptual relations between Jur-IWN, CLO and DOLCE.

CLO and Jur-IWN contain some of the following legal notions (Gangemi et al. 2005):

- Law
- Social norm
  Legal norm expressed_by a NormativeText and realised_by a Document.
- Regulations
- Types of norms
  Constitutive norms
  Regulative norms
- Modal Descriptions. Some classes of legal modal descriptions are:
  Legal rights
  Duty, Privilege, Immunity, etc.
  Legal Powers
  Legal Empowerments
  Faculty/Implicit Permission
  Explicit Permission
- Legal Roles. Legal Functions are Legal Roles played_by legal subjects.
- Legal Agents
- Legal Information Objects

- Legal Cognitive Objects
- Legal Facts
- Crimes

Moreover, Jur-WordNet and CLO were also taken into account for the development of the Project LOIS (Legal Ontologies for Knowledge Sharing),[50] which was aimed "at creating a JurWordNet in five European languages" (Gangemi et al. 2003a).[51] The LOIS database, a multilingual lexicon, is composed by about 35,000 concepts in five European languages: English, German, Portuguese, Czech, and Italian, linked by English (around 5,000 concepts for each language, see Dini et al. (2005), Tiscornia (2007) and Peters et al. (2007)).[52]

The knowledge acquisition process for the LOIS Project was based in semi-automatic methods and is explained thoroughly at Tiscornia (2007).[53] Basically, concepts imported from Jur-IWN were identified within a corpus of Italian legislation and assessed by experts, definitions were extracted from legal handbooks, and European Directives (consumer protection law) were used in different languages to extract the a multilingual set of terms to be aligned.[54] See Fig. 4.6 for an overview of the LOIS architecture.

[50]EDC-22161 (2003–2006). The project LOIS had several partners: ITTIG (coordinator), Italy, The Academy of Science of Czech Republic, University of Wien, Austria, University of Leiden, The Netherlands, University of Evora, Portugal, University of Sheffield, UK, Ellis Publishing, The Netherlands, C.E.L.I., Torino, Italy, C.E.S.I. Multimedia, Milano, Italy, GoNetwork, Pisa, Italy.

[51]"Within the lexical database of LOIS the Italian JWN is used as the ILI to map the language specific word-nets" (Schweighofer and Liebwald 2007). Two ontologies have been integrated "to a greater or lesser extent" in the LOIS lexical database: the foundational ontology DOLCE2.1-Lite-Plus and the Core Legal Ontology. On one hand, DOLCE2.0-Lite-Plus was already aligned with WordNet 1.6 Noun Synsets, on the other, the Core Legal Ontology helps the structuring of ILI legal concepts (Peters et al. 2007).

[52]"However, original hopes were a bit disappointed as the development of the ontology was very time-consuming and difficult. The number of 5,000 descriptors is now considered as too low for a broad legal application. Besides that, more work has to be done on the qualitative structuring of various concepts that will require even to a higher extent lawyers with excellent conceptual knowledge of the domain. Besides these shortcomings, the LOIS thesaurus provides a good basis for next steps to a Comprehensive Legal Ontology" (Schweighofer and Liebwald 2007).

[53]"In the LOIS project, various methods for building the lexical ontology were used. The main part has been developed manually (...) At the moment, the LOIS project follows a combination of semi-automatic methods to achieve a sufficient level of quality" (Schweighofer and Liebwald 2007).

[54]"In European Community legislation, a unique situation is created regarding legal meaning. All language versions of regulations and directives are deemed to be authentic. Thereby, they are de iure equivalent to each other. Thus, for instance, the meaning of the Dutch version of a European directive is deemed identical to the meaning of the English or Greek version of that directive" (Dini et al. 2005). "Once alignment had been established, legal equivalence was assumed and each set of corresponding terms in different languages were automatically linked to one unique identifier. An additional legal relation `implemented_as` defines the link between a European legal concept and its implementation in national legislation. As to legal concepts from European legislation, the Identifier acts as the Interlingual Index item" (Tiscornia 2007).

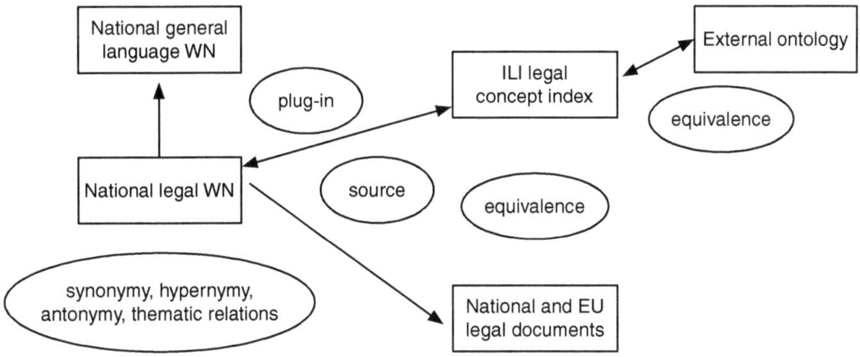

Fig. 4.6 The general architecture of LOIS (Tiscornia 2007)

In the LOIS project, the lexical resources were translated into OWL to allow consistency checking, and was used as an important source of knowledge in the development of a question-answering system for juridical documents (Curtoni et al. 2005; Quaresma and Rodrigues 2005).

Finally, Gangemi et al. (2005) and Gangemi (2009) is currently defining CODeP (Conceptual or Content Design Patterns) on top of the DOLCE foundational ontology library, the Core Legal Ontology (CLO) and JurWordNet. These patterns may be found in expert's documents and may be used to support ontology design.[55]

4.2.2.9 European VAT Regulatory Ontology: Topical Ontology of Fraud and Topical Ontology of VAT

The FFPOIROT project[56] aims at compiling for several languages (Dutch, Italian, French and English) a computationally tractable and sharable knowledge repository for the financial forensics domain. "The goal of the project is to build a detailed

[55]Current work focuses on building a tool that assists development, discussion, retrieval, and interchange of CODePs over the Semantic Web, and towards establishing the model-theoretical and operational foundations of CODeP manipulation and reasoning" (Gangemi 2007). For more information regarding conceptual ontology design patterns consult Gangemi (2005) and Blomqvist (2007, 2010) and to access the repository of content ontology design patterns visit: http://wiki.loa-cnr.it or http://www.ontologydesignpatterns.org

[56]Financial Fraud Prevention Oriented Information Resources using Ontology Technology (IST 2001-38248), visit http://starlab.vub.ac.be/research/projects/poirot, retrieved August 18, 2010, for more information. The ontologies were modeled by the Department of Applied Linguistics (Centrum voor Vaktaal en Communicatie, Belgium) and STARLab (Vrije Universiteit Brussel, Belgium). For relevant information see: Kerremans et al. (2005a, c), Kerremans and Zhao (2005), and Zhao and Leary (2005b).

ontology of European Law, preventive practices and knowledge of the processes of financial fraud within the European Union" (Leary et al. 2003), especially focused on unauthorised online investment solicitation and VAT fraud.

The FFPOIROT ontology was to be used on one hand "with software tools to automate the launching of queries that will find suspect websites and to optimise the web information retrieval results" and, on the other hand, to be part of a knowledge system that asks the user a few questions and then supplies all the necessary information and forms for VAT compliance (Kingston et al. 2003). However, it was envisioned that the ontology could also be used in the future to support "future police-oriented query systems, in a non-technical user-friendly, attractive, and comprehensive manner" (Kingston et al. 2003).

The ontology had to be able to describe concepts for several uses, mainly, supporting queries to find suspect websites, VAT compliance, fraud detection and prevention in EU transactions.[57] To model the ontologies, first, the Termontography approach was followed: "a method designed for compiling multilingual termbases which can be integrated in ontological architectures" (Geentjens et al. 2006). Later, the user requirements of this project were focused on the ORM modellers, who followed the DOGMA ontology paradigm and its derived ontology engineering methodology AKEM (and used the DOGMAmodeler tool).[58] Also, a study was carried out regarding the suitability of ontology reuse. Candidates for reuse were FOLaw, FBO and LRI-Core (see Kingston and Vandenberghe (2003)), and SUMO's financial ontology and the ontology of services, and McCarthy's REA (economic Resources, Events and Agents) ontology (see Kingston et al. (2005)). Finally, SUMO was taken into account for the construction of the ontologies (Zhao and Leary 2005b).

Finally, two "topical" ontologies were produced: the Topical Ontoloy of VAT (which contains 173 terms, 66 roles and 276 lexons (Kerremans and Zhao 2005; Zhao and Leary 2005b)), and the Topical Ontology of Fraud[59] (which modelled 760 lexons and had several versions). The Topical Ontology of VAT conceptualized the "concepts and relations used in several VAT applications for document management,

[57]Ontology requirements identified by the Joseph Bell Centre for Forensic Statistics and Legal Reasoning (University of Edinburgh, UK) are detailed in Kingston et al. (2003): (1) representing national and supranational law regarding online investments and VAT – key requirement that involves the representation of goals as intention, motives and capabilities of actors, plans as actions and sequences of actions, and legal and administrative rules together with definitions and sanctions for fraud in different EU countries –, (2) representing postulates of legal rules – a rule consists of a number of conditions –, (3) representing products or commodities, (4) representing commercial transactions, (5) representing VAT invoices, (6) representing indicators – types of evidence that can be identified which indicate a risk of fraud –, (7) including knowledge of companies and their structure, (8) including knowledge of individuals and their relationships, (9) including knowledge of databases and their communication formats, (10) representing websites, and (11) thesaurus and other support for natural language processing tools.

[58]For the user requirements see Kingston et al. (2003).

[59]FF POIROT, Introduction to topical ontology of fraud: http://starlab.vub.ac.be/research/projects/poirot/contents/FraudOntology.htm, retrieved August 18, 2010.

monitoring, question-answering, etc." (Kerremans and Zhao 2005), and was based mainly on the structure of the website of the Taxation and Customs Union of the European Union and the Directive 77/388/EEC. The core concepts identified were: VAT, taxable person, VAT scheme, VAT exemption, zero-rated good and VAT rate. This VAT Ontology was represented in XML and XLS. The Topical Ontology of Fraud was based on "publicly available knowledge resources" such as published research on fraud issues (Zhao and Leary 2005b). This ontology was aimed at capturing a working typology of frauds, a descriptive model of frauds, an argumentation model of frauds, a lifecycle model of frauds, and expressions of frauds. The particular uses of this ontology were knowledge management and sharing, case reasoning on frauds and fraud detection.

Other related application ontologies, such as VAT fraud prevention application ontology, investment fraud detection application ontology and customer fraud investigation application ontology, were later also developed. The final architecture of the ontologies developed for the project was of a layered structure based on SUMO and other domain ontologies (finance, economics and legislation domains). See Fig. 4.7 for an overview of the integration between the different ontological lawyers.

Regarding their availability, the ontologies "are of confidential nature due to the real life cases used and the underlying hard-earned know-how. The consortium restricted access to them, in conjunction with these technical factors, affects its possible technological, social and economic impacts to the public domains" (Zhao and Leary 2005b). Moreover, very few deliverables of the project related either to the *topical* or the *application* ontologies were made public.

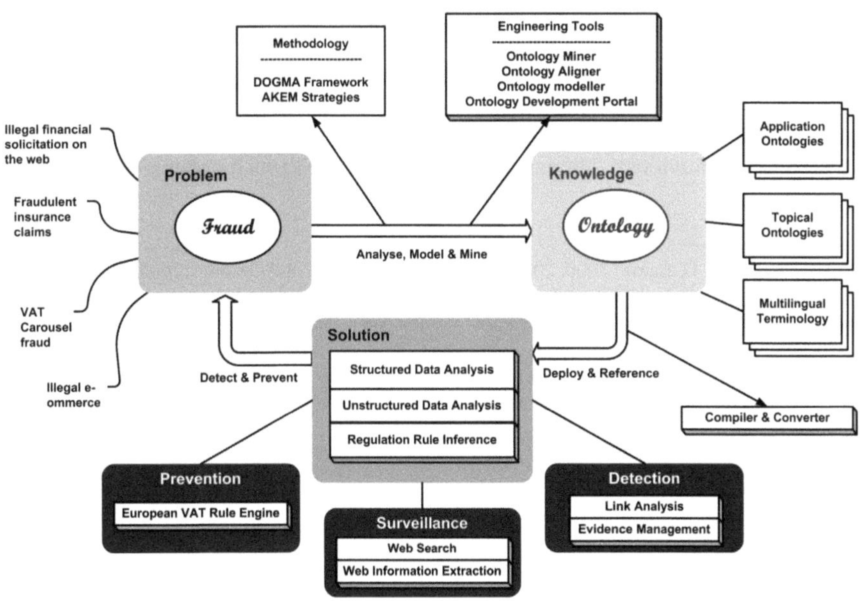

Fig. 4.7 FFPOIROT ontology layer (Zhao and Leary 2005b)

4.2.2.10 Lame's Ontology of French Law

The Ontology of French Law by Lame (2002) aimed at aiding the search and retrieval of legal information.[60] The construction methodology was based on a terminological analysis of a corpus of 57 codes of French Law, a bottom-up method, inspired by the work of Aussenac-Gilles et al. (2000a) and Moens (2001).[61] The methodology followed the following steps: (1) extraction of domain terms (118,000 terms initially), (2) identification of lexical relations between terms, (3) modelization the hierarchical knowledge of the domain, (4) modelization the structural knowledge of the domain, and (5) modelization de knowledge regarding the functions of the norms. It must be taken into account that the author took both the role of knowledge engineer and of domain expert.[62] The terms were obtained using several term extractors (such as Syntex). From an initial list of 118,000 legal terms, a list of 16,681 fundamental legal terms was finally considered.

> L'ontologie que nous obtenons est una *ontologies conceptuelle*, ou ontologie *pré-computationelle*, dans le sens oü elle définit des concepts et des relations entre concepts dans un langage non formel et non opérationnel (...) L'usage auquel est dédiée notre ontologie ne nécessite pas, de notre point de vue, sa spécification dans un langage formel et opérationnel de represéntation des connaissances (Lame 2002).

The ontology was implemented in a system to support the refinement of queries for its evaluation.[63] The users of the system acted as the evaluators, and the evaluation took place while assessing the usefulness of the ontological resource to guide and aid in search refinement. Results of this evaluation may be consulted in (Lame 2002).

Later, taking into account that "[s]ince the initial ontology is meant to be included in a Web site to allow intelligent access to documents and to interact with end users in a request expansion system", it was important to keep the ontology updated. In Lame and Desprès (2005) a further ontology was built from a new code (Research Code), following the same above-mentioned methodology and was aligned to the previously obtained ontology (from the French codes), "using coarse

[60]Main developer: G. Lame (2000, 2001, 2002, 2005) and Lame and Desprès (2005). Nevertheless, the work of updating the legal ontology was "performed by a pluridisciplinary group of researchers gathered for a 1 year work session in Paris: Action Spécifique Ontologies du Droit et Langage Juridique" (Lame and Desprès 2005). Also, the ontology was represented in XML and was, initially, made available at http://ontologie.w3sites.net. It is no longer available at this site. Lists of terms obtained during the knowledge acquisition process may be found in the appendices of Lame (2005).

[61]57 codes in Lame (2005), 58 codes in Lame (2002).

[62]"[n]otre position d'ingénieur de la connaissance et d'expert du domain nous a permis d'avoir una vision globale sur la tâche que nous avons définie de qualifiation sémantique des relations linguistiques établies entre les termes de la ressource ontologique" (Lame 2002).

[63]"Le principe fondamental de ce processus d'évaluation est de mettre la ressource ontoloquique en contexte, c'est-à-dire de l'intégrer dans un système d'aide à la reformulation de requête" Lame (2002).

techniques" and the participation of legal experts. "Both ontological resources (the initial ontology and the new ontological resource) were XML files. The updating of the source ontology consisted in including the elements in the source ontology, these elements being described by appropriate XML markers" (Lame and Desprès 2005).

4.2.2.11 IPROnto (Intellectual Property Rights Ontology) and the Copyright Ontology

As most initiatives regarding web-based management of intellectual property (multimedia) worked at the syntactic level and the meaning of the expressions was usually provided in separate *rights data dictionaries*, which made difficult their automatic processing (MPEG-21, ODRL, Creative Commons, etc.), the authors of IPROnto advocated the use of ontologies to specify in a machine-readable form the domain of intellectual property rights (IPR), also referred to as digital rights management (DRM) in the area of e-commerce of multimedia content.

> Our idea is to facilitate the automation and interoperability of IPR frameworks integrating both parts, the Rights Expression Language and the Rights Data Dictionary. These objectives can be accomplished using ontologies, which provide the required definitions of the rights expression language terms in a machine-readable form. Thus, from the automatic processing point of view, a more complete vision of the application domain is available and more sophisticated processing can be carried out (Delgado et al. 2003.)

Regarding the methodology followed for the development of IPROnto,"[s]ince a lot of work has been done in the area of IPR representation and definition, we started the development of our ontology (...) from selected specifications. The `<indecs>` framework was incorporated as the "core IPR specific part" Delgado et al. (2002), the results of the Imprimatur project (Barlas 1995) were also taken as a reference towards the IPR business model, and previous work of the Distributed Multimedia Applications Group[64] was also incorporated. Finally, the upper ontology SUMO was chosen to root all the domain conceptualization. The legal aspects of the ontology were taken from the WIPO (World Intellectual Property Organisation) common framework (see Fig. 4.8). This ontology was used in the NewMARS project,[65] which implemented a broker-based application for digital content management. The IPROnto ontology was initially formalized in DAML+OIL (Delgado et al. 2003) and is available now in OWL-DL.[66]

IPROnto was a preliminary version of the more complete Copyright Ontology (CO). This Copyright Ontology was modeled focusing on three different parts, that

[64] Distributed Multimedia Applications Group: http://dmag.ac.upc.edu

[65] See García et al. (2004) regarding this project.

[66] IPROnto was modeled by the Departament de Tecnologia, Universitat Pompeu Fabra and the Departament d'Arquitectura de Computadors, Universitat Politécnica de Catalunya. See, for further information, (Delgado et al. 2003; García et al. 2005). IPROnto has $\mathcal{ALCHI}$ expressivity, and was developed with the Protégé ontology Editor. It contains 113 classes and 54 properties, and is available at: http://dmag.ac.upc.edu/ontologies/ipronto/index.html, retrieved August 18, 2010.

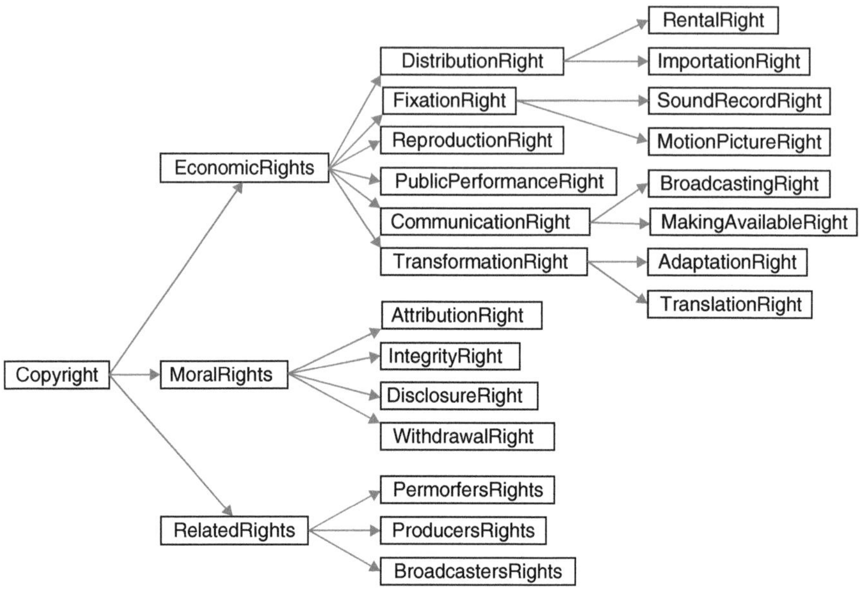

Fig. 4.8 Copyright hierarchy (García 2006)

concentrated on different portions of the problems in the copyright domain: the Creation Model (a basis for the other the conceptualization of the other two models, which defines the different forms a creation can take – work, manifestation, fixation, instance, performance and communication –), the Rights Model (which follows the recommendations of WIPO) and the Action Model (the primitive actions that can be performed on the Creation Model concepts) (García and Gil 2006). The Copyright Ontology is aimed at reasoning towards licence checking (García and Gil 2009, 2010).

The Copyright Ontology was implemented in OWL-DL (García and Gil 2006) as "[t]he main objective has been to provide a straightforward and efficient implementation geared towards an extensive use of DL (Description Logic) reasoners" (García and Gil 2006). Also, "[i]n order to implement the rules and axioms included in the conceptual model, SemanticWeb rules have been used" (García 2006).[67]

For the development of the Copyright Ontology, the METHONTOLOGY methodology was followed (García 2006), and the knowledge was acquired from WIPO recommendations and treaties, Copyright Law handbooks and conceptualized in three different parts, in which "[t]he core concepts of the ontology are those that formalise the notion of creation" (García 2006) and are inspired in top ontologies

[67] The Copyright Ontology is available from http://rhizomik.net/ontologies/2006/01/copyrightonto.owl, retrieved August 18, 2010. CO was modeled by R. García, see García and Gil (2006, 2007, 2009) and García (2006).

(such as SUMO, DOLCE and LRI-Core). Also, concepts from these top ontologies are used to enrich the CO. Further, "[s]ome specific concepts that lay outside the scope of the copyright ontology have been reused from external domain ontologies": collective, time, location, content characteristic and current measure (García 2006). The DL reasoner Pellet was used to reason about the Copyright Ontology in the Semantic Digital Rights Management System.[68]

CO was evaluated "using ontology evaluation tools like the ones provided by some ontology editors or reasoners" (García 2006).[69] The ontology was also evaluated indirectly, generating ontologies for MPEG-21 and ODRL, the main rights expression languages. From these evaluation ODRLOntos (Open Digital Rights Language Ontologies) and MPEG21Ontos (MPEG-21 Ontologies, RELOnto) emerged.[70]

4.2.2.12 Customer Complaint Ontology (CContology)

"The *customer complaint ontology* (CContology) intends to capture the knowledge elements (present in a so-called *conceptualization*) of the 'customer complaint management' domain. Its core covers a semantic description of complaints that could be issued by any legal person against any other legal person (NGO, company, natural person, government, etc.). It comprises business models, categories of complaints and resolutions, 'best-practice' business rules, etc." (Jarrar et al. 2003). This ontology was aimed at supporting extensibility and multilinguality in the CC-form (a standard form for establishing online customer complaint mechanisms, specifically a European online complaint platform).[71] Therefore, a complaint form (CC-form) was based on the semantics represented in the CContology. Therefore the purposes of the ontology were:

1. to enable sharedness within stakeholders and consistent implementation (and interoperation) of their software complaint management systems based on the CContology;
2. to allow enforcement of valid information structures, as the CContology supports business rules;
3. to play the role of core domain ontology (Jarrar et al. 2003).

---

[68]http://rhizomik.net/semdrms, retrieved November 10, 2008.

[69]Towards Copyright Ontology evaluation, the Protégé editor was used. "This kind of evaluation has been performed during the ontology formalisation phase, which has not been documented in this work as it has been automatically performed by the ontology modelling tools that have been employed" (García 2006).

[70]Visit http://dmag.ac.upc.edu/ontologies/odrlonto/index.html and http://dmag.ac.upc.edu/ontologies/relonto/index.html, both retrieved August 18, 2010, for more information and downloads.

[71]CCFORM Thematic Network project, IST-2001-34908, 5th framework. For more information regarding this project consult: http://www.fedma.org/cc-form.71634.en.html, retrieved August 18, 2010.

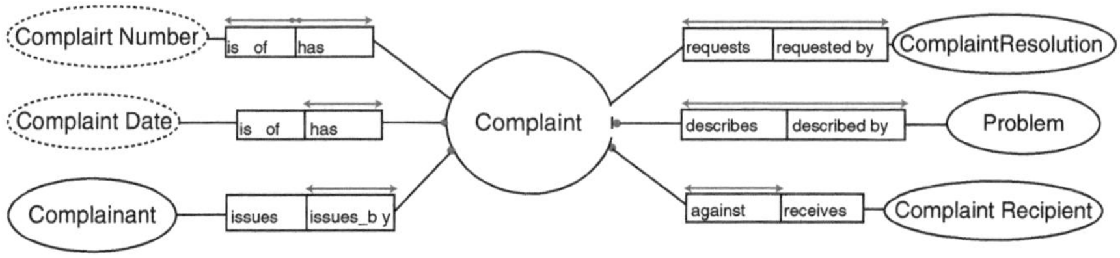

Fig. 4.9 The Complaint module

The CContology is modularized into seven *ontological commitment modules*: Complaint, Complainant, Recipient, Address, Complaint Problems, Complaint Resolutions and Contract. (Fig. 4.9 depicts the Complaint module.) It was developed in English as *native* language, although conceptual translations were made available for 11 other European languages (a multilingual *lexicalization* of an ontology) (Jarrar 2005).

For the development of the CContology, the DOGMA approach was taken into account. First, the ontology base was developed, establishing conceptual relations with the participation of domain experts,[72] and taking into account the requirements of a CC-form (Jarrar et al. 2003; Jarrar 2005). Then, the ontological commitments were developed.[73] The final axiomatization consisted of about 220 concepts and 300 lexons (Jarrar 2005).

The CContology was built and approved by all topic panels in the CCForm community, nevertheless, while this community is representative for a sizable cross-section of the domain, it is not a standardization body or holds a position for the *de facto* enforcement of this ontology as a generally agreed semantic specification. "[I]n its current state it can only be considered a proposal (...) However, we claim the approach presented in this paper is designed to initiate and drive such a process" (Jarrar et al. 2003).[74]

[72]"Ontology development and maintenance is not a single-person effort. Adequate ontologies are normally built, reviewed, and maintained by several types of knowledge experts. For example, our experience in building a 'Customer Complain Ontology', reported in chap. 7 [in Jarrar (2005)], shows that some parts of the ontology - specifically those that capture knowledge about customer regulations -should be built and evaluated by lawyers" (Jarrar 2005).

[73]The DOGMAModeler tool was used towards formalization in ORM, the conceptual graphical modelling notation used by DOGMAModeler. See Jarrar (2007) for further information on ORM. Context (in the CContology the "customer complaint context"), terms and their glosses (220 terms) and lexons ("represent taxonomies of complaint problems, complaint resolutions, etc.) are the three representation units.

[74]CContology was modeled by STARLab (Vrije Universiteit Brussel). For relevant publications see: Jarrar et al. (2003) and Jarrar (2005, 2008). Initially the CContology was implemented in the CC-form demo portal, although "[t]his portal (which was not an official deliverable in the project) is no longer available due to copy-right issues" (Jarrar 2008). Nevertheless, the CContology may be downloaded at: http://www.jarrar.info/CContology, retrieved August 18, 2010.

4.2.2.13 BEST Ontologies

The BEST-project (Batna Establishment using Semantic web Technology) aims at providing laymen with information regarding their best alternative to a negotiated agreement (BATNA), thus, to gain knowledge regarding what the outcome of a court decision in a similar case would be. This information may offer laymen, in the field of Dutch tort law, insights regarding their positions for negotiation.[75] The system supports users by retrieving relevant case law on liability, this retrieval is based on terms provided by the user (layman) that match terms provided in stored case law through the use of ontologies (Wildeboer et al. 2007; Uijttenbroek et al. 2008).

The aim of the Ontology of Dutch Tort Law (referred to as BEST-user Ontology In van Laarschot et al. (2005)) is to support users to describe their case (Klein et al. 2006).[76]

> The resulting ontology will have two different viewpoints: the layman's and the expert's viewpoint in the field of law. The layman will give a case description in terms that are understandable from a layman's viewpoint and the ontology will 'translate' that case description into expert terms that can be used for the reasoning component (van Laarschot 2005).

The methodology followed for the development of the ontology was the proposed by Noy and McGuinness (2001). The knowledge acquisition and conceptualization processes are detailed in van Laarschot (2005). First, recommended books and relevant Tort Law legislation are consulted, together with think aloud sessions with law students. Then, a hierarchical structure based on Tort Law articles is developed, which constitutes the basis for the development of the legal expert's ontology. The common sense or layman's part of the ontology is constructed from the retrieval of case descriptions from http://www.rechtspraak.nl.[77] Also, although several legal

---

[75]The BEST project is funded by the Netherlands Organisation for Scientific Research and is part of the ToKeN research programme (01-02-2005/01-07-2010, 634.000.436B). Visit: http://www.best-project.nl for further details.

[76]However, in the description of the Ontology of Dutch Tort Law by van Laarschot (2005), more reasoning capabilities were established: [i]n this Ontology of Dutch Tort law "all possible case descriptions in tort law can be expressed plus it must be able when a given one of these case descriptions to determine (after reasoning) which party is liable, on what grounds a party is liable and the corresponding article numbers". Therefore, "The role of the BEST-ontology is reasoning and problem solving" (van Laarschot 2005).

[77]"Since I am a layman in the field of law myself, the first thing to do is knowledge acquisition. I try to achieve that by: reading a recommended book about the unlawful act and the sections in Dutch law concerning tort law, doing a think aloud session with a Master student in law and getting a lot of help and advice from a PhD student of Law, who's main task is to analyze the domain of tort law. Together, we try to understand the domain of tort law as best as possible. Then a hierarchical structure will be made of the domain of tort law. This hierarchical structure will only contain article numbers. A domain in law seldom stands alone; it will refer to definitions or articles of another domain of law. These also have to be modelled in the hierarchical structure. Then we will use the hierarchical structure to build the legal or expert's part of the ontology. For the common sense or layman's part of the ontology a number of well-chosen case descriptions will be extracted from

core ontologies (FOLaw, FBO, CLO and LRI-Core) were analysed for reuse, none was finally reused (van Laarschot 2005). The OilEd editor was used to model the ontology in OWL DL, Swoop was used as a debugger and FaCT as reasoner. Protégé was also used but was found not to perform properly (van Laarschot 2005).

The ontology included concepts from Tort law (hierarchy of article numbers and grounds for liability), kinds of damage (damage concerned with objects and concerned with people), entities subject to law and objects in tort law and is formalized in OWL (about 300 classes and 50 relations) (van Laarschot 2005; van Laarschot et al. 2005). Ontology evaluation was performed against the established requirements, the initial competency questions and several test cases (instantiation) (van Laarschot 2005).[78]

The current development of the BEST system (Fig. 4.10), envisions the development of two separate and mapped ontologies, an ontology with layman concepts, and a legal ontology (the BEST horseshoe), through text analysis statistics (*fingerprints*).[79,80]

Although a system was built upon this first conceptualizations, an improved second version of this system has recently been produced, the BestPortal,[81] with the BestMap ontology,[82] which allows the specification of context-aware mappings between vocabularies as SKOS concepts (Hoekstra 2009a).

4.2.2.14 The Ontology of Professional Judicial Knowledge

The Ontology of Professional Judicial Knowledge (OPJK) is a legal professional ontology grounded on empirical data and expert knowledge, and it was developed towards enhancing search and retrieval (Casellas 2008). This ontology is used by the IURISERVICE system, designed to provide Spanish judges in their first appointment with on-line access to an FAQ (Frequently Asked Questions) system, which contains a repository of practical questions (issues) with their corresponding answers. The aim of the system was to discover the best semantic match between the user's

www.rechtspraak.nl. These will give a good idea of how to express a case in layman terms and the problems that arise in transforming them into legally valid statements, which can be used in reasoning" (van Laarschot 2005).

[78]The BEST-User ontology is available from http://www.best-project.nl/ontology/BEST.daml, retrieved August 18, 2010.

[79]The description of the system is as follows: "[f]irst a case description is entered by the layman user. An ontology with layman concepts is used to structure the input and guides the user by entering relevant aspects of the case at hand. The laymen ontology is mapped to a second, legal ontology that is used for indexing case law" (Uijttenbroek et al. 2008).

[80]More current information regarding the BEST project developments may be found in Uijttenbroek et al. (2007a, b, 2008) and Hoekstra (2009a). Ontology visualizations are provided with TopBraid Composer.

[81]BestPortal: http://sembweb.cs.vu.nl/best-portal

[82]BestMap: http://www.best-project.nl/owl/bestmap.owl, both retrieved August 18, 2010.

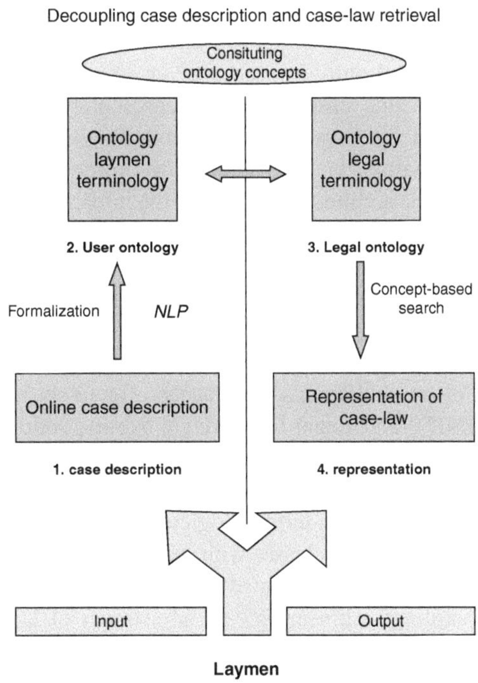

Fig. 4.10 Schematic overview of the BEST-project (Uijttenbroek et al. 2008)

question [input question] (formulated in natural language) and a stored question, so as to offer an answer that satisfies the user. (Benjamins et al. 2005c; Casellas et al. 2007). The ontology was developed in OWL with the Protégé ontology editor, and the methodological approach taken was characterized by the participation of legal experts in the all stages of the process, and by the ethnographic acquisition of data (Vallbé 2009; Casellas 2009). The construction of this ontology is detailed as a case study in Chap. 5.

4.2.2.15 LKIF Core Ontology

LKIF is a Legal Knowledge Interchange Format developed at the Estrella Project[83] in order to "enable the translation between legal knowledge bases written in different representation formats and formalisms" and to act "as a knowledge representation formalism that is part of a larger architecture for developing legal knowledge systems" (Hoekstra et al. 2007).[84]

[83]Estrella project (IST-2004-027665), http://www.estrellaproject.org. See Boer et al. (2007) for a specification of the Legal Knowledge Interchange Format.

[84]Also MetaLex XML is, as LKIF, a knowledge interchange format of sources of law and references to sources of law. It has been based from best practices from amongst other versions

Within the LKIF development effort, an ontology of basic legal concepts, LKIF-core, is being developed and formalized in OWL-DL towards several purposes, "[a] legal ontology can play an important role in the translation of existing legal knowledge bases to other representation formats," "can support the process of knowledge acquisition and modelling in the legal domains" (Hoekstra et al. 2007). But mainly, the LKIF Core Ontology contains 'basic concepts of law' and is part of a generic architecture to enable the interchange of knowledge (LKBS).[85] Thus, LKIF-Core is directed at supporting legal inference, knowledge acquisition, knowledge exchange and semantic annotation (Hoekstra et al. 2009).

The ontology is structured in modules and layers. Three layers can be distinguished in the ontology: Top Level (that borrows most classes from LRI-Core), Intentional Level (that includes concepts and relations which describe behaviour "of rational agents that can be effectively influenced by the law" (Hoekstra et al. 2007)) and Legal Level (legal agents, actions rights and powers – modified from Rubino et al. (2007), also described in the list of ontologies below – and legal roles and concept definitions). "We adhere to a rather restrictive view on what an ontology should contain: terminological knowledge, i.e., intensional definitions of concepts, represented as classes with which we interpret the world" (Hoekstra et al. 2007).

"The construction of LKIF-Core followed a combination of methodologies for ontology engineering," an adjustment of Uschold and Grüninger (1996b), within others, with the following steps: (1) identification of purpose and scope, (2) ontology capture, (3) ontology coding, (4) integration with existing ontologies, and (5) evaluation" (Hoekstra et al. 2007; Breuker et al. 2007; Hoekstra et al. 2009). The ontology capture stage is explained as follows.

> The Estrella consortium includes representatives of the three kinds of experts [citizens, legal professionals and legal scholars]. Each partner was asked to supply their 'top-20' of legal concepts. Combined with terms we collected from literature (jurisprudence and legal text-books) we obtained a list of about 250 terms. As such a number is unmanageable as a basic set for modelling, we asked partners to assess each term from this list on five scales: level of abstraction, relevance for the legal domain, the degree to which a term is legal rather than common-sense, the degree to which a term is a common legal term (as opposed to a term that is specific for some sub-domain of law), and the degree to which the expert thinks this term should be included in the ontology. The resulting scores were used to select an initial set of 50 terms plus those re-used from other ontologies [LRI-Core and LLD] Hoekstra et al. (2007).[86]

---

of MetaLex schema, Akoma Ntoso schema and Norme in Rete schema, and it has been inspired also from the experiences of LexDania, CHLexML, FORMEX, and R4eGov. Earlier descriptions of MetaLex can be found in Boer et al. (2002) and Winkels et al. (2003). The European Committee for Standardization has adopted the latest proposal as a prenorm and a workshop is open to participation (Boer et al. 2008). Latest proposals can be viewed at http://www.metalex.eu. Description of the interfacing between MetaLex and LKIF may be consulted at Boer et al. (2008).

[85]Due to its knowledge interchange purpose "[i]t is dependent on the (potential) users what kind of vocabulary is aimed at" (Hoekstra et al. 2007).

[86]The lists of concepts can be found in the Appendix of Breuker et al. (2007). These "terms formed the basis for the identification of clusters and the development of the LKIF Core ontology" (Hoekstra et al. 2007). These clusters were: Expression, Norm, Process, Action, Role, Place,

The developers expected to reuse concepts from existing upper and core ontologies, although "it turned out that the amount of re-use and inspiration was rather limited" (Hoekstra et al. 2007). Some of the ontologies taken into account were: SUMO, DOLCE, CYC, LRI-Core, LLD and CLO (see Hoekstra et al. (2009)). The number of typical legal concepts in the LRI-Core ontology, for example, was found to be "disappointingly small" (Hoekstra et al. 2007). Nevertheless, LRI-Core was used as an inspiration for the development of the LKIF Core Ontology.

This ontology was tested with the instantiation of the EU Directive 2006/126 on driving licences,[87] "a relatively straightforward regulation, in which at least two types of normative statement are recognisable – definitional and deontic" (Hoekstra et al. 2007, 2009). Also, regarding the knowledge acquisition process, "[t]he list of terms will be subjected to a more rigorous empirical study, whereby we will consult a group of legal professionals (taking courses in legal drafting), and law students. By applying statistical cluster analysis, we might be able to identify the properties of the scales used (...) and whether the statistical clusters have some resemblance to the clusters we have identified based on theoretical considerations" (Hoekstra et al. 2007). Also, a specialization of LKIF Core in the domain of university library regulations was used to evaluate legal assessment with the OWL Judge Protégé plug-in (van de Ven et al. 2008).

The ontology is formalized in OWL-DL.[88] LKIF-Core version 1.0.2 had 206 classes and 113 object properties. The current available version (1.0.3) contains 155 classes and 97 object properties.[89]

4.2.2.16 The Legal Case Ontology

The Legal Case Ontology "could be used to make explicit implicit knowledge of legal cases which legal professionals have; it could be used as a tool to build a database of cases; which a database of cases we could apply automated case-based reasoning rules and query the knowledge-base; with a web-based tool, case representation and reasoning could be done over the Internet" Wyner and

Time, and Mereology, which were further specified following a middle-out strategy. A final total of 14 modules was obtained after discussion and reuse (Legal Role, Legal Action, Rules, Time Modification, Core and Top – based on LRI-Core – were added). They are integrated in the LKIF-Core ontology module, which acts as *entry point* (Breuker et al. 2007).

[87]EU Directive 2006/126/EC of the European Parliament and of the Council of 20 December 2006 on driving licences (OJ L403, 30/12/06).

[88]LKIF-Core version 1.0.2 had $\mathcal{SHIN}(\mathcal{D})$ expressivity, and used Protégé 3.2/4.0 and TopBraid Composer (Hoekstra et al. 2007) as ontology editing tools. Moreover, OWL2 expressiveness was also studied.

[89]The LKIF Core Ontology and relevant documentation are available from: http://www.estrellaproject.org/lkif-core, retrieved August 18, 2010. See also Hoekstra et al. (2007), Breuker et al. (2007), Hoekstra (2009b), Hoekstra et al. (2009). A Protégé 4 plugin for legal assessment based in LKIF-Core is being developed (Hoekstra et al. 2009).

Hoekstra (2010). Thus, this ontology represents legal case concepts such as: `Case`, `Decision`, `Jurisdiction`, `Participant`, `Evidence`, `Legal_Concept`, or `Legal_Document`, based on previous experiences in legal case based reasoning and argumentation schemes.[90] Although LKIF Core Ontology was examined, it was not finally reused. The formalization of the concept `Party` is described below:

```
<!-- http://www.best-project.nl/owl/legal-case-ontology.owl#Party -->

<owl:Class rdf:about="&legal-case-ontology;Party">
    <owl:equivalentClass>
        <owl:Class>
            <owl:unionOf rdf:parseType="Collection">
                <rdf:Description
                    rdf:about="&legal-case-ontology;Defendant"/>
                <rdf:Description
                    rdf:about="&legal-case-ontology;Plaintiff"/>
            </owl:unionOf>
        </owl:Class>
    </owl:equivalentClass>
    <owl:equivalentClass>
        <owl:Restriction>
            <owl:onProperty
                rdf:resource="&legal-case-ontology;party_of"/>
            <owl:someValuesFrom
                rdf:resource="&legal-case-ontology;Case"/>
        </owl:Restriction>
    </owl:equivalentClass>
        <rdfs:subClassOf rdf:resource="&legal-case-ontology;Participant"/>
</owl:Class>
```

The property case Popov v. Hayashi[91] has been instantiated to illustrate the annotation and reasoning possibilities of the Legal Case Ontology. This ontology is formalized in OWL 2 with the Protégé ontology editor (with the ACE View plug-in), following "current guidelines for ontology development," especially best practices established at Hoekstra (2009b).[92]

Finally, as a summary, Table 4.4 below includes a list of ontologies and information regarding their purpose, subject-matter, level of generality, formality, methodology, participation of legal experts, tools, evaluation, availability and applications. When, from the literature consulted, it has not been possible to obtain the information a "—" will appear. Due to the lack of space, purpose

[90]This ontology is available at: http://wyner.info/research/ontologies/LegalCaseOntology_v9.owl, retrieved August 18, 2010.

[91]Popov v. Hayashi, 2002 WL 31833731 (Ca. Sup. Ct. 2002).

[92]Previous work on the ontology for legal case-based reasoning (LCBR Ontology) and other related work may be found at Wyner (2007), Wyner and Bench-Capon (2007) and Wyner (2008, 2009). This LCBR Ontology was formalized in OWL-Lite using Protégé (the ontology was tested with the reasoner Pellet 1.3). "As the ontology is web-based and provided in the context of an open-source European Project (ESTRELLA), our object is to allow public use and development of the ontology" (Wyner 2007).

Table 4.4 List of legal ontologies

	Purpose	Subject	Level	Formality	Methodology	KA	Tools	Evaluation	Application	Availability
FBO	S.E. (KA and R)	S/D	Core	Frame-based Ontolingua	–	Legal theory	Ontolingua	–	FRAMER CLIME POWER	Yes (article)
FOLaw	S.E. (KA and R) and T.I.	S/D	Core	Ontolingua	–	Legal theory	Ontolingua	–	ON-LINE PROSA Causati-ONT	–
O.D.I. States of Affairs	T.I. and S.E. (KA)	S/D	Core	First-order language	–	Legal theory	–	–	Yes (article)	–
CLIME Ont.	I.S.	S	Domain	Own	Own	MARPOL and BV doc.	Own (Protégé)	MILE (experts)	CLIME (MILE) KDE	No
KB Model of Law	T.I.	S/D	Core	own	–	Legal theory	–	–	(Dutch Penal Law)	Yes (article)
LRI-Core	S.E. (KA and R)	S	Upper/ core	DAML+OIL/ RDF OWL-DL	Yes (consistency)	Cognitive Science Studies	Protégé	–	e-Court (OCN-NL) DIRECT Copyright Ont. EU employee O.	No (see LKIF)
OCN-NL	I.S.	S	Domain	DAML+OIL (OWL?)	–	LRI-Core (reuse)	–	–	e-Court	–

(continued)

Table 4.4 (continued)

	Purpose	Subject	Level	Formality	Methodology	KA	Tools	Evaluation	Application	Availability
Jur-IWN and LOIS ont.	Com. and I.S.	S	Core/domain (linguistic)	own (JWN) OWL(Lois)	own	Legal texts, queries (ITALIGURE), EU Directives, reuse (CLO)	–	Yes (consistency, expert revision of terms)	NormeInRete LOIS DALOS AGO Ont. CODeP	–
CLO	S.E. (KA and R)	S	Core	OWL	own	Legal theory, reuse (DOLCE)	Protégé	Yes (consistency)	Jur-IWN LOIS DALOS CODeP	Yes
TOF and TOV	I.S and R.P.S.	D/S	Domain	XML/XLS	Termonthography DOGMA and AKEM	Public literature (research) and Requirements by experts (TOF) and EU Directive and official website (TOV)	–	–	FFPoirot	No
Ont. French Law	I.S. (B.N.)	S	Domain	XML	Aussenac-Gilles et al. (2000b) and TERMINAE	58 French codes domain expert as ontology engineer	Term extractors (Syntex)	Yes (system implementation and comments by users)	Website	No

(continued)

Table 4.4 (continued)

	Purpose	Subject	Level	Formality	Methodology	KA	Tools	Evaluation	Application	Availability
IPROnto	Int.	S	Domain	DAML+OIL OWL-DL	–	PR specifications (WIPO) and reuse (SUMO)	Protégé	Yes (consistency)	NewMars Copyright Ont.	Yes
Copyright Ont.	Int. and R.P.S.	S/D	Domain	OWL-DL Semantic-Rules	Methontology	PR specifications (WIPO) and reuse (IPROnto, LRI-Core, SUMO, DOLCE)	Protégé	Yes (translation of specifications and consistency)	–	Yes
CCOntology	Com. and S.E. (KA)	S	Domain	ORM	DOGMA	CCFORUM experts and documents	Dogma Modeler	expert approval	CCFORM	Yes
BEST Ontologies	R.P.S., I.S., com.	S	Domain	OWL	Initially Noy and McGuinness (2001)	Doctrine LLM/PhD law students text analysis (fingerprints)	OilED TopBraid	Requirements and CQ Test portal	BEST portal	Yes

(continued)

Table 4.4 (continued)

	Purpose	Subject	Level	Formality	Methodology	KA	Tools	Evaluation	Application	Availability
OPJK	I.S.	S	Domain	OWL	own, inspired by Uschold and Grüninger (1996b)	Ethsnography text analysis expert discussion	Protégé text analysis and OL tools	Yes (experts)	Iuriservice	Yes (on de-mand)
LKIF-Core	Int. and S.E. (K.A. and R.P.S.)	S	Upper/ Core	OWL-DL	own, inspired by Uschold and Grüninger (1996b)	Brainstorming (lists of terms) and inspiration (FOL, LRI-Core)	Protégé TopBraid Com-poser	Yes Requir-ements and consistency (future expert ev.)	LKIF archi-tecture	Yes
LCO	K.A., R., R.P.S.	S	Domain (some core con-cepts)	OWL 2	best practices (Hoekstra 2009b)	Previous LCBR knowledge and inspiration (LKIF)	Protégé ACE View	Yes Instantiation	–	Yes

and subject-matter have been abbreviated.[93] While we do not claim to have a complete and thorough view of all the literature regarding each of the ontologies, information has been sought wherever it has been possible and most literature has been consulted. Nevertheless, some relevant information may still be missing.

4.2.3 More Legal Ontologies

Many other legal ontologies have been developed so far. The following is a further list of other relevant legal ontologies being built in the field.[94]

1. **e-POWER ontology**[95]: The POWER ontology was developed to aid the formalization of legislation with the e-POWER Method: (1) translation of legislation and regulations in basic concepts (conceptualization) and (2) representation of these concepts into executable specifications. "In the first step an *ontology of legislation and regulations* is used. The basic concepts in this ontology are definitions, actions and norms" (van Engers et al. 2000) (emphasis added). This ontology was based on FBO. The ontology and the method were used "to improve the speed and efficiency with which the Dutch Tax and Customs

[93]Purpose: interoperability (int.), systems engineering (SE), knowledge acquisition (KA), reuse (R), indexing and search (IS), reasoning and problem solving (RPS), theoretical investigation (TI), and communication (com.). Subject-matter: static (S) and dynamic (D).

[94]Many contributions refer nowadays to the use of legal ontologies, however there are few specific details about their development processes. Some of these are Costa et al. (1999), Peek (1997), Singh (1999), Desprès and Delforge (2000), Zeleznikow and Stranieri (2001), Boella et al. (2001), Jouve et al. (2003), Ryan et al. (2003), Shaheed et al. (2005), Kayed (2005), Boella et al. (2005), Yan et al. (2006), Abramowicz et al. (2007), Saravanan et al. (2007), Gray (2007), Winkels et al. (2007), da Rosa Alves et al. (2007), Gray et al. (2007), Loukis (2007), Schweighofer and Liebwald (2007), Adams (2008), Khadraoui et al. (2008), Liebwald (2009), Rahmouni et al. (2009), Pazienza et al. (2009), Sonntag (2009), Stadlhofer et al. (2009), Charalabidis and Metaxiotis (2009), Zurek and Kruk (2009), Kharbili and Stolarski (2009), Barbagallo et al. (2010) and Luz Clara et al. (2010). Finally, other contributions such as the Multi-lingual and multi-jurisdictional RDF Dictionary for the legal world by M. Muller (see Muller (2001), the Dictionary Workgroup at LegalXML by J. McClure (see also McClure (2007) and the European Legal RDF Dictionary are relevant for this research. (Visit: http://rdfdictionary.sourceforge.net, http://www.legalxml.org, and http://www.lexml.de/eu/index.htm). Further, see some legal database providers which offer *semantically-enhanced* search in their search engines, although few information is available with regards to the development or technical details: LawMoose (MooseBoost: http://www.lawmoose.com/index.cfm?HomeCommunity=WorldLaw, retrieved August 18, 2010; LexisNexis Total Patent for patent research: http://www.lexisnexis.com/media/press-release.aspx?id=125674399689744, retrieved August 18, 2010; La Ley Digital con expansión semántica (sinónimos): http://www.atencionclientes.com/FAQ/LALEY/FAQ_Buscar_Sinonimos.htm, retrieved August 18, 2010.

[95]E-Power Project (Program for an Ontology-based Working Environment for Rules and Regulations) was partially funded by EC as IST Project 2000-28125.

Administration (DTCA) can implement decision support systems for internal use and for its clients. Ontologies have also proven their usefulness for efficient and effective analysis of draft legislation, allowing the DTCA to give immediate feedback to drafts of the new income tax law of 2001" (Boer et al. 2003). It was represented in UML ("[w]ithin the UML package, the important concepts found in the legislation are modelled as types and attributes. As opposed to the more often used classification of concepts in classes, the use of types allows introducing redundant concepts, and is independent of the way the data will be structured in later applications" (van Engers 2004). However, as it was not suitable for ontology integration, OWL was used towards norm representation and comparison (Boer et al. 2003). The e-POWER ontology was developed by the Department of Computer Science and Law, University of Amsterdam and Dutch Tax and Customs Administration (DTCA). For relevant documentation consult: van Engers et al. (2000, 2001, 2002), van Engers and Glassée (2001), van Engers and Vanlerberghe (2002), Boer et al. (2003) and van Engers (2004).

2. **The Ontology of Cyberspace** by Koepsell (2000). An informal ontology, proposed from a philosophical approach (applied ontology), intended to offer understanding of cyberspace and to clarify intellectual property law regarding that particular domain. "While philosophers have not yet adequately addressed the ontological problems presented by cyberspace, the legal system has been grappling with the practical problems raised by the emergence of computerized media" (Koepsell 2000). The author presents the legal ontology of intellectual property, the legal ontology of software and the commonsense categories of cyberspace in order to propose a new internally consistent ontology of cyberspace and intellectual property.[96]
3. **e-COURT ontologies**. A number of specialized ontologies were developed in order to cover all the topics the e-COURT Project[97] had to model: (a) criminal law terminology (described in Sect. 4.2.2.7, OCL.NL), (b) trial content and

[96]The list includes this ontology because, although it is informal, it provides a basis for the formalization of intellectual property rights, in a similar but more theoretical way as IPROnto, CO, or the Ontology of Licenses. Moreover, Smith (2003) also indicates that "the lessons drawn from information systems ontology can support the efforts of those philosophers who have concerned themselves not only with the development of ontological theories, but also – in a field sometimes called 'applied ontology' (such as does Koepsell (2000)) – with the application of such theories in domains such as law, or commerce, or medicine."

[97]e-Court European Project (IST-2000-28199). "The e-COURT project is a European project 2 that aims at developing an integrated system for the acquisition of audio/video depositions within courtrooms, the archiving of legal documents, information retrieval and synchronized audio/video/text consultation. The University of Amsterdam is responsible for the role of (legal) ontologies in the e-COURT system" (Breuker et al. 2002a). Partners: Project Automation S.p.A. (Italy), Ministero della Giustizia (Italy), SchlumbergerSema (Spain), CRYPTOMAThiC A/S (Denmark), INTRASOFT International S.A. (Luxembourg), Consiglio Nazionale delle Ricerche (Italy), Université Paul Sabatier (Toulouse 3, France), Universiteit van Amsterdam (The Netherlands), Ministry Of Justice (Poland).

criminal court procedure, and (c) document description entities. Moreover, "[i]n e-COURT ontologies are developed for the Italian, the Polish and the Dutch jurisdictions" (Breuker et al. 2002b). Protégé-2000 was used as ontology editor and the ontologies were formalized in RDF(S)/OIL. These ontologies were linked to the LRI-Core ontology in order to "prevent incoherence and to supply a more or less uniform point of view on these ontologies" (Breuker et al. 2002b).

4. **AGO IR Ontology** an ontology for the web information retrieval system of the Portuguese Attorney General's Office (AGO). The development of the ontology followed a following a specific methodology based in NLP techniques (Saias and Quaresma 2003a, b, 2005). Nevertheless, an existing top-level legal ontology from the Portuguese AGO (6,000 classes and 10,000 relations) was reused. The results form the LOIS project (described in Sect. 4.2.2.8) were expected to be useful. The language chosen for formalization was first DAML+OIL (Saias and Quaresma 2002).
5. **Italian Crime Ontology** by Asaro et al. (2003). Offers a domain conceptualization of Crime-related concepts in Italian Criminal Law to "achieve a homogeneous conceptual structure in the various projects" (Minerva Project, Ithca Project and P.M. Daedalus)[98], to "add domain knowledge to the support tools," to "manage documents by means of metadata," to "identify and suggest crime hypothesis to the judge, for example, by scanning documents by means of shallow parser" and, to "mark semantically the criminal laws by using the XML language." The conceptualization includes also the concepts related to crime not committed and crime attempt. At the first stage UML class diagrams were used towards formalization. Further formalization will take DOLCE into account. The ontology was build through the analysis of articles 42–49 of the Penal Code by legal experts (a Magistrate at Lucca Court (C. Asaro) took part in the development of the ontology) (Asaro et al. 2003).
6. **Multi Tier Contract Ontology (MTCO)**. MTCO is a layered ontology structure for representing contractual domain perspectives in order to enable human-to-human communication. "The conceptual meanings and interpretations of the contractual obligations inherent in a business contract are analyzed and represented in the multi tier contract ontology" (Kabilan and Johannesson 2003). The ontology is conformed by several layers: Upper Level Core Contract Ontology (components of a business contract in order to be legally valid),[99] Specific Domain Level Contract Ontology (specific contract types) and Template

[98]See, for example, Asaro and Nissan (2001) on the Daedalus Project.

[99]For example, "the UCLC Ontology [Upper Level Core Contract Ontology] defines the generic concepts and semantic relationships between contracts, its participants the actors, the roles they undertake within the scope of the contract, the object for which they undertake the contract. Consideration, the commitments they make, obligations, the expected business actions that will fulfill the obligations, performance" (Kabilan et al. 2005).

Level Contract Ontology (a group of pre-defined contractual obligations and their fulfillment patterns). At first, they were presented as conceptual models using UML, and later they were formalized in RDFS/DAML (for an extensive description of this formalization see Kabilan (2003)). Knowledge acquisition regarding the legal contractual domain was perform from available literature, standards and recommendations, and the input of various legal experts (lawyers, and judges) (Kabilan 2003). This UML-RDFS/DAML conversion was used as proof of concept.[100] The development methodology was inspired by Gruber (1993a) and Noy and McGuinness (2001). For the formalization Protégé-2000 and DUET were used. The ontology may be used towards deducing contract workflow models, monitor and track obligation fulfillment and for "automated or semi-automated wizard like tools to help monitor contracts or to interpret the required actions for fulfilling obligations" (Kabilan and Johannesson 2003).

7. The **Legal Ontology using a General Ontology**. The authors demonstrate the possibility of the development of a legal domain ontology with the help of an existing general ontology. The DODDLE environment (with WordNet enhancement) is used for the development of the legal ontology. See Kurematsu et al. (1998a), Yamaguchi and Kurematsu (1998), Sugiura et al. (2004), Kurematsu et al. (1998b), Aoki et al. (1998) and Sugiura et al. (2003).
8. **EU Employee Legal Ontology** by Desprès and Szulman (2004), an ontology constructed from the European Council Directive 2001/23/EC (in French). The ontology construction was based on the TERMINAE method and tool and reuses some top-level distinctions from DOLCE and core level concepts from LRI-Core. The first version of the ontology included 100 concepts and 30 "roles."
9. **Tax Ontology** by Melz and Valente (2004). The ontology formalizes the US Internal Revenue Code (IRC) for a broad range of applications. "Ontologizing the IRC would allow a broad range of tax-related applications to be built, including help systems, auditor agents and question-answering systems" (Melz and Valente 2004). However, the ontology will play two roles: "organize and structure information, and semantic indexing and search." A proposal. modellers: USC Information Institute (ISI, USA).
10. **e-Government Ontology (OCML)**, and later the E-Government Upper Level Ontology, by Domingue et al. (2004) and Gugliotta et al. (2005). The initial e-Government ontology modelled concepts relevant to the provision of community services and information (e-government), based on a previous taxonomy created by the Essex County Council (seamless UK). The e-Government Upper Level Ontology, based on the previous one, reused concepts from DOLCE+.

[100] "We tested our conceptual models on novices to software design principles including legal experts and business strategy and policy makers. Proof-of-concept implementation for transformation of UML conceptual models into machine-understandable ontology formats like RDFS and DAML have been carried out successfully" (Kabilan 2003).

Some of the e-government ontology concepts included: `law`, `administration-of- justice`, `courts`, `legal-advice`, `criminal-law`, `offenders`, etc. The ontology was modelled in OCML but it could be exported to RDF(S) and OWL.[101]

11. **CausatiONT** ontology by Lehmann et al. (2004, 2005). An ontology regarding causation in Law for Artificial Intelligence purposes. CausatiONT "was envisioned as part of the Functional Ontology of Law (FOLaw)" (Lehmann et al. 2005) in order to allow automatic legal reasoning. Legal theory notions of *responsibility* and *causation* were taken into account for the construction of CausatiONT and its top level is based on the concept `Noesis` and its three subconcepts `Dimension`, `Entity` and `Category`. The ontology was developed using Protégé-2000.
12. The **SIAP Legislative Ontology** (LO) by Costilla et al. (2005). An ontology that includes legislative concepts and "it makes possible the definition of semantic rules for the knowledge inference mechanisms" (Costilla et al. 2005), to be used by the Parliamentary Integrated Management System (SIAP) of the Madrid Autonomous Community Parliament [Asamblea de Madrid]. Developed with Protégé 2000, expressed in OWL.
13. **OnProc** by Blaquier-Ascaño (2006). An ontology to aid the automatization of juridical processes and allow information retrieval on them. It was based on Cuban Procedural Law, although it holds generality objectives. The modelling used a previous computational model regarding juridical processes, funded on petri nets (RPCIPETT) in PNML (XML founded) language. They have used a mixed top-down/bottom-up process. formalized in OWL DL, using Protégé. It is being tested by Civil law experts.
14. **BDSG Ontology** by Abou-Tair and Berlik (2006). The authors formalize the German Personal Data Protectio Act (Bundesdatenschutzgesetz, BDSG) with OntoStudio, where rules are represented in F-Logic. This ontology is aimed at reasoning over access control to data sources (Abou-Tair 2006). Moreover, "[b]y constructing the BDSG-Ontology we profit from well-known experience in the field of AI and law, like FOLaw's and CausatiONT ontologies" (Abou-Tair 2006).[102]
15. **LegLOPD ontology** by Mitre et al. (2006). This ontology modelled concepts from the Spanish Data Protection Act (LOPD), reused concepts from the LRI-Core ontology, and the development process of the LegLOPD ontology followed the TERMINAE method. Although legal experts are not referred to, the authors state that "designers should become experts in privacy legislation

[101] The ontology is described in http://dip.semanticweb.org/documents/D9.3Annex-eGovermentontologyOCML.pdf, retrieved August 18, 2010. Recent development are described in Gugliotta et al. (2008). Information on the Operational Conceptual Modelling Language (OCML) language may be found at http://technologies.kmi.open.ac.uk/ocml/, retrieved August 18, 2010.

[102] A example (demonstration) may be found at: http://pi.informatik.uni-siegen.de/whois/BDSG_Ontology_Demo, retrieved August 18, 2010.

in order to interpret their precepts," and that [p]rivacy legislation are huge and complex, making quite difficult its interpretation by non-experts" (Mitre et al. 2006).

16. **REIMDOC project legal ontologies for e-Government.**[103] The EGO Ontology Model reuses the first two layers of LRI-Core and includes several Real-estate Transaction Ontologies (the Person Ontology, the Civil Personality Ontology, the Organisation Ontology, the Location Ontology, the Tax Ontology, the Contract Model Ontology, the Jurisprudence Ontology, the Real-estate Transaction Verifications Ontology, the Real-estate Ontology, the Legislation Ontology, the Real-estate Transaction Ontology and the Documentation Ontology[104]). These ontologies have been developed following the METHONTOLOGY methodology and using the WebODE workbench and will be used in the EgoIR, information retrieval system. Galindo (2007) emphasises that "the development of this type of programmes can be outstandingly promoted if philosophers of Law participate," as did in this project. The REIMDOC effort and the EGO Model are currently also being adapted not only to the Spanish legal system but also to the Mexican legal system. See Gómez-Pérez et al. (2005, 2006), Ortiz-Rodríguez et al. (2006), Galindo (2007), Ortiz-Rodríguez and Villazón-Terrazas (2006) and Ortiz-Rodríguez (2007) for further insight and discussions.
17. **ONTOLEGIS** and **ONTOJURIS** ontologies by Drumond et al. (2006a,b, 2007) to be used by the INFONORMA multi-agent recommender system. ONTOLEGIS represents the structure of a "juridical-normative instrument" and ONTOJURIS represents "the knowledge about the juridical domain" (Drumond et al. 2006a). OWL and Protégé have been used as format and tool, respectively.
18. **OntoPrivacy** by Cappelli et al. (2007). A modelization of a glossary of keywords (manually created by an expert) from the Italian Personal Data Protection Code to support the metaSearch (mS) tool and allow retrieval and visualization. It consisted of a domain ontology together with an top level ontology consisting of a universal class `Thing` and five main classes: `Events`, `Scenes`, `Non-Physical Objects`, `Physical Objects` and `Roles`. The ontology was developed following a bottom-up approach. LRI-Core, CLO and Legal-RDF Vocabularies had been taken into account. OntoPrivacy is also used in the Law Making Environment (LME) project (Cappelli et al. 2007; Bartalesi Lenzi et al. 2007; Lenzi et al. 2009).

[103]The REIMDOC Spanish Project aims at developing "tools that allow the legal document to be modelled in electronic support and its semantic retrieval to facilitate the government-citizen document transaction" Gómez-Pérez et al. (2005). Visit: http://reimdoc.atosorigin.es

[104]The EGODO ontology (based on the EGO Ontology Model) was not listed in the original 11 Real-estate Transaction Ontologies. See (Ortiz-Rodríguez 2007) for a detailed account of the Documentation Ontology.

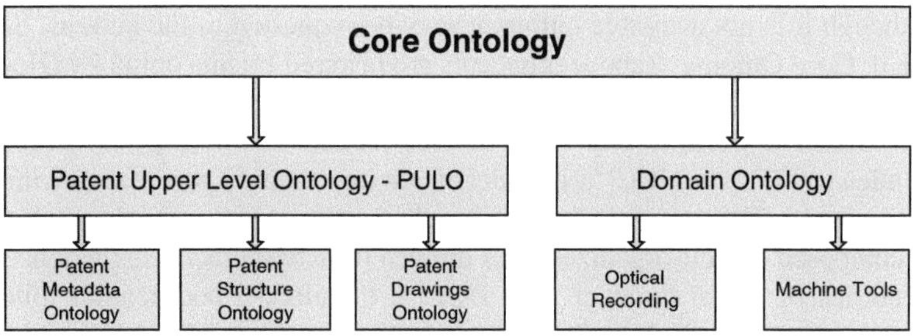

Fig. 4.11 PATExpert Ontologies (Figure from http://mklab.iti.gr/project/patexpert)

19. **PATExpert Ontologies**[105]: Patent Upper Level Ontology (PULO) (which includes the Patent Metadata Ontology, the Patent Structure Ontology and the Patent Drawings Ontology) and the Domain Ontology (which includes the Core Domain Ontology, the Auto Domain Ontology and the Patent Classification Ontology) (Giereth et al. 2007). See the current organization of the modules in Fig. 4.11. Wordnet in English, French and German is also included. The ontologies are expressed in OWL, and SUMO is reused as upper-level ontology.
20. **Ontology of Fundamental Legal Concepts** by Sartor (2006) and Rubino et al. (2006, 2007). Sartor (2006) introduced a set of fundamental legal concepts which not only include deontic modalities, but also obligative rights, permissive rights, *erga-omnes* rights, normative conditionals, liability rights, different kinds of legal powers, potestative rights, resultive declarations, and sources of the law, with the purpose of providing a coherent and integrated account and of offering more appropriate foundations for the notion of power. The Ontology of Fundamental Legal Concepts is based on the work of Sartor (2006) and organizes these concepts in a taxonomy (class hierarchy) initiated by Normative Judgement and Norms. Classes and subclasses in the ontology are related with the 'state', `exercised_through`, `power_holder`, concerned, bearer and towards object properties and the `conditioned_by` datatype property. More abstract concepts, if needed, are assumed to the authors to be imported from top or core ontologies such as DOLCE and LRI-Core. "[T]he proposed ontology may be useful for semantic access to digital legal information and for the representation of legal knowledge" (Rubino et al. 2007). Also, the aim of the ontology is to contribute to the clarification of "the legal theoretical concepts such as deontic modalities, obligative rights, permissive rights, liberty rights, liability rights, different kinds of legal powers, potestative rights (rights to produce legal results) and sources of law" (Rubino et al. 2006). The ontology is represented in OWL-DL, using the editor Protégé (OWL Plugin), developed following the methodological approach of Noy and McGuinness (2001), and,

[105]The PATExpert project: http://www.patexpert.org. Ontologies are available at: http://mklab.iti.gr/project/patexpert, retrieved August 18, 2010.

although it is not available online, it may be requested to the authors. Several LKIF Core Ontology (above) concepts are inspired by this ontology (Hoekstra et al. 2008).[106]

21. **US Uniform Commercial Code (UCC) Article II ontology** by Bagby and Mullen (2007). The UCC "is a model of two important factors that may improve its potential for adaptation through ontologies into AI systems. First, the UCC is composed of well-organized rules derived from best practice experience from centuries of actual conduct. The UCC is therefore a codification following practice significantly bridging the gap between prescribed conduct and actual behavior. As a result, an ontology based on the UCC is already more robust because it includes many details from experience. Second, the UCC has a form of modular composition, again derived from experience, enabling manageable analysis and ontological representation" (Bagby and Mullen 2007). The ontology, to be used to analyse contract requirements, has been formalized in OWL using Protégé as editor and Jess (a Java expert system shell) as reasoner. It has been evaluated through simulation using "real cased enhanced hypotheticals." Developers: College of Information Sciences and Technology, Pennsylvania State University, USA.
22. **Legal Taxonomy Syllabus** by Ajani et al. (2007a, b).[107] The Legal Taxonomy Syllabus takes a comparative law perspective to the modelling of legal terms and concepts from European Union Directives (several legal experts participate in this initiative). Recent contributions on this topic may be found at Ajani et al. (2009, 2010)
23. **Generic Ontology for Digital Content Licensing** (Ontology of Licenses) by Nadah et al. (2007). "Our approach is to model a generic level by means of an ontology describing the concepts and relations that are useful to define and declare licenses. Such an ontology would make it possible to declare generic licenses that reflect content holders intentions. The next step would then be the translation of this generic license – expressed with our ontology – into licences expressed with specific terms of the existing REL operational standards" (Nadah et al. 2007). This work is developed within the Medialex project.[108] The task is to handle "copyright questions and context description and expression by all users and copyright balance maintenance within creative content electronic delivery" (Nadah et al. 2007). Methodology: (1) Identification of concepts used by existing standards (ODRL, XrML and Creative Commons), (2) define a global use case to test the model, and (3) linking

[106]Developers: The Law Department, European University Institute and CIRSFID, University of Bologna, Italy. See Sartor (2006) and Rubino et al. (2006, 2007).

[107]More information on the Legal Taxonomy Syllabus may be found at: http://www.eulawtaxonomy.org, retrieved August 18, 2010.

[108]RIAM Program 2005–2008 (http://www.medialex-digitalrights.org). Developers: Université de Technologie de Compiègne (Centre de Recherche de Royallieu), CERSA-CNRS (University Paris 2) and Direction de la Recherche et de l'Expérimentation (Institut National de l'Audiovisuel). Previous work may be found in de Rosnay (2003).

the ontology to a legal dictionary. In Nadah et al. (2007) the ontology was composed of about a hundred concepts, divided into five classes (Defined situation, Context Information, License's Party, and Action).

24. **Consumer Protection Ontology**, developed within the DALOS project by Agnoloni et al. (2007), Francesconi and Tiscornia (2008) and Agnoloni et al. (2009).[109] This project is aimed at providing legal drafters and decision-makers with control over the legal language at European level, developing legislative drafting tools enhanced with linguistic and ontological resources. This project uses the results of the LOIS project (the database of 35,000 concepts in five European languages), but focuses on the consumer protection domain. It provides a lexical layer (Italian, English, Spanish and Dutch) and an ontological layer, which contains the conceptual representations of the domain at a language-independent level (Agnoloni et al. 2007). These two layers are linked by the `hasLexicalization` and `hasConceptualization` relationships. The DALOS domain ontology imports top-level notions from CLO. T2K is used towards ontology learning and the ontology is formalized in RDF/OWL.
25. **Oral Hearing Ontology**, an ontology regarding the Oral Hearing Civil Procedure in Spain developed to support the automatic classification of audiovisual judicial records and its search and retrieval. Legal experts are involved in the acquisition and conceptualization of knowledge regarding usual practise during oral hearings in civil trials. The ontology is developed in the context of the e-SENTENCIAS project. The aim of this project is to develop a software-hardware system for the global management of the multimedia contents produced by Spanish civil courts. Protégé and OWL are used as tools and representation formalism, respectively. See Gracia et al. (2007), Binefa et al. (2007), and Casanovas et al. (2007b).
26. The **Ontology of Greek Public Administration Procedures** by Savvas and Bassiliades (2008), which represents the types of documents produced, the units of public administration and the flow of the documents in the units. Documents are formalized in OWL and procedures in OWL-S service models. The ontology is to be used by the architecture of the Administrative Procedures Knowledge Portal. The ontology has been tested in a case study.
27. **Legal case repository of ontologies**: Legal Case Ontology, Legal Issues Ontology, Legal Roles Ontology by Shen et al. (2008). The Legal Case Ontology will be used "to generate marked-up case reports that target electronic storage and automated or semi-automated production of paper-based reports. To enable the generation of paper-based reports, the case ontology needs to cover surface information of a case, such as the dates, the title, the roles, the decisions and etc. Furthermore, the case ontology is also required to facilitate intelligent information searching of legal cases through extracting

[109] DALOS (DrAfting Legislation with Ontology-bases Support) e-Participation project (01-01-2007/30-04-2008) website: http://www.dalosproject.eu

deep semantics contained in legal case report" (Shen et al. 2008). Basically, it is aimed at conceptual information retrieval. In order to build the ontology, head-notes of case reports and statutes were used as knowledge resource. Also, "[i]nstead of using one monolithic ontology, breaking an ontology into several relatively loosely-coupled sub-ontologies can bring many benefits such as low maintenance and high reusability" (Shen et al. 2008). WordNet and other generic ontologies have been imported. The process followed to create the ontologies is: (1) conceptual extraction, (2) class and property identification, (3) class taxonomy, (4) OWL implementation (Protégé).[110]

28. **ALIS IP ontology** by Cevenini et al. (2008). The development of this Intellectual Property (IP) ontology takes into account the results from the development of IPROnto, although takes two perspectives for the development of the IP ontology: legal (French IP law) and technical. This IP ontology will be used within the ALIS[111] system (aimed at providing reliable access to the European IP law domain) to "(1) to improve the management of the repository of legal documents, (2) to improve the versatility of the document retrieval system, (3) to create a common layer between legal and game theory concepts, and (4) to create a general 'common' language to enable the modules and the web services of the ALIS architecture to exchange information" (Cevenini et al. 2008). The ontology was built from the selection of relevant copyright terms: `Author`, `Work Of Mind`, (`Collective`, `Of Collaboration`, `Single` and `Composite`), `Moral Rights`, `Economic Rights`, etc. Noy and McGuinness (2001) was followed as methodological approach, both

---

[110]The separate ontologies Legal Issue Ontology (hierarchy of legal issues within each category of legal statutes) and Legal Role Ontology (role duties and rights in legal cases) are not further described in Shen et al. (2008). Developers: Department of Computer Systems, Faculty of Information Technology, University of Technology, Sydney (Australia). The Legal Case Ontology development is inspired by the results of SALOMON (Moens et al. 1997) and JUSTICE (Osborn and Sterling 1999b), which "proposed a data model using DTD (Document Type Definition) in their legal case knowledge base. The concepts such as jurisdiction, judge, parties and facts are extracted from case head-notes or abstract to form a case descriptor. The case knowledge base is composed of marked up XML or SGML instances based on the proposed DTD. However, their data models that are built on the DTD can only achieve limited semantics annotation due to the fact that XML only provides a surface syntax for structured documents, but imposes no semantic constraints on the meaning of these documents" (Shen et al. 2008). A Legal Case Ontology (LegalCase.dtd) was also developed for the JUSTICE system, which consisted of 76 concepts covering possible concepts in legal case headnotes (including facts, law and order) (Osborn and Sterling 1999a, b).

[111]ALIS, Automated Legal Intelligent System, Project (IST-IST-2004-2.4.9), and is a STREP Project funded by the European Commission under the 6th Framework. The Consortium is coordinated by ORT France and the project partners are: Imperial College London, Sineura SPA, Atos Origin SA, CBKE (Research Centre for Legal and Economical Aspects of Electronic Communication), SIVECO Romania SA, Exalead SA, Technical University Darmstadt, Alma Consulting Group, CIRSFID (University of Bologna), and the Gesica Paris Friedland law firm. For more information, visit: http://www.alisproject.com

Protégé (OWL language) and TopBraid Composer were used as ontology editing tools, and LKIF-core ontology (`Manifestation` and `Expression`) was reused. No evaluation results are offered, although a comparative table between IPROnto and IP ontology is presented. Finally, "[a] part from enriching ALIS IP ontology with all the concepts of French IP law, in the future we are planning to develop ALIS ontology involving the corresponding ontologies on patent law and trademark law. Afterwards, these three legal ontologies will be consolidated into unique ontology which will constitute the framework of general IP ontology" (Cevenini et al. 2008).

29. **Minimal Model for Economic Crimes** by Jedrzejek et al. (2009). This ontology is formalized in OWL language with the Protégé editor and organized in several modules (e.g. Person, Document, LegalProvision, Action, etc.) to represent concepts related to the financial crime domain, in particular to fuel laundering. This ontology is used by the FuelFlowViz tool in order to analyse transactions between companies to uncover fuel laundering cases.[112]
30. **Ontología Jurídica Libre [Free Legal Ontology]** is developed at Laboratorio del Procomún (in RDF, at MediaLab Prado with the participation of lawyers – Javier de la Cueva –), within the project Kelsen. This project is directed at developing Open Government principle-based structured databases towards legal information management.[113]
31. **Mediation Core Ontology** by Poblet et al. (2009). This ontology is used in the ONTOMEDIA mediation platform, and represents practical knowledge and concepts from the mediation domain (e.g. `MediationRole`, which includes `Disputant`, `Mediator`, `ServiceProvider`, etc.). The knowledge is acquired with the participation of experts (mediators and lawyers) and the ontology has been formalized in OWL-DL with the Protégé ontology editor.
32. **EuroVoc SKOS** by Polo et al. (2008) of Fundación CTIC.[114] EuroVoc is maintained by the Publications Office of the European Union, and is a multilingual thesaurus that covers the activities of the European Union (e.g. law and legislation). The EuroVoc Thesaurus is used by many institutions and databases (e.g. EURLex, the European Union Law database)[115] and is now semantically enhanced with the SKOS/RDF standard.

[112]This ontology is available at: http://www.man.poznan.pl/~jolac/MinimalModel/MinimalModel.owl, retrieved August 18, 2010.

[113]The latest release of the ontology may be found at http://purl.org/derecho/vocabulario#, retrieved August 18, 2010. More information on the Kelsen Project may be found at http://derecho-internet.org/proyectos/kelsen, retrieved August 18, 2010.

[114]More information may be found at: http://idi.fundacionctic.org/classifications_endpoint/eurovoc, retrieved August 18, 2010. Also, the description of the semantically enhanced EuroVoc may be found in http://eurovoc.europa.eu/drupal/?q=es/ontology, retrieved August 18, 2010.

[115]EurLex: http://eur-lex.europa.eu/en/index.htm

33. **The NEURONA Ontologies** by Casellas et al. (2010) and Meroño-Peñuela et al. (2010). The Neurona Ontologies are application oriented ontologies, and model the necessary knowledge for the development of a data protection compliance application that offers reports regarding the correct application of security measures to files containing personal data. The construction of the ontologies was, thus, focused on the acquisition of conceptual domain knowledge extracted from the legal documents and protocols and from the interaction with the legal experts, the methodology used in the development of OPJK was taken into account. The design of this ontological system is based on a central Data Protection Knowledge Ontology, which contains the core concepts of the system (such as `Data`, `Consent`, `Purpose`, `Security_Measures`, `Security_Degree`, etc), and a Data Protection Reasoning Ontology, which structures the required classification reasoning towards assessing Data Protection compliance. Both ontologies are being modeled with the Protégé ontology editor and using the OWL-DL ontology language.
34. **Ontology of Vehicles**, based on the Brazilian Traffic Code, by Freitas et al. (2010). The Ontology of Vehicles (OWL) is developed, following the METHONTOLOGY process, to open a discussion about the deficiencies and inconsistencies of legal norms and regulations, and to propose legal ontology modelling as a means to improve the quality of legislation. A semantic law checker prototype will be implemented in the future (DOLCE upper ontology and OntoClean method could be used).

4.3 Some Conclusions of the Analysis

As it may be observed, legal ontologies are a popular field of research, its development and quantity increasing over the years. From the lists above, most of the initial ontologies were directed towards theoretical investigations or knowledge acquisition and reuse, and were built mainly at the core level, while latter ontologies are built with particular applications in mind, especially towards semantic indexing, search and retrieval, and represent mainly domain static knowledge. Reuse is not a main feature in the development of legal ontologies, nevertheless, FBO (e-Power ont.), LRI-Core (OCN-NL, Copyright ont., EU employee ont., OntoPrivacy, Ontology of Fundamental Legal Concepts, LKIF-Core, LegLOPD), CLO (JWN, Lois, OntoPrivacy), and LKIF-Core (ALIS IP ont.) have sometimes been reused. The reuse of upper ontologies is not widespread, although some ontologies, such as CLO (DOLCE), IPROnto (SUMO), Copyright Ont (DOLCE, SUMO), EU employee ont. (DOLCE), Patent Ont. (SUMO), Ontology of Fundamental Legal Concepts (DOLCE), e-Gov Ontology (DOLCE+), took some into account.

Nowadays, most ontologies are also being formalized with some of the W3C standard languages: RDF(S) or OWL (in the past ONTOLINGUA, LOOM and

Table 4.5 Languages used for legal ontology formalization

Ontolingua	XML	RDF/S and SKOS	DAML+OIL	OWL/OWL2
FBO and FO-Law	TOF, TOV and Ontology French Law	e-Court O. (RDF(S)/OIL), Multi Tier Contract O. (RDFS/DAML), Consumer Protection Ontology (RDF/OWL), O.J. Libre (RDF), and EuroVoc SKOS	OCL-NL, LRI-Core, IPROnto, AGO IR O.	LRI-Core (OWL-DL), LOIS, IPROnto (OWL-DL), Copyright O. (OWL-DL), BEST-Ont., LKIF-Core (OWL-DL), OPJK, Legal Case Ontology, SIAP Legislative O., OnProc (OWL-DL), Ontolegis and Ontojuris, PATExpert O., Ont. Fundamental Legal Concepts (OWL-DL), US UCC, Legal Case Repository of Ont., Oral Hearing O., Greek Public Adm. O. (OWL/OWL-S), ALIS IP O., e-Gov O. (OCML-OWL), BDSG O. (OWL and F-Logic), LegLOPD, MMEC Ont., MCO, Neurona Ont. and Ont. Vehicles

DAML+OIL were also used). Moreover, Protégé seems to be the most preferred tool for ontology editing, as it is freely available and kept up to date (Table 4.5).[116]

Other relevant issues have to be noted regarding the construction process (Table 4.6). First, most developers do not offer an account of the methodological steps followed or insight into the knowledge acquisition process itself, including both the acquisition of the knowledge and its validation. Those who describe the steps taken have generally adopted a methodology of their own, rather than following an established one. This observation is consistent with the findings of Paslaru and Tempich (2006) in a survey regarding several aspects of the development of ontologies (e.g., methodology and tools used).[117] "The survey pointed out that only a small percentage of ontology-related projects follow a systematic approach to

[116] At least 22 of the above-mentioned ontologies have been developed, at some point, with the use of Protégé: CLIME Ont., LRI-Core, CLO, IPROnto, Copyright Ont., LKIF-Core, OPJK, e-Court Ont., Multi Tier Contract Ont., SIAP Legislative Ont., Ontolegis/Ontojuris, Ontology of Fundamental Legal Concepts, US UCC, Legal Case Ont., Oral Hearings Ont., ALIS IP ont., Legal Case Repository of Ont., legLOPD, Minimal Model of Economic Crimes ont., Mediation Core Ont., and NEURONA ontologies. Other tools referred to are: OilEd (the initial BEST ont.), TopBraid Composer (LKIF-Core, ALIS IP ont., BEST ont.), DODDLE (Legal On. with General ont.), WebODE (Real Estate Transactions Ont., or OntoStudio (BDSG ont.)).

[117] The survey included 34 projects which involved ontology modelling. "(...) the respondents are representative for the community of users and developers of semantic technologies. They were IT practitioners, researchers and experts from various disciplines, affiliated to industry or academia, who were involved in the last 3–4 years in ontology building projects in areas such

Table 4.6 Methodologies used (explicitly) towards ontology modelling

Own method	Dogma	Noy and McGuiness	Terminae	Methontology
CLIME o., JWN, CLO, LKIF-Core (Uschold and Grüninger 1996b), AGO IR o., OnProc, OntoPrivacy, Consumer Protection o., Legal Case Repository, OPJK, Oral Hearing Ont., Legal Tax. Syllabus, Mediation Core Ont., Neurona Ont., and Italian Crime Ont. (e-Gov Ont. and EuroVoc convert pre-existing materials)	TOF/TOV and CCOnt.	BEST-User o., Multi Tier Contract O. (also (Gruber 1993a), Ontology of Fundamental Legal Concepts and ALIS IP o.	Ontology French Law, EU employee o. and LegLOPD	Copyright O., Real Estate Transactions O. and Ont. Vehicles

ontology building, and even less commit to a specific methodology. Most of the projects are executed in an ad-hoc manner".[118]

Second, regarding knowledge acquisition, most initial legal (core) ontologies (e.g., FBO, FOLaw) were built upon insights provided by legal theory. In a very early discussion regarding ontologies in AI and Law, Valente and Breuker (1994c) proposed not only that ontologies could be beneficial for AI and Law in general and that AI and Law could be used as a testbed for legal theories, but also that the best source for ontological commitments for AI and Law ontologies were "in particular the legal theories that identify in their theories a number of 'fundamental concepts' and the like (such as the ones by Kelsen, Hart, Bentham and Hohfeld." In particular, FBO, FOLaw, the Ontology of Law as Dynamic Interconnected System of States of Affairs, and the Knowledge-based Model of Law were largely influenced by normativism, legal positivism, or analytical jurisprudence, especially by the works of Hart (1961) and Kelsen (1991).[119]

Currently, a good number of legal ontologies developed are text-based (term extraction and ontology learning), and legal experts are consulted at times, rather

as skill management, human resources, medical information systems, legal information systems, multimedia, Web services, and digital libraries" (Paslaru and Tempich 2006).

[118]Paslaru and Tempich (2006) discovered from the interviews that 80% of the projects did not follow a particular ontology engineering methodology.

[119]The legal system as *system*, the concept of *norm*, together with the contributions from deontic logic have influenced these approaches. Hart inspired FBO, FOLaw, and the Knowledge-based Model of Law. Kelsen inspired FBO, FOLaw, the Ontology of Law as Dynamic Interconnected System of States of Affairs, and the Knowledge-based Model of Law. Other relevant and cited contributors were the logicist G.H. von Wright (FBO and the Ontology of Law as Dynamic Interconnected System of States of Affairs), and the Scandinavian realist A. Ross (FBO and the Ontology of Law as Dynamic Interconnected System of States of Affairs), within others.

Table 4.7 (Explicit) participation of experts in legal ontology development

Ontology	Expert participation
O. Law as dynamic interconnected system of states of affairs	Legal experts as ontology engineer
Mommer's Knowledge-based Model of Law	Legal expert as ontology engineer
Lame's O. French Law	Legal experts (knowledge acquisition towards ontology updating)
JWN/Lois/CLO	Legal experts (validation of terms)
CCOntology	Legal experts (conceptualization, evaluation)
BEST initial ontology	Law students (knowledge acquisition)
LKIF-Core ontology	Legal experts (list of terms)
OPJK ontology	Legal experts (acquisition, conceptualization-formalization, evaluation)
Italian Crime Ontology	Legal experts (knowledge acquisition and conceptualization)
Multi Tier Contract Ontology	Legal experts (knowledge acquisition)
OnProc	Legal experts (testing)
Legal Taxonomy Syllabus	Legal experts (knowledge acquisition comparative law perspective)
Reimdoc Project Ontologies (Real Estate Transactions Ontology)	Legal Philosophers (knowledge acquisition and conceptualization)
OntoPrivacy	Legal experts (knowledge acquisition)
Ontología Jurídica Libre	Legal experts, acquisition/conceptualization/formalization (lawyers)
Ontology of Fundamental Legal Concepts	Legal expert as ontology engineer
Oral Hearing Ontology	Legal experts (knowledge acquisition and conceptualization)
Mediaton Core Ontology	Legal experts (lawyers and mediators), knowledge acquisition
Neurona ontologies	Legal experts (acquisition, conceptualization, evaluation)

vaguely, towards knowledge acquisition or evaluation. Thus, legal expertise (academic or professional) plays at most a secondary role in the lifecycle development process of most legal ontologies, and, only in some cases, legal experts have been explicitly involved in the knowledge acquisition or evaluation processes. Table 4.7 below includes the list of 19 legal ontologies which explicitly state the participation of experts in legal ontology development, within the 50 legal ontologies listed above.[120]

[120]Whilst, within the consulted publications, it was not explicitly stated that legal experts had participated in the development of Jur-IWN, CLO and Consumer Protection Ontology, legal experts did participate in the development of the LOIS database, and, in general, several legal experts were employed by the ITTIG research centre.

Moreover, this even seems to suggest that top down approaches to ontology building would require an expert-based or legal theory-based approach while bottom-up developments would not.[121] Lately, the citizen's view of law has been considered as relevant as legal expert's for legal core ontology modelling.[122]

This lack of explicit involvement of legal expertise[123] in the development of legal ontologies could jeopardize their central characteristics: its sharedness. Not only procedural but also conceptual knowledge may be extracted from legal experts (Schreiber et al. 1999; Milton 2007). Therefore, in general, the use of well-established knowledge acquisition techniques and the participation of legal experts in corpus preparation should be a desirable feature of the process of developing a legal ontology. It is true that different requirements may be set for core ontologies aimed mainly at knowledge reuse and acquisition, and for domain ontologies aimed at representing knowledge towards a specific application (and thus, aimed at producing particular results). It is also true that not all ontologies may require knowledge acquisition from legal experts and other techniques, such as ontology learning from texts, may be preferable. Nevertheless, advice on relevant documentation by legal experts ought then to be considered.

Finally, and related to the comments above, the relevant documentation offered by most legal ontologies hardly provides evaluation insights or results. When present, evaluation consists on consistency checking or its system implementation (no metrics provided). This is in the same line as the findings of Paslaru and Tempich (2006). In their survey, "in 40% of the cases the results of the process were not nominally evaluated. In the remaining ones, 95% have been manually evaluated by their authors without the help of a methodical approach. Three ontologies have

---

[121]"Another top-down way to elaborate an ontology can be to get together some experts of the domain and ask them to agree on a unique point of view on their specialities, this unique point of view being the basis of an ontology. The main difficulty is then the time; it is long for experts to agree. The second way to build an ontology is a bottom-up method. This method consists on extracting from appropriate documents all the elements needed to compose an ontology" (Lame 2001).

[122]For the developers of LKIF-Core, the view of the citizens is taken into account because this group has to "understand legal sources and legal procedures to plan their activities" (Breuker et al. 2007). "Although these populations have different uses and views on legal concepts, we assumed that the different perspectives involved are not conflicting: the legal system –the 'professionals' – and society – the citizens are in permanent interaction. The results of this interaction are not limited to the participants in courtrooms but are a major subject in news reporting. The views of legal scholars are very important because they develop abstract terms that may articulate a legal core ontology" (Breuker et al. 2007). In this case, the knowledge acquisition process was based on asking each partner (either 'expert citizen' or 'legal expert') to supply their 'top-20' *legal* concepts, together with a combination of terms collected from jurisprudence and legal text-books (without specifying the jurisdiction or legal domain).

[123]Either towards knowledge elicitation or as documentation supervision, advice, validation or evaluation.

been evaluated through external expert judgement." We believe, that legal ontology development would benefit from the use of evaluation methodologies, and especially from the participation of legal experts in validation.

As mentioned also in Chap. 3, these criticisms share many similarities with the criticisms most developers of legal knowledge based systems received during the 1980s and the beginning of the 1990s. Authors such as Greenleaf et al. (1987) criticised the lack of legal knowledge or legal domain understanding of most of LKBS developing teams, at the time.[124] His criticisms were rooted in the widespread use of legal sources (statutes, case law, etc.) directly as the knowledge for the knowledge base, instead of including in the knowledge base the 'expert' knowledge of lawyers or legal professionals.[125] This author encouraged developers towards fostering the direct construction of knowledge bases by legal experts (Table 4.8).

> "The traditional method of acquiring knowledge for an expert system makes use of the so-called 'knowledge engineer', a person who is wholly familiar with the representations of knowledge which are internal to the expert system and who is skilled at extracting knowledge from the domain expert and translating it into the internal representation. There are several problems with this process. First, it is very easy for the knowledge engineer to believe that he or she knows a great deal about the domain (...) The second problem with the 'domain expert-knowledge engineer-expert system' paradigm is simply one of time and money. (...) We will argue below that it is possible to devise representation schemes which will allow lawyers to be their own knowledge engineer" (Greenleaf et al. 1987).

Moles (1992) also criticized several literature, especially took into account the work of Sergot et al. (1986)[126] and Kowalski and Sergot (1990), regarding the development of legal expert systems (LKBS) for the fact that they had not included legal experts in the development team, and that in order to avoid complex modelling,

---

[124] "Perhaps it should not be necessary to include a section which describes some of the fundamental problems of building expert systems in law, yet it is clear that there are a number of systems which have been built or are being built by people whose primary interest and training is in computer science and who fundamentally misunderstand the nature of law and legal reasoning. It is particularly strange that law should suffer in this way, since the standard texts on building expert systems emphasize the importance of capturing the knowledge of an expert in the domain area. Yet, people who would not dream of beginning construction of a medical expert system without the firm support of a medical physician will happily go to work on a legal system. The reason, of course, lies in the widespread misconception that law is a simple system of rules and that legal inference consists of a simple deductive application of these rules. Since most expert systems are rule based, the translation job seems easy" (Greenleaf et al. 1987).

[125] "[A] system which fails to include this knowledge is unlikely to be very 'expert'" (Greenleaf et al. 1987).

[126] "Sergot and others made much of the point that most of the BNA was translated by a student, without any expert legal assistance. Their constant references to the use of non-legal expertise is seen by them to be unproblematic, and to be a virtue rather than a vice. They assume that an expert will only contribute to the 'accuracy' of the knowledge base and fail to appreciate that an expert may have a great many useful things to say about how one goes about the process of interpretation including the way in which the knowledge is structured" (Moles 1992).

Table 4.8 (Explicit) evaluations performed in existing legal ontologies

Ontology	Evaluation
CLIME Ontology	MILE implementation (experts)
LRI-Core	Consistency
JWN/Lois	Consistency, expert validation of terms
CLO	Consistency, norm comparison (EC directives)
Ontology of French Law	Implementation (user comments)
IPROnto	Consistency
Copyright Ontology	Consistency
CCOntology	Expert approval
BEST initial ontology	Requirements, competency questions
LKIF-Core ontology	Consistency, requirements
OPJK ontology	consistency, CQ, validation, evaluation (SUS)
Multi Tier Contract Ontology	UML-RDFS/DAML conversion
US UCC	Simulation
Ontology Greek Public Administration Proceedings	Case study application
SIAP Legislative Ont.	SIAP system implementation
BDSG ontology	Demonstration (example)
Minimal Model Economic Crimes ont.	FuelOwlViz implementation
NEURONA ontologies	competency questions, NEURONA tool implementation

they made naive assumptions such as: law is based on rules, rules may be applied deductively, there is no need for legal expertise, etc.

> The problem can, of course, be avoided by: (1) pretending that knowledge can be detached from its social context; (2) assuming that signs (or 'rules') carry this expert substance; (3) and that the human process of interpreting signs is not essential to the knowledge represented. The price to be paid is in the avoidance of responsibility, and hiding behind a false and misleading technicalism (Moles 1992).

These criticisms fostered the initial widespread use of legal theory towards LKBS development during the late 1990s, later also towards ontology development, although the participation of legal experts (e.g., professionals) in the development of LKBS remained low.[127] In particular, Valente and Breuker (1994b) were clear about their preference for legal theory rather than legal expertise: "Of course one can create a conceptualization of legal phenomena 'from scratch' or based on personal experience of lawyers, but the perspectives and conceptualizations used in Legal Theory have the advantage of having been discussed and debugged in the course of years, for a research community whose work is centered on these problems."

[127] See, regarding the interest for legal theory: Valente and Breuker (1994a, c), Bench-Capon (1994), Brouwer (1994), Gordon (1994), Greinke (1994), den Haan and Winkels (1994) and Wahlgren (1994). Most of these contributions conform the proceedings of the JURIX'94 conference dedicated to 'The relation with legal theory'.

Moreover, according to Casanovas et al. (2004), as general theories of Law are directed to offer a single coherent body of general legal concepts which represent legal knowledge, in legal ontology building Law has been mostly conceived as (a) a set of related static and dynamic norms, (b) as a set of interrelated rights and duties, (c) as a set of institutional rules and facts, or (d) as a set of states of affairs, events and rules. As a consequence of this analysis, these authors suggested that the design of legal ontologies might not only require the representation of normative knowledge or coherent normative systems but also the representation of legal practical knowledge. Therefore Casanovas and colleagues (Casanovas et al. 2004; Benjamins et al. 2004; Casanovas et al. 2006) advocated the elicitation and encoding of professional legal knowledge (PLK) and the construction of ontologies of professional legal knowledge.

The modelling process of the Ontology of Professional Judicial Knowledge (OPJK) presented in the following chapter will take into account these discussions and follow an approach inspired by a sociological perspective to the study of Law (empirical-data based acquisition and elicitation of professional judicial knowledge). The Ontology of Professional Judicial Knowledge developed for the IURISERVICE application is aimed at representing conceptual judicial knowledge towards semantic indexing and search. Therefore, the knowledge acquisition process and the development process will be based on the acquisition of professional judicial conceptual knowledge through semi-structured interviews and its validation and evaluation by legal experts. This empirical perspective taken regarding knowledge acquisition may offer the possibility of analysing modelling difficulties raised by the interaction with other theoretical perspectives based on general theories of Law, and by the general difficulties offered by an initial term-based approach.

Chapter 5
Modelling Judicial Professional Knowledge: A Case Study

5.1 The Ontology of Professional Judicial Knowledge

In this chapter, the development process of the Ontology of Professional Judicial Knowledge (OPJK) for the IURISERVICE system will be fully described. The purpose of the Ontology of Professional Judicial Knowledge is to semantically enhance the search and retrieval capabilities of IURISERVICE, a web-based application that supports legal decision making during the on-call period of Spanish newly recruited judges. This chapter will, therefore, outline the difficulties encountered during this process, mainly regarding the preparation of textual material, the reuse of upper concepts (middle-out strategy), and practical discussions about expert conceptual knowledge modelling (theoretical and practical – expert and professional – knowledge interaction) will be also discussed.

This notion of professional legal ontology, as described by Casanovas et al. (2004), is based on the idea that "professional knowledge is developed as a product of professional action, and it establishes itself through work and performance in the profession, not merely through accumulation of theoretical knowledge, but thorough the integration, tuning and restructuring of theoretical knowledge to the demands of practical situations and constraints" (Bromme and Tillema 1995). Professional and expert knowledge (experts and professionals) are necessarily and closely related:

> Current expert research, however, often overlooks the fact that expert activity is mostly professional activity, and that the information processed in its course belongs mainly to the culture of the respective profession. The application of expertise is thus also linked to enculteration within a profession (Bromme and Tillema 1995).

The development process of the OPJK ontology follows the methodological steps established in Chap. 3: Specification of requirements, knowledge acquisition, conceptualization, formalization, evaluation, and refinement. In particular this chapter describes the acquisition and organization of the corpus acquired from ethnographic data for term extraction, the use of different tools available for the construction of the ontology, the methodology finally used, the problems encountered during the

N. Casellas, *Legal Ontology Engineering: Methodologies, Modelling Trends, and the Ontology of Professional Judicial Knowledge*, Law, Governance and Technology Series 3, DOI 10.1007/978-94-007-1497-7_5, © Springer Science+Business Media B.V. 2011

extraction of conceptual knowledge and the formalization of this knowledge for its automatic management. The purpose of this detailed description is to explore the limitations and possibilities of a socio-legal perspective with regards to the study of law and legal professions for legal ontology construction, based on the acquisition of ethnographic data, textual analysis for ontology learning, and the participation of legal experts or professionals in legal ontology construction.

5.2 Requirements and Knowledge Acquisition

This section will present the specification of the requirements of the Ontology of Professional Judicial Knowledge, and the description of the knowledge acquisition process for the OPJK ontology in order to extract the knowledge that will be conceptualized and formalized in the following section.

5.2.1 Initial Research and Ethnography

The need for the IURISERVICE system and its initial design was established as a result of a thorough ethnographic survey carried out with the collaboration of the Spanish General Council of the Judiciary (CGPJ). The Spanish Young Judges [*Jueces Jóvenes en España*] survey[1] was conducted during 2002, involved five Spanish Universities,[2] and its main objective was to gather information towards the implementation of a support network for judges.

In-depth interviews were made by judges still in training to a set of 129 judges with less than 4 years of experience, out of the total set of 352 young judges who had completed their studies at the Spanish School of the Judiciary between 1997–1999 and occupied at the time their first appointment. The questionnaire was designed by senior judges of the Spanish School of the Judiciary, experts of the Documentation Office and team members of the research group. To perform a comparative analysis a set of 139 senior judges was selected.

The questionnaire contained both open-ended and closed questions tackling several areas. Table 5.1 below includes some of the questions included in the questionnaire, adapted from Ayuso et al. (2003) and Álvarez et al. (2005).

Some of the results provided some insight towards which problems could a system for judges in their first appointment offer support. The analysis of the open-ended question "Explain the two most important doubts that you had during the

[1]Detailed information regarding this survey can be found at Ayuso et al. (2003) and Álvarez et al. (2005). Also Casanovas et al. (2004) includes some references to the data.

[2]Universitat Autónoma de Barcelona (UAB), Universitat de Barcelona (UB), Universitat Politècnica de Catalunya (UPC), Universidad de León, and Universidad de Burgos.

Table 5.1 Questionnaire

Domains	Number of questions	Examples
Training evaluation	18 closed questions, 3 open-ended questions	What is your opinion about the education received at the Law School? What is your opinion regarding the current system of access to the profession? What changes do you suggest in the training at the Spanish School of the Judiciary? Have you used the on-line continuous training system of the CGPJ?
Professional activity	13 closed questions, 16 open-ended questions	What was the most complex professional problem that you had during the first 3 months of appointment? Do you comment your cases if complex with other peers? Do you use Internet?
CENDOJ services	5 closed questions	Do you use the personal attention service of CENDOJ? Do you use legal databases?
Relationships	26 closed questions, 4 open-ended questions	Do you think that people are right when they say that "Justice is very slow"? Do you keep professional relationships with judges from your own class?
Comments on the profession	7 closed questions, 3 open-ended questions	What do you think it is a "good judge"? Why did you become a judge? Do you take your work home?

first three months as a judge," reported that their questions referred to mostly to the on-call period [*guardia*] (Benjamins et al. 2005c).[3] During that period, usually a week, the judge must be available 24 h a day for any case that reaches the judicial office. This on-call period doubts referred mostly to practical situations regarding, for example, who is to keep the belongings of a detainee or a corpse? Or what is to be done when the prosecutor or the coroner does not attend an appointment? This on-call problems did not appear in the responses of the interviewed senior judges, suggesting that this type knowledge was probably acquired with the day-to-day practice of the profession. Accordingly, the theoretical training that applicants endure to access judicial appointments[4] does not contain this more 'practical'

[3]The lexical analysis offered "guardia" as the lexical form most characteristic for that open-ended question (Ayuso et al. 2003) in the group of young judges during their first appointment.

[4]Currently, access to the judicial profession in Spain is exam-based. As an example, the 2008 first exam included 100 test questions from a set temario consisting of Constitutional Law (31 temas), Civil Law (98 temas), Criminal Law (62 temas), Civil Procedure Law (62 temas), Criminal Procedure Law (37 temas), Commercial Law (33 temas) and Administrative and Labour Law (37 temas). This information may be consulted at http://www.poderjudicial.es

knowledge, neither does the training at the Spanish School of the Judiciary.[5] This is also consistent with the findings of the survey regarding the changes proposed to the training received in the Spanish Judicial School at Barcelona: judges in their first appointment suggested educational changes towards offering a more practical teaching approach rather than the current focus on theoretical study (Ayuso et al. 2003).

This, together with the fact that most judges in their first appointment declared to comment with peers (especially more experienced peers) their cases frequently (11.8%) or sometimes (72.7%), was thought to provide a ground for such a support system.[6] Problems regarding on-call situations at late hours were difficult to consult or comment with others and access to a Frequently-Asked Questions (FAQ) repository containing this type of material could be of use, especially during the first months of appointment.

Therefore, some results obtained in the Spanish Young Judges Survey in 2002 offered some grounds for the development of an FAQ system for judges in their first appointment, which could offer support towards problems raised during the on-call period. Nevertheless, the questionnaire supplied no further information regarding other requirements of such system or the knowledge that ought to contain regarding the problems faced during the on-call period. A second survey was designed in order to obtain such information.

In this section, the findings of the survey towards obtaining the set of requirements for the decision-support tool, the ontology requirements specification and the process of knowledge acquisition are outlined, together with an account of an initial modelization, which offered initial insights and inspired several improvements.

5.2.2 *Specification of Requirements*

From the experience of the Spanish Young Judges survey, a further questionnaire and ethnographic campaign were designed, and performed during 2004. 124 newly

[5]Once the written and oral examinations have been passed, the judges start the period of training at the Spanish Judicial School: 9 months of theoretical training at the School and 5–6 months of practical training under the supervision of a juez tutor. The main teaching at the Spanish Judicial School, according to their program, is directed to the discussion of cases relevant for Juzgados de Primera Instancia e Instrucción (first appointment courts) regarding: Constitutional Law, European Union Law, Civil Law, Criminal Law and Procedural Law. Some insight on Accounting, Forensic Medicine and Organic Law – the legal framework of the judicial profession –. More practical subjects, such as Judgment drafting, Relation with the press, Gender discrimination, Informatics, Legal English and French, Learning an official language of Spain (Catalan, Galician or Basque), Justice and Society, Mediation and The Judge on its first appointment are paid a secondary attention and are, sometimes, voluntary. Second year training takes place not only in judicial courts but also in other relevant administrations: Registro Civil, Registro Mercantil, Registro de la Propiedad, Inspección de Trabajo, etc. For more information see Consejo del Poder Judicial (2007).

[6]The judges in their first appointment which declared not to comment their cases were the 9.4% of the total. 6.1% of the set interviewed gave no answer to that question (Ayuso et al. 2003).

appointed judges around Spain conformed the sample (from a total of 248 judges of the 52th Class), and the semi-structured interviews were entirely carried out by the research team of the Institute of Law and Technology at the Universitat Autònoma de Barcelona (UAB). The new questionnaire was also organized in five sections, concerning professional training, professional activity, professional relationships, quality of life, and personal data. This time, the questionnaire contained some of the 2002 questions, together with questions more directed towards gathering information on the requirements that a would-be system ought to have. Information regarding complex cases in civil or criminal law was included again, together with the inquiry regarding their comments with peers about the cases, and the use of Internet. However, new questions such as, "Could you explain specific doubts or problems that came up during the on-call period?," "What kind of professional information do you usually look for in the Web?," and "What would you expect from a web service/software that would provide professional assistance to judges?" were added.

According to the findings presented in Vallbé (2009) (initially analysed in Casanovas et al. (2004)), the use of Internet was widespread among the interviewed judges, and the information search was mostly job-related, being the official websites (official legislative publications, the judicial power website, etc.) the sites most visited. Computer skills were generally at user level, and mainly regarding the use of text processors, databases and e-mail. The majority of interviewees also desired a system that could solve "doubts," although "corporate information," "judges' forum," and "doctrine" were also considered issues that a system could also offer.[7] Finally, in this survey, also a list of practical problems (in the form of questions) was gathered from the judges interviewed.

5.2.2.1 IURISERVICE Requirements

From the findings of the first and the second surveys, the technological partner iSOCO and the research team assumed that:

- Judges in their first appointment had to solve several practical problems during their first months of work, mostly occurring during the on-duty period, either on their own or with the counsel of more experienced judges, if available.
- This knowledge was acquired mainly by practice.
- A repository of possible solutions based on experience towards practical problems could offer valuable support for the newly appointed judges.
- Also, a system which stored and managed this professional knowledge could be useful to the judicial profession itself in order to distribute, maintain, and avoid inconsistencies of this practical knowledge shared by the professionals.

[7] The most up-to-date analysis of the data is contained in Vallbé (2009), although more information regarding the data and the results may be found in Casanovas et al. (2004, 2005b).

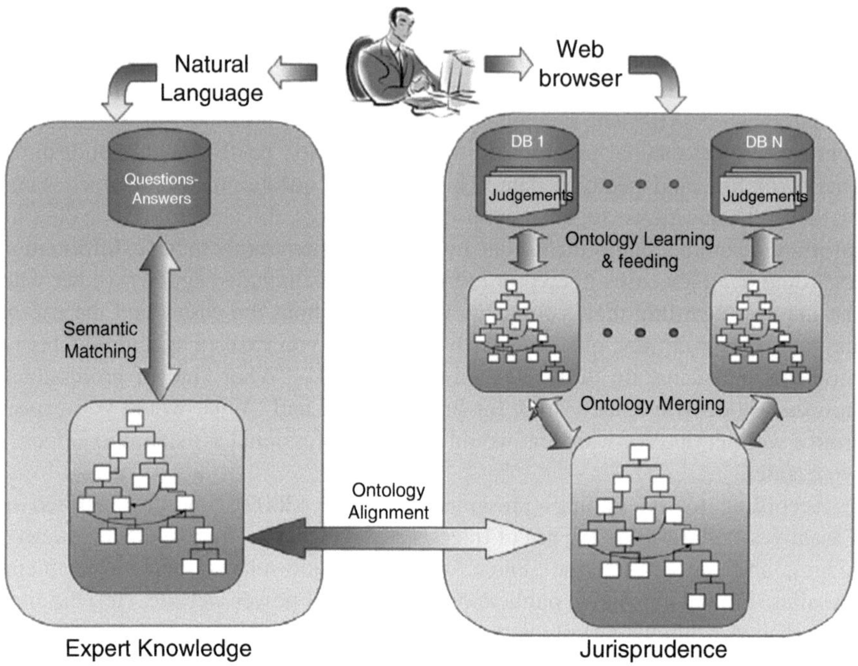

Fig. 5.1 IURISERVICE architecture in the SEKT project

- As use of the Internet/Intranet was widespread among judges, a web-based FAQ system with a simple natural language interface could be both easily accessible by judges and easily maintained by the Judicial School (rather than an installable software).
- If a system was to provide efficient support in a reliable manner, the construction of the repository of knowledge and its accuracy and validity (answers to questions regarding practical problems of the judicial profession) were critical.
- If the system was to be of use during the on-call period where situations require quick answers, time and accuracy were also critical issues.
- The decision as to whether the question of the user is similar to an FAQ stored question should be based on semantics rather than on simple keyword matching (Fig. 5.1).

Therefore, the IURISERVICE application was designed to provide on-line access to an FAQ (Frequently Asked Questions) system that permits the user to search for the practical questions in a repository of stored questions. The lists of questions gathered from the interviews provided the input list of questions for the system and, together with the answers that senior judges of the Spanish School of the Judiciary have provided, they conform the repository of the system. The aim of the system was to discover the best semantic match between the user's question or input question (formulated in natural language) and a stored question, so as to offer an answer that satisfies the user. Time and accuracy are critical issues and, to that end, the main research has been based on the possibility of modelling the legal knowledge contained in the repository of questions through the use of ontologies. In order to find the question-answer pair that best matches the input question, the system would be enhanced with an ontology and semantic distance calculation.

The participation in the SEKT European project as a case study offered more insight into particular user needs and other methodological and technological support. The SEKT (Semantically Enabled Knowledge Technologies) integrated project, co-funded by the EU 6th Framework programme, had a duration of 36 months and involved a large consortium of academic institutions and business companies.[8] The Legal case study (IDT-UAB and iSOCO) was focused on the improvement of IURISERVICE and its initial OPJK ontology with the technologies and insights from the different partners involved in the project.

The ontological expertise of the partners of the project provided (a) methodological support for distributed ontology construction with the DILIGENT methodology (DIstributed, Loosely-controlled and evolvInG Engineering of ONTologies, by AIFB), (b) upper level support with the development of the PROTON (PROTo Ontology, developed by Ontotext Lab as a light-weight upper-level ontology), (c) ontology mapping support (University of Innsbruck), (d) ontology inconsistency detection (UvA), and (e) offered the opportunity to use several semi-automatic ontology learning tools (TextToOnto and Text2Onto – Ontoprise GmbH and AIFB –, and OntoGen – JSI –). Moreover, the technological expertise of the SEKT partners influenced the technological development of the IURISERVICE system with the incorporation of domain detection technology (TextGarden, by JSI), the use of the KAON2 infrastructure for ontology management (AIFB), the support from GATE technology[9] for natural language processing (NLP group – University of Sheffield –), together with the integration of the system into SIP, the SEKT Integration Platform (Empolis GmbH). Also, the IURISERVICE FAQ system was experimentally extended with a Jurisprudence Knowledge System which used further SEKT technology, such as the search and browse technology (BT) and

[8]SEKT project (IST-IP 2003-506826), Dr. John Davies from British Telecom was the Project Coordinator, Dr. Rudi Studer from the University of Karlsruhe was the Technical Coordinator, and Paul Warren, also from British Telecom, was the Project Manager. Partners: British Telecommunications Plc. (UK), Empolis GmbH (Germany), Jozef Stefan Institute (Ljubljana, Slovenia), University of Karlsruhe (Institute AIFB, Germany), University of Sheffield (NLP Group, UK), University of Innsbruck (Austria), Intelligent Software Components S. A. (iSOCO, Spain), Kea-pro GmbH (Switzerland), Ontoprise GmbH (Intelligente Lösungen für das Wissensmanagement, Germany), Sirma AI Ltd (Bulgaria), Vrije Universiteit Amsterdam (Netherlands), and Autonomous University of Barcelona (IDT, Spain). For more information visit http://www.sekt-project.com. The SEKT vision was to develop and exploit the knowledge technologies underlying Next Generation Knowledge Management, integrating fundamental research, development of components and input from real world case studies in the public and private sectors: Siemens case study (Improving Individual Productivity), British Telecom case study (Reducing Overheads of Knowledge Creation and Maintenance), and the Legal case study (Decision Support for Legal Professionals).

[9]Visit, GATE (General Architecture for Text Engineering) at http://gate.ac.uk

name entity extraction and knowledge generation technology (NLP group), for the retrieval of relevant case law.

Finally, more insight regarding user needs was gathered with the support of the Kea-pro partner and the realization of a questionnaire and a choice-based analysis carried out by legal experts familiar with the judicial setting. The results of the questionnaire (14 participants) showed positive feedback concerning the use of an FAQ application. The choice-based analysis (12 participants: 6 legal experts and 6 senior judges of the Spanish Judicial School) aimed at elicit the importance of several features offered by the FAQ system to the users: recall, precision, time and the possibility of browsing related rulings. The greatest majority of respondents attached more weight to precision (i.e., the ratio of relevant number of retrieved documents to the total number of documents retrieved) than to recall (i.e., the ratio of relevant documents retrieved to the total number of relevant documents in the database). Nevertheless, some also demanded high recall rates. Finally, a Google-like response time was desired, while delays of more than 5 min were considered unacceptable.[10] For further information consult Bösser and Melchior (2006) and Bösser et al. (2009).

The IURISERVICE prototype included several search and score algorithms designed to locate the best match (question-answer pair) for the input question, organized around an architecture based on an adaptive multistage search chain, which is based on a variation of the "chain of responsibility" pattern:

1. the search process is subdivided into several cooperative stages;
2. at each stage, the system applies an algorithm that reduces the incoming target FAQs at that stage;
3. each stage is premised with the believe that the FAQ question that matches the input question belongs to the outcome set of FAQ's at that stage;
4. the multistage search algorithm allows the system to stop when the FAQ target has been reduced considerably (beyond a parameterized threshold).

Therefore, all stages need not be necessarily exhausted and the system may also show the best score results before completing all available search steps. At the same time, the key technologies used in the architecture, which enable these design considerations to be met, are: Natural Language Processing (morphological analysis), Thesaurus Processing (exact and synonym matching), Ontology Processing (domain locator and additional understanding), Cache Proxy (control computational repetitions and memory recovery).[11]

The overall design of the system is based on the need for effectiveness: the system ought to be able to locate the best possible matching FAQ question to the user's input question that tackles the problem. The use of semantic technologies, through the use of ontologies, in the system is aimed at providing more accurate searches than the

[10]Delays up to 5 min were considered acceptable if the delay increased precision and recall.

[11]For more detailed information regarding the architecture of the system see Blázquez et al. (2005) and Casanovas et al. (2005a, 2006).

Table 5.2 Effectiveness measurements (Casellas et al. 2007)

	Keywords	Keywords and semantic distance
Success	28.57%	45.71%
Failure	71.43%	54.29%

Table 5.3 Efficiency measurements (Casellas et al. 2007)

	Average response time (ms)	Average keyword time (ms)	Average semantic distance (ms)
Without caching	6652	3747	2095
With caching	2925	2,852	73

basic keyword search. The results from an preliminary performance evaluation on an initial development of the OPJK ontology (see more information regarding this development in Sect. 5.2.3.2) showed that semantic distance and ontology usage could improve both effectiveness (precision of user's query response) and (average time to respond to a query) efficiency measurements. Tables 5.2 and 5.3 below describe the results obtained in those measurements (Casellas et al. 2007).

5.2.2.2 Ontology Requirements

The ontology to be developed was to provide better search capabilities than the mere keyword search and to be designed towards semantic indexing and search in the IURISERVICE web-based application. This ontology, the Ontology of Professional Judicial Knowledge, ought to represent the relevant concepts related to the problems that take place during the on-call period. The ontology contains domain specific knowledge, the professional knowledge gathered by experience from the practice during on-call periods. This knowledge has been acquired during the semi-structured interviews taken during the 2002 and 2004 surveys (mainly 2004).

As explained, some questions included in the interviews were aimed at eliciting the problems that judges faced in their first appointment ("Could you explain specific doubts or problems that came up during the on-call period?"). The judges in their first appointments described in the form of questions or problem explanations, several problems they faced during the on-call period that required counselling of peers or could not be easily solved at that time. From these, a corpus of nearly 800 practical questions is the main knowledge source towards term extraction and ontology learning.

5.2.2.3 Methodological Requirements

The OPJK ontology is interested in modelling static knowledge about the conceptual structure of the domain concepts, rather than in the dynamic knowledge involved in the questions themselves. The system is to offer searching support towards the best possible stored answer in the repository, and would not require to fully exploit OWL's inferencing capabilities. The answers to the doubts and problems expressed in the questions contained in the respository have been already provided by the Spanish School of the Judiciary, which is to keep and maintain the repository of knowledge. Moreover, it is important for the usability of the system to try to represent the conceptual structure contained in the questions as they are perceived by the judges. This conforms the part of the world that the OPJK ontology wants to represent and, in this sense, we agree with the comments from Bylander and Chandrasekaran (1987) and van Heijst (1995), acknowledging that the intended purpose of the ontology influences the acquisition of the knowledge, its conceptualization and encoding.

For this, the construction of the ontology is focused on the acquisition of conceptual domain knowledge extracted from the corpus of questions containing practical problems obtained from the surveys. As mentioned in Chap. 3, knowledge acquisition is as an important stage as is conceptualization or evaluation; the knowledge conceptualized requires to be well-grounded and documentation of the sources used should be provided. Ontology methodologies ought to include specific guidelines to support knowledge acquisition, as the lack of guidelines or even reference towards knowledge acquisition techniques undermines its importance within the ontology development process and may cause several problems: lack of knowledge acquisition effort, lack of sharedness of the knowledge encoded, and lack of reuse of the resulting ontology.

The selection of knowledge sources and the use of adequate knowledge acquisition techniques may offer reuse and sharedness and may support the development of ontologies, especially the conceptualization and evaluation steps. Certainly, not all ontologies will require the participation of experts, although in all cases the choice of information sources for knowledge extraction is key, together with the supply of that information. The Ontology of Professional Judicial Knowledge is built upon the practical questions that had been faced by judges in their first appointments due to certain lack of practical expertise. This repository of questions constitutes a source of knowledge (completed with their answers) that will be accessible in IURISERVICE and the OPJK ontology is to provide semantic enhancement for their search.

For these reasons, we would like to take into account the recommendations from Schreiber et al. (1999), Sure (2003) and Milton (2007) towards knowledge acquisition and complete them with the detailed guidelines from Noy and McGuinness (2001), Gómez-Pérez et al. (2003), de Nicola et al. (2005) and Suárez-Figueroa et al. (2007) towards the specification of a methodology for the construction of the Ontology of Professional Judicial Knowledge. The proposed methodology would have several steps, in a cyclic modelling approach (validation/evaluation). These steps have been established from the analysis of the most detailed and complete methodologies (see table) relevant for the case at hand: (1) preparatory phase (specification of ontology requirements), (2) development phase (knowledge acquisition – experts, documents, reuse –, conceptualization – classes, relations, properties, instances –, expert validation and formalization), and (3) evaluation phase (internal consistency, requirements, competency questions and expert evaluation).

Finally, legal experts (academics and professionals) will participate in the extraction of knowledge, conceptualization and validation of the knowledge extracted, the modelling decisions taken, and the final OPJK ontology.

Sources of Knowledge

During the initial grouping and the conceptualization phase other knowledge sources, apart from the corpus of questions, may be of use to support modelling decisions. First, a list of competency questions can be used to guide the extraction of relevant concepts.

Establishing a list of competency questions is complex, as the concepts of the ontology ought only to represent the contents of the IURISERVICE database of questions, and they have yet to be analysed. Nevertheless, due to the nature of the setting (judicial office), the experience of the development of the first OPJK ontology prototype during the SEKT project, and the requirements of the IURISERVICE tool, some questions can be initially set to guide the extraction and conceptualization of knowledge:

- Which are the problematic situations?
- Which people are involved? What procedural roles are involved? What professionals are involved?
- What type of organizations are involved?
- Which documents and other information sources are involved?
- Which judicial procedures are mentioned?
- Which relevant relations exist between these situations, people, organizations, procedures and documents?

Second, although the list of questions is the main source of knowledge towards knowledge acquisition, other sources may be used to support the modelling phase. Most of these sources are related to the theoretical and practical knowledge acquired by judges during their career development and training both at the Faculty and at the Spanish School of the Judiciary, and regarding the organizational context of the judicial setting.

- The full contents of the questionnaires from both survey and the transcriptions of the complete interviews.
- The vast information contained regarding the Spanish Judiciary in the website of the General Council of the Judiciary: organization of the judiciary in Spain, access materials, relevant legislation regarding the organization of the judiciary, etc. (http://www.poderjudicial.es).
- Specialised handbooks on the judicial setting and organization: VillaGómez et al. (2003), Toharia and García (2005) and Arnaiz et al. (2005).

- Specialised textbooks on Civil, Criminal and Procedural Law Ramos-Méndez (1997a, b, 2006), Montero-Aroca et al. (2005a, b, c, 2007, 2008) and Cortés-Domínguez and Moreno-Catena (2008a, b).
- Civil, Criminal and Procedural Law codes.
- Dictionaries, mainly *Diccionario de la Lengua Española de la Real Academia Española* (http://buscon.rae.es), Moliner (2000), or Alcaraz-Varó and Hughes (2006).[12]

Tools for Knowledge Extraction, Conceptualization and Formalization

Towards the acquisition of conceptual knowledge from the corpus of questions (in Spanish), several tools may be used in order to gather as much information as possible to aid the conceptualization step, taking into account that Spanish is to be the input language. TERMINAE, YOSHIKODER, ANTCONC and DOODLE could offer further added insights to TextToOnto and Text2Onto. The lists of relevant extracted terms would support the conceptualization process and concepts will be specified or generalised when possible.

The Protégé ontology editor was again chosen for the formalization of the ontology. Its most important feature are its easy-to-use interface, the many plug-ins offered (e.g. graph view, OWL, etc.), on-going development effort, and widespread use among legal ontology engineers.

Reuse Requirements

The OPJK ontology is intended to aid indexing and search in a very specific domain: practical problems in first instance courts. Nevertheless, top concepts from upper and core ontologies such as DOLCE Lite (CLO), SUMO, PROTON, and LKIF-Core will be taken into account to support a middle-out construction strategy: ontology learning from texts together with upper conceptual guidance.

Other Design Requirements

Although most complex modelling decisions would be discussed by the team of domain experts and ontology engineers, most acquisition, conceptualization and formalization tasks would be placed under the responsibility of a domain expert trained in ontology engineering, The methodological requirements established will

[12]Also sources in different languages are taken into account: *Enciclopèdia Catalana* and *Gran Diccionari de la Llengua Catalana* (http://www.enciclopedia.cat), *Collins English Dictionary and Thesaurus* (http://www.collinslanguage.com), *Cambridge Dictionaries Online* (http://dictionary.cambridge.org).

support the accountability of the development decisions taken in order to validate and evaluate the final ontology. Moreover, the initial conceptualizations will be validated by legal experts.

Some naming conventions will also be observed. Classes will begin with capital letters, instances and relations will begin with lower case. Instances are an important feature of the ontology. Concepts will allow semantic search and semantic distance calculation, instances will mainly represent the terms already contained in the stored questions, together with synonyms that the input queries may also contain to refer to them, and, thus, allow indexing. We do not specify the number of concepts/instances that the ontology will finally contain, although recommended by Sure (2003). The number needs to represent the database (questions), and it is difficult to assess without the analysis of the documents. However, a low number of classes and a higher number of instances is expected.

Furthermore, as the aim of the system is not to offer a reasoned solution to the problem, only to guide the search towards the best possible stored answer in the repository (senior judges of the Spanish School of the Judiciary have provided answers to each of the question), the domain knowledge contained in the ontology might be represented in a lightweight manner, with the use of OWL as representation language. The use of such language could foster future reusability or allow ontology merging and alignment (as most legal ontologies and top level ontologies are formalized using OWL).

Finally, a brief description, inspired by the Ontology Requirements Specification Document, of the main OPJK requirements will be included in the OWL file of the Ontology of Professional Judicial Knowledge to provide relevant information towards use or reuse (see Table 5.4). These requirements will be modified or specified according to the final development of the ontology.

5.2.3 Knowledge Acquisition

As stated above, the main corpus for judicial professional knowledge modelling was acquired through semi-structured interviews and is constituted by nearly 800 practical questions formulated by the newly recruited judges. The interviews were recorded by the team of researchers, with the consent of the judges involved. Later, the recorded interviews were transcribed by the team. Finally, the questions regarding on-call problems were extracted from the transcripts of the interviews and organized in a corpus. In this way, three protocols for further analysis were gathered: one corpus included the completed questionnaires, a second corpus included all transcribed questionnaires, and a final corpus contained all the on-call doubts and problems formulated by the judges during the interviews.

This last corpus, the set of questions, contains the professional judicial knowledge gathered during daily practice at courts and constitute the repository of the application. The questions contain mainly problems or doubts arisen during the

Table 5.4 Requirement documentation for OPJK

Purpose	Search and indexing for the IURISERVICE web-based application. The Ontology of Professional Judicial Knowledge (OPJK) ought to represent the relevant concepts related to the problems that take place during the on-call period in Spanish first instance courts. The ontology contains domain specific knowledge, professional knowledge, gathered by experience from the practice during on-call periods with semi-structured interviews.	
Methodological approach	These steps have been established from the analysis of the most detailed and complete methodologies: (1) preparatory phase (specification of ontology requirements), (2) development phase (knowledge acquisition – experts, documents, reuse –, conceptualization – classes, relations, properties, instances –, expert validation and formalization), and (3) evaluation phase (internal consistency, requirements, competency questions and expert evaluation).	
Sources of Knowledge	**Competency questions**	Which are the problematic situations? Which people are involved? What procedural roles are involved? What professionals are involved? What type of organizations are involved? Which documents and other information sources are involved? Which judicial procedures are mentioned? Which relevant relations exist between these situations, people, organizations, procedures and documents?
	Other sources	The full contents of the questionnaires from both survey and the transcriptions of the complete interviews. The vast information contained regarding the Spanish Judiciary in the website of the General Council of the Judiciary: organization of the judiciary in Spain, access materials, relevant legislation regarding the organization of the judiciary, etc. (http://www.poderjudicial.es). Specialised handbooks on the judicial setting and organization: VillaGómez et al. (2003), Toharia and García (2005) and Arnaiz et al. (2005). Specialised textbooks on Civil, Criminal and Procedural Law Ramos-Méndez (1997a, b, 2006), Montero-Aroca et al. (2005a, b, c, 2007, 2008) and Cortés-Domínguez and Moreno-Catena (2008a, b). Civil, Criminal and Procedural Law codes. Dictionaries, mainly Diccionario de la Lengua Española de la Real Academia Española (http://buscon.rae.es) and Moliner (2000).
Tool support	Towards the acquisition of conceptual knowledge from the corpus of questions, several tools may be used, taking into account that Spanish is to be the input language. TERMINAE, YOSHIKODER, ANTCONC and DOODLE could offer further added insights to TextToOnto and Text2Onto.	
Ontology editor	Protégé	
Reuse	Reuse of top concepts from upper ontologies such as DOLCE Lite (CLO), SUMO, PROTON, and LKIF-Core.	

on-call period, although they also include other complex cases that junior judges had to face during their first year of practice. As an example,

- A doctor phoned to inform of someone who is not quite well and that would require internment (confinement). He asks for a court order on the phone. Can I grant it?
- Police is asking for a search warrant to enter a property to unblock a drainpipe, as the owner does not let them in. Should I grant that warrant?
- What is to be done if, while on-call, a corpse removal needs to be performed and there is not forensic doctor available?

In order to gain some more insight towards the general contents of these questions, ALCESTE and also ONTOGEN offered information regarding the subdomains or areas of knowledge included in the questions.

ALCESTE (see Sect. 3.3.2.2) offers a particular analysis of the "topography of a discourse" by creating, confronting and representing different lexical worlds. The analysis of the different lexical worlds that supplies the results of ALCESTE might be useful not only for the understanding of the particular content of the questions (the subdomains or areas of specific knowledge contained in the judicial professional domain), but also to support future conceptual decisions.

The program identifies the vocabulary in the different context units and relates them. In other words, it connects those contexts having common words, finds the strongest vocabulary oppositions and extracts some categories of representative statements. In this case, the analysis of the corpus of questions returns seven classes or lexical worlds.

- Class 1 (15.38%) includes terms such as: enforcement [ejecución], deposit [depósito], seizure of assets [embargo], sentence [condena], decision [resolución], notification [notificación], and auction [subasta]. These terms are generally related to enforcement proceedings.
- Class 2 (20.36%) is expressed by office [oficina], civil servant [funcionario], court [juzgado], deputy [adjunto], work [trabajo], police [policia], courtroom [sala]. They may be considered to be representative of the judicial administration.
- Class 3 (15.84%) includes restrainment [alejamiento], mistreatment [malo, trato], victim [víctima], woman [mujer], order [orden], measure [medida], protection [protección], violence [violencia], and son [hijo], as terms, which are representative of gender violence issues.
- Class 4 (11.76%) relates to internment [internamiento], corpse [cadaver], emergency [urgencia], doctor [médico], removal [levantamiento], on-call [guardia], autopsy [autopsia], which are issues related to internment, corpse removal and incapacitation issues (on-call issues).
- Class 5 (6.79%) includes terms such as: regulation [disposción], comission [comisión], competent [competente], summons [requerimiento], foreign [extranjero], transfer [traslado], detention [detención]. It may refer specially to immigration proceedings.
- Class 6 (18.10%) refers mainly to judicial proceedings, as includes: trial [juicio], oral [verbal], monitorio [type of civil proceeding], joinder [acumular], celebration [celebración], rapid [rápido], audience [vista], lawyer [abogado], solicitor [procurador].

- Class 7 (11.76%) is expressed by to determine [determinar], to qualify [calificar], evidence [prueba], identify [identificar], to rule [resolver], to proceed [tramitar], appeal [recurso], expert [pericial], act [acto]. This class refers mainly to judicial acts or situations.

Moreover, ALCESTE's hierarchical classification of classes informs of relevant existing relations between Classes 6 and 7, which strongly relates judicial proceedings to judicial acts, and between Classes 4 and 5, which seems to suggest that the most representative words of these two classes could be typical of on-call situations. Finally, Class 3, although is slightly related to all the other classes, is more detached as represents all situations, processes, decisions, acts within a specific area: gender violence.

ONTOGEN (see Sect. 3.3.2.2) was used on the corpus of questions to suggest concepts and relations, while the instances of those concepts were the questions themselves. This semi-automatic classification of the questions into different concepts (or topics) produced the following main topics: `Oficina_Judicial` [court office], `Violencia_Domestica` [gender violence], `Extranjeria` [immmigration], `Proceso` [process], and `Familia` [family]. A total of 17 classes (root, main topics and subtopics) were semi-automatically learnt by the OntoGen tool (see Table 5.5 and Fig. 5.2). This topic ontology (Question Topic Ontology) was used to support question classification within the IURISERVICE system. See, for more details, Blázquez et al. (2005), Casellas et al. (2007) and Casellas (2008).

5.2.3.1 Upper-level Ontological Support

The content of the interviews, the context of the judicial setting, the insight provided by ALCESTE and ONTOGEN analyses, and the competency questions laid may be used to analyse different upper and core ontologies to decide which upper concepts may be reused towards knowledge acquisition. In particular, the established competency questions are mainly interested in the acquisition of information regarding roles (professionals, etc.), problematic situations, documents, procedures, and courts or other administrations and organizations. Therefore, the representation that some of the upper and core ontologies (LKIF-Core, CLO, SUMO,[13] and

[13]SUMO is an effort from the Standard Upper Ontology Working Group at IEEE, a non-profit professional association for the advancement of technology: Visit http://suo.ieee.org for more information regarding the development of SUMO. This upper ontology "is a collection of approximately 1,000 well-defined and well-documented concepts, interconnected into semantic network and accompanied by a number of axioms" (Sevcenko 2003). See also Niles and Pease (2001).

Table 5.5 QTO topic and subtopic classification

Topic	Subtopics
Process	Competence conflicts, enforcement proceeding, quick trial, comision rogatoria
Judicial office	Public prosecution, hearing video recording
Gender violence	Restraining order
Immigration	Expulsion and extradition
Family	Internment and incapacitation, autopsy and corpse removal, minors

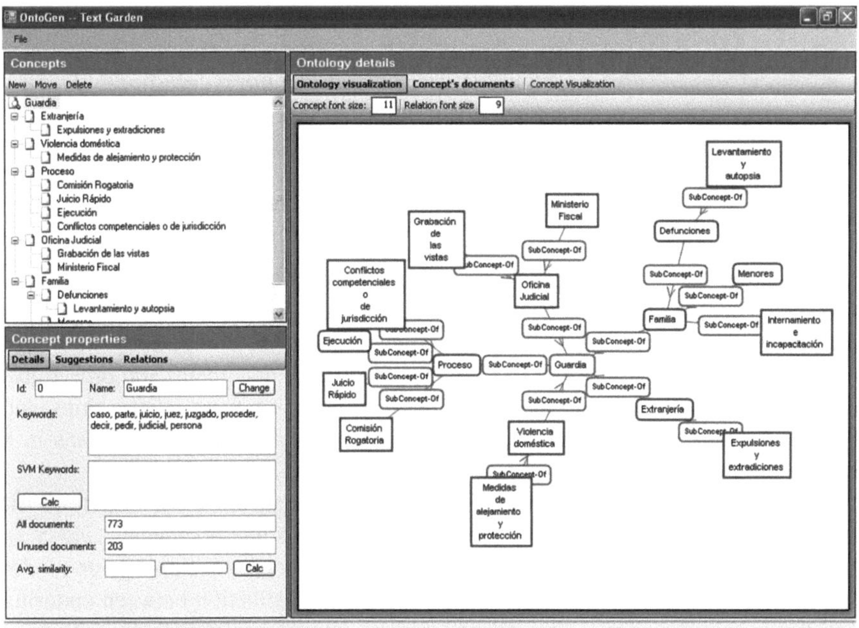

Fig. 5.2 QTO in OntoGen's interface

PROTON[14]) have made of such concepts could be useful for our knowledge acquisition and conceptualization steps.

At a first glance, the upper categories of the analysed upper and core ontologies contain some organizational similarities. LKIF is organized in different super-classes including `Abstract_Entity`, `Mental_Entity`, `Physical_Entity`, `Agent`, `Change`, `Medium`, `Occurrence`, and `Qualified`. DOLCE contains two main categories `abstract` and `spatio-temporal-particular`, which has `endurant` and `perdurant` as subclasses. SUMO is organized in two

[14]PROTo ONtology, (PROTON, in OWL Lite) was developed during the SEKT European Project (SIRMA AI, Ltd.) as a general-purpose domain-independent ontology. A light-weight upper-level ontology to serve as modelling basis (Terziev et al. 2005).

main categories `Abstract` and `Physical` that, in turn, contains `Object` and `Process`. Finally, PROTON is organized in three main categories comprising: `Abstract`, `Happening` and `Object`. Nevertheless, each upper, top or foundational ontology has different theoretical commitments.[15] Below, a more detailed description of each of the selected upper ontologies is offered.

Regarding the analysis of the above-mentioned upper ontologies, the main issue is that the revision and comparison of these upper ontologies is very complex, as also is the assessment of the ontological commitments made by each of them. DOLCE and LKIF-Core (LRI-Core) declare a (not shared) cognitive approach[16] but share their interest for the legal domain. SUMO integrates existing views from several existing upper ontologies (such as Sowa's – Sowa (1995, 2000) –), avoiding commitments to a view of the world, in a large structure, and PROTON offers a domain-independent naive formalization towards multi-purpose uses. Moreover, naming differences make comparisons difficult, for example, `Process` in SUMO is defined in a similar way to `Happening` in PROTON, and `stative (process/state)` in DOLCE is defined similarly to PROTON's `Situation/Event`, as they offer the same examples.

Therefore, the best option towards reuse for the construction of the Ontology of Professional Judicial Knowledge was to compare how each of the ontologies formalizes the different conceptual ideas mentioned in the competency questions: roles, organizations, situations (problematic situations), documents and procedures (processes). Their formalization would offer insight on their relationships and boundaries in order to extract the knowledge from the corpus of questions in a middle-out manner.

LKIF-core offers an interesting and simple formalization for situations (if understood as actions), procedures, roles, organizations and documents (Fig. 5.3). DOLCE Lite+ (with CLO and extensions) is a very complex ontology or modularized set of ontologies, based on the philosophical distinction between enduring (continuants) and perduring (occurrents) entities. Therefore, DOLCE formalization implies many modelling decisions based on a particular philosophical view, which has been criticized by Breuker and Hoekstra (2004a) in the area of legal ontologies. Nevertheless, CLO offers interesting approaches to modelling legal acts and facts, and legal roles (Fig. 5.4). SUMO is also a very large and complex ontology, containing more than 1,000 concepts. In this case, the OWL translation of SUMO includes 630 classes. Finally, PROTON appears to be a very simple ontology, when compared to LKIF-Core, DOLCE Lite/CLO and SUMO. Very few concepts and relations are formalized in the first two modules of PROTON (28 classes). The developers of PROTON asserted that some of the design principles were domain-independence, light-weight logical definitions, and alignment with popular

[15] See Oberle et al. (2007) for a discussion regarding upper ontology commitments regarding a descriptive vs. revisionary approach, multiplicative vs. reductionist ontology, possibilism vs. actualism, and endurantism vs. perdurantism.

[16] See Breuker and Hoekstra (2004a) and Breuker et al. (2005).

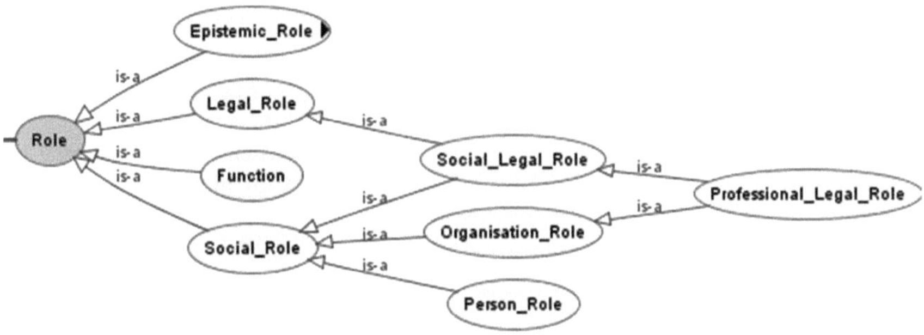

Fig. 5.3 Role in LKIF

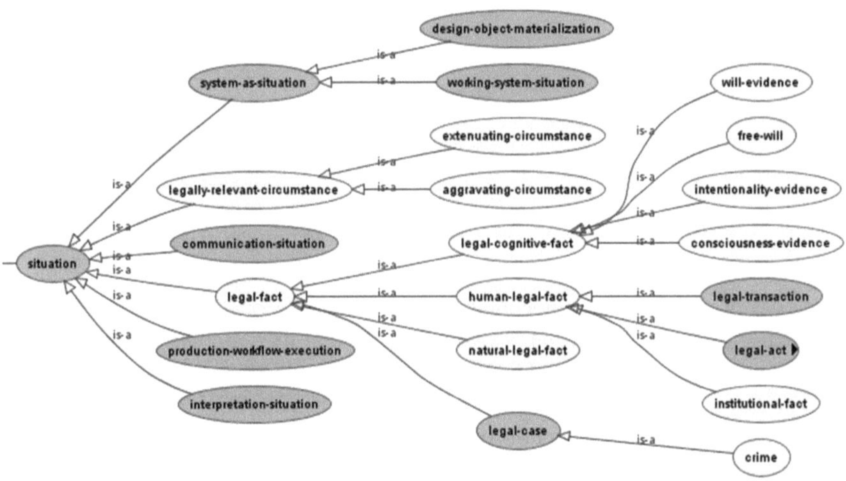

Fig. 5.4 Situation in DOLCE Lite + (extensions/CLO)

standards (Terziev et al. 2005) and, therefore, does not include the modelization concepts from the legal domain. Moreover, the analysis of the ontology shows that the conceptual representation formalized in PROTON is focused towards the representation of corporate knowledge for enterprise knowledge management.

Each of the above-mentioned ontologies offered some arguments towards reuse and some interesting views on the formalization of document, process, situation, role and organization. LKIF-Core offers an interesting cognitive-based approach that includes the representation of agents (organizations and persons) playing roles and performing actions, which is interesting for the representation of knowledge in the judicial setting (Fig. 5.3). DOLCE-CLO offers an extensive representation of concepts related to the legal domain to allow extensive reasoning capabilities. SUMO offers a functional view on the representation of organizations, finally, PROTON provides simplicity.

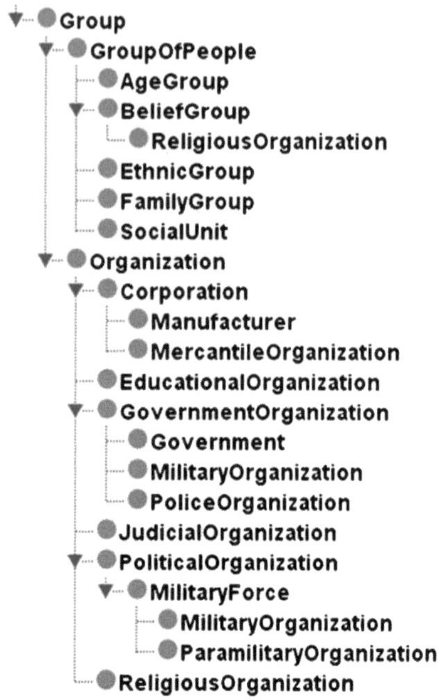

Fig. 5.5 Group and organization in SUMO

However, reusing the conceptualization offered by one of them implies the acceptance of the model of the "existing" world that they represent. For example, the concept `Role`, which could include important instances such as `prosecutor` or `plaintiff` is modeled very differently: in PROTON is a subclass of `Situation`, in turn a subclass of `Happening`, something that happens (not `Abstract` nor `Object`). For DOLCE-CLO `Role` is a `Concept`, which is a `Social_Object`, a non-agentive and non-physical endurant, in the sense that does not adopt plans and has no mass. LKIF-Core conceptualizes role as a subtype of `Mental_Entity` (but not an `Abstract_Entity`) which `is_played` by some `Thing`, and in SUMO is modelled as a relationship that specifies the status of a `CognitiveAgent` within an `Organization` or `Group`. This example shows the difficulty of certain conceptualization and formalization decisions and the different implications of reusing an upper ontology for our particular domain ontology development (Fig. 5.5).

The main interest of OPJK is the representation of the conceptual knowledge contained in the set of questions stored in the IURISERVICE FAQ to provide enhanced semantic indexing and search. The rationale behind the complex knowledge acquisition process based on semi-structured interviews was to acquire the conceptual knowledge from the experience of judges. Therefore, the rationale of OPJK is to try to represent the concepts included in the questions as used by the judges. Reusing or deciding a conceptualization beforehand may jeopardize the construction process of the ontology based on the knowledge extracted from the questions. Moreover, the computational limitations of the IURISERVICE system, aimed at indexing and search could not require a complete use of all their reasoning capabilities.

Due to these limitations and requirements, the conceptualization and formalization will take into account the concepts of *role*, *document*, *process*, *situation/action* and *organization* (*agent*), inspired by the analysis of these upper ontologies. From the analysis of the corpus of questions and the insights provided by the additional sources and the experts' validation, the content of these concepts and relations holding between them will be defined. Then, mappings between similar OPJK concepts and concepts represented in PROTON, DOLCE-CLO, SUMO or LKIF-Core could be provided to explore further reasoning capabilities.

5.2.3.2 Term Extraction and Ontology Learning from Text

The results of the analysis of these different upper-level ontologies supports the use of roles, situations, documents, organizations and processes (or procedures) as some top-level concepts to be taken into account during the ontology learning process (a middle-out approach). Moreover, the interesting contributions offered by each of the ontologies towards the clarification of some of those concepts will also be taken into account if that knowledge was finally required.

The main knowledge source is the corpus of the questions obtained from the interviews and stored in the database of the system. This corpus is used as the text for automatic term extraction and knowledge acquisition. The language of the textual data is Spanish, and the questions are available in Word document format, in.txt document format, after lemmatization.[17]

Several textual analysis and ontology learning programs could be used towards knowledge acquisition from the corpus of questions: TextToOnto, Text2Onto, TERMINAE, AntConc, Yoshikoder and Doodle.

In the course of the SEKT project, the corpus of questions was used as the input text for the extraction of terms using TextToOnto and Text2Onto for an initial ontology development. The main issues with both tools, apart from the retrieval of verbs and adverbs in the case of TextToOnto and the retrieval of concepts with little meaning in the case of Text2Onto, were the complex management of the results and the exportable possibilities offered of the results (Fig. 5.6). Due to these results, at that time, a manual development of the ontology was performed based on the detection of concepts by a team of legal experts from each of the questions contained in the list. The lists of terms provided by the tools were used as reference towards relevance. This team of domain experts from the Institute of Law and Technology (Barcelona) shared the development with the ontology engineers of the iSOCO company (Madrid). The distributed modelling environment (ontology engineers and domain experts) forced distance discussions and cooperative modelling that required to take into account methodological support. The DILIGENT

[17]The lemmatization of the corpus of questions improved the results obtained, see Vallbé et al. (2007). More details on these analysis with TextToOnto and Text2Onto may be found in Casellas (2008). Stopwords could also be removed.

Domain	Range	Confidence
pago	asociación	1.0
juicio	hurto	1.0
si	falta	1.0
fábrica	persona	1.0
defecto	vicio	1.0
cuestión	incidente	1.0
cancelación	entrega	1.0
¿Cómo	procedimiento	1.0
límite	¿Cuáles	1.0
consecuencia	procedimiento penal	1.0
medio	¿Cuáles	1.0
¿Cuáles	criterio	0.75
¿Cuáles	límite	0.25
¿Cuál	papel	0.17647058823529413
¿Cuál	límite	0.17647058823529413
¿Cuál	trámite	0.11764705882352941
¿Cuál	procedimiento	0.11764705882352941
¿Cuál	frase	0.058823529411764705
¿Cuál	diferencia	0.058823529411764705
¿Cuál	baremo	0.058823529411764705
¿Cuál	criterio	0.058823529411764705
¿Cuál	delimitación	0.058823529411764705
¿Cuál	Juzgado	0.058823529411764705
¿Cuál	instrucción	0.058823529411764705

Fig. 5.6 Screenshot for the concept subclass extraction in Text2Onto

methodology (DIstributed, Loosely-controlled and evolvInG Engineering of ONTologies) methodology was followed to support such relations (Pinto et al. 2004, 2005; Tempich et al. 2007; Casanovas et al. 2007a).

The manual extraction and conceptualization proved very time consuming, also did the collaborative development of the ontology as the tools available at the moment did not sufficiently support the process. Nevertheless, a first ontology was developed in RDF using Protégé's latest version, which could allow the system to perform several user validation steps towards improvement and evaluation. The construction process followed, then, a middle-out strategy (with the reuse of the top-level module of the PROTON ontology); selected terms contained in the questions were included in the ontology, formalized at first in RDF (or in a repository of synonyms), and were generalized or specified when necessary (Casellas et al. 2005). This initial OPJK-RDF ontology contained around 100 concepts and 400 instances, and modeled the conceptual knowledge contained in nearly 200 questions.

Therefore, for the final development of the Ontology of Professional Judicial Knowledge, the decision of retaking the process was made, taking full advantage of the experience and the evaluation results towards the establishment of more accurate ontology requirements regarding the use of term extraction tools, other sources of information, and methodological support.

While the TERMINAE and DODDLE tools could not support Spanish term and concept extraction, Yoshikoder and AntConc[18] provided frequency wordlists

[18]AntConc supports the loading of files containing stop words to clean the input document.

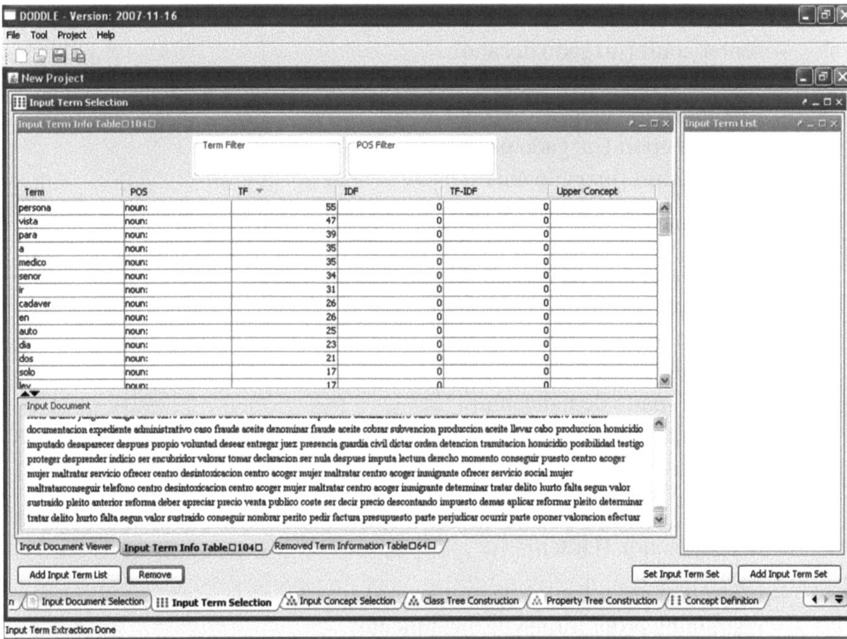

Fig. 5.7 Input term selection from the lemmatized document in DODDLE

(Fig. 5.7). Further, it was found necessary to obtain more information regarding each of terms included in the list. Some terms such as base [base] did not offer sufficient relevant meaning, other terms such as *violenc*e [violencia] and *domestic* [doméstica], which appeared separately but with the same frequency, where considered after a review of the content to be a multiple term *domestic violence [violencia doméstica], and some terms suggested synonimia (case [caso], matter [asunto],* situation [situación]). Therefore, AntConc's cluster analysis was performed on most terms in order to obtain more information regarding: (a) terms with low or no relevancy for the domain, (b) multiple terms (N+Adj, N+prep+N, and N+prep+N+Adj forms), and (c) the contexts of use of the terms.

(a) Some terms were found to have no specific meaning (or too many different meanings, none relevant enough) in the context of practical problems in the judicial domain, and were removed from the list.
(b) A large list of relevant multiple terms was obtained and added to the list. As a summary:

- Court [Juzgado]:
  - competent court [juzgado competente]
  - criminal law court [juzgado de lo penal]
  - assigned court [juzgado de destino]

  - on-call court [juzgado de guardia]
  - senior court [juzgado decano]
  - court of administrative area [juzgado del partido judicial]
  - foreign court [juzgado extranjero]
  - criminal court [juzgado penal]
  - unique court [juzgado único]

- Party [Parte]:

  - accusation party (prosecution) [parte acusadora]
  - buying party (buyer) [parte compradora]
  - opposite party [parte contraria]
  - defendant [parte demandada]
  - plaintiff [parte demandante]
  - reporting pary [parte denunciante]
  - enforcement party [parte ejecutante]
  - damaged party [parte perjudicada]

- Order/Injunction [Orden]:

  - protection order [orden de protección]
  - restraining order [orden de alejamiento]
  - search warrant [orden de entrada y registro]
  - arrest warrant [orden de detención]
  - search and arrest warrant [orden de búsqueda y detención]
  - European arrest warrant [orden de detención europea = orden europea de detención]
  - extradition warrant [orden de extradición]
  - active extradition warrant [orden de extradición activa]
  - internment order [orden de internamiento]
  - preventive inprinsonment order [orden de prisión preventiva]

(c) Contexts of use of terms provided insight to the different uses of particular terms, the possible synonyms of a term (according to the context of use). For example, **Trial** [juicio], as procedure, appears frequently in the questions. The usage of the term suggests that there are other terms in the corpus that are used in a similar way: *lawsuit* [pleito], *process* [proceso], and *proceeding* [procedimiento] are also used similarly. Figure 5.8 below gives an example of the relations between these terms.

(d) Finally, some extracted terms acquire complete meaning when considered as part of a complex or multiword concept. (For example, [partido] is judicial (administrative) area [partido judicial]. *Protection* [protección] is used in *injuction of protection* [orden de protección].)

With all these new information, the list of terms was revised in order to construct the grouping and a first conceptual tree of terms. The initial extensive list of terms was finally reduced to a working list of 477 terms.

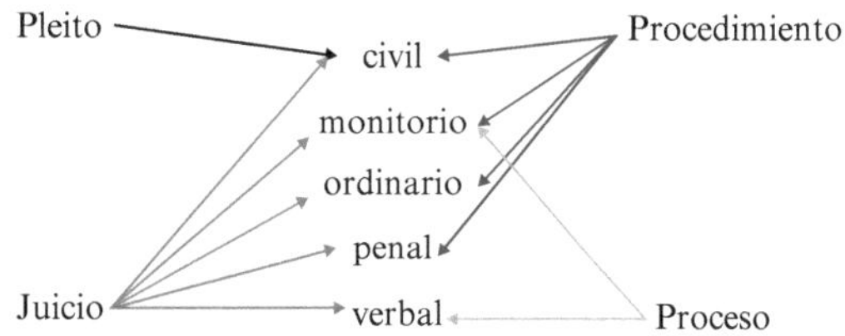

Fig. 5.8 [juicio], [proceso], [procedimiento], [pleito] and their relations

5.2.4 *Acquisition of Conceptual Domain Knowledge*

Once the conceptual extraction has been performed and as much information as possible has been acquired on the corpus of questions, we proceed at grouping and organizing the concepts in a taxonomy, taking into account the content of the corpus of questions (practical problems), the context of the questions (the judicial setting) together with background theoretical knowledge acquired during the training period of judges (from academic textbooks, legislation and examination and training course syllabuses).

Also, the established competency questions regarding the roles, situations, documents, procedures and organizations involved in the problems described by the corpus of questions and the insights given by the analysis of the upper ontologies of Sect. 5.2.3.1 will support the organization of the first set of clusters. Finally, concept definitions will be provided during the conceptualization process, after a first validation by legal experts has been provided on an initial grouping of relevant concepts.

5.2.4.1 Grouping and Initial Taxonomical Relations

Roles

From the initial list, 56 terms were classified as roles involved in the practical problems included in the corpus of questions. Within this group, four groups were clearly identified: a group including legal roles together with a subgroup including all procedural roles, a group of professional roles, and a group of roles played within the family setting. Nevertheless, some terms could belong to more than one group at a time.

Organizations and Other Agents

From the list, 50 terms related to organizations were extracted, and a differentiation is made regarding group and organization, taking into account the insights from the top ontologies. Second, regarding the group of organizations several subgroups may be identified according to their main focus of activity or function (inspired by SUMO).

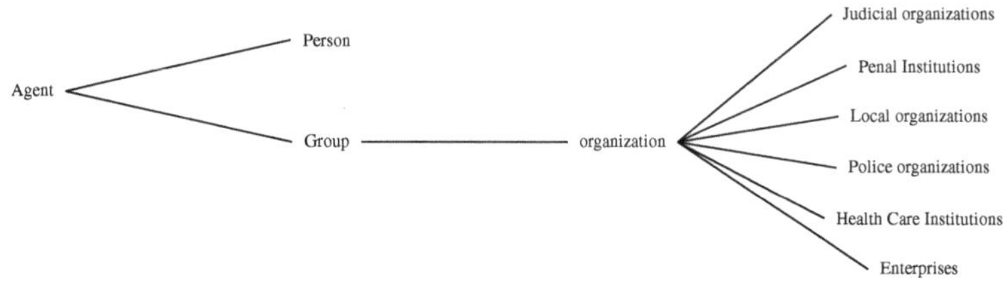

Processes, Situations and Documents

The distinction between processes, situations or actions and documents is not straightforward, and there are several issues involved, that may be observed from the data:

1. Judicial processes include a sum of procedural moments and have a temporal duration, and some processes may include not only moments but also other shorter processes. For example, an ordinary civil procedure includes an oral hearing.
2. Some procedural documents are the result of procedural actions and/or short procedures and, in the questions, judges refer to either of them, for example a notificación is used as a document in "to receive a notification" and as a process in "carry out the notification."
3. Finally, some terms may refer at the same time to a process and to a action. For example, deshaucio or incapacitación ("he señalado el desahucio para mañana" and "tengo una demanda de desahucio.")

A first grouping is attempted within the remaining set of 368 terms which include procedures, situations and documents. For this initial distinction we take into account procedural law textbooks (tables of contents) and the program for the examination of judges. A total of 231 terms could be initially grouped into either Process, Situation and Document. Nevertheless, several difficulties arised.

- Still some terms (60) could be related to more than one group at a time (e.g., proceeding [diligencia], communication [comunicación], notification [notificación], claim [reclamación], purchase contract [compraventa], appeal [recurso], celebration [celebración], etc.). The distinction among Document [Documento], Situation [Situación] and Process [Proceso] was difficult to clarify.
- A further list of 77 terms could not be classified in any of the previous groups, rendering other classifications necessary (e.g. time, place, objects, etc.).

A validation by legal experts, comprising legal academics and professionals, was sought to clarify some of these difficulties, and to offer new possibilities for classification.

5.2.4.2 Preliminary Validation by Legal Experts

A group of seven legal experts (two legal professionals and five legal academics) were asked two different types of questions. On one hand, to review the classification of some concepts and, on the other, to classify themselves certain concepts into the groups given. From their validation, several outputs were obtained.

First, regarding the review of the lists of Role and Organization, the general contents of both groups were widely accepted as valid (belonging to them). However, some expressed the need to include (or take into account) the theoretical distinction between natural persons (Persona Física) and legal persons (Persona Jurídica).

Second, the experts were asked to consider the occurrences of Trial [Juicio], Process [Proceso], Proceeding [Procedimiento], and Lawsuit [Pleito] within the corpus of questions and to give their opinion as whether they could be regarded as similar (synonyms for the ontology). Most experts considered that, for practical purposes, they could be considered synonyms although, theoretically, all denoted different, although complementary, aspects of process. Specially, Pleito was generally used to refer to the oral part of the process.[19]

Third, Situation [Situación] was not considered to be a too clear concept for grouping to most experts and they suggested other terminologies such as: act [acto], legal act [acto jurídico] or action [acción].

Nevertheless, although in the previous discussions the different experts mostly agreed, in other cases there was wide disagreement regarding the classification of terms, especially within some distinctions in the category of organizations, roles and the categories of processes-situations-documents.

- **Organizations**. First, the experts were asked to review the concept *Judicial Office* [Oficina Judicial] and to offer more adequate solutions for that concept within the group of organizations. Although it is part of the judicial organization, it is not involved with judicial decision-making process, it is rather an organization for the management of courts and tribunals. Most experts made this differentiation and offered solutions such as divide judicial organization in two further groups: órganos jurisdiccionales and órganos de gestión. Moreover, some experts included the need to conceptualize Administración, Administración Pública, Poder Judicial, etc, to clarify these distinctions.
- **Roles**. The experts were asked to classify a list of concepts into several subgroups of Role: Legal Role, Procedural Role (included in Legal Role), Family Role and Professional Role. The interest was placed also in their opinion regarding the relation between Legal Role, Procedural Role and Professional Role. The results showed that the experts believed that most concepts belonged to more than one set at a time. Two specific problems were encountered. First, concepts such as Juez, Abogado, Procurador, etc. were classified as belonging to Legal Role and

[19] For a discussion of the theoretical relations between these terms see Montero-Aroca et al. (2005a).

Professional Role (some experts included them also in Procedural Role). Second, a further group of concepts containing Victima, Agresor, Titular, Ejecutante, etc. were sometimes classified as Legal Role and others as Procedural Role. Both problems suggested that the differences between Legal and Procedural role should be clarified before attempting the conceptualization. In this sense, some concepts classified as Family Roles or Professional Roles were also classified as Legal Roles (husband [marido], doctor [médico]). This suggested that, in fact, the concepts related to roles, were all relevant for the legal field in a general sense, and it would be more useful to consider directly the category of Judicial Roles (including Procedural Roles).

- **Process-Act-Document**. Our impression that most documents could also be classified as processes and situations (acts) was certified. The explanation being that most actions taken during judicial processes are largely documented (written form). Nevertheless, the experts offered several solutions to solve these problems. First, as the importance of documenting the acts and procedures carried out by the courts and the parties is of outmost relevance for the due process of law (e.g., 24 Constitución Española, 145–168 Ley de Enjuiciamiento Civil 1/2000, de 7 de enero, art. 141–162 de la Ley de Enjuiciamiento Criminal) the classification terms into the category of documents could take preference to their classification into either processes or acts. Second, they agreed that factual situations and legally relevant actions (either criminal or civil) could be classified in a simple manner as Acts. Finally, that the distinction between processes and subprocess (or macro and micro processes) was acceptable from a practical point of view, but the theoretical distinction between processes and procedural stages (fases procesales) ought to be taken into account in a complex formalization, as was widely used in Spanish Procedural Law.

Finally, some suggestions from the experts were directed to a more precise conceptualization, rather than to grouping. For example, several experts suggested relations between Process, Subprocess, Situation, Document and Role based on the following theoretical and epistemological structure: within a process, there are several consecutive phases that usually finalizes with a formal document, produced by an agent performing a certain role. Moreover, some suggested that some terms were to be regarded not as instances or concepts but as attributes of those concepts (on-call court [juzgado de guardia] or competent court [juzgado competente], for example).

The conceptualization of these groupings and the relations between them is performed in the next section, and the list of terms included in the ontology is extended (to include more than 900 terms). Conceptualization and instantiation will be the first activities to be realised, as well as providing working definitions for the main concepts. As noticed with this preliminary validation by experts, there is a difficulty to accommodate theoretical classifications with the more bottom-up and text-based view taken for this work. Therefore, the decision is to perform a conceptualization in different stages, so other less application based and more theoretically grounded distinctions suggested by legal experts may be incorporated and evaluated for the functioning of the system.

5.3 Conceptualization and Formalization

This section conceptualizes the terms extracted from the knowledge acquisition and first grouping stages, and offers working definitions for the main concepts (see a detailed description in Casellas (2008)).[20] In order to be able to be able to technically evaluate, in the future, the search enhancement capabilities of the different modelling decisions taken during the conceptualization process, conceptualization and formalization are performed in several stages of complexity.[21]

The conceptualization offered in this chapter was formalized in OWL using the Protégé ontology editor to allow future reuse or enrichment.[22]

5.3.1 *Classes, `rdfs:subClassOf` Relations, and Instances*

In the following subsections describe the conceptualization and formalization of the main classes and their subclasses of the Ontology of Professional Judicial Knowledge: `Role`, `Agent`, `Document`, `Process` and `Act`.

5.3.1.1 Role

Most roles present in the questions and relevant for the system are, in fact, legal roles. The distinction between legal roles and non-legal roles was not sufficiently relevant. Therefore, importance was placed on the judicial setting and the `Role` group was divided into `Judicial_Role`, `Family_Role` and `Professional_Role`. Figure 5.9, below, shows a graphic representation of the `Role` class in Protégé.

---

[20]These definitions are inspired by the use of the terms in the corpus of questions (supported by relevant literature) and are based on the definitions offered by several reputed dictionaries (e.g. Collins, Oxford, Moliner (2000), Alcaraz-Varó and Hughes (2006)), and from definitions contained in the given top ontologies, and Spanish legislation, when appropriate.

[21]Two versions of the ontology, regarding only expressivity but also complex conceptual decisions, will be available. At first, a class hierarchy will be established (classes, subclass relations —`rdfs:subClassOf`—, and instances), enriched with further `owl:ObjectProperty` (`owl:subPropertyOf` and `owl:inverseOf`) constructs to establish relations between the classes. Later, `owl:equivalentClass`, `owl:sameAs` constructs, and multiple class subclasses or multiple class instances will be discussed in order to formalize, for example, the conceptualization of instances that may be declared as members of more than one class or classes which share instances. The inclusion of these constructs will take into account the purpose of the IURISERVICE search system, the input received from the validation and the suggestions by the legal experts, and their formalization will modify the simplicity of the initial class hierarchy modeled.

[22]Versions 3.3.1, 3.4 (beta) and 4.0 (beta) are used. GraphViz (OWLViz) was used to provide graphical representations of the formalized ontology.

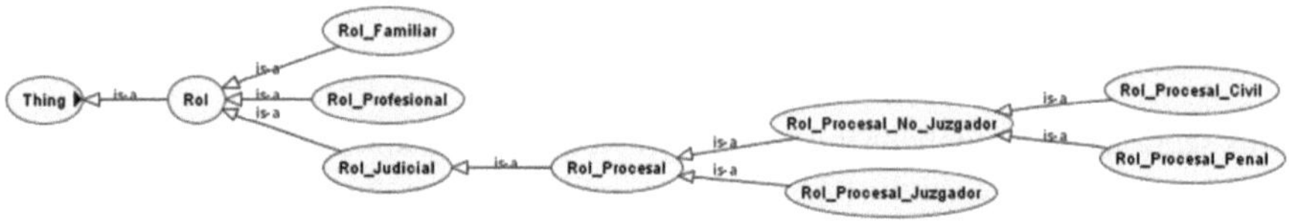

Fig. 5.9 Role class in Protégé

- Role [Rol]: The part played by an agent in a particular setting.
- Judicial_Role [Rol_Judicial]: The part played by an agent in the judicial setting.
- Procedural_Role [Rol_Procesal]: The part played by an agent in a judicial process.
- Decision_Maker_Procedural_Role [Rol_Procesal_Juzgador]: The part played by an agent who takes judicial decisions in a judicial process.
- Non_Decision_Maker_Procedural_Role [Rol_Procesal_No_Juzgador]: The part played by a non judicial decision-making agent in a judicial process.
- Criminal_Procedural_Role [Rol_Procesal_Penal]: The part played by an agent in a criminal procedure.
- Civil_Procedural_Role [Rol_Procesal_Civil]: The part played by an agent in a civil procedure.
- Family_Role [Rol_Familiar]: The part played by an agent in the family setting.
- Professional_Role [Rol_Profesional]: A professional part played by an agent.

5.3.1.2 Agent

Regarding Organization, the grouping is performed from the concept of Agent, which includes individually considered agents (Person) and collective agents (Group and Organization). See Fig. 5.10. The definition of Judicial_Organization, Penal_Institution, and Local_Administration requires the analysis of relevant legislation.[23]

- Agent [Agente]: A person or thing that performs actions, that acts or has the power to act.
- Person [Persona]: An individual human being.
- Group [Grupo]: A number of persons or things considered collectively.

[23]Ley Orgánica 1/1979, de 26 de septiembre, General Penitenciaria, Ley 30/1992, de 26 de noviembre de Régimen Jurídico de las Administraciones Públicas y del Procedimiento Administrativo Común, Constitución Española, and Ley Orgánica 6/1985, de 1 de julio, del Poder Judicial.

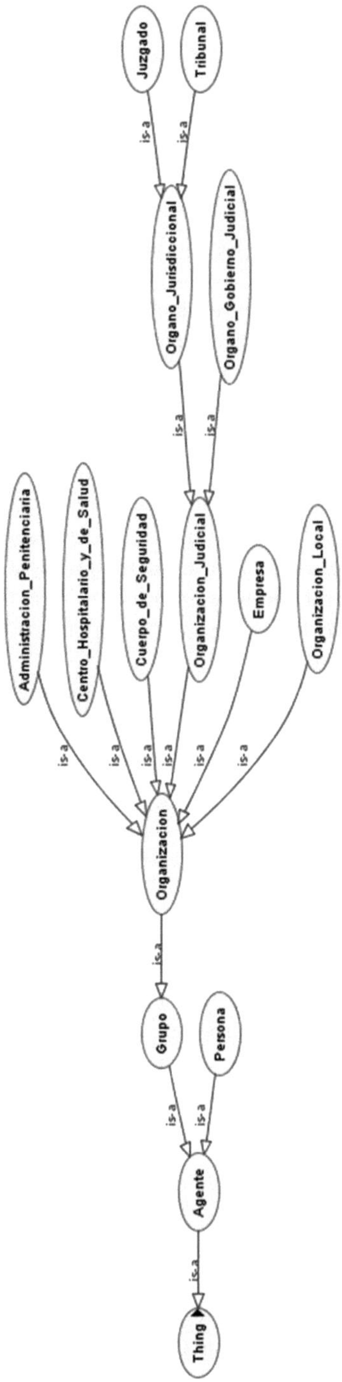

Fig. 5.10 Agent class in Protégé

- `Organization` [`Organización`]: A group of people who work together in a structured way for a shared purpose.
- `Judicial_Organization` [`Organizacion_Judicial`]: The organization of the administration of justice.
- `Judicial_Government_Organization` [`Organizacion_Gobierno_Judicial`]: The organizations in charge of the management of the administration of justice.
- `Judicial_Decision_Organization` [`órgano_Jurisdiccional`]: The organizations responsible for judicial decision-making within the administration of justice.
- `Bench`[24] [`Tribunal`]: Judicial body which hears and makes decisions on legal cases, a court of justice with more than one decision-maker.
- `Court` [`Juzgado`]: Judicial body which hears and makes decisions on legal cases, a court of justice with one decision-maker.
- `Local_Administration` [`Organizacion_Local`]: organization responsible for the local management of services and execution of laws.
- `Penal_Institution` [`Administración_Penitenciaria`]: An organization responsible for social rehabilitation and reintegration into society of convicts, the custody of persons under arrest (inspired by Ley Orgánica 1/1979, de 26 de septiembre, General Penitenciaria).
- `Police_Organization` [`Cuerpo_de_Seguridad`]: organization responsible for keeping law and order.
- `Health_Care_Institution` [`Centro_Hospitalario_y_de_Salud`]: Health-care centers.
- `Enterprise` [`Empresa`]: A business organization.

5.3.1.3 Document

`Document` may be defined, more generally, as any support to data. In this sense, we take into consideration towards conceptualization and definition the view of the Criminal Code art. 26, which states that a document will be considered as any material support that expresses or incorporates data, facts or stories which may be of any legal relevance.[25] In order to conceptualize and define the classes, several legislative documents have been taken into account, especially the Civil Code and the Ley 1/2000, de 7 de enero, de Enjuiciamiento Civil. This Act conceptualizes

[24]"Court in which more than one judge sits" (Alcaraz-Varó and Hughes 2006).

[25]Art. 26, Código Penal: "A los efectos de este Código se considera documento todo soporte material que exprese o incorpore datos, hechos o narraciones con eficacia probatoria o cualquier otro tipo de relevancia jurídica."

procedural documents (demanda, contestación, informe) and public and private documents (with regards to their proof values).[26]

Finally, in order to avoid again the formalization of tangled hierarchies (Rector et al. 2004), multiple inheritance or multiple instantiation, `Judicial_Communication` and `Appeal` are here formalized only as subclasses of `Procedural_ Document`. Nevertheless, although the instances of those classes may also be considered acts or (micro)processes within the judicial setting, and this feature will be addressed when adding complexity to this initial formalization (Fig. 5.11).

- `Document` [`Documento`]: Any material support that expresses or incorporates data, facts or stories.
- `Legal_Document` [`Documento_Jurídico`]: Any document that expresses or incorporates data, facts or stories, with legal relevance.
- `Legislative_Document` [`Documento_Legislativo`]: Any document that expresses or incorporates legal rules.
- `Procedural_Document` [`Documento_Procesal`]: Any document that expresses or incorporates data generated during a judicial procedure.
- `Judicial_Decision` [`Resolución_Judicial`]: A decision of a court of law.
- `Judgement` [`Sentencia`]: Motivated judicial decision.
- `Interlocutory_Order` [`Auto`][27]: Motivated judicial decision regarding secondary or executive issues of a judicial process.
- `Procedure_Decision` [`Providencia`]: Judicial decision regarding the management of judicial processes, which does not require motivation.
- `Judicial_Comunication` [`Comunicación`]: Document that establishes communication between the judicial Organization and private parties, other judicial organizations and administrations.
- `Appeal` [`Recurso`]: Document or set of documents presented to challenge a ruling, a judicial decision.
- `Public_Legal_Document` [`Documento_Jurídico_Público`]: Document authorised by notaries (official deeds), public registrars (e.g., Land Registry), and other public officials or civil servants in the exercise of their official appointment (excluding judicial decisions).

[26] Public and private documents are conceptualized and defined differently, although compatible, in the Civil Code and the Civil Procedure Act. The Civil Procedure Act takes into account the documents from the point of view of presenting evidence. In that view, judicial decisions are included within public documents. Here, we will consider that judicial decisions are not considered by the junior judges as public documents used in the evidence process, but as documents/decisions which they themselves produce in a judicial process. Therefore, the conceptualizations suggested by both the Civil Code and the Civil Procedure Act have been taken into account, although modified for the content of the corpus.

[27] *Auto* may also be translated as: order, court order, writ, decree and warrant within the judicial domain (Alcaraz-Varó and Hughes 2006). Nevertheless, providencia may be translated also by the terms order, court order and writ.

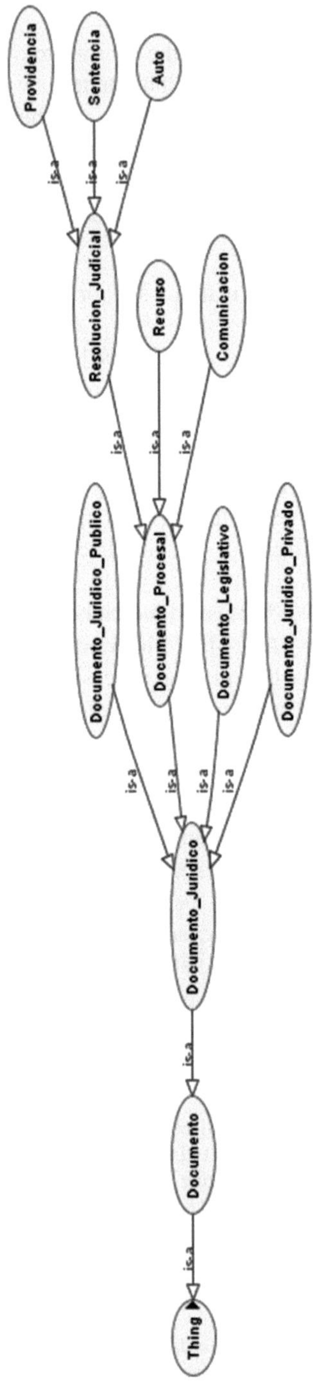

Fig. 5.11 Document class in Protégé

- `Private_Legal_Document` [`Documento_Jurídico_Privado`]: Documents not included within the `Public_Legal_Document` definition, documents without public or official endorsement.

5.3.1.4 Process

Process or procedure is here understood as a set of successive actions or sets of actions of a phenomena (the judicial decision-making process), and are classified into `Macroprocess` and `Microprocess`. The conceptual difference between them is based on the consideration of *procedural stages*, and the idea of *dependence*. Although some judicial processes are complete sets of actions, they depend on or are part of a more general process. For example, a `Trial` or a `Hearing` are established procedures (with precise temporal duration, conformed by a set of actions, etc.), but generally exist within the framework of a more general process, for example, the ordinary civil process. The challenge of a judicial decision (an appeal) is also a process itself, although it is not possible without the previous existence of a more general process, for example, (again) the ordinary civil procedure. For the conceptualization, both the Civil Procedure Act and the Criminal Procedure Act have been revised, together with other relevant legislation.

`Microprocess` are considered, therefore, processes that conform stages of a (macro)process. Nevertheless, their possible conceptualization as `parts_of` or `stages_of Macroprocess`, could be taken into account for a more accurate conceptualization.

- `Procedure` [`Proceso`]: A series of actions.
- `Macroprocess` [`Macroproceso`]: A judicial process considered as a complete and independent set of actions (a framework).
- `Civil_Macroprocess` [`Macroproceso_Civil`]: A civil judicial process considered as a complete and independent set of actions (a framework).
- `Criminal_Macroprocess` [`Macroproceso_Penal`]: A criminal judicial process considered as a complete and independent set of actions (a framework).
- `Microprocess` [`Microproceso`]: A judicial process considered as an incomplete and dependent set of actions (taking place within a framework).
- `Joinder` [`Acumulación`]: The process of joining counts, parties, or processes in a judicial process.
- `Enforcement_Proceeding` [`ejecución`]: The process of enforcing (executing) an court ruling (although other title deeds may also be enforced).
- `Appeal_Procedure` [`Impugnación`]: The process of challenging a ruling, a judicial decision.
- `Habeas_Corpus` [`Habeas_Corpus`]: A procedure, regulated by Ley Orgánica 6/1984, de 24 de Mayo, Reguladora del Procedimiento Habeas Corpus, to decide whether the detention of a person is lawful.

- Inquisitorial_Investigation [Instrucción]: Process of investigation of facts and preparation for the criminal trial.
- Service_Of_Process [Comunicación]: Procedure employed to give legal notice of a certain procedural act to a person (such as a defendant), another court or administrative body.
- Hearing [Vista]: Process of appearing before a court.
- Trial [Juicio_Oral]: Process of appearing before a court in a criminal procedure.
- Interim_&_Precautionary_Process [Proceso_Cautelar]: Procedure to adopt measures that are deemed necessary to ensure the effectiveness of the judgement that may be granted (in civil proceedings) or to limit (criminal proceedings).
- Evidence [Prueba]: Procedures of proof.

5.3.1.5 Act

Act [Acto], defined as something done or performed, an action, a static event, is of special importance within the judicial setting, taking into special consideration the acts performed during a procedure, Procedural_Act. This type of Act, a term preferred by legal experts during the validation process, and highly used by relevant literature (see Ramos-Méndez (2006) and Montero-Aroca et al. (2007)), would define actions performed during a judicial procedure expressing the will of the court, the parties or third parties and have certain requirements regarding form, time, or place, and may be null if not complied with. The difficulty of conceptualizing procedural acts, and acts in general, corresponds to the difficulty of distinguishing between documents, procedures and acts in the judicial setting. Procedural acts are performed during a (micro)procedure and are usually expressed in a documented form (a required formality).

Therefore, some procedural acts, may have a specific procedure and be expressed in a specific document which bear the same name. For example, denuncia is an instance of Procedural_Document, but could also be considered an instance of Procedural_Act (or of a subclass named, for example, Incoation_Act, which takes place during the Inquisitorial_Investigation stage. Further, in order to clarify the relationship between Act and Process, it may be necessary to include a superclass of both concepts (such as Event, Occurrence or Happening) as the class of "anything which takes place," as both, Act and Process may occur, take place or *happen*. Therefore, Act and Process will conceptualize a simplified difference between dynamic and static events (inspired by PROTON and DOLCE top ontologies). A Process would then be defined a set or a series of different actions (acts or other procedures). See Fig. 5.12.

- Act [Acto]: Something done or performed, an action, a static event.
- Legal_Act [Acto_Jurídico]: An action, the manifestation of a will, aimed at creating, regulation, modifying or extinguishing legal relations.

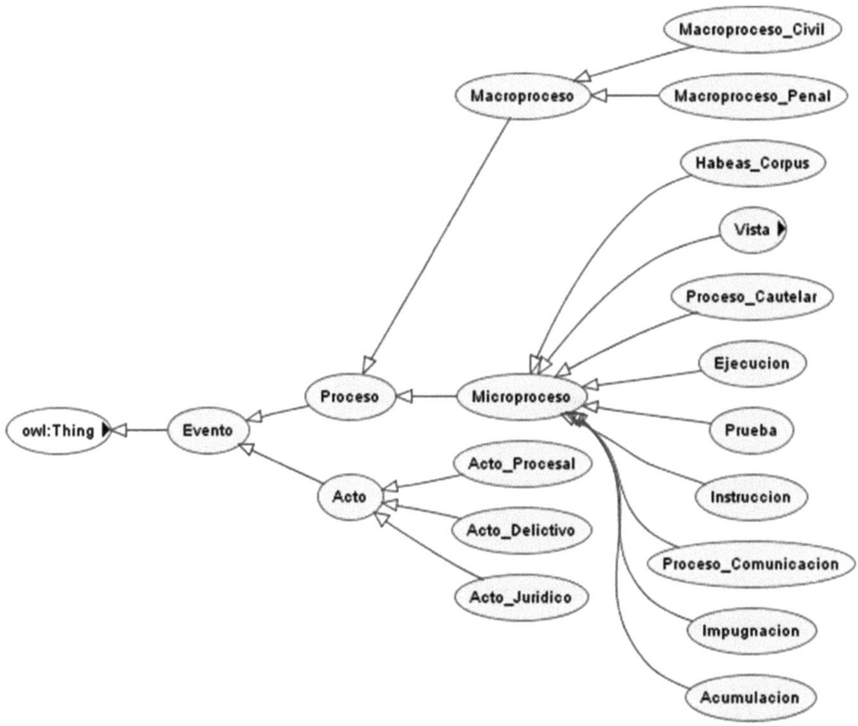

Fig. 5.12 `Process` and `Act` classes in Protégé

- `Procedural_Act` [`Acto_Procesal`]: Actions performed during a judicial procedure expressing the will of the court, the parties or third parties and have certain requirements regarding form, time, or place, and may be null if not complied with.
- `Criminal_Act` [`Acto_Delictivo`]: A public wrong or crime (based on the list of criminal acts –offences– provided by the Ley Orgánica 10/1995, de 23 de noviembre, del Código Penal.)

5.3.2 `owl:ObjectProperty` and Further Constructs

Several relationships (`owl:ObjectProperty`) may be established between the classes of the OPJK ontology, which may enhance search and indexing and the representation of the judicial professional domain. These relationships try to take into account the reality of the judicial setting, as also suggested by the legal experts during validation (see Sect. 5.2.4.2). Agents may take on several roles, which, in turn, may perform certain acts and issue documents. These acts generally

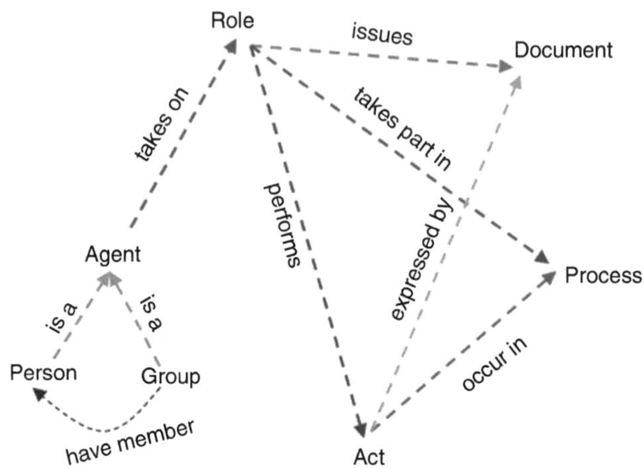

Fig. 5.13 Main relationships between concepts

occur within a process and are expressed by documents. Finally, roles take part in processes and groups have members (persons). Figure 5.13 below includes a graphical representation of these relationships.

Therefore, an initial set of `owl:ObjectProperty` constructs is formalized: `takesOn`, `issuesA`, etc. Moreover, the relationship of membership between persons and groups (organizations) is also formalized with the `isMemberOf` property and its inverse. Finally, we believe relevant to include a preliminary formalization of the relationship existing between processes, as a process may have subprocesses, formalized with the object property `hasSubprocess` (with no inverse). Table 5.6 offers the list of the above-mentioned `owl:ObjectProperty` with their inverses (`owl:inverseOf`) that may be established between the main conceptualized classes:

More specifically, Agents may take on several judicial roles, which, in turn, may perform certain procedural acts and issue procedural documents. These procedural acts generally occur within a process (microprocess or macroprocess) and are expressed by legal documents. Also, procedural roles take part in micro and macroprocesses. For example, the following specific relationships ought to be taken into account:

- Certain judicial organizations carry out decision maker procedural roles;
- Judicial decisions are passed by decision maker procedural roles;
- Procedural documents formalize procedural acts;
- Civil procedural roles participate in civil macroprocesses;

Table 5.6 Object properties (and their inverse) in OPJK

Domain	Object property	Range
Agent	takesOn	Role
Role	isTakenOnBy	Agent
Role	performsA	Act
Act	isPerformedBy	Role
Act	occursIn	Process
Process	consistsOf	Act
Document	expressesA	Act
Act	isExpressedBy	Document
Role	issuesA	Document
Document	isIssuedBy	Role
Role	takesPartIn	Process
Process	isTakenPartBy	Role
Group	hasMember	Person
Person	isMemberOf	Group

5.3.2.1 `owl:subPropertyOf`

In order to add further complexity to the Ontology of Professional Judicial Knowledge, these relationships are further formalized as `owl: subPropertyOf` constructs, specific for the judicial setting, are also conceptualized, and described in Table 5.7. Finally, the formalized `owl:ObjectProperty` and `owl:subPropertyOf` have been analysed in order to add further property characteristics,[28] (such as `owl:TransitiveProperty`, `owl:Functional Property`).

The property `hasSubprocess` is defined as transitive, because we may consider that if a process Z is a subprocess of Y, and Y is a subprocess of X we may conclude that Z is also a subprocess of X. Also, the relation existing between `Judicial_Decision` and `Decision_Making_Procedural_Role` formalized in the `owl:subPropertyOf` construct `isPassedBy` could be considered functional.

[28]Using a `TransitiveProperty` "one defines a property P to be a transitive property, this means that if a pair (x, y) is an instance of P, and the pair (y, z) is also instance of P, then we can infer the pair (x, z) is also an instance of P" (Dean et al. 2004). A `FunctionalProperty` "is a property that can have only one (unique) value y for each instance x, i.e. there cannot be two distinct values y1 and y2 such that the pairs (x, y1) and (x, y2) are both instances of this property" (Dean et al. 2004).

Table 5.7 `owl:subPropertyOf` (and their inverses) in OPJK

ObjectProperty	subPropertyOf	ObjectProperty
carriesOut isCarriedOut	subPropertyOf	takesOn isTakenOnBy
passesA isPassedBy	subPropertyOf	issuesA isIssuedBy
formalizesA isformalizedBy	subPropertyOf	expressesA isExpressedBy
executesA isExecutedBy	subPropertyOf	performsA isPerformedBy
realisesA isRealisedBy	subPropertyOf	performsA isPerformedBy
Domain	subPropertyOf	Range
Judicial_Decision_Organization	carriesOut	Decision_Maker_Procedural_Role
Decision_Maker_Procedural_Role	isCarriedOut	Judicial_Decision_Organization
Decision_Maker_Procedural_Role	passesA	Judicial_Decision
Judicial_Decision	isPassedBy	Decision_Maker_Procedural_Role
Procedural_Document	formalizesA	Procedural_Act
Procedural_Act	isformalizedBy	Procedural_Document
Civil_Procedural_Role	executesA	Civil_Macroprocess
Civil_Macroprocess	isExecutedBy	Civil_Procedural_Role
Criminal_Procedural_Role	realisesA	Criminal_Macroprocess
Criminal_Macroprocess	isRealisedBy	Criminal_Procedural_Role

5.3.2.2 Further Constructs

The formalization of multiple class instances,[29] multiple class subclasses,[30] instance equivalence (`owl:sameAs`), and class equivalence or even the use

[29]The main formalization difficulty was to offer solutions for the conceptualization of instances which may belong to more than one class at the same time or classes which share their instances because instances in OPJK are, in fact, linguistic units. The instance is the term itself, e.g., the term `auto_de_alejamiento` is the instance itself, not the particular auto issued by a specific judge for a concrete situation. As linguistic units, their meaning will be further defined by the class and the context of use (*semantic distance calculations*) of the term both in the questions asked at the IURISERVICE system and the questions stored within the system. The interest is thus placed in the search capabilities and enhancement possibilities offered by ontological engineering, nevertheless, if OPJK was to be used for further reasoning purposes, current OPJK instances might be formalized as classes, to allow further instantiation. Moreover, Smith et al. (2004) acknowledges the fact that in building ontologies, the distinction between a *class* and an *instance* or *individual* may be *blurred* because of the different levels of representation. "In certain contexts something that is obviously a class can itself be considered an instance of something else. For example, in the wine ontology we have the notion of a Grape, which is intended to denote the set of all grape varietals. `CabernetSauvingonGrape` is an example instance of this class, as it denotes the

of owl:intersectionOf offers solutions to several problems faced during the first domain conceptualization. On one hand, the formalization of multiple class subclasses or instances for some of the instances of Role could be useful in order to conceptualize those instances which belong to more than one subclass of Role. As mentioned, multiple class instantiation could offer solutions, for example, for the formalization of the instance judge [juez], which is an instance of both Professional_Role and Judicial_ Role, coroner [forense], which is an instance of both Professional_Role and Procedural_Role, and heir [heredero], which is an instance of Family_Role and Civil_Procedural_Role. Or the creation of tangled hierarchies with the formalization of multiple class subclasses such as Judicial_Professional_Role and Procedural_Professional_Role) could offer a different solution for the same conceptualization.

Moreover, multiple class instantiation, instance equivalence or class equivalence, and owl:intersectionOf construcs provide a useful solutions for modelling the relationships held between the Document, Process, and Act classes, for declaración, denuncia, and demanda are both instances of Document (Procedural_Document) and Act (Procedural_Act). Therefore, the previous initial class hierarchy was enriched with typical OWL DL axioms (Smith et al. 2004), together with multiple class instantiation and instance equivalences (owl:sameAs) constructs.

For example, in Sect. 5.3.1.3 we have already described the conceptual relations held between the Document, Process, and Act classes. For example, declaración, denuncia, and demanda are both instances of Document (Procedural_Document) and Act (Procedural_Act). Several formalization perspectives could be taken regarding this issue. For example, the formalization of instances which are declared to be a member of more than one class:

```
<Prueba rdf:about="#autopsia">
        <rdf:type rdf:resource="#Acto_Procesal"/>
</Prueba>

<Rol_Profesional rdf:about="#magistrado">
        <rdf:type rdf:resource="#Rol_Procesal_Juzgador"/>
</Rol_Profesional>
```

Different from the situation were an instance may be declared as member of more than one class, there are also few cases of instances which may be considered

actual grape varietal called Cabernet Sauvignon. However, CabernetSauvignonGrape could itself be considered a class, the set of all actual Cabernet Sauvignon grapes."

[30]As Rector et al. (2004) advocated "a policy in which primitives form a skeleton of pure trees" we will avoid the creation of tangled hierarchies based on the description of multiple owl:subclass classes. Furthermore, multiple class instantiation, the declaration of instances as members of more than one class could offer an initial modelling solution for most situations were an instance may be considered as being a member of two classes.

to be the same. In this case, instance equivalence has been used to formalize those instances that, although have different URI references, are, in fact, identical individuals.[31] In order to formalize these situations the `owl:sameAs` construct have been used, and 51 same individual axioms have been included.

Therefore, for conceptualization and computational reasons, two versions of the Ontology of Professional Judicial Knowledge were produced. OPJK version 1.0 formalized a class hierarchy (`rdfs:subClassOf`) with corresponding instances and properties, and OPJK version 2.0 added `owl:equivalentClass`[32] and `owl:disjointWith` axioms, multiple class instances, together with `owl:sameAs` constructs to the conceptualization formalized in OPJK 1.0.[33]

5.3.3 *Some Last Comments*

In this section we have presented the initial conceptualization and formalization of the Ontology of Professional Judicial Knowledge for the enhancement of the IURISERVICE search system with semantic capabilities. Two versions of OPJK have been produced in order to facilitate computation capabilities and to obtain significant technical evaluation results in the future.

OPJK version 1.0 includes 56 classes, 55 `rdfs:subClassOf` relations and 913 instances, together with a total of 25 `owl:ObjectProperty` axioms (10 `owl:subPropertyOf` and 12 `owl:inverseOf`), 1 transitive and 1 functional `owl:ObjectProperty`.

OPJK version 2.0 includes, as well, 2 `owl:equivalentClass` and 77 `owl:disjointWith` axioms, around 80 multiple class instantiation constructs, and, finally, 51 `owl:sameAs` axioms.[34]

---

[31]"The built-in OWL property `owl:sameAs` links an individual to an individual. Such an `owl:sameAs` statement indicates that two URI references actually refer to the same thing: the individuals have the same 'identity' (Dean et al. 2004)."

[32]"A class axiom may contain (multiple) `owl:equivalentClass` statements. `owl:equivalentClass` is a built-in property that links a class description to another class description. The meaning of such a class axiom is that the two class descriptions involved have the same class extension (i.e., both class extensions contain exactly the same set of individuals)" (Dean et al. 2004).

[33]The formalization of OPJK v.2.0 has required the use of version 4.0 (beta) of the Protégé editor.

[34]OPJK versions 1.0 and 2.0 have a DL expressivity of $\mathcal{ALHIF}+$ and $\mathcal{SHOIF}$, respectively. $\mathcal{AL}$, the Description Logic base language, "is the smallest DL language that can be detected by Pellet" (d'Aquin et al. 2007). $\mathcal{ALHIF}+$ includes class hierarchies, property hierarchies, inverse properties, and functional and transitive properties. $\mathcal{SHOIF}$ includes also the formalization of disjoint axioms, `owl:sameAs` instances, together with `owl:equivalentClass` and multiple class instantiation (although they do not add DL complexity themselves). While OWL Lite is based on inverse and functional properties and property hierarchies, transitive properties, nominals and qualified cardinality restrictions express OWL DL (Baader 2003). Therefore OPJK 1.0 is formalized in OWL Lite and OPJK 2.0 in OWL DL.

The construction process of the Ontology of Professional Judicial Knowledge and its formalization has been based on the terminology, information and knowledge contained in the corpus of questions. The judicial knowledge contained in these questions expresses practical problems faced by judges in their fist appointment during their on call court period. In order to conceptualize and formalize the terms extracted from the corpus, we have supported our modelling decisions on materials used by judges for their knowledge acquisition process: course syllabus, legislation, and doctrine. Moreover, several upper and core ontologies have been revised in order to obtain a set of top concepts for grouping and supporting middle-out conceptualization.

Nevertheless, there are several representational aspects that have not been resolved by this approach, and that ought to be taken into account for further working purposes and experiments:

1. **Object and datatype properties**. Although some properties have already been formalized, the OPJK ontology could be further extended with more object and datatype properties. As suggested by the legal expert's validation, some of the terms currently formalized as instances may, in fact, be conceptualized as datatype properties. Nevertheless, this extension would require changes or additions in the current conceptualization.

   As an example, `Decision_Maker_Procedural_Role` could take the values `competent` or `incompetent`. The OPJK ontology may benefit from this further modelization.[35] Finally, instances such as `minor`, `boy`, `girl`, etc. could benefit from the conceptualization of a concept `Age` and a related `owl:DatatypeProperty`. However, the evaluation first will demonstrate the use of the current `owl:ObjectProperty` formalization and the need for the representation of further complex properties.
2. **Adding even more complexity to OPJK**. More complexity could be added with the formalization of further class and property constraints (`owl:someValues From` and cardinality) or enumerated classes `owl:oneOf` (for example, `Court` and `Bench`). `owl:someValuesFrom` could be used to add property-based restrictions to those classes where for each instance of that class there exists at least one value for the property that fulfills it (for example: `Decision_Maker_Judicial_Role dicta some Judicial_Decision` or `Microprocess consistsOf some Procedural_Act`). Also, cardinality constraints could be set on the `owl:ObjectProperty hasMember`, and with the use of this restriction, we may express in the OPJK ontology the fact that `Court` ought to have a

[35]Nevertheless, the formalization of this datatype property would bring about, for example, a legal theoretical discussion regarding the adequate conceptualization of legal concept *competency*. Taking Rector et al. (2004) into account, this formalization could perhaps be solved creating a `Value_Type` class, with a sublcass `CompetencyVT`, which, in turn, had `Competent` and `Incompetent` as subclasses. This formalization would, in practice, probably provide a sufficient formalization, but would not include the discussion about the nature of this legal concept.

maxCardinality of "1" and a minCardinality of "1" (while for the concept Bench, a minCardinality ought to be set to "3").

3. **Granularity**. Some terms, currently conceptualized as instances, could be formalized as classes, improving the granularity of OPJK. For example, the class Contract (contrato_de_compraventa, contrato_de_leasing, etc.), or the classes Judge and Magistrate (subclasses of Decision_Maker_Procedural_Role). Moreover, Procedural_Act could be further conceptualized in, for example, Commencement_Act, Preparatory_Act, Investigation_Act, etc.
4. **Remodelling decisions**. Other modelling decisions could have been made regarding, especially, the conceptualization of Organization and Microprocess. Organization does not take into account traditional theoretical distinctions between the executive (government), legislative and judicial powers and their relation to the, so called, public administrations (e.g., the Administration of Justice). Microprocess are related to Macroprocesses by the involvesA and isInvolvedIn properties. However, their relation would benefit from the inclusion in the OPJK ontology of the formalization of mereological relations (e.g., part_Of, such as the Mereology module from the LKIF-Core Ontology (Breuker et al. 2007; Hoekstra et al. 2007),[36] or the Mereotopology conceptualization in SUMO.[37]
5. **Extracted and non included terms**. A list of nearly 100 relevant extracted terms (e.g., over the set frequency threshold of "4") have not yet been included in the current ontology, as these terms would require the conceptualization of new upper ontological classes, and may require the addition or modification of owl:ObjectProperty constructs. Some of these terms are: environment [medio ambiente], domicile [domicilio familiar], price [precio], vehicle [vehículo], drug [droga], province [provincia], flat [piso], capital of province [capital de provincia], etc.
6. **Conceptual interpretation and legal ontology development**. Some of the concepts that have not yet been included in the current versions of the OPJK ontology, could offer several interpretations and result in many modelling possibilities, according to legal theory analysis: competency (as mentioned above) [competencia], jurisdiction [jurisdicción], *mens rea* [culpa], obligation [obligación], emergency [urgencia], exception [excepción], impartiality [imparcialidad], just [justo], error [error], etc.
7. **Upper ontology alignment or mapping**. From the main OPJK concepts modelled it could be possible to "find[ing] relationships between entities belonging to different ontologies" (Euzenat et al. 2004) for the alignment of the OPJK ontology with SUMO, PROTON, DOLCE/CLO or LKIF-Core. As mentioned

[36] "The mereology module defines mereological concepts such as parts and wholes, and typical mereological relations such as part of, component of, containment, membership, etc." (Breuker et al. 2007).

[37] See, for example, http://virtual.cvut.cz/kifb/en/concepts/part.html, retrieved August 18, 2010.

in Sect. 5.2.3.1, most of these upper ontologies refer to the conceptual ideas of `Agent`, `Document`, `Role`, `Process`, and `Act`. LKIF-Core models the `Agent` `Document`, `Role` classes; DOLCE/CLO models the `Agent`, `Event`, and `Stative` classes; SUMO models the `Process` and `Agent` classes; and PROTON models the `Agent`, `Situation`, and `Event` classes. Their corresponding conceptualizations may differ and an in-depth analysis of those concepts could suggest alignment possibilities.[38]

In the next Sect. 5.4, different evaluations will be performed on the OPJK versions: consistency checking, requirements and competency questions revision, and expert evaluation.

5.4 Evaluation and Refinement

This section focuses on the evaluation and refinement activities of the Ontology of Professional Knowledge, conceptualized and formalized in Sect. 5.3. The results from these different evaluations will fuel the refinement of the Ontology of Professional Judicial Knowledge, described at the end of this chapter.

Evaluation is a recursive process; different evaluative activities may take place during the ontology modelling lifecycle; for example, validation activities already took place after the knowledge acquisition process. Nevertheless, evaluative activities are of special importance prior to implementation. Findings during evaluation may require ontology refinement, further knowledge acquisition, and, as a consequence, also further conceptualization. Evaluation is thus understood as a cyclic activity and ontology refinement, might require further evaluation (Sure 2003).

At this stage, ontology evaluation involves different types of evaluative activities: a purpose evaluation, and an ontological evaluation (verification and validation). As the Ontology of Professional Judicial Knowledge models conceptual expert professional legal knowledge, validation activities require the involvement of legal professionals or *experts* to validate the shareability of the conceptualization formalized under the established requirements.

"Evaluation of ontologies refers to the correct building of the content of the ontology, that is, ensuring that its definitions (a definition is written in natural language and in a formal language) correctly implement ontology requirements and competency questions or perform correctly in the real world" (Gómez-Pérez 2001).

Evaluation (validation, verification and assessment) and quality measurement of ontologies are currently an important topic of research, especially towards ontology

[38]References regarding ontology matching, aligning and mapping may be found in Kalfoglou and Schorlemmer (2005), de Bruijn et al. (2004) and Euzenat et al. (2004). Also, P. Shvaiko and J. Euzenat: Ontology Matching. http://www.ontologymatching.org, retrieved August 18, 2010), may be consulted for further reference.

assessment and comparison for reuse purposes.[39] Recently, the organization of the EON (Evaluation of Ontologies and Ontology-based tools) and OntoContent workshops series,[40] together with new evaluation and measurement proposals, demonstrate the relevance of this activity both for ontology development and comparison for reuse. OntoClean (Guarino and Welty 2002, 2004), OntoQA (Tartir et al. 2005), and the work of Gómez-Pérez (2001); Gómez-Pérez et al. (2003) and Vrandečić and Sure (2007) and Vrandečić and Gangemi (2006), are some examples of these proposals.

The set of methodologies described in Chap. 3 include, generally, an evaluation stage, although different proposals regarding its actual performance are offered. Grüninger and Fox (1995) proposed an ontology evaluation based on the competency questions set for the development of the ontology. Gómez-Pérez (2001) proposes a life-cycle evaluation, based on the implementation of the requirements, and the validation of definitions, consistency, completeness and conciseness. User assessment is envisaged as an evaluation activity towards ontology reuse. Sure (2003) proposes a technology-focused evaluation (formal language – syntax – and consistency), a user-focused evaluation (requirements specification document, including competency questions), and an ontology-focused evaluation (including verification and validation). CommonKADS loosely includes the participation of experts in several validation steps (e.g., communication model validation, user-interface development). Finally, UPON and OntoLearn include the participation of domain experts in the validation phase, and in the validation cycle of ontology learning and extraction (Velardi et al. 2005; Sclano and Velardi 2007), respectively. Nevertheless, most of the above-mentioned expert involvements within ontology validation are described rather vaguely.[41]

The evaluation of the Ontology of Professional Judicial Knowledge will include, then, a purpose-focused evaluation and an ontology-focused evaluation. The evaluation of the purpose will be based on the analysis of the specification of requirements and competency questions established in this chapter against the final OPJK ontology. The ontology-focused evaluation will comprehend also the verification of the correctness of an ontology, and the validation of the representation offered. Sure (2003) refers to them as the evaluation of "building the system right" and "building the right system", respectively. Language conformity, consistency checking will

---

[39]Some authors refer to this step as *ontology evaluation*, although the main purpose of this assessment is ontology reuse rather than the conceptual and quality improvement of a particular ontology (Gómez-Pérez et al. 2003; Hartmann et al. 2005; Brank et al. 2005). *ONTOMETRIC*, for example, is a tool that "allows the users to measure the suitability of the existent ontologies, regarding the requirements of their systems" (Lozano-Tello et al. 2003). See also Gangemi et al. (2006).

[40]Visit the 5th International EON Workshop at http://km.aifb.uni-karlsruhe.de/ws/eon2007, retrieved August 18, 2010, and the 6th OntoContent workshop at http://www.onthemove-conferences.org/index.php/ontocontent2010, retrieved August 18, 2010.

[41]Other methods for ontology evaluation may also be found in Hartmann et al. (2005) and Brank et al. (2005).

verify the correctness, whilst a legal expert's analysis of the taxonomy constructed (together with the revision of its natural language definitions, instantiation and class relations) will validate the representation offered of the knowledge contained corpus of questions used by the IURISERVICE search engine. This legal expert's validation plays a similar role to *usability inspection* for a software product, as introduced in Chap. 3. "Usability inspection methods is a generic name for a set of cost-effective ways of evaluating user interfaces to find usability problems" (Nielsen 1994b).

5.4.1 Purpose-Focused Evaluation

The overall design of the IURISERVICE system is based on the need for effectiveness to search the best possible matching stored question to the user's input question. Due to this requirement, the Ontology of Professional Judicial Knowledge required the representation of the relevant concepts related to the problems that take place during the on-call period. This knowledge regarding practical problems was acquired during the semi-structured interviews taken during the 2002 and 2004 surveys (mainly 2004). To fulfill this requirement, the knowledge acquisition, grouping and conceptualization stages have been based on a corpus of text containing the complete set of practical questions conforming this professional knowledge.

The methodological steps recommended by most ontology development methodologies (Noy and McGuinness 2001; Sure 2003; Gómez-Pérez et al. 2003) and knowledge acquisition techniques (Schreiber et al. 1999; Sure 2003; Milton 2007) have been carefully followed and accounted for: (1) preparatory phase (specification of ontology requirements), (2) development phase (knowledge acquisition – experts, documents, reuse –, conceptualization – classes, relations, properties, instances –, validation and formalization), and (3) evaluation phase.

Definitions have been provided for each formalized class and naming conventions have been followed (classes begin with capital letters, instances and relations begin with lower case – relations have no spaces between words and further words begin in capital letters –).

Finally, a set of competency questions was established in order to support modelling decisions and guide the knowledge extraction process. The following were the established competency questions:

- **Question 1.** Which are the problematic situations?
- **Question 2.** Which people are involved? What procedural roles are involved? What professionals are involved?
- **Question 3.** What type of organizations are involved?
- **Question 4.** Which documents and other information sources are involved?
- **Question 5.** Which judicial procedures are mentioned?
- **Question 6.** Which relevant relations exist between these situations, people, organizations, procedures and documents?

The aim of the system is not to offer a reasoned solution to the problem, only to guide the search towards the best possible stored answer in the repository (senior judges of the Spanish School of the Judiciary have provided answers to each of the question). Therefore, the competency questions guide the definition of the contents of the list of terms extracted that ought to be present in the Ontology of Professional Judicial Knowledge, and the description of the properties (relations) established between the derived concepts.

The classes and instances formalized under the `Act` class are the *problematic situations* included in Question 1. Question 2 is represented in the contents of the class `Role` and its subclasses `Judicial_Role` (`Procedural_Role`), `Family_Role`, and `Professional_Role`. Nevertheless, the people involved (from Question 2) is formalized together with the organizations involved (from Question 3) under the `Agent` class. The documents and information sources included in Competency Question 4 conform the contents of the `Document` class and the judicial procedures referred in Question 5 are included in the formalization of `Process`. Finally, `rdfs:subClassOf` and `owl:ObjectProperty` describe some of the main relations encountered between acts, roles, documents, agents and processes.

5.4.2 *Ontology-Focused Evaluation*

The ontology-focused evaluation is directed at both establishing the correctness of the construction of the ontology, and the validation of the knowledge that the OPJK ontology represents.

5.4.2.1 Language Conformity and Consistency Checking

The domain knowledge contained in the ontology is first represented in a lightweight manner, and complexity is added with the use of OWL as representation language in the following versions of the Ontology of Professional Judicial Knowledge. The use of the Protégé knowledge acquisition tool and ontology editor allows consistency checking through the Pellet reasoner,[42] and prevents the incorrect usage of the OWL language in the construction of ontologies (Sure 2003).

OPJK version 1.0, with $\mathcal{ALHIF}+$ expressivity (detected by Pellet in Protégé 4.0 beta), includes classes, relations (properties) and instances: a total of 56 classes, 913 instances, 25 `owl:ObjectProperty` axioms (1 transitive and 1 functional properties), and 10 `rdfs:subPropertyOf` and 12

[42]Pellet supports reasoning with OWL-DL ($\mathcal{SHOIN}(\mathcal{D})$ and $\mathcal{SROIQ}(\mathcal{D})$), and also performs concept satisfiability, classification and realisation. Pellet may be downloaded from: http://pellet.owldl.com

`owl:inverseOf` axioms. OPJK version 2.0, with $\mathcal{SHOIF}$ expressivity, includes 2 `owl:equivalent Class` axioms, 77 `owl:disjointWith` axioms, around 80 multiple class instantiation constructs, and 51 `owl:sameAs` axioms. All OPJK versions are found consistent by the Pellet reasoner used by the Protégé editor.[43]

5.4.2.2 Legal Expert's Validation

Debriefing sessions were set for different groups of legal experts (professionals and academics) in order to inform them of the purpose of the Ontology of Professional Judicial Knowledge, its requirements and the process of conceptualization followed, based on the corpus of questions provided by the judges in their first appointment during the surveys carried out during 2004. At the end of these debriefing sessions, the experts were required to answer a questionnaire evaluating different features of the OPJK ontology and, to provide suggestions for improvement.[44] Finally, the experts were also asked to answer a tailored version of the System Usability Scale (SUS) questionnaire.

A total of 9 legal experts (academics, professionals and researchers) working at or collaborating with the Faculty of Law of the Universitat Autònoma de Barcelona took part in the evaluation. From these legal experts, 7 had 6 or more years of working experience (3 experts had 10 years or more). Regarding the area of expertise, there were experts in substantive law – public and private law –(3), procedural law (2), and in the areas of legal theory, legal sociology or legal history (4). Finally, from the total of participants, 3 were legal professionals (2 lawyers and 1 judge), 3 were legal researchers (Law and Technology), and 3 were legal academics.

The initial questionnaire contained a total of 48 questions regarding several aspects of the conceptualization: concepts, definitions, instances, and relations. The evaluation of the complete ontology (56 classes, 913 instances, 24 `owl:Object Property` axioms (10 `rdfs:subPropertyOf` and 12 `owl:inverseOf`), 2 `owl: equivalentClass` axioms, 77 `owl:disjointWith` axioms, 80 multiple class instantiation constructs, 51 `owl:sameAs` axioms) was considered a lengthily and time consuming activity with respect to the limited access to experts'

[43]Nevertheless, Pellet version 1.5.2 used in Protégé version 3.3.1 ignores the assertion `owl:sameAs` as the use of this construct for individuals is acknowledged not to be supported by the reasoner. Pellet built-in version used by Protégé version 4.0 (beta) supports reasoning with `owl:sameAs` constructs.

[44]"The participants in the debriefing should include the evaluators, any observer used during the evaluation sessions, and representatives of the design team. The debriefing session would be conducted primarily in a brainstorming mode and would focus on discussions of possible redesigns to address the major usability problems and general problematic aspects of the design. A debriefing is also a good opportunity for discussing the positive aspects of the design, since heuristic evaluation does not otherwise address this important issue" (Nielsen 2005).

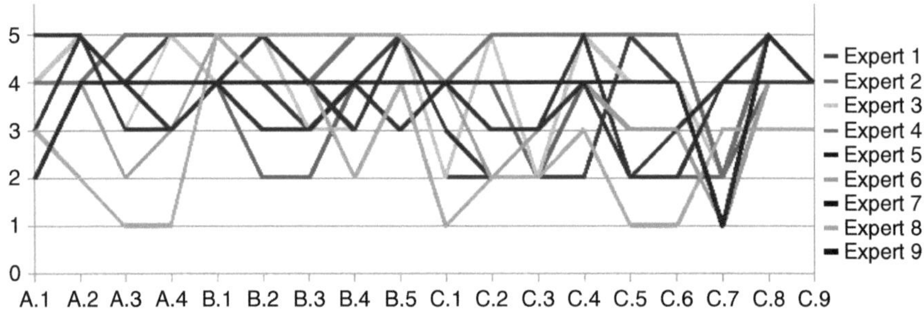

Fig. 5.14 Expert level of agreement regarding class hierarchy and concept definitions

time. Therefore, the evaluation was designed to include the validation of the complete taxonomical structure (56 classes), and the revision of 14 concept definitions, 49 instance classifications, 9 property relations, 4 multiple class instantiations, and 4 equivalent instance relations. The specific contents of the questions were chosen by their modelling complexity, based on the previous validation experience and discussions (Sect. 5.2.4.2), and conceptualization difficulties (Sect. 5.3). The experts expressed their opinion regarding their agreement with the conceptualization according to the following scale: 1 (highly disagree), 2 (disagree), 3 (indifferent), 4 (agree), and 5 (highly agree). Finally, the evaluation of the features was carried out on these different levels of the ontology separately, as suggested by Brank et al. (2005). The evaluation questionnaire may be consulted in Appendix C.

First, legal experts performed an evaluation of each of OPJK main classes and some of the natural language definitions provided for them: `Agent`, `Document`, `Act`, `Process`, and `Role`. The experts highly agreed or agreed with 27.78% and a 36.11%, respectively, to the taxonomical conceptualization of classes, which represented a 63.89% of general agreement. Nevertheless some high disagreement (5.56%) was also expressed.[45] Then, the experts were asked to evaluate the natural language definitions provided for some of the most characteristic concepts of the OPJK ontology with relation to the judicial setting: `Judicial_Decision_Organization`, `Procedural_Role`, `Legal_Document`, `Legal_Act`, `Criminal_Act` and `Procedural_Act`. Also, the definitions provided for `Macroprocess`, `Microprocess` and `Family_Role` were included to validate their acceptance. The following Fig. 5.14 shows the degree of agreement of each of the experts regarding all the questions included in the first section of the validation: class hierarchy conceptualization (A), and concept definitions (B and C).[46]

[45]There was no wide disagreement between the experts regarding a specific class, although the `Agent` class obtained a "high agree" from 8 out of 9 experts.

[46]B questions referred to the definitions of the main classes and C to definitions of some relevant subclasses.

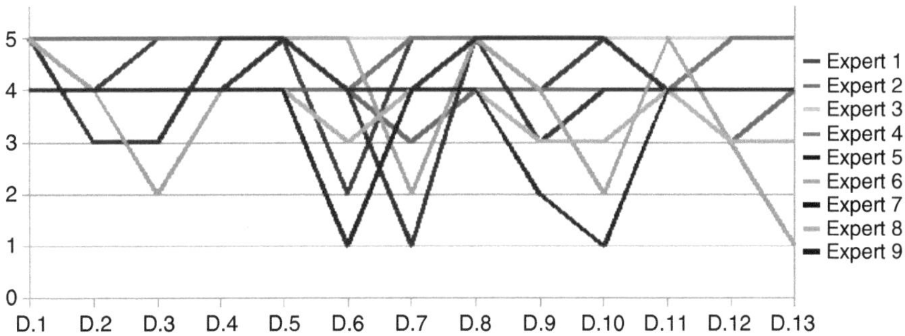

Fig. 5.15 Expert level of agreement regarding instantiation

Judicial_Organization (C1), Family_Role (C3), Microprocess (C6), and Legal_Act (C7), were the definitions most disagreed upon. Finally, the overall agreement of the experts with the questions included in this first section (class definitions and conceptualization) was of 62.96%, including "high agree" and "agree"(while high disagreement represented a 4.32%).

The next section of the evaluation questionnaire included 13 questions related to the classification of instances. For example, the experts were asked about their agreement regarding the classification of donation and purchase as instances of Legal_Act, or plaintiff, defendant, complainant as instances of Criminal_Procedural_Role. The overall level of agreement on the classification of instances, taking into account results from both "high agree" and "agree" options, was of the 82.9%. Nevertheless, as Fig. 5.15 below expresses, most experts "disagree" and "highly disagree" with the instantiation of judicial_office as Judicial_Government_Organization (D6), and of town_hall and social_services as Local_Organization (D7). Also the instantiation examples provided for class Procedural_Document (D9), and class Public_Legal_Document (D10) present a relevant level of disagreement between the experts.

In the following section of the evaluation questionnaire, the experts were required to evaluate several relations established between the conceptualized classes, and to express their degree of agreement with several owl:Object_Property and rdfs:subPropertyOf constructs and with a set of multiple class instantiation and owl:sameAs constructs. A total of 75.82% of general agreement (35.95% "highly agree" and 39.87% "agree") was obtained. Regarding the set of Object_Property and subPropertyOf constructs, (e.g. Agent takesOn Role, Act occursIn Process, Group hasMember Person, Procedural_ Document formalizes Procedural_Act, and DecisionMaker_Judicial_Role performs Decision_Making_Procedural_Role), Group hasMember Person (E4) offered some of the lowest scores (see Fig. 5.16). The last set of questions of the evaluation questionnaire comprehended the validation of multiple class

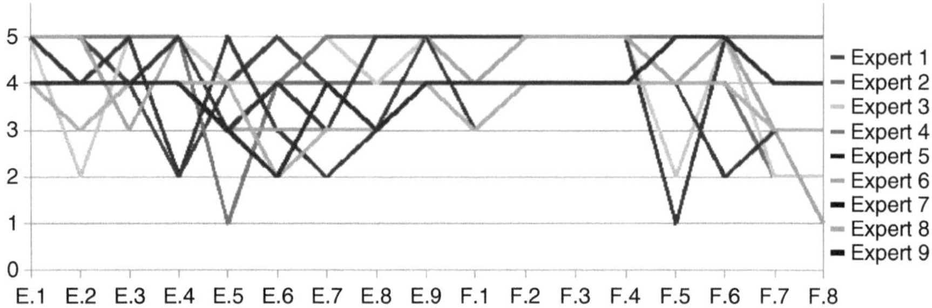

Fig. 5.16 Expert level of agreement regarding properties and other constructs

Table 5.8 Evaluation results

	Groups of questions						
Levels	A	B	C	D	E	F	Totals
High agreement	27.78%	35.56%	17.28%	38.46%	34.57%	37.50%	32.41%
Agreement	36.11%	42.22%	37.04%	44.44%	40.74%	38.89%	40.51%
Indifferent	19.44%	15.56%	14.81%	9.40%	16.05%	9.72%	13.19%
Disagreement	11.11%	6.67%	24.69%	4.27%	7.41%	11.11%	10.65%
High disagreement	5.56%	0.00%	6.17%	3.42%	1.23%	2.78%	3.24%
Totals	100.00%	100.00%	100.00%	100.00%	100.00%	100.00%	100.00%

instantiation and `owl:sameAs` constructs. `medida_de_proteccion sameAs auto_de_proteccion` (F7) and `medida_de_alejamiento sameAs auto_de_alejamiento` (F8) presented a significant level of disagreement.[47]

In total, the experts were asked to validate 48 items. Their overall levels of agreement with the general conceptualization offered (class, subclass, instantiation, properties, etc.) was of 72.92% (high agreement 32.41% and agreement 40.51%) in total. Table 5.8 above includes all the specific results.

Finally, during the debriefing sessions the experts made several relevant suggestions, generally related to the taxonomical classifications and concept definitions showing the lowest scores, for the improvement of the OPJK ontology. In general, the taxonomical structure of `Process` and `Act` was found rather complex. Also, although the class structure for `Organization` and `Role` was considered correct, minor revisions could provide major improvement. Moreover, slight changes in labels and definitions could offer clarity and foster expert understanding and agreement. These suggestions were taken into account towards OPJK refinement (see Casellas (2008) for specific details).

[47] The experts considered that the `sameAs` construct confused form with content, in this particular case.

5.4.2.3 Usability Questionnaire: Shareability

As mentioned in Chap. 3 and in Sect. 5.4 within this chapter, experimentally we will make use of a usability questionnaire in order to evaluate the understanding and agreement felt by the legal experts regarding the Ontology of Professional Judicial Knowledge as a whole. At the end of the above expert validation, the experts were asked to respond the System Usability Scale.

The System Usability Scale, developed by (Brooke 1996), is a ten-item Likert scale (stating the degree of agreement or disagreement), elaborated initially to evaluate system's usability. The use of this questionnaire is recommended by the UsabilityNet project website as "[i]t is very robust and has been extensively used and adapted. Of all the public domain questionnaires, this is the most strongly recommended." Also, in a comparison between different questionnaires to assess usability (regarding websites) it was found that "one of the simplest questionnaires studied, [SUS], yielded among the most reliable results across sample sizes."

The scale has here been translated into Spanish and tailored to evaluate the understanding and sharedness of the contents of the ontology, regarding its purpose.[48] The original sense of the questions have been maintained as far as the tailoring allowed. For example, question 3: "I found the system was easy to use" has been modified as "I found the ontology easy to understand."

The overall results of the SUS questionnaire were of the 69.44% in total (specific results may be found in Fig. 5.17), which may suggest a high level of agreement with the general OPJK conceptualization. Furthermore, a comparison between the global results within the previous validation and the SUS results shows a high degree of similarity (72.92% and 69.44%, respectively). This may also suggest that the use of a well-designed *shareability* questionnaire, based on the idea of usability questionnaires for software products, could offer support towards the establishment of quality measures in expert-based ontology evaluation.

5.4.2.4 Comparative Evaluation: Additional Metrics

As mentioned in the introduction to this section there are several approaches to the establishment of metrics towards a comparative ontology evaluation for reuse purposes. Moreover, research carried out to identify the usage of semantic documents and ontologies in the current Web, also offers metrics for comparison. Although these approaches mainly require similar purpose existing ontologies for the comparison, some of these metrics may offer additional information regarding the Ontology of Professional Judicial Knowledge (OPJK).

For example, d'Aquin et al. (2007) offered an analysis of almost 25,500 ontologies and semantic documents, and compared the level of expressiveness of

---

[48]The method has been widely used and evaluated and tailored for other purposes, e.g., the evaluation of websites (see Tullis and Stetson (2004)).

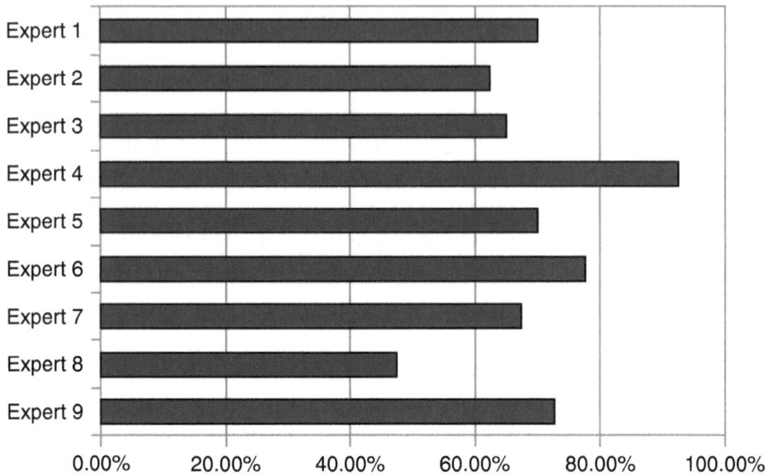

Fig. 5.17 Results from the SUS questionnaire

the language used in these ontologies and the richness of their representation, taking into account the density of properties, instances and classes.[49] $\mathscr{AL}$ and $\mathscr{AL}(\mathscr{D})$ were found to conform the expressivity of 94% of the ontologies and semantic documents analysed. Moreover, d'Aquin et al. (2007) discovered that "transitive and functional properties, which are features of OWL Lite, are rarely used". From the analysis of all entities (classes, properties, and individuals) present in the documents extracted, the authors calculated the total average **P-density** (number of properties per class), **H-density** (number of super-classes per class), and **I-density** (number of instances per class). Table 5.9 compares those results with the results obtained with the Ontology of Professional Judicial Knowledge and shows that OPJK versions are, in general, above average regarding their density.[50]

Also OntoQA offers a set of metrics in order to evaluate relationship, attribute, class and inheritance richness, and average population of instances and class importance, within others. From all the metrics proposed, class importance or instance distribution may offer useful information for ontology refinement to "get a consistent coverage of all classes in the schema" (Tartir et al. 2005).[51]

[49]For more data see also M. d'Aquin, The use of DL expressivity in Semantic Web Documents, http://watson.kmi.open.ac.uk/blog/2007/10/19/1192796480480.html, retrieved August 18, 2010. For other approaches, see also (Wang et al. 2006; Ding and Finin 2006).

[50]d'Aquin et al. (2007) describes that "a class is considered to possess a property if it is declared as the domain of this property". Therefore we will consider that all property related axioms are properties (b) and only those counting as `ObjectPropery` domain axioms (as counted by Protégé 4.0) are considered to be domain relations (d).

[51]"Formally, the importance (*Imp*) of a class *Ci* is defined as the number of instances that belong to the subtree rooted at *Ci* in the KB (*Ci*(*I*)) compared to the total of instances in the KB (*I*)" (Tartir et al. 2005).

Table 5.9 Density measures comparison with results from d'Aquin et al. (2007)

Measures	Value		
		OPJK	
	d'Aquin et al. (2007)	OPJK v1.0	OPJK v2.0
Total number of classes (a)	161,264	56	56
Total number of properties (b)	76,350	73	73
Total number of individuals (c)	984,526	913	913
Total number of domain relations (d)	32,572	25	25
Total number of sub-class relations (e)	106,729	55	55
Total number of instance relations (f)	1,114,795	913	1051
Average **P-density** (d/a)	**0.20**	**0.44**	**0.44**
Average **H-density** (e/a)	**0.66**	**0.98**	**0.98**
Average **I-density** (f/a)	**6.90**	**16.30**	**18.76**

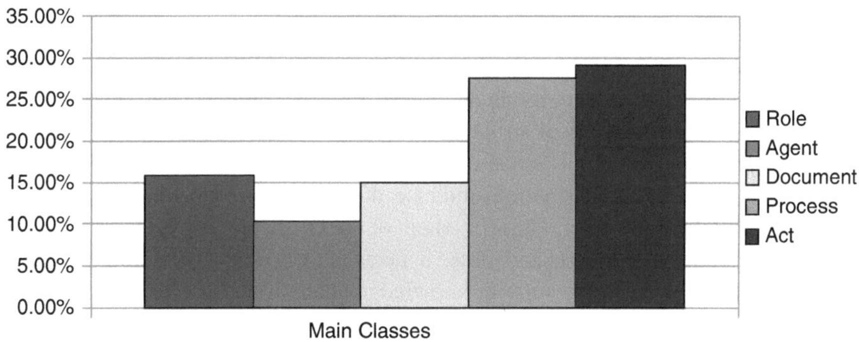

Fig. 5.18 Instance distribution in OPJK

Figure 5.18 contains OPJK (v1.0) instance distribution. `Process` and `Act` contain nearly 60% of the total of instances. These results show the importance of these two conceptual classes within the judicial setting and also suggest the need to revise the granularity and instantiation of the class `Document`.

Finally, it may also be discovered that 8 of the 56 classes contain nearly 50% of the total number of instances (see Fig. 5.19 below), and that 21 classes have under 1% of instances (of the total of classes which have instances). The classes which contain nearly 50% of the total number of instances are `Judicial_Act`, `Criminal_Procedural_Role`, `Interlocutory_Order`, `Enforcement_Proceeding`, `Professional_Role`, `Criminal_Act`, `Civil_Macroprocess`, and `Procedural_Act`. This may suggest that these classes ought to be further divided or that relevant subclasses might be available.

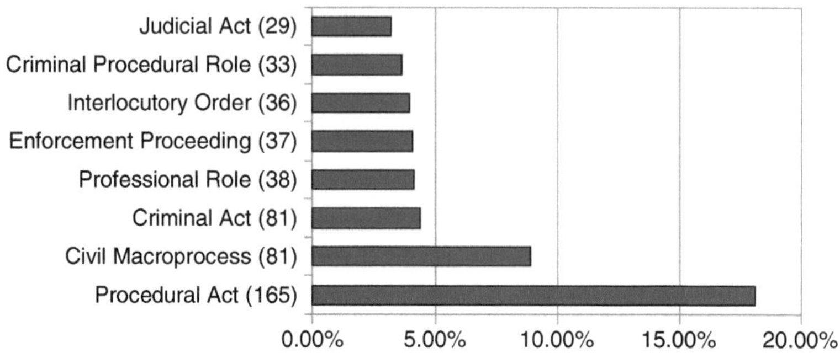

Fig. 5.19 OPJK classes with the most number of instances (over 3%)

5.4.3 *Refinement*

The results obtained from the expert evaluation of the ontology involve the refinement of several aspects of the Ontology of Professional Judicial Knowledge. As mentioned, the experts made several relevant suggestions regarding the complexity of the taxonomical structure of `Process` and `Act`, the clarification of the `Organization` and `Role` classes, within others. Moreover, the metrics obtained from instance distribution, indicate that there is room for improvement regarding OPJK's granularity. The refinement of the OPJK ontology requires further knowledge acquisition effort, and thus, it takes into account the documentation established in Sect. 5.2.2, to support knowledge acquisition based on the expert's suggestions.

5.4.3.1 Class Refinement

Class Refinement includes the addition of classes, class relabeling and definition modification. `Macroprocess` and `Microprocess` ought to be relabelled and redefined. Moreover their subclasses should be revised to offer a fine-grained structure. For example, Montero-Aroca et al. (2005a, 2008) distinguishes between civil or criminal processes, and declarative, enforcement or precautionary processes. Moreover, the author also distinguishes between ordinary and especial processes. According to Montero-Aroca et al. (2008) a process may be either civil or criminal, ordinary or especial and declarative, enforcement or precautionary, with respect to the legal area involved, the content or object of the process and a certain moment in time. Cortés-Domínguez and Moreno-Catena (2008b) distinguish, within civil processes, between declarative processes (ordinary processes – ordinary and verbal procedures – and especial processes (Cortés-Domínguez and Moreno-Catena 2008a)), precautionary processes, and enforcement proceedings. In addition, Ramos-Méndez (1997a), for example, offers a classification of the civil procedure within several stages such as allegations [alegaciones], evidence [prueba], conclusion [conclusión], and appeal [recursos]. Finally, Moreno-Catena and Cortés-Domínguez (2008) distinguishes within the declarative stage of the criminal process [Instrucción], intermediate stage [fase intermedia], and oral trial [juicio oral] (which includes evidence [prueba]).[52]

The `Act` class would benefit from an initial distinction between `Fact` and `Legal_Act`, which in turn demands a subclass conceptualization. Also a fine-grained `Act` class is necessary (see in Fig. 5.20). Montero-Aroca et al. (2005a, 2008) organizes procedural acts within party acts, jurisdictional organization acts, including judicial decisions ([providencias], [autos], [sentencias], [resoluciones orales]), clerck acts ([diligencias], [decretos]) and judicial communications (with the parties and with other judicial organizations). Moreover, relevant handbooks (Moreno-Catena and Cortés-Domínguez 2008; Montero-Aroca et al. 2005b, 2007) not only include references to the roles which perform the acts, but include references to the acts by the function or the purpose they accomplish or the stage where they are performed, such as the above-mentioned communication acts, but also the investigation acts, the allegation acts, evidence acts, enforcement acts, etc.[53]

`Agent` could be clarified introducing the `Legal_Person`, `Natural_Person` and `Public_Administration` classes (see Fig. 5.21). As it is also suggested by LRI-Core/OCN.NL. Although the distinction was not initially included, from the comments of the experts it could be noticed that such a distinction could offer clarity and granularity to the `Agent` class. Further, the Spanish Civil Code (art. 35) organizes a taxonomy of legal persons [personas jurídicas], as oposed to natural persons [personas físicas]. Public corporations, associations and foundations are understood as legal persons. Public corporations or legal public persons are somehow related to the concept of Public Administration. Moreover, associations

[52]Therefore, `Precautionary_Proceeding` and `Enforcement_Proceeding` could be either conceptualized as a `Judicial_Process` or as a `Procedural_Stage` at the same time, depending on the perspective taken. Both options are grounded on relevant literature in the area, however, and taking into account the previous modifications suffered by `Legal_Act` and `Procedural_Role`, modifying also the `Precautionary_Proceeding`, and `Enforcement_Proceeding` classes would now result in a more coherent taxonomical approach. In the new formalization provided, `Judicial_Process` has three subclasses: `Declarative_Process`, `Precautionary_Proceeding`, and `Enforcement_Proceeding`. This distinction adds granularity to the OPJK ontology, without leaving aside the main distinction between civil and criminal processes (`Civil_Process` and `Criminal_Process` are formalized as subclasses of `Declarative_Process`).

[53]Therefore `Procedural_Act` could have a set of subclasses based on the roles performing the acts: `Jurisdictional_Act`, `Party_Act`, etc. Or a set of subclasses based on the corresponding `Microprocess`: `Communication_Act`, `Investigation_Act`, `Allegation_Act`, `Enforcement_Act`, `Precautionary_Act`, etc. Both classifications may be integrated, although it is complex to establish sharp distinctions between them, and it would require further multiple class instantiation or the formalization of more `equivalentTo`. The final implemented modification of the `Role` class of the OPJK ontology takes into account the subclassification of acts regarding their subject (their role).

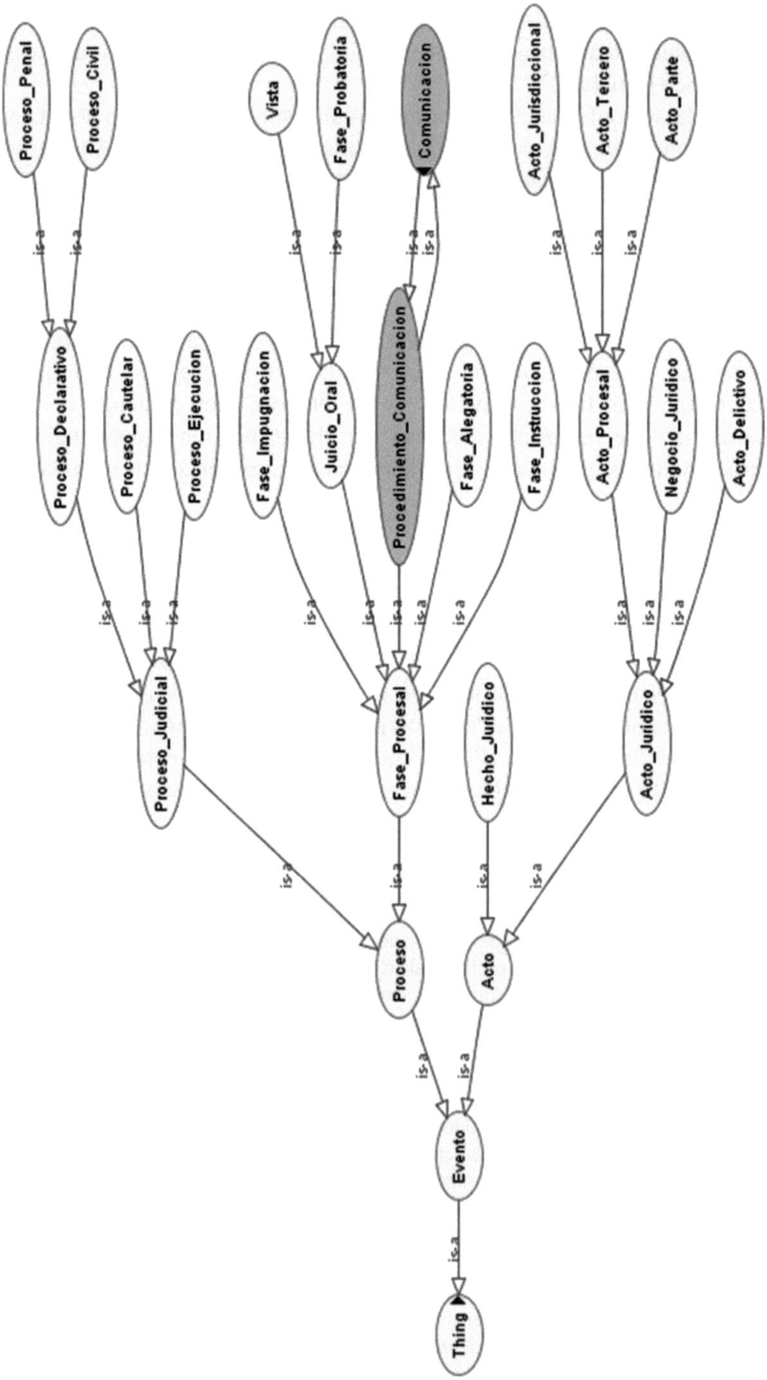

Fig. 5.20 Refined Act and Process classes

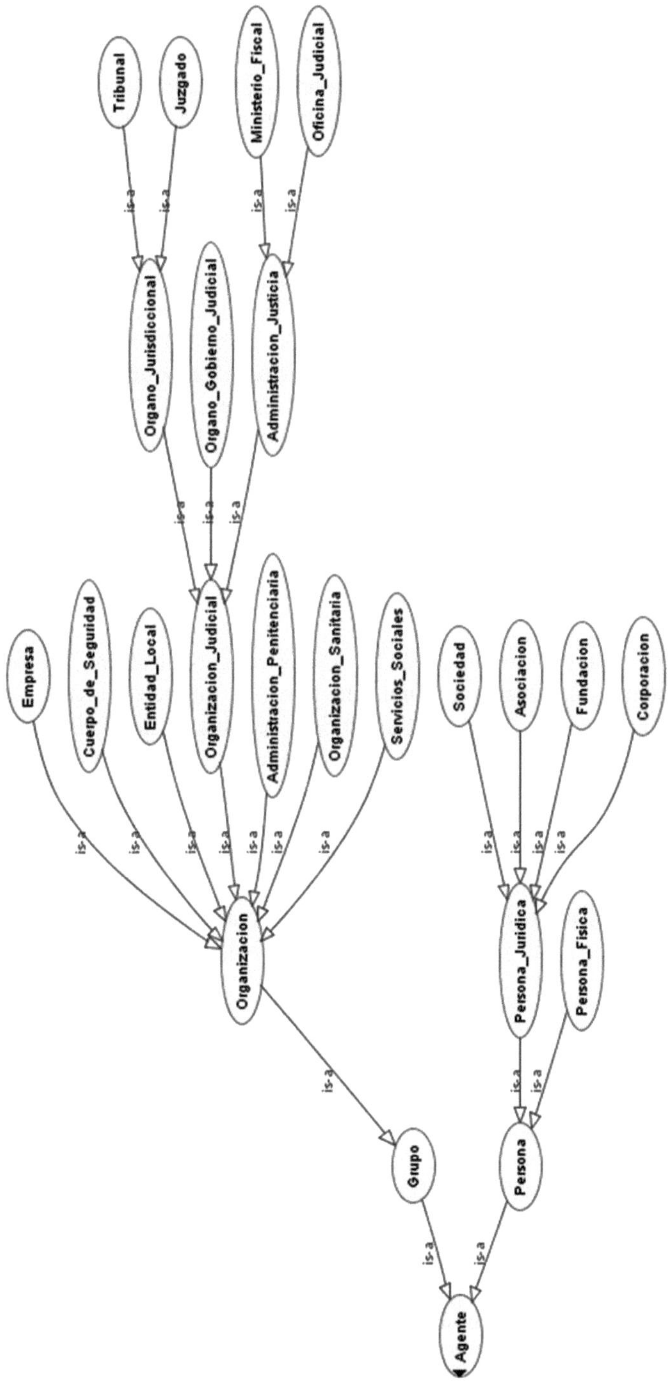

Fig. 5.21 Refined Agent class

may have a public or a private interest, the latter being generally referred to as companies [sociedades], which may be either civil or commercial.[54]

With regards to the `Role` class relabeling and clarification between the classes `Judicial_Role` and `Procedural_Role` are required. Finally, some improvement within `Document` definition and relabeling is recommended (see Fig. 5.22).

5.4.3.2 Property Refinement

Once the classes have been revised, `Object_Property` relations and `rdfs:subPropertyOf` constructs have to be modified or added accordingly. For example, changes in the classes `Civil_Procedural_Role`, `Criminal_Procedural_Role`, and `Procedural_Document` require the modification of their relationships with other classes. All prior relations are maintained, and several others are added, due to the addition of new classes and new relational possibilities. The following table (Table 5.10) shows all changes incorporated in the Ontology of Professional Judicial Knowledge.

5.4.3.3 Instance Refinement

Due to several changes at the class level, several modifications are required regarding instance classification. First, the creation of new classes, such as `Natural_Person` and `Social_Services`, causes a new distribution of instances mainly from parent classes. Also, instances belonging to classes which have disappeared are redistributed. Second, instances from the `Appeal` class, which was `equivalentTo Appeal_Process` are formalized as being members of more than one class. Moreover, the creation of `Staff_Role` favours a more than one class membership for instances of the `Professional_Role`. Finally, some classes are instantiated and some instances are conceptualized as classes (e.g., `Habeas_Corpus`, `Association`, etc.). The list below includes a brief account of the changes:

- 7 instances moved from `Person` to `Natural_Person`.
- 4 instances moved from `Organization` to `Ministerio_Fiscal`.
- 1 instance moved from `Organization` to `Oficina_Judicial`.
- 3 instances moved from `Local_Administration` to `Social_Services`.
- 26 instances moved from `Event` to `Legal_Fact`.
- 10 instances moved from `Jurisdictional_Role` to `Judge`.

[54]"Artículo 35 Código Civil. Son personas jurídicas: (1) Las corporaciones, asociaciones y fundaciones de interés público reconocidas por la Ley. Su personalidad empieza desde el instante mismo en que, con arreglo a derecho, hubiesen quedado válidamente constituidas. (2) Las asociaciones de interés particular, sean civiles, mercantiles o industriales, a las que la ley conceda personalidad propia, independiente de la de cada uno de los asociados."

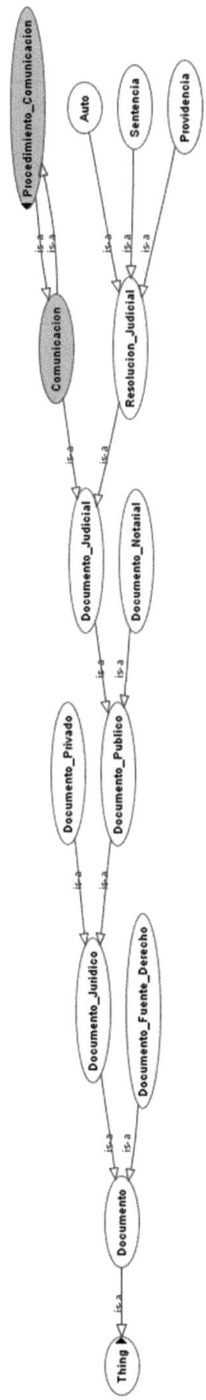

Fig. 5.22 Refined Document class

Table 5.10 Modifications in owl:ObjectProperty and rdfs:subPropertyOf constructs

Domain	ObjectProperty	Range	Modification type
Legal_Person	isOfType	Organization	Added
Organization	hasPersonality	Legal_Person	Added
Judicial_Process	consistsOf	Procedural_Stage	Added
Procedural_Stage	happensIn	Judicial_Process	Added
Domain	**subPropertyOf**	**Range**	**Modification type**
Judicial_Decision_Organization	carriesOut	Jurisdictional_Role	Modified
Jurisdictional_Role	isCarriedOut	Judicial_Decision_Organization	Modified
Jurisdictional_Role	passesA	Judicial_Decision	Modified
Judicial_Decision	isPassedBy	Jurisdictional_Role	Modified
Judicial_Role	executesA	Judicial_Process	Modified
Judicial_Process	isExecutedBy	Judicial_Role	Modified
Judicial_Role	realisesA	Procedural_Stage	Modified
Procedural_Stage	isRealisedBy	Judicial_Role	Modified
Legal_Document	formalizesA	Legal_Act	Modified
Legal_Act	isformalizedBy	Legal_Document	Modified
Ministerio_Fiscal	adoptsA	Procedural_Role	Added
Procedural_Role	isAdoptedBy	Ministerio_Fiscal	Added
Jurisdictional_Role	executesA	Jurisdictional_Act	Added
Jurisdictional_Act	isExecutedBy	Jurisdictional_Role	Added

- 2 instances moved from Jurisdictional_Role to Magistrate.
- 13 instances moved from Procedural_Role to Staff_Role (multiple class instances of also Professional_Role.
- From Judicial_Role, 23 instances have been moved to Procedural_Role, 44 instances have been moved to Party_Role, 4 instances have been moved to Third_Party_Role, and 3 instances have been moved to Postulation_Role.
- 1 instances moved from Procedural_Stage to Allegation_Stage.
- From Process, 13 instances have been moved to Judicial_Process, 69 instances have been moved to Civil_Process, 16 instances have been moved to Criminal_Process, 24 instances have been moved to Precautionary_Process, and 37 instances have been moved to Enforcement_Proceeding.
- 26 instances moved from Acto to Legal_Fact.
- 8 instances of Private_Document are now also instances of Legal_Transaction.

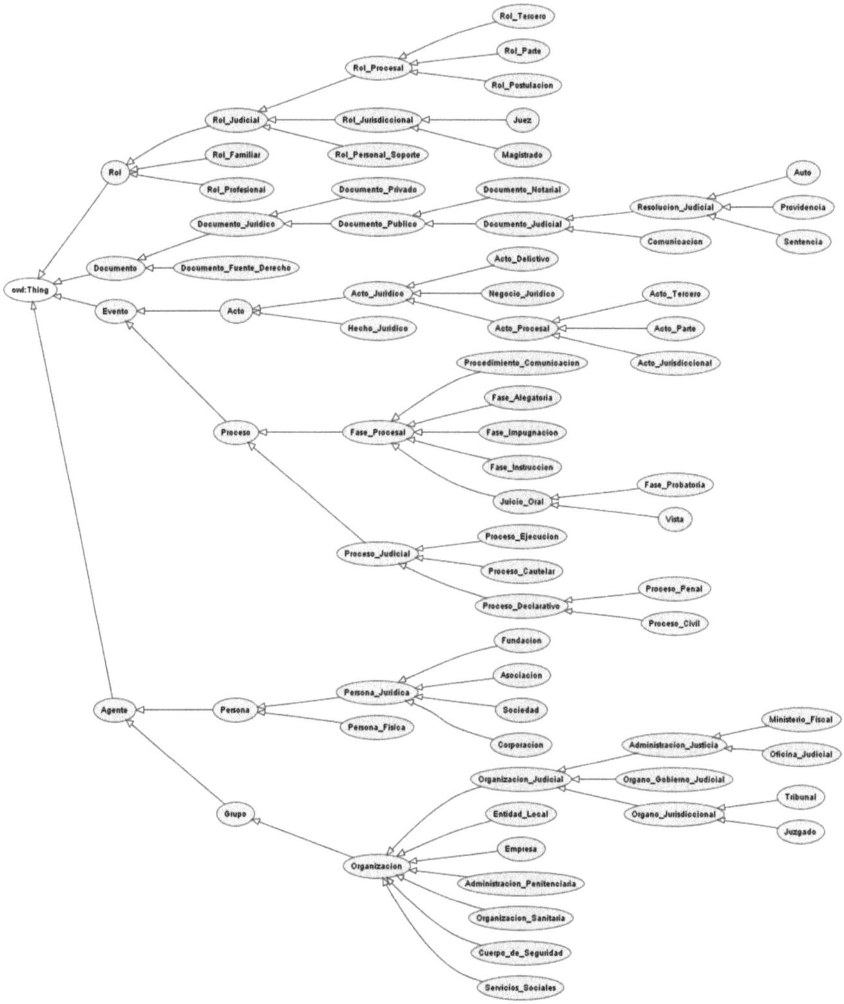

Fig. 5.23 OPJK v1.1 in Protégé

- From Procedural_Act, 53 instances have been moved to Party_Act, 26 instances have been moved to Third_Party_Act, 45 instances have been moved to Jurisdictional_Act, and 36 instances have been moved to Legal_Transaction (Fig. 5.23).

5.4.4 Discussion: A Socio-Legal Approach

This chapter offered the description of all the methodological steps towards the development of the Ontology of Professional Judicial Knowledge. From the specification of requirements and the knowledge acquisition phase, towards the conceptualization and formalization of the OPJK concepts and relations. In particular, it also described in detailed the evaluation activities of the OPJK ontology and its refinement. The OPJK ontology has been developed in collaboration with the Spanish School of the Judicary to enhance search and retrieval capabilities of a Web-based frequently- asked-question system (IURISERVICE) containing a repository of practical knowledge for Spanish judges in their first appointment. The knowledge was elicited mainly from an ethnographic survey in Spanish First Instance Courts, and followed a middle-out approach to ontology development.

Towards evaluation, as seen in Sect. 5.4, different purpose and ontological evaluative tasks have been carried out at this stage of the ontology development. Favourable results were obtained by the analysis of the specification of requirements and competency questions, language conformity, and consistency checking. However, special interest has been placed in the performance of a legal expert validation.

This expert validation included both a specific validation of OPJK classes, subclass relationships, properties and instances and a more general and experimental validation based on a usability questionnaire. The results of these validations suggested that there was room for improvement regarding class conceptualization which could offer more granularity and foster understanding and shareability amongst experts. The total results from both questionnaires showed a high degree of similarity (72.92% and 69.44%, respectively), which may suggest that the use of a well-designed *shareability* questionnaire, based on the idea of usability questionnaires for software products, could offer support towards expert-based ontology evaluation.

With the evaluation results and the expert's suggestions the Ontology of Professional Judicial Knowledge was refined, several classes were added or modified (e.g., relabelled), some instances were redistributed, properties and dijoint axioms were modified or added. At the moment, OPJK version 2.1 (2.0 refined) includes a total of 74 classes and 912 instances, 31 `owl:ObjectProperty` axioms (14 `rdfs:subPropertyOf`, 15 `owl:inverseOf`, 1 transitive and 1 functional `owl:ObjectProperty`). This ontology also includes (as distinct from OPJK v 1.1) 1 `owl:equivalentClass` axiom, 75 `owl:disjointWith` axioms, around 100 multiple class instantiation constructs, and 53 `owl:sameAs` axioms.[55]

The current refined versions of the ontology are still consistent, and the metrics regarding P-density, H-density and I-density still show that OPJK versions may be considered above average, if compared with the results obtained by the analysis of d'Aquin et al. (2007). Nevertheless, the results from the refined versions of the ontology are slightly lower than the previous results largely due to an increment in the number of classes (Table 5.11).

Moreover, a further evaluation of instance distribution metrics shows the improvement of the distribution regarding the previous analysis (see Fig. 5.19),

[55]OPJK versions 1.1 and 2.1 have still a DL expressivity of $\mathcal{ALHIF}+$ and $\mathcal{SHOIF}$, respectively,as detected by Pellet in Protégé 4.0.

Table 5.11 Density measures comparison with previous results from Table 5.9

Measures	Value		
		OPJK	
	d'Aquin et al. (2007)	OPJK v2.0	OPJK v2.1 (ref.)
Total number of classes (a)	161,264	56	74
Total number of properties (b)	76,350	73	93
Total number of individuals (c)	984,526	913	912
Total number of domain relations (d)	32,572	25	31
Total number of sub-class relations (e)	106,729	55	73
Total number of instance relations (f)	1,114,795	1051	1065
Average **P-density** (d/a)	**0.20**	**0.44**	**0.42**
Average **H-density** (e/a)	**0.66**	**0.98**	**0.98**
Average **I-density** (f/a)	**6.90**	**18.75**	**14.40**

where 8 out of 56 classes contained nearly 50% of the total number of instances, and that the `Procedural_Act` class contained around the 18% of the total of instances of OPJK.[56] With the refinement of the OPJK ontology the distribution of instances is improved, especially within the `Procedural_Act` class, now with a total of 6.14% of the total of instances. Also, for example, 15 classes, instead of 12, reach the threshold of 2%. See Table 5.12 below for an overview of instance distribution in OPJK after refinement. Nevertheless, the distribution among the main classes remains very similar (`Role` 15.79%, `Agent` 10.30%, `Document` 11.95%, `Process` 29.17%, and `Act` 29.93%). OPJK version 2.1 may be found in Appendix D.

The OPJK ontology has been at this stage evaluated against its purpose and its content (language conformity, consistency and expert evaluation) obtaining favourable results. Nevertheless, there are several issues that ought to be taken into account regarding conceptualization limitations and further evaluation. The decisions and difficulties encountered during the conceptualization, formalization and refinement processes show several problematic situations in the modelization of the legal domain for the construction of the Ontology of Professional Judicial Knowledge. This main difficulties encountered are: (a) the integration of a text-based approach for ontology construction with legal dogmatics or/and legal theory, (b) compatibility issues between different ontological views regarding the structure of the Law for the conceptualization of the Spanish judicial domain, and (c) the effects of a purpose-based perspective in conceptualization decision-making.

As it is described in Sect. 5.2.3, the knowledge acquisition process for the construction of the Ontology of Professional Judicial Knowledge is based on the extraction of terms from a corpus of questions regarding practical on-call problems, formulated by Spanish judges in their first appointment during semi-structured

[56]This calculation is performed on OPJK version 1.1 (1.0 refined), which does not contain multiple class instantiations.

Table 5.12 Instance distribution in OPJK after refinement

Class	%	Class	%
Group	0.66%	**Event**	2.85%
Organization	1.00%	**Criminal Act**	4.39%
Penitentiary	0.55%	**Procedural Act**	6.14%
Security Forces	0.88%	**Jurisdictional Act**	5.92%
Enterprise	0.66%	**Party Act**	5.81%
Local Entity	0.33%	Third Party Act	1.75%
Judicial Organization	0.22%	**Legal Transaction**	3.10%
Public Prosecutor	0.44%	**Legal Fact**	2.85%
Judicial Office	0.11%	Process	1.10%
Judicial Governing Body	0.88%	Procedural Stage	0.88%
Jurisdictional Organization	0.10%	Allegation Stage	1.53%
Court	1.86%	Appeal Process	1.86%
Bench	0.55%	**Investigation Process**	2.30%
Health Care Organization	0.77%	Oral Trial	0.44%
Social Services	0.33%	**Evidence Stage**	2.52%
Natural Person	0.76%	Hearing	0.33%
Association	0.11%	Judicial Process	0.88%
Company	0.11%	**Precautionary Process**	2.63%
Document	1.00%	Declarative Process	1.42%
Legal Source Document	1.54%	**Civil Process**	7.56%
Legal Document	0.44%	Criminal Process	1.75%
Private Document	1.10%	**Enforcement Proceeding**	3.95%
Public Document	0.44%	Role	1.64%
Judicial Document	1.43%	Judicial Role	0.88%
Communication	1.21%	Family Role	1.53%
Judicial Decision	0.77%	Procedural Role	1.53%
Interlocutory	2.63%	**Party Role**	4.82%
Judgment	1.10%	Third Party Role	0.33%
Notary Document	0.33%	**Professional Role**	5.00%

interviews. The modelization task presented in this and the previous chapters offers the possibility to discuss the advantages and drawbacks of taking a sociological modelization perspective based on the conceptualization of data obtained from ethnographic fieldwork (bottom-up), and the complexity of establishing clear connections with legal dogmatics or legal theory approaches based on positivist views of the Law (top-down).

The elicitation of conceptual knowledge from this textual corpus of questions is central for the modelization of OPJK. Due to extensive lists of terms produced by term extraction and ontology learning tools in the initial stage of the process, the conceptualization was initially organized around some upper level concepts borrowed from existing upper and core level ontologies. With the support of these upper level concepts (`Agent`, `Document`, `Act`, `Process`, and `Role`), and relevant legislation and literature we organized the conceptual knowledge contained in the textual corpus into an initial hierarchy of concepts (classes). Later, the suggestions and the evaluation of legal experts brought about some requirements for the representation of certain dogmatic or theoretical conceptualizations not included in this first modelization.

The refinement of the initial class hierarchy for the representation of some of those concepts was a very complex task and hard to achieve. First, terms used in practice and made explicit during the interviews could or could not coincide with their dogmatic or theoretical views. For example, `auto` and `orden`. From the list of questions, `auto_de_alejamiento` and `orden_the_alejamiento` were used in the same situations, within the same linguistic structure, therefore they seemed to be interchangeable. Nevertheless, when legal experts were asked about considering these two instances as the (`owl:sameAs`), most experts considered that the content (the order) ought not to be confused with the form ([auto]). Also, the purpose of the ontology and the results from the extraction of terms indicated the relevancy of a group of procedural documents (initially formalized as the `Procedural_Document` class), which was found nonexistent as a concept by the experts, and therefore it was suppressed in the refinement of the OPJK ontology. This suppression also caused the deletion of the `Appeal_Document` subclass, and blurred the relevancy of the documents produced by the parties or third parties during a process which, for the dogmatic definition, could not be considered public documents.

Second, as suggested by the `Procedural_Document` situation, the decision to model a certain concept from a certain ontological point of view may cause conceptual mismatches and conceptualization problems. For example, most experts suggested the conceptualization of "Public Administration." Nevertheless, the conceptualization of this particular concept combines a legal view with a political view regarding the organization of the State, and then, other related concepts may also become relevant, for example, the separation of powers (Judiciary, Executive, and Legislative), within others. With the conceptualization of Public Administration, modellers ought to decide if `Health_Care_Organization` (which may be public or private), `Local_Entities` (which may have administrative and executive tasks) or a particular `Enterprise` (which may be regulated by private or public law) are subclasses of Public Administration. Therefore, we could also state that several ontological views are possible regarding the legal domain, depending on the point of view or area of expertise taken into account. As a further example, the conceptualization of `Court`, `Bench`, and `Public_Prosecution` offered also several ontological difficulties. Courts and Tribunals (bench) are invested in the Spanish legal system, with the jurisdictional function or the judicial power (jurisdiction). The CGPJ [Consejo General del Poder Judicial] is the governing body of this jurisdictional organizations although it is not itself considered "jurisdictional." Nevertheless, the Public Prosecution [Ministerio Fiscal] is considered by the act which establishes its functions "a body integrated in the Judicial Power with functional autonomy",[57] although it is obvious that, Public Prosecution is no subjected to the govern of the CGPJ and that its structure is largely related to the Ministry of Justice.

This situation described above relates to the conceptualization difficulties raised by the purpose of the Ontology of Professional Judicial Knowledge. The OPJK ontology is envisioned and designed to be used in the IURISERVICE application towards search and indexing. Therefore, class hierarchy is defined towards semantic distance calculation purposes and instantiation is modelled to favour term matching, both from the input at the IURISERVICE's web search interface (search), and from the data stored in the system for the retrieval of the most relevant question-answered pair (indexing). This purpose-based bias had effects on the ontological decisions taken. For example, these search and indexing requirements affected the instantiation of `notification` as a multiple class instance of `Document` and `Process`. The modelization of `notification` in an ontology for a reasoning system, would surely require a different solution to this conceptual problem. Moreover, the representation of central *reasoning* concepts such as jurisdiction or competency, or the establishment of specific relations between legal facts and legal acts (legal qualification), between jurisdictional organizations (competency and case distribution) has been set aside.

From all these discussions, we may conclude that the use of core concepts from legal dogmatics and legal theory might offer support towards legal ontology construction in a middle-out manner, avoiding bottom-up modelling difficulties, in the same manner as did the use of `Agent`, `Document`, `Act`, `Process`, and `Role`). Nevertheless, the adoption of top-level concepts (legal or not) implies the assumption of several ontological commitments, and in the case of legal core level concepts, these commitments may represent the view of a particular legal theoretical perspective, based on Legal Positivism, Legal Realism, Legal Pragmatism, Legal Sociology, Critical legal Theory, etc. Therefore, legal ontological commitments adopted from legal theory ought to be documented (not only made explicit by the conceptualization itself) and made available to facilitate the exploration of those commitments and to facilitate legal ontology reuse.

Furthermore, we may also conclude that the purpose of the ontology represents a bias for the conceptualization of a particular domain (as much as the legal perspective taken), and that legal ontology construction and reuse would benefit from their explicit account in the appropriate documentation. In our case, we have introduced the OPJK ontology requirements as comments of the ontology in the owl file. This comments then may be visualized in the Protégé editor, as in Fig. 5.24. (See, also, the OPJK final ontology requirements specification documentation in Table 5.13.)

[57] Ley 50/1981, de 30 de diciembre, por la que se regula el Estatuto Orgánico del Ministerio Fiscal, art. 2: "El Ministerio Fiscal es un órgano de relevancia constitucional con personalidad jurídica propia, integrado con autonomía funcional en el Poder Judicial, y ejerce su misión por medio de

Fig. 5.24 OPJK documentation (requirements) in Protégé

Finally, the modelization task presented in this chapter offers an attempt to model an ontology based on an empirical perspective based on term extraction from data obtained during ethnographic fieldwork, influenced by a sociological approach to the study of Law, and presents the difficulties faced towards ontology refinement with the suggestions offered by legal experts. Further work will be focused on investigating the connections between the expert's view of the Law and their theoretical background knowledge acquired at the Law School, which may be based on legal dogmatics and inspired by specific legal theory constructs based on normativist or positivist views of the Law. Moreover, future work will consist on the implementation of the ontology within the IURISERVICE system for its technical evaluation (performance tests), in order to evaluate its technical capabilities. Also several comparative evaluations ought to be performed, first, between the refined and

---

órganos propios, conforme a los principios de unidad de actuación y dependencia jerárquica y con sujeción, en todo caso, a los de legalidad e imparcialidad."

Table 5.13 Final ontology requirements documentation

Purpose	Search and indexing for the IURISERVICE web-based application. The Ontology of Professional Judicial Knowledge (OPJK) represents relevant concepts related to the problems that take place during the on-call period in Spanish first instance courts. The ontology contains domain specific knowledge, professional knowledge, gathered by experience from the practice during on-call periods with semi-structured interviews.	
Methodological approach	(1) preparatory phase (specification of ontology requirements), (2) development phase (knowledge acquisition –experts, documents, reuse–, conceptualization –classes, relations, properties, instances–, expert validation and formalization), and (3) evaluation phase (internal consistency, requirements, competency questions and expert evaluation, using SUS usability questionnaire).	
Sources of Knowledge	**Competency questions**	Which are the problematic situations? Which people are involved? What procedural roles are involved? What professionals are involved? What type of organizations are involved? Which documents and other information sources are involved? Which judicial procedures are mentioned? Which relevant relations exist between these situations, people, organizations, procedures and documents?
	Other sources	The full contents of the questionnaires from both survey and the transcriptions of the complete interviews. Corpus of questions (list of 800 questions). Specialised handbooks on the judicial setting and organization: VillaGómez et al. (2003), Toharia and García (2005) and Arnaiz et al. (2005). Information contained regarding the Spanish Judiciary in the website of the General Council of the Judiciary (http://www.poderjudicial.es). Specialised textbooks on Civil, Criminal and Procedural Law Ramos-Méndez (1997a, b 2006), Montero-Aroca et al. (2005a, b, c, 2007, 2008) and Cortés-Domínguez and Moreno-Catena (2008a, b). Civil, Criminal and Procedural Law codes. Dictionaries, mainly Diccionario de la Lengua Española de la Real Academia Española (http://buscon.rae.es) and Moliner (2000)
Tool support	YOSHIKODER, and ANTCONC towards term extraction, TextToOnto and Text2Onto for further input.	
Ontology editor	Protégé (versions 3.3.1, 3.4 (beta), and 4.0 (beta)).	
Reuse	Use of top general concepts suggested by the analysis of (DOLCE Lite/CLO, SUMO, PROTON, and LKIF-Core): Agent, Role, Document, Process, and Act.	

initial versions, then, between the more and less expressive versions of the Ontology of Professional Judicial Knowledge, in order to evaluate if the refinement applied to the ontology improves its results, and the utility of some formalized constructs.

Chapter 6
Some Final Remarks and Issues for Discussion

6.1 Comments on the State-of-the-Art

The representation of legal expert knowledge through ontologies is an area of interdisciplinary research were the disciplines of Law, Knowledge Management and Artificial Intelligence converge. This book explored some of the existing boundaries between these areas of study, the development of legal ontologies, for legal information search and retrieval, legal knowledge representation and management, or legal reasoning and argumentation. Further, this book also proposes a socio-legal approach to the study of law and traditional KBS design, that takes into account expert-based knowledge acquisition techniques, for an ontology-based representation of conceptual legal knowledge. As proof of concept, the development of the Ontology of Professional Judicial Knowledge, for the IURISERVICE web-based application, which supports legal decision making during the on-call period of Spanish newly recruited judges, is described in Chap. 5.

Ontologies allow the formal representation of meaning in order to share with computers the flexibility, intuition and capabilities of the conceptual structures of the human natural language, and, thus, making information machine-readable is just one step towards the envisaged possibility of global knowledge sharing and reusing (Berners-Lee et al. 2001). Moreover, they also offer changeability (in software design), ease of use (for development and editing), and reasoning capabilities (Meroño-Peñuela et al. 2010). In fact,"[a]pplications that combine data in new ways and allow users to make connections and understand relationships that were previously hidden are very powerful and compelling" (Segaran et al. 2009), and semantic modeling offers advantages over the use of relational databases or XML descriptions:

- when it requires flexibility (a graph data model, a non-hierarchical tree-like structure), or scalability(Berners-Lee 1998);
- when data models are not well understood (Segaran et al. 2009) (e.g. relational database schemas are not public);

N. Casellas, *Legal Ontology Engineering: Methodologies, Modelling Trends, and the Ontology of Professional Judicial Knowledge*, Law, Governance and Technology Series 3, DOI 10.1007/978-94-007-1497-7_6, © Springer Science+Business Media B.V. 2011

- when the usage patterns are not predictable (e.g. *schema migration* problems in relational databases) (Segaran et al. 2009);
- when data is distributed over several sources (Allemang and Hendler 2008);
- when we could benefit from the use of public access points (SPARQL end-points) or Linked Data URLs.

Nowadays, ontologies are used to implement semantic content in different types of applications: knowledge engineering and KBS development, natural language applications, database and information retrieval systems, multi-agent systems, etc. In fact, the Semantic Web vision has influenced the definition of *ontology* and broadened its scope. Nevertheless, ontology definitions and purposes were initially related to the development of application and domain independent ontologies for knowledge sharing and reuse, mainly as knowledge interchange formats for knowledge-based systems.

Aside from the analysis of ontology definitions, the first chapters included an overview of typologies (purpose, level, etc.), methodologies, tools, and languages used towards ontology development.

In general, as described in Chap. 2, reusability has been considered the main objective for the development of ontologies, and most typologies are organized in levels of reusability, understood as levels of generality. It is usually believed that the more general the ontology is the less commitments offers to a domain and, therefore, the more reusable it becomes across domains and applications. Also knowledge sharing, the agreement on the conceptualization, is an important feature of ontologies. Nevertheless, the specific level of formality required, together with the relationship between the representation of problem solving (task, method, etc.) knowledge and domain knowledge have been issues undergoing discussion. Moreover, the analysis of legal ontologies from Chap. 4 suggests that, although there is certainly a level of ontology reuse in this domain, the degree of reuse remains low. This may be due to the specificity of the legal terminology (e.g. domain, language, etc.), the differences between legal systems (e.g. interpretation, common law vs. civil law systems), or application requirements (e.g. search vs. reasoning), etc.

Regarding ontology methodologies, Chap. 3 described many methodological approaches towards ontology engineering and other evaluation or knowledge acquisition techniques. Most methodologies follow a cyclic modelling approach, a recursive and incremental cycle of steps, including: a preparatory step (initial feasibility study, specification of requirements); a development step (knowledge acquisition activities, ontology conceptualization, formalization, evaluation and refinement); and an application step (implementation and maintenance activities). Nevertheless, few ontology methodologies give nowadays precise guidelines or recommendations regarding requirements specification, knowledge acquisition, ontology evaluation, and documentation support (reuse).[1]

[1]Guidelines are given, for example, in Suárez-Figueroa et al. (2007, 2009a) and Spyns et al. (2008).

Moreover, although some methodological approaches rely mainly on bottom-up approaches to knowledge acquisition for ontology development, most lifecycle ontology methodologies offer, in fact, an open approach with various concurrent possibilities (top-down, middle-out, bottom-up). As Suárez-Figueroa et al. (2007) point out "[r]esearch on methodologies for the Ontology Engineering field is in its 'adolescence' since this field is only 10 years old." Ontology engineering is still an open area of research, as is the application of ontology methodologies in the legal domain.

With regards to ontology modelling tools and languages, Protégé ontology editor offers an easy-to-use interface (with graphical visualisation capabilities), consistency checking support, language and domain independence, and a long history of development, together with free availability. Also the NeOn Toolkit offers a complete set of features, although it is mostly directed towards collaborative ontology development, and both tools support the OWL 2 language. Protégé, freely available and kept up to date, seems to be the most preferred tool for ontology editing, although other editors such as the NeOn toolkit, or TopBraid Composer are also used.

Nowadays, most legal ontologies are also being formalized with W3C standard languages, with a growing preference for the OWL language (in the past also ONTOLINGUA, LOOM and DAML+OIL were also used). The use of RDF and OWL could therefore be recommended as they are currently widely used in ontology development and might offer grounds for reuse and extensibility. The choice between RDF/S and OWL (including OWL 1 sublanguages and OWL 2 profiles) ought to depend on the required expressive power and the computational and/or implementational needs of the particular application in mind. Nevertheless, the wide usage of OWL as the preferred ontology language in the development of legal ontologies for a wide variety of purposes (search and retrieval, knowledge acquisition, reasoning, etc.) could suggest that OWL constructs better support for the representation of legal knowledge, that its adoption is tool-based rather than requirement-based (as most up-to-date freely- available ontology editors support this format), or that reuse of available OWL ontologies influence this choice. Further research on the specific purpose and application requirements of legal ontologies in relation to the ontology language used, could offer more insight regarding the influence that tool availability or ontology reuse have on the choice of language.

The analysis of ontologies, methodologies and tools offered a list of criteria for the further analysis of the existing legal ontologies and trends in current legal ontology construction directed at answering the following preliminary research questions:

1. How are existing legal ontologies modelled?
   (a) Which knowledge acquisition techniques and development methodologies are used?
   (b) How does legal theory or thought influence ontology construction?
   (c) How is the acquired knowledge or the resulting ontology evaluated?
2. What is the role of experts and legal expertise in legal ontology construction?

As derives from the analysis described in Chap. 4, most of the initial ontologies were directed towards theoretical investigations or knowledge acquisition and reuse, and were built mainly at the core level, while more recent ontologies are built generally with particular applications in mind, especially towards semantic indexing, search, and retrieval. Nevertheless, in current legal ontology development there are few explicit accounts or insights into the methodological steps followed towards legal knowledge acquisition and conceptualization, and those who describe the steps taken have generally adopted a methodology of their own. It is important that such methodological steps are made explicit to enable future reuse and interoperability.

Regarding knowledge acquisition, most initial legal core ontologies (e.g., FBO, FOLaw) were built upon insights provided by legal theory. In particular, FBO, FOLaw, the Ontology of Law as Dynamic Interconnected System of States of Affairs, and the Knowledge-based Model of Law were largely influenced by normativism, legal positivism, and analytical jurisprudence, especially by the works of Hart (1961) and Kelsen (1991). In general, legal expertise (academic or professional) plays a secondary role in legal ontology development. Only in a few cases, although with rather vague descriptions, legal experts have been involved in the knowledge acquisition or the ontology evaluation processes. Table 6.1 includes a list of legal ontologies described in Chap. 4 which explicitly declare either the participation of legal experts or the inclusion of legal expertise, their methodological approach or some evaluation results or insights.

These results correspond to the vagueness also encountered in the analysis of expert involvement in ontology validation activities from a methodological point of view (Chap. 3). Moreover, the initial top-down construction of legal core ontologies based on general theories of Law, due to the criticisms suffered by legal knowledge based systems development, seems to have suggested that text-based modelling or bottom-up approaches might not require extensive expert support.

> Another top-down way to elaborate an ontology can be to get together some experts of the domain and ask them to agree on a unique point of view on their specialities, this unique point of view being the basis of an ontology. The main difficulty is then the time; it is long for experts to agree. The second way to build an ontology is a bottom-up method. This method consists on extracting from *appropriate* [emphasis added] documents all the elements needed to compose an ontology (Lame 2001).

As mentioned in Chap. 4, the lack of explicit involvement of legal expertise in the development of legal ontologies, either towards knowledge elicitation or as documentation supervision, advice, validation or evaluation, could jeopardize their sharedness. The use of well-established knowledge acquisition techniques and the participation of legal experts in corpus preparation should be a desirable feature of the process of developing a legal ontology, although different requirements may be set for core and domain ontologies. Therefore this book includes as a proof of concept (Chap. 5) the description of a methodological approach followed for the development of the Ontology of Professional Judicial Knowledge, based on the following ideas:

1. a sociological approach to the study of legal knowledge, related to human-centred methods for systems design, and traditional knowledge elicitation techniques

Table 6.1 (Explicit) evaluations, methodologies and expertise in existing legal ontologies

Ontology	Evaluation	Methodology	Expertise
O. Law as dynamic interconnected system of states of affairs	–	–	X
Mommer's knowledge-based model of law	–	–	X
CLIME ontology	X	Own	–
LRI-core	X	–	X
JWN/Lois	X	Own	–
CLO	X	Own	–
Ontology of French law	X	Terminae	X
TOF & TOV	–	Dogma	–
IPROnto	X	–	–
Copyright Ontology	X	Methontology	–
CCOntology	X	Dogma	X
BEST-user ontology	X	Noy et al. 2001	X
OPJK	X	Own	X
LKIF-core ontology	X	Own	X
Legal Case Ontology	–	Own	–
AGO IR Ontology	–	Own	–
Italian Crime Ontology	–	Own	X
Multi tier contract Ontology	X	Noy et al. 2001	X
OnProc	–	Own	X
Reimdoc project ontologies (Real estate transactions Ontology)	–	Methontology	X
OntoPrivacy	–	Own	X
Consumer protection Ontology	–	Own	X
EU employee Ontology	–	Terminae	–
Ontology of fundamental legal concepts	–	Noy et al. 2001	X
e-Government Ontology	–	Own	–
SIAP Legislative Ontology	X	–	–
Oral hearing Ontology	–	Own	X
US UCC	X	–	–
Legal Taxonomy Syllabus	–	Own	X
BDSG Ontology	X	–	–
Legal case repository	–	Own	–
Ontology Greek public administration proceedings	X	–	–
Minimal model economic crimes	X		
ALIS IP Ontology	–	Noy et al. 2001	–
EuroVoc SKOS	–	Own	–
LegLOPD	–	Terminae	–
Mediation Core Ontolgy	–	Own	X
Ontología Jurídica Libre	–	–	X
Neurona Ontologies	X	Own	X
Ontology of Vehicles	–	Methontology	–

in KBS design, as support towards knowledge acquisition and the selection of knowledge sources for bottom-up legal ontology development, and validation;
2. the need to ground knowledge acquisition in relevant empirical data about the legal domain modelled in the construction of legal professional ontologies;
3. legal expert participation as a useful tool for legal ontology development, specially for ontology evaluation;
4. tailored *usability* methods for ontology evaluation may offer quality measurements towards understanding and *sharedness* of the resulting ontology.

6.2 The Socio-Legal Expert-Based Approach to Ontology Development

The IURISERVICE application (see Fig. 6.1) was designed to provide on-line access to an FAQ (Frequently Asked Questions) system that permits the user to search for the practical questions in a repository of stored questions. The lists of questions gathered from the interviews provided the input list of questions for the system and, together with the answers that senior judges of the Spanish School of the Judiciary have provided, they conform the repository of the system. The aim of the system is

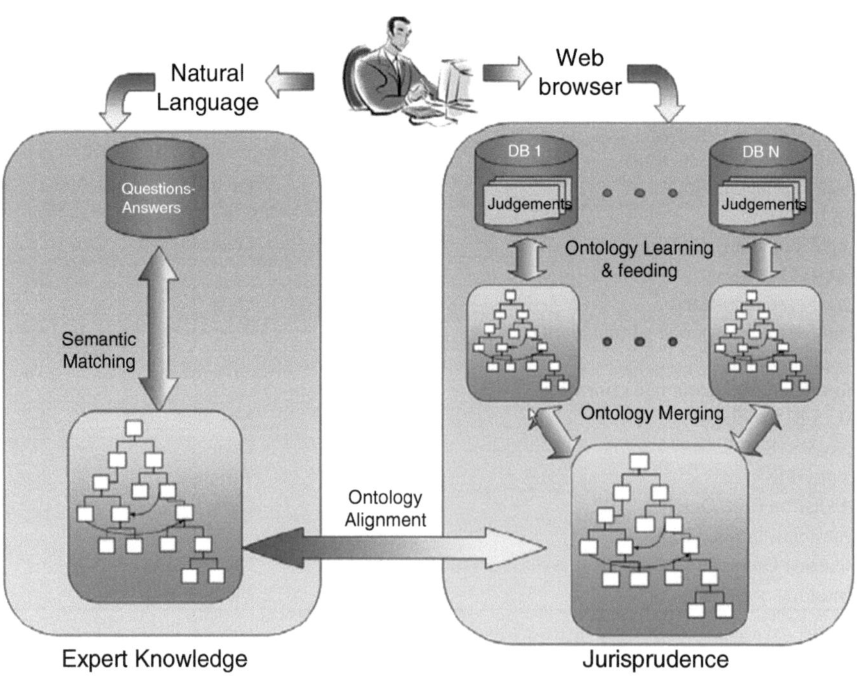

Fig. 6.1 IURISERVICE FAQ architecture

to discover the best semantic match between the user's question or input question (formulated in natural language) and a stored question, so as to offer an answer that satisfies the user. Time and accuracy are critical issues and, to that end, the main research has been based on the possibility of modelling the legal knowledge contained in the repository of questions in the Ontology of Professional Judicial Knowledge.

For this reason, the Ontology of Professional Judicial Knowledge is interested in modelling knowledge about the conceptual structure of the domain concepts, rather than in the dynamic or problem-solving knowledge involved in practical problem resolution, as the answers to the doubts and problems expressed in the questions contained in the repository have been already provided by the Spanish School of the Judiciary, which is to keep and maintain the repository of knowledge. Moreover, it is important for the usability of the system to represent the conceptual structure contained in the questions as they are perceived by the judges.

The *appropriateness* of the corpora selected towards term extraction and ontology learning, together with the validation of those extracted terms is of utmost importance in bottom-up ontology construction. The careful selection of knowledge sources, the use of adequate knowledge acquisition techniques, and a life-cycle human-centred design and usability evaluation may offer sharedness and give overall support to the development of legal ontologies. Ontology engineering could benefit from the perspective that the sociological study of law may offer and, in general, from taking a human-centred perspective in legal ontology development life-cycle, especially towards the construction of domain ontologies for areas of knowledge which require the modelling of conceptual professional or expert knowledge.

For example, theoretically guided empirical studies or the use of tailored *usability* methods for ontology evaluation could offer support towards ontology development, knowledge sharing, reuse, and the establishment of certain quality measurements and aid the evaluation of modelling decisions, prior ontology implementation. We understand that many ontology building methodologies only intend to "address the very basics of ontology development" (Noy and McGuinness 2001) and thus avoid reference to knowledge acquisition for practical needs. Nevertheless, the lack of guidelines or even reference towards knowledge acquisition techniques undermines its importance within the ontology development process and may cause several problems: lack of knowledge acquisition effort, lack of sharedness of the knowledge encoded, and lack of reuse of the resulting ontology.

Therefore, the conceptualization process of the Ontology of Professional Judicial Knowledge was based on a previous and careful knowledge acquisition stage, which comprehends the acquisition of relevant terminology related to practical problems faced by judges in their first appointment, followed by the process of term extraction from the corpus of questions – problems – faced by judges. The acquisition of this corpus – for term extraction – was, thus, the result of a thorough ethnographic campaign to gather relevant conceptual and domain knowledge from the professional practice of judges, which tried to ensure the quality (relevance) of the input data. 124 newly appointed judges from all around Spain conformed the sample (from a total of 248 judges of the 52th Class), and the semi-structured interviews were performed the research team of the Institute of Law and Technology at the Universitat Autònoma de Barcelona (UAB). The questionnaire was organized in five sections, concerning professional training, professional activity, professional relationships, quality of life, and personal data. This time, the questionnaire contained some of the 2002 questions, together with questions more directed towards gathering information on the requirements that a would-be system ought to have. Information regarding complex cases in civil or criminal law was included, together with the inquiry regarding their comments with peers about the cases, and the use of Internet. Nevertheless, relevant knowledge was obtained from the answers to the question, "could you explain specific doubts or problems that came up during the on-call period?." This knowledge acquisition stage was driven by the purpose of the OPJK ontology: to represent the concepts involved in the usual problems encountered by judges for the semantic enhancement of the search and retrieval capabilities of the Frequently Asked Questions system IURISERVICE. The set of competency questions focused on the acquisition of knowledge regarding problematic situations during the on-call period: people or professional roles involved; relevant documents or judicial procedures (and their respective relations), etc. At this point, the knowledge acquisition process continued with the preparation of the corpus, containing nearly 800 practical questions formulated by the newly recruited judges, for term extraction and ontology learning. ALCESTE and OntoGen were used to supply subdomain information, TextToOnto, Text2Onto, AntConc, and Yoshikoder were used as term extraction tools, and some upper ontologies (LKIF-Core, CLO, SUMO and PROTON) were analysed to offer middle-out development support.

Each of these ontologies offered arguments towards reuse. LKIF-Core offered an interesting cognitive-based approach that includes the representation of agents (organizations and persons) playing roles and performing actions, which was interesting for the representation of knowledge in the judicial setting. DOLCE-CLO offered an extensive representation of concepts related to the legal domain to allow extensive reasoning capabilities. SUMO offered a functional view on the representation organizations, finally, PROTON provided simplicity. However, their reuse implied the acceptance of the model of the "existing" world that they represented and, as the main interest of the knowledge acquisition process to acquire the conceptual knowledge from the experience of judges. The reuse of upper conceptualizations and the acceptance of their (philosophical) commitments was not considered appropriate at that moment due to the sociological perspective taken based on empirical data analysis. Nevertheless, in order to aid the grouping and initial conceptualization stages, the generally accepted concepts of role, document, process, situation/action and organization (agent), relevant for the competency questions were taken into account.

Yoshikoder and AntConc offered the list of 477 terms (later extended to include more than 900 terms), which supplied the initial terminological knowledge for term grouping, conceptual modelling and ontology formalization. Grouping took into account several knowledge sources, including relevant literature and legislation, and was complemented by an initial expert validation. Also, in order to conceptualize and formalize the terms extracted from the corpus, all modelling decisions were supported by materials used by judges for their knowledge acquisition process: course syllabus, legislation and doctrine. Moreover, to be able to technically evaluate, in the future, the search enhancement capabilities of the different modelling decisions taken during the conceptualization process, conceptualization and formalization were performed in several stages of complexity.

At this stage, the evaluation of the conceptualization and formalization activities consisted of a purpose evaluation and an ontological evaluation based on the involvement of legal professionals or experts to validate the shareability of the conceptualization formalized under the established requirements.

The evaluation of the purpose was based on the analysis of the specification of requirements and competency questions established in Sect. 5.2.2 against the final OPJK ontology. The methodological steps recommended by most ontology development methodologies (Noy and McGuinness 2001; Sure 2003; Gómez-Pérez et al. 2003; de Nicola et al. 2009; Suárez-Figueroa et al. 2009a) and knowledge acquisition techniques (Schreiber et al. 1999; Sure 2003; Milton 2007) had been carefully followed and accounted for: (1) preparatory phase (specification of ontology requirements), (2) development phase (knowledge acquisition – experts, documents, reuse –, conceptualization – classes, relations, properties, instances –, validation and formalization), and (3) evaluation phase. Definitions had been provided for each formalized class and naming conventions have been followed. Finally, the competency questions guided the definition of the contents of the list of terms extracted, and the description of the properties (relations) established between the derived concepts.

Regarding ontology-focused evaluation, first, the use of the Protégé knowledge acquisition tool and ontology editor allowed consistency checking through the Pellet reasoner, and prevented the incorrect usage of the OWL language in the construction of the Ontology of Professional Judicial Knowledge.

Second, we performed a legal expert's analysis of the taxonomy constructed (together with the revision of its natural language definitions, instantiation and class relations) to validate the representation offered of the knowledge contained corpus of questions used by the IURISERVICE search engine. Debriefing sessions were set for a total of nine legal experts (academics, professionals and researchers) working at or collaborating with the Faculty of Law of the Universitat Autònoma de Barcelona, and were informed of the purpose of the Ontology of Professional Judicial Knowledge, its requirements and the process of conceptualization followed, based on the corpus of questions provided by the judges in their first appointment during the surveys carried out during 2004. At the end of these debriefing sessions, the experts answered a questionnaire evaluating different features of the OPJK ontology and, to provide suggestions for improvement. This initial questionnaire contained a total of 48 questions regarding several aspects of the conceptualization: concepts, definitions, instances, and relations. In total, the experts were asked to validate 48 items, and their overall levels of agreement with the general conceptualization offered (class, subclass, instantiation, properties, etc.) was of the 72.92% (representing the sum of high agreement 32.41% and agreement 40.51% responses).

Regarding the lowest scores, the experts made several relevant suggestions for the improvement of the OPJK ontology. In general, the taxonomical structure of `Process` and `Act` was found rather complex. Also, although the class structure for `organization` and `Role` was considered correct, minor revisions could provide major improvement. Moreover, slight changes in labels and definitions could offer clarity and foster expert understanding and agreement.

Third, the experts were also asked to answer a tailored version of the System Usability Scale (SUS) questionnaire, an experimental validation which played a similar role to *usability inspection* for a software product. The overall results of the SUS questionnaire were of the 69.44% in total, which may suggest a high level of agreement with the general OPJK conceptualization. Furthermore, a comparison between the global results within the previous validation and the SUS results shows a high degree of similarity (72.92% and 69.44%, respectively).

Fourth, and finally, the metrics inspired by d'Aquin et al. (2007) and Tartir et al. (2005) offered a comparative positive overview of the OPJK ontology with respect to 25,500 semantic documents extracted from the web, and suggested the need for adding more granularity to the OPJK ontology.

The results from the different evaluation activities were taken into account towards OPJK refinement, several classes were added or modified (e.g., relabelled), some instances were redistributed, properties and disjoint axioms were modified or added. At the end of this process, the Ontology of Professional Judicial Knowledge included a total of 74 classes and 912 instances, 31 `owl:ObjectProperty` axioms (14 `rdfs:subPropertyOf`, 15 `owl:inverseOf`, 1 transitive and 1 functional `owl:ObjectProperty`). This ontology also includes (as distinct from OPJK v 1.0) 1 `owl:equivalentClass` axiom, 75 `owl:disjointWith` axioms, around 100 multiple class instantiation constructs, and 53 `owl:sameAs` axioms.

The current refined versions of the ontology are still consistent, and the metrics regarding P-density, H-density and I-density still show that OPJK versions may be considered above average, if compared with the results obtained by the analysis of d'Aquin et al. (2007), although the results from the refined versions of the ontology are slightly lower than the previous results largely due to an increment in the number of classes. Finally, distance distribution was improved, with respect to previous measurements.

6.3 Issues for Discussion

The OPJK ontology has been at this stage evaluated against its purpose and its content (language conformity, consistency and expert evaluation) with positive results. Nevertheless, there are several issues that ought to be taken into account regarding conceptualization limitations and further evaluation.

First, the decisions and difficulties encountered during the conceptualization, formalization and refinement processes offer several issues for future discussion in the legal ontology modelling and research; especially, the integration of bottom-up and top-down approaches, the influence of other areas of expertise or domains of knowledge, and the effects of a purpose-based perspective for legal ontology construction.

The knowledge acquisition process for the construction of the Ontology of Professional Judicial Knowledge based on the extraction of terms from a corpus of questions regarding practical on-call problems, offers the possibility to discuss the advantages and drawbacks of taking a sociological modelization perspective (bottom-up), and the complexity of establishing clear connections with legal dogmatics or general legal theory approaches (top-down). As discussed in Chap. 3 although most lifecycle ontology methodologies offer an open approach towards the choice of top-down, middle-out, or bottom-up ontology development, there are no suggested guidelines to support such choices. To what extent are the bottom-up and top-down perspectives to legal ontology modelling compatible? How could they relate? How much does this choice influence the outcome of the development process?

Further, and in relation to text-based approaches to the development of legal ontologies, some authors believe that in the area of Artificial Intelligence and Law, "little attention has been devoted both to techniques coming from the NLP community, and to research efforts concerned with the analysis of legal language peculiarities. In particular, it has been overlooked how understanding the characteristics of this specialised language can help to shed light on the main difficulties of extracting semantic information out of legal documents" (Venturi 2010).

These questions raise, in turn, a discussion on the appropriateness and possibilities offered by the middle-out approach, a combination of both, the top- down and bottom-up approaches, or described to "define the more salient concepts first and then generalize and specialize them appropriately" (Noy and McGuinness 2001). As discussed in Chap. 5, in the legal domain, the appropriate salient concepts for a particular ontology development project are part of the ontology requirements that influence a modelling decision, and may involve core legal concepts, general domain concepts, low-level upper concepts, "intermediate legal concepts",[2] etc. Moreover, as mentioned in the ontology learning experience described in Chap. 5, middle-out approaches raise an important question that has not been sufficiently addressed: what are the relationship and trade-offs between linguistic-based approaches to the development of legal ontologies and top or core ontology reuse? What methodologies may be employed to minimize these trade-offs?

These questions are complex, but some of the explored answers to these questions involve the participation of legal experts in ontology learning activities (e.g. evaluation of upper or core ontologies, selection of terms, grouping, etc.) as depicted

[2] See, for example, Ashley and Brüninghaus (2003).

in Chap. 5, the lexicalization of concepts in the ongoing work of Francesconi and Tiscornia (2008) and Francesconi et al. (2010a) in the DALOS knowledge organisation system development,[3] the ontology enrichment and extension by NLP techniques applied by (Peters 2009), or the methodological aspects from comparative legal analysis employed in building multilingual conceptual dictionaries (Ajani et al. 2010), within others.

A second discussion evolves from the practical experience in the development of the Ontology of Professional Judicial Knowledge. From specific discussions regarding OPJK conceptualizations, such as that the terms used in practice and made explicit during the interviews could not coincide with their dogmatic or general theoretical views, or that the purpose of the ontology and the results from the extraction of terms indicated the relevance of a group of procedural documents which was found nonexistent as a concept by the experts, a more general discussion arises, that may also originate further possible and fruitful research.

For example, we may suggest the idea that the legal sociology approach based on empirical data studies for ontology construction could represent, not only a bottom-up approach to ontology construction, but also a usability approach, while the general legal theory approach could represent reusability approaches to ontology engineering. This perspective could open a distinct discussion, a legal theoretical discussion, regarding one of the classical ontology development discussions, a view not based on the upper-core-domain-application distinction (see Fig. 6.2), but based on knowledge acquisition and grounding for legal ontology development. The related *legal* knowledge acquisition bottleneck discussion could also be explored.

A third discussion, related with the previous one, revisits the notion of legal ontological commitment, together with the effects of these commitments in legal ontology construction and reuse, and the requirements for additional documentation. From the experiences derived from the development of the Ontology of Professional Judicial Knowledge for the IURISERVICE system towards indexing and search we may open again the discussion regarding the effects of a purpose-based perspective in conceptualization decision-making, or on the different ontological requirements (even commitments) necessary towards search ontologies or reasoning ontologies, or usable *vs* reusable ontologies.

This could be somehow related to the Ontology Library proposal by Visser and Bench-Capon (1998a), and its indexing mechanism (intra and inter-ontology features). The authors envisioned the development of a legal ontology library were the users needed "to be able to browse and compare, the competing ontologies starting with the top-level concepts. This will once alert them to the fundamental

[3]"In the DALOS KOS, the two layers are connected by relationships mapping concepts to their linguistic counterpart, i.e. terms: this mapping is implemented through the hasLexicalization relationship, which from a monolingual perspective maps a given concept to the term(s) expressing it, whereas from a cross-lingual perspective it maps a given concept to the multilingual terminological variants conveying it" (Francesconi et al. 2010b).

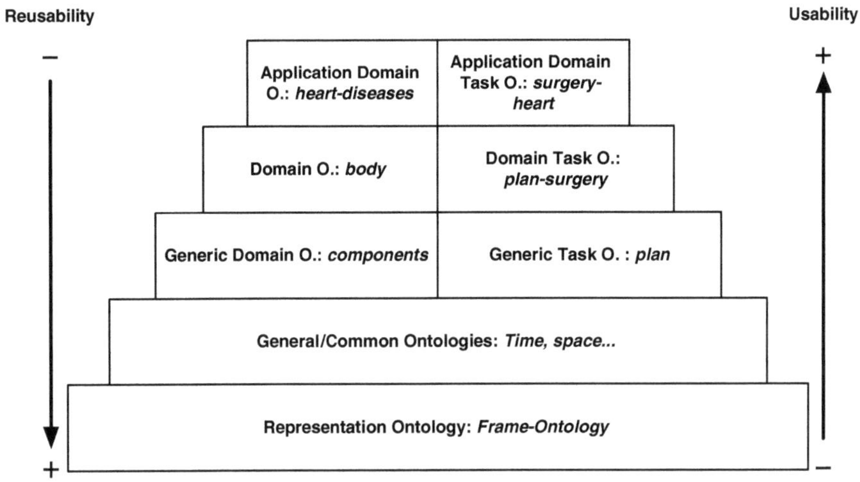

Fig. 6.2 Graphical representation of the usability-reusability trade-off by Benjamins and Gómez-Pérez (1999) (also in Gómez-Pérez et al. (2003)

design choices to be made, and enable them to decide which one is most in accord with their own conceptualization. Armed with this knowledge, they will then be able to select a more refined ontology which conforms to this conceptualization, using the other indexing questions." Towards this library of legal ontologies, it could be interesting to reuse or explore the successful strategies followed by the biomedical community or the Gene Ontology experience. Biomedical ontology repositories in the biomedical domain such as the OBO foundry[4] and the BioPortal[5] could provide some source of inspiration for similar approaches in the legal domain.[6] Could such joint effort be effective in the legal domain? Although there are evident differences between the medical and the legal communities, both areas share a requirement of expert-based and technical language.

[4]OBO Foundry: http://www.obofoundry.org/

[5]BioPortal: http://bioportal.bioontology.org/

[6]"The GO project has developed three structured controlled vocabularies (ontologies) that describe gene products in terms of their associated biological processes, cellular components and molecular functions in a species-independent manner. There are three separate aspects to this effort: first, the development and maintenance of the ontologies themselves; second, the annotation of gene products, which entails making associations between the ontologies and the genes and gene products in the collaborating databases; and third, development of tools that facilitate the creation, maintenance and use of ontologies," http://www.geneontology.org/GO.doc.shtml

In fact, the experiences in the medical domain[7] in relation to ontology development could offer a starting point for comparative research and methodological insight for the construction of expert or professional knowledge-based legal ontologies.

In addition, the influence of other areas of expertise or domains of knowledge in legal ontology construction ought to be further explored. For example, the relations between: legal ontology and legal epistemology (Breuker and Hoekstra 2004b), legal knowledge and common sense knowledge (Breuker and Hoekstra 2004a) or world knowledge (Valente and Breuker 1994a), legal knowledge and layman's knowledge of the legal domain (Uijttenbroek et al. 2008), the influence of Open Data initiatives and Linked Data efforts in the legal domain,[8] conceptual legal representations and deontic logics/ operators or the combination of legal ontologies and rules (Antoniou and Wagner 2003; Uszok et al. 2004; Paschke et al. 2005; Linehan 2007),[9] and the representation of legal knowledge and organisational or political science concepts. In this regard, the ongoing work in the design of autonomous agents and multi-agent systems (MAS), and specifically in legal electronic institutions and normative multi-agent systems, can offer interesting results.[10] These discussions could also turn to a more profound discussion regarding the capabilities of OWL for the representation of certain reasoning aspects the legal domain, or the possibilities of incorporating the legal flavour in OWL (see, for example Hoekstra (2008, 2009b) and Hoekstra and Breuker (2008)).

Finally, although the use of ontologies and the implementation of the Semantic Web vision may offer great advantages to information and knowledge management, there are great challenges and problems to overcome. First, the problems related to knowledge acquisition techniques and bottlenecks in software engineering are

[7]"In many ways, the medical-informatics research community should become more concerned with identifying reusable ontologies, tasks, and problem-solving methods, not only because making these abstractions explicit leads to better knowledge engineering, but also because the study of these abstractions is the essence of medical informatics. In some regards, the most reusable and sharable end points of medical-informatics research are not specific computer-based artifacts, but rather insights into the structure of biomedical knowledge and methods for applying that knowledge in the clinic or laboratory. New computational architectures that will allow us to define and examine knowledge-level abstractions are important not only for building robust decision-support systems, but also for developing and validating our theories regarding biomedical knowledge and its organization" (Musen 1992).

[8]See for example: Govtrack.us (http://www.govtrack.us/), or legislation.gov.uk (http://www.legislation.gov.uk/).

[9]See the proceedings from the DEON (Deontic Logic in Computer Science) Workshops at: http://www.defeasible.org/deon2010/, and the materials provided by the Rule Markup Initiative as an example (http://ruleml.org/).

[10]See, for example the COIN (Coordination, Organizations, Institutions and Norms in Agent Systems) Workshops (http://coin-aamas2011.iiia.csic.es/, or the CLIMA (Computational Logic in Multi-Agent Systems) Workshops (http://centria.di.fct.unl.pt/events/climaXII/index.html), as an example.

also inherent in ontology engineering, and ontology development is quite a time-consuming and complex task. Moreover, the notion of *sharedness*, used in AI ontology definitions, might require some revision, and the establishment of a clear distinction between the agreement on a conceptualization (and collaborative development, concept negotiation, etc.) and a shared conceptualization (shared knowledge). From our point of view, sharing a conceptualization constitutes a deeper notion than merely agreeing on a given conceptualization. In this sense, and inspired from the OPJK expert evaluation activities based on the use of tailored usability methods, the development of a well-designed *shareability* questionnaire, based on the idea of usability questionnaires for software products, could offer support towards the establishment of quality measures in expert-based ontology evaluation. At the same time, the more general methodological professional-centred approach to legal ontology construction based on the sociological study of the domain, clear specification of ontology requirements, the validation of initial results prior to conceptualization and pre-technical evaluation, and the production of appropriate accompanying ontology documentation should be further specified.

Still, how can we better evaluate the content of ontologies? Current research is focused on overcoming these problems through the establishment of gold standards in concept extraction and ontology learning from texts, and the idea of collaborative development of legal ontologies, although these techniques might be unsuitable for the development of certain types of ontologies. Also, evaluation (validation, verification, and assessment) and quality measurement of ontologies are currently an important topic of research, especially ontology assessment and comparison for reuse purposes. Finally, once created, how are these ontologies to evolve? How are ontologies to be maintained over time?

Legal ontology engineering faces many important challenges. Moreover, the possible limitations of legal ontologies are substantial. Nevertheless, the potential of legal ontologies is immense, and legal professionals and legal experts have a central role to play in the successful development of legal ontologies and legal semantic applications.

References

Abou-Tair, D. e. D. I. 2006. A framework ensuring privacy in a distributed environment. In *PST '06: Proceedings of the 2006 International Conference on Privacy, Security and Trust*, 1–6. NewYork: ACM.

Abou-Tair, D. e. D. I., and S. Berlik. 2006. An ontology-based approach for managing and maintaining privacy in information systems. In *On the move to meaningful internet systems 2006: CoopIS, DOA, GADA, and ODBASE*, ed. R. Meersman and Z. Tari. *Lecture notes in computer science*, Vol. 4275, 983–994. Berlin/Heidelberg: Springer.

Abramowicz, W., P. Stolarski, and T. Tomaszewski. 2007. Reasoning using polish commercial companies code ontology. In *Legal knowledge and information systems. JURIX 2007: The Twentieth Annual Conference*, ed. A. R. Lodder and L. Mommers. *Frontiers in artificial intelligence and applications*, Vol. 165, 163–164. Amsterdam: IOS Press.

Adams, W. A. 2008. A transdisciplinary ontology of innovation governance. *Artificial Intelligence and Law* 16(2):147–174.

Agnoloni, T., L. Bacci, E. Francesconi, W. Peters, S. Montamegni, and G. Venturi. 2009. A two-level knowledge approach to support multilingual legislative drafting. In *Law, ontologies and the Semantic Web. Channelling the legal information flood* (IOS Press ed.), ed. J. Breuker, P. Casanovas, M. Klein, and E. Francesconi. *Frontiers in artificial intelligence and applications*, Vol. 188, 177–198. Amsterdam: IOS Press.

Agnoloni, T., L. Bacci, E. Francesconi, P. Spinosa, D. Tiscornia, S. Montemagni, and G. Venturi. 2007. Building an ontological support for multilingual legislative drafting. In *Legal knowledge and information systems. JURIX 2007: The Twentieth Annual Conference*, ed. A. R. Lodder and L. Mommers. *Frontiers in artificial intelligence and applications*, Vol. 165, 9–18. Amsterdam: IOS Press.

Ajani, G., G. Boella, L. Lesmo, M. Martin, A. Mazzei, D. P. Radicioni, and P. Rossi. 2009. Legal taxonomy syllabus version 2.0. In *3rd workshop on legal ontologies and artificial intelligence techniques joint with 2nd workshop on semantic processing of legal text (LOAIT 2009), Co-located with the 12th International Conference on Artificial Intelligence and Law (ICAIL 2009)*, ed. N. Casellas, E. Francesconi, R. Hoekstra, and S. Montemagni. *IDT series*, Vol. 2, 9–17. Barcelona: IDT/Huygens Editorial.

Ajani, G., G. Boella, L. Lesmo, M. Martin, A. Mazzei, D. P. Radicioni, and P. Rossi. 2010. Multilevel legal ontologies. In *Semantic processing of legal texts: Where the language of law meets the law of language*. ed. E. Francesconi, S. Montemagni, W. Peters, and D. Tiscornia. *Lecture notes in computer science*, Vol. 6036, 136–154. Berlin/Heidelberg: Springer

Ajani, G., G. Boella, L. Lesmo, A. Mazzei, and P. Rossi. 2007a. Multilingual ontological analysis of european directives. In *ACL '07: Proceedings of the 45th Annual Meeting of the ACL on Interactive Poster and Demonstration Sessions*, 21–24. Morristown: Association for Computational

N. Casellas, *Legal Ontology Engineering: Methodologies, Modelling Trends, and the Ontology of Professional Judicial Knowledge*, Law, Governance and Technology Series 3,
DOI 10.1007/978-94-007-1497-7,

Ajani, G., L. Lesmo, G. Boella, A. Mazzei, and P. Rossi. 2007b. Terminological and ontological analysis of European directives: Multilinguism in law. In *Proceedings of the Eleventh International Conference on Artificial Intelligence and Law (ICAIL 2007)*, June 4–8, Palo Alto, 43–48. New York: ACM Press.

Al-Debei, M., and G. Fitzgerald. 2010. The design and engineering of mobile data services: Developing an ontology based on business model thinking. In *Human benefit through the diffusion of information systems design science research*, ed. J. Pries-Heje, J. Venable, D. Bunker, N. Russo, and J. DeGross. *IFIP advances in information and communication technology*, Vol. 318, 28–51. Boston: Springer.

Al-Debei, M. M., and G. Fitzgerald. 2009. OntoEng: A design method for ontology engineering in information systems. In *Proceedings of the International Workshop on "Ontology-Driven Software Engineering", ACM SIGPLAN International Conference on Object-Oriented Programming, Systems, Languages, and Applications (OOPSLA)*, October 2009, Florida.

Alberts, L. K. 1994. Ymir: A sharable ontology for the formal representation of engineering-design knowledge. In *Formal design methods for CAD*, ed. J. S. Gero and E. Tyugu, *IFIP transactions*, Vol. B-18, 3–32. New York: Elsevier.

Alcaraz-Varó, E., and B. Hughes. 2006. *Diccionario de términos jurídicos*. Editorial Ariel. Barcelona.

Aldewereld, H., F. Dignum, A. García-Camino, P. Noriega, J.-A. Rodríguez-Aguilar, and C. Sierra. 2006. Operationalisation of norms for usage in electronic institutions. In *Proceedings of AAMAS'06*, May 8–12, Hakodate. New York: ACM.

Allemang, D., and J. Hendler. 2008. *Semantic Web for the working ontologist. Modeling in RDF, RDFS and OWL*. Burlington: Morgan Kaufmann.

Allen, L. E. 1996. From the fundamental legal conceptions of hohfeld to legal relations: Refining the enrichment of solely deontic legal relations. In *Deontic logic, agency and normative systems, DEON '96: Third International Workshop on Deontic Logic in Computer Science*, ed. M. A. Brown and J. Carmo, 1–26. Sesimbra, Portugal

Allen, L. E., and C. S. Saxon. 1994. A-hohfeld: A language for robust structural representation of knowledge in the legal domain to build interpretation-assistance expert systems. In *Deontic logic in computer science: Normative system specification*, ed. J.-J. C. Meyer and R. J. Wieringa, 205–224. Chichester: Wiley.

Allen, L. E., and C. S. Saxon. 1995. Better language, better thought, better communication: The a-hohfeld language for legal analysis. In *ICAIL '95: Proceedings of the 5th International Conference on Artificial Intelligence and Law*, 219–228. New York: ACM Press.

Álvarez, R., M. Ayuso, and M. Bécue. 2005. Statistical study of judicial practices. In *Law and the Semantic Web. Legal ontologies, methodologies, legal information retrieval, and applications*, ed. V. R. Benjamins, P. Casanovas, J. Breuker, and A. Gangemi. *Lecture notes in artificial intelligence*, Vol. 3369, 25–35. Berlin/Heidelberg: Springer.

Anthony, L. 2005. AntConc: Design and development of a freeware corpus analysis toolkit for the technical writing classroom. In *International Professional Communication Conference* 10–13 July, 729–737.

Antoniou, G., E. Franconi, and F. van Harmelen. 2005. Introduction to Semantic Web ontology languages. In *Reasoning web*, ed. N. Eisinger and J. Maluszynski. *Lecture notes in computer science*, Vol. 3564, 1–21. Berlin Heidelberg: Springer.

Antoniou, G., and F. van Harmelen. 2004a, April. *A Semantic Web primer. Cooperative information systems*. Cambridge: MIT Press.

Antoniou, G., and F. van Harmelen. 2004b, March. Web ontology language: OWL. In *Handbook on ontologies*, ed. S. Staab and R. Studer, 67–92. Heidelberg: Springer.

Antoniou, G., and F. van Harmelen. 2008. *A Semantic Web primer*. 2nd ed. *Cooperative information systems*. Amsterdam: MIT Press.

Antoniou, G., and G. Wagner. 2003. Rules and defeasible reasoning on the Semantic Web. In *Rules and rule markup languages for the Semantic Web*, ed. M. Schroeder and G. Wagner. *Lecture notes in computer science*, Vol. 2876, 111–120. Berlin/Heidelberg: Springer. doi:10.1007/978-3-540-39715-1_8.

Aoki, C., M. Kurematsu, and T. Yamaguchi. 1998. LODE: A legal ontology development environment in Proceedings of The Pacific Knowledge Acquisition Workshop (PKAW'96), Coogee, Sydney, Australia.

Arnaiz, A., R. López, and M. Loredo. 2005. *Organización judicial*. Vol. 1, *Colección de esquemas de derecho procesal*. Valencia: Tirant Lo Blanc.

Asaro, C., M. Biasiotti, P. Guidotti, M. Papini, M. Sagri, and D. Tiscornia. 2003. A domain ontology: Italian crime ontology. In *Proceedings of the ICAIL 2003 Workshop on Legal Ontologies and Web Based Legal Information Management*, 1–7.

Asaro, C., and E. Nissan. 2001. The daedalus system: A tool for the Italian investigating magistrate. *Computers and Artificial Intelligence* 20(6):1–40.

Ashley, K. D. 2009. Ontological requirements for analogical, teleological, and hypothetical legal reasoning. In *ICAIL*, 1–10. New York: ACM.

Ashley, K. D., and S. Brüninghaus. 2003. A predictive role for intermediate legal concepts. In *Proceedings of the 16th Annual Conference on Legal Knowledge and Information Systems (JURIX'03)*, Utrecht, ed. D. Bourcier. Amsterdam: IOS Press.

Aussenac-Gilles, N., B. Biébow, and S. Szulman. 2000a. Corpus analysis for conceptual modelling. In *Workshop on Ontologies and Texts, Knowledge Engineering and Knowledge Management: Methods, Models and Tool, (EKAW'2000)*, October 2009, Juan-les-pins.

Aussenac-Gilles, N., B. Biébow, and S. Szulman. 2000b. Revisiting ontology design: A method based on corpus analysis. In *Proceedings of EKAW 2000*, ed. R. Dieng and O. Corby, Vol. 1937, 172–188. Berlin/Heidelberg: Springer.

Ayuso, M., M. Bécue, R. Álvarez, O. Valencia, R. Álvarez, M. L. Hernández, and M. Santolino. 2003, Septiembre. Jueces jóvenes en españa (2002). análisis estadístico de las encuestas a los jueces en su primer destino (promociones 48/49 y 50). análisis comparativo con jueces de mayor experiencia. SEC-2001-2581-C02-01/02 informe interno Report n2, Consejo General del Poder Judicial [General Council of the Judiciary].

Baader, F. 2003. *Description logic terminology*, Chapter Appendix 1, 485–495. Cambridge: Cambridge University Press.

Baayen, R. 2008. *Analyzing linguistic data: A practical introduction to statistics*. Cambridge/New York: Cambridge University Press.

Bach, D., R. Meersman, P. Spyns, and D. Trog. 2010. Mapping OWL-DL into orm/ridl. In *On the move to meaningful internet systems 2007: OTM 2007 Workshops*, ed. R. Meersman, Z. Tari, and P. Herrero. *Lecture notes in computer science*, Vol. 4805, 742–751. Berlin/Heidelberg: Springer.

Baer, P. D., K. Kerremans, and R. Temmerman. 2006. The termontography workbench: A protégé-based tool for the compilation of multilingual terminological resources. In *Proceedings of the 9th International Protégé Conference (Poster and Demo Session)*, Stanford, July 23–26, 2006.

Baer, P. D., K. Kerremans, and R. Temmerman. 2008. Constructing ontology-underpinned terminological resources. A categorisation framework api. In *Proceedings of the 8th International Conference on Terminology and Knowledge Engineering*, Copenhagen, 18–21 August 2008.

Baer, P. D., R. Meersman, and R. Temmerman. 2009. Termontography and DOGMA for knowledge engineering within prolix. In *Proceedings of the Confederated International Workshops and Posters on the Move to Meaningful Internet Systems: ADI, CAMS, EI2N, ISDE, IWSSA, MONET, OnToContent, ODIS, ORM, OTM Academy, SWWS, SEMELS, Beyond SAWSDL, and COMBEK* , Vilamoura, 2009, ed. R. Meersman, P. Herrero, and T. Dillon. *Lecture notes in computer science*, Vol. 5872, 534–543. Berlin/Heidelberg: Springer.

Bagby, J., and T. Mullen. 2007. Legal ontology of sales law application to ecomerce. *Artificial Intelligence and Law* 15:155–170.

Baglioli, C., E. Francesconi, and G. Sartor, eds. 2007. *Proceedings of the V Legislative XML Workshop*. Florence: European Press Academic Publishing.

Barbagallo, A., A. D. Nicola, and M. Missikoff. 2010. eGovernment ontologies: Social participation in building and evolution. *Hawaii International Conference on System Sciences* 0:1–10.

Barlas, C. 1995. The imprimatur project. In *KnowRight '95: Proceedings of the Conference on Intellectual Property Rights and New Technologies*, 264–272. Munich: R. Oldenbourg Verlag GmbH.

Bartalesi Lenzi, V., C. Biagioli, A. Cappelli, R. Sprugnoli, and F. Turchi. 2007. Meta data driven legislative information retrieval based on semantic and pragmatic knowledge models. In *Proceedings of the 2nd International Conference on Metadata and Semantics Research*, Corfu, October, 11–12th, 2007.

Bench-Capon, T. 1990. *Knowledge representation: An approach to artificial intelligence*. London: Academic Press.

Bench-Capon, T. 1994. Legal theory and legal kbs: A computer scientist's perspective. In *Legal knowledge based systems (JURIX'94) the foundation for legal knowledge systems: The relation with legal theory*, ed. H. Prakken, A. Muntjewerff, and A. Soeteman, 33–42. Lelystad: Koninklijke Vermande. ISBN 90 5458 190 5.

Bench-Capon, T. 2001. Task neutral ontologies, common sense ontologies and legal information systems. In *Proceedings of the Second International Workshop on Legal Ontologies (LEGONT) in JURIX 2001*, ed. R. Winkels, 15–19. Amsterdam: IOS Press.

Bench-Capon, T., and P. Visser. 1996. Deep models, ontologies and legal knowledge based systems. In *Proceedings of JURIX'96, Legal Knowledge Based Systems (Foundations of Legal Knowledge Systems)*, ed. R. van Kralingen, H. van den Herik, J. Prins, M. Sergot, and J. Zeleznikow, 3–14. Tilburg: Tilburg University Press.

Bench-Capon, T. J. M., and P. R. S. Visser. 1997. Ontologies in legal information systems; the need for explicit specifications of domain conceptualisations. In *Proceedings of the 6th International Conference on Artificial Intelligence and Law (ICAIL'97)*, 132–141. New York: ACM Press.

Benjamins, V. R., P. Casanovas, J. Breuke, and A. Gangemi. 2005a. Law and the Semantic Web: An introduction. In *Law and the Semantic Web. Legal ontologies, methodologies, legal information retrieval, and applications [Outcome of the Workshop on Legal Ontologies and Web-Based Legal Information Management, June 28, 2003, Edinburgh, UK & International Seminar on Law and the Semantic Web, November 20–21, 2003, Barcelona, Spain]*, ed. V. R. Benjamins, P. Casanovas, J. Breuker, and A. Gangemi. *Lecture notes in computer science*, Vol. 3369, 1–17. Berlin/Heidelberg: Springer.

Benjamins, V. R., P. Casanovas, J. Breuker, and A. Gangemi, eds. 2005b. *Law and the Semantic Web. Legal ontologies, methodologies, legal information retrieval, and applications [outcome of the Workshop on Legal Ontologies and Web-Based Legal Information Management, June 28, 2003, Edinburgh, UK & International Seminar on Law and the Semantic Web, November 20–21, 2003, Barcelona, Spain]. Lecture notes in computer science*, Vol. 3369, Berlin/Heidelberg: Springer.

Benjamins, V. R., P. Casanovas, J. Contreras, J. M. López-Covo, and L. Lemus. 2005c. Iuriservice: An intelligent frequently asked questions system to assist newly appointed judges. In *Law and the Semantic Web. Legal ontologies, methodologies, legal information retrieval, and applications [Outcome of the Workshop on Legal Ontologies and Web-Based Legal Information Management, June 28, 2003, Edinburgh, UK & International Seminar on Law and the Semantic Web, November 20–21, 2003, Barcelona, Spain]*, ed. V. R. Benjamins, P. Casanovas, J. Breuker, and A. Gangemi. *Lecture notes in computer science*, Vol. 3369, 205–222. Berlin/Heidelberg: Springer.

Benjamins, V. R., J. Contreras, P. Casanovas, M. Ayuso, M. Bécue, L. Lemus, and C. Urios. 2004. Ontologies of professional legal knowledge as the basis for intelligent it support for judges. *Artificial Intelligence and Law* 12(4):359–378. Presented first at *ICAIL 2003 Workshop on Legal Ontologies & Web Based Legal Information Management*.

Benjamins, V. R., J. Contreras, and O. C. A. Gómez-Pérez. 2002. Six challenges for the Semantic Web. Presented at *Semantic Web Workshop, at the Eighth International Conference on Principles of Knowledge Representation and Reasoning (KR2002)*, Toulouse, April 22–25, 2002.

Benjamins, V. R., and A. Gómez-Pérez. 1999. Knowledge-system technology: Ontologies and problem-solving methods. *Knowledge and Information Systems*, Retrieved November 10, 2008. http://hcs.science.uva.nl/usr/richard/pdf/kais.pdf [submitted].

Bernaras, A., I. Laresgoiti, and J. Corera. 1996. Building and reusing ontologies for electrical network applications. In *Proceedings of the 12th European Conference on Artificial Intelligence (ECAI'96)*, ed. W. Wahlster, 298–302. Budapest, Hungary: Wiley.

Berners-Lee, T. 1998, September. Why RDF model is different from the XML model. http://www.w3.org/DesignIssues/RDF-XML.html

Berners-Lee, T. 2000. Semantic Web on XML. Keynote presentation for XML 2000.

Berners-Lee, T. 2003. Foreword. In *Spinning the Semantic Web: Bringing the world wide web to its full potential*, ed. D. Fensel, J. A. Hendler, H. Lieberman, and W. Wahlster, xii–xxiii. Cambridge: MIT Press.

Berners-Lee, T., and M. Fischetti. 1999. *Weaving the Web: The original design and ultimate destiny of the world wide web by its inventor*. New York: Harper.

Berners-Lee, T., J. Hendler, and O. Lassila. 2001, May. The Semantic Web. *Scientific American* 284(5):34–43.

Biasiotti, M., E. Francesconi, M. Palmirani, G. Sartor, and F. Vitali. 2008. Legal informatics and management of legislative documents. In *GC working papers*, ed. G. Sartor, Vol. 2, Global Centre for ICT in Parliament. Rome, Italy.

Biébow, B., and S. Szulman. 1999. TERMINAE: A linguistics-based tool for building of a domain ontology. In *Proceedings of the 11th European Workshop (EKAW'99)*, ed. D. Fensel and R. Studer, *Lecture notes in artificial intelligence*, Vol. 1621, 49–66. Berlin/Heidelberg: Springer.

Binefa, X., C. Gracia, M. Monton, J. Carrabina, C. Montero, J. Serrano, M. Blázquez, R. Benjamins, E. Teodoro, M. Poblet, and P. Casanovas. 2007. Developing ontologies for legal multimedia applications. In *Proceedings of the Workshop on Legal Ontologies and Artificial Intelligence Techniques (LOAIT 2007) at the International Conference on AI and Law (ICAIL'07)*, ed. P. Casanovas, M. A. Biasiotti, and E. F. M. T. Sagri, 87–101, Stanford, June 4.

Bing, J. 1984/1991. *Handbook of legal information retrieval (in cooperation with T. Fjeldvig, T. Harvold and R. Svoboda)*. Revised ed. Amsterdam: North-Holland Publishing Company.

Bing, J. 2010. Chapter Let there be LITE: A brief history of legal information retrieval. In *A History of legal informatics*, ed. Paliwala, A. *LEFIS series*, Vol. 9, LEFIS, Zaragoza: Prensas Universitarias de Zaragoza.

Bizer, C., T. Heath, and T. Berners-Lee. 2009. Linked Data – the story so far. *International Journal on Semantic Web and Information Systems* 5(3):1–22.

Blaquier-Ascaño, M. I. 2006. OnProc: Una ontología para el proceso jurídico. In *Congreso Internacional INFO 2006*. La Habana, Cuba: Instituto de Información Científica y Tecnológica (IDICT).

Blázquez, M., M. Fernández, J. M. García-Pinar, and A. Gómez-Pérez. 1998. Building ontologies at the knowledge level using the ontology design environment. In *Proceedings of the Eleventh Knowledge Acquisition Workshop (KAW98)*. Banff: Voyager Inn.

Blázquez, M., R. Peña-Ortiz, J. Contreras, R. Benjamins, P. Casanovas, J.-J. Vallbé, and N. Casellas. 2005, December. D10.3.1 legal case study: Prototype. Sekt ist-2003-506826 deliverable, SEKT, EU-IST Project IST-2003-506826, Intelligent Software Components S.A. (iSOCO) and Universitat Autonoma de Barcelona (UAB).

Blomqvist, E. 2007. Semi-automatic ontology engineering using patterns. In *The Semantic Web*, ed. K. Aberer, K.-S. Choi, N. Noy, D. Allemang, K.-I. Lee, L. Nixon, J. Golbeck, P. Mika, D. Maynard, R. Mizoguchi, G. Schreiber, and P. Cudré-Mauroux, *Lecture notes in computer science*, Vol. 4825, 911–915. Berlin/Heidelberg: Springer.

Blomqvist, E. 2010. Ontocase – a pattern-based ontology construction approach. In *On the move to meaningful internet systems 2007: CoopIS, DOA, ODBASE, GADA, and IS*, ed. R. Meersman and Z. Tari. *Lecture notes in computer science*, Vol. 4803, 971–988. Berlin/Heidelberg: Springer.

Blythin, S., M. Rouncefield, and J.A. Hughes. 1997. Never mind the ethno' stuff, what does all this mean and what do we do now: ethnography in the commercial world. *Interactions* 4(3):38–47.
Boella, G., L. Favali, and L. Lesmo. 2001. An action-based ontology of legal relations. In *Proceedings of the Eigth International Conference on Artificial Intelligence and Law (ICAIL'01)*, May 21–25, St. Louis, 227–228. New York: ACM Press.
Boella, G., L. Lesmo, and R. Damiano. 2005. On the ontological status of norms. In *Law and the Semantic Web. Legal ontologies, methodologies, legal information retrieval, and applications [outcome of the Workshop on Legal Ontologies and Web-Based Legal Information Management, June 28, 2003, Edinburgh, UK & International Seminar on Law and the Semantic Web, November 20–21, 2003, Barcelona, Spain]*, ed. V. R. Benjamins, P. Casanovas, J. Breuker, and A. Gangemi. *Lecture notes in computer science*, Vol. 3369, 125–141. Berlin/Heidelberg: Springer.
Boella, G., and L. van der Torre. 2004a. An agent oriented ontology of social reality. In *Proceedings of Formal Ontologies in Information Systems FOIS-2004*, 210–221. Amsterdam: IOS Press.
Boella, G., and L. van der Torre 2004b. Attributing mental attitudes to roles: The agent metaphor applied to etrade organizations. In *Proceedings of ICEC04*. New York: ACM.
Boer, A., M. di Bello, K. van den Berg, T. Gordon, A. Förhécz, and R. Vas. 2007. Specification of the legal knowledge interchange format. Deliverable 1.1 D.1.1, ESTRELLA project (IST-2004-027655).
Boer, A., R. Hoekstra, R. Winkels, T. van Engers, and F. Willaert. 2002. Metalex: Legislation in XML. In *Proceedings of Fifteenth Annual Conference of Legal Knowledge and Information Systems (Jurix'02)*, ed. T. Bench-Capon, A. Daskalopulu, and R. Winkels. *Frontiers in artificial intelligence and applications*, 1–10. Amsterdam: IOS Press.
Boer, A., T. van Engers, and R. Winkels. 2003. Using ontologies for comparing and harmonizing legislation. In *Proceedings of the International Conference on Artificial Intelligence and Law (ICAIL)*. Edinburgh: ACM Press.
Boer, A., R. Winkels, and R. Hoekstra. 2001. The CLIME ontology. In *Proceedings of the Second International Workshop on Legal Ontologies (LEGONT) in JURIX 2001*, ed. R. Winkels, 37–47. Amsterdam: IOS Press.
Boer, A., R. Winkels, and F. Vitali. 2008. Metalex XML and the legal knowledge interchange format. In *Computable models of the law*, ed. P. Casanovas, G. Sartor, N. Casellas, and R. Rubino, *Lecture notes in artificial intelligence*, Vol. 4884, 21–41. Berlin/Heidelberg: Springer.
Borst, W. N. 1997. *Construction of engineering ontologies for knowledge sharing and reuse*. Ph.D. thesis, University of Twente.
Bösser, T., N. Casellas, E.-M. Melchior, I. Thurlow, and J.-J. Vallbé. 2009. User quality and business benefit of semantic knowledge management applications. In *Semantic knowledge management*, ed. J. Davies, M. Grobelnik, and D. Mladenic, 231–244. Berlin Heidelberg: Springer.
Bösser, T., and E. Melchior. 2006. *D8.2.2 user needs and opportunities for business process improvement with knowledge technology*. SEKT IST-2003-506826 Deliverable 8.2.2, SEKT, EU-IST Project IST-2003-506826, Kea-Pro, GmbH, Springer (Switzerland).
Bourcier, D., P. Casanovas, M. D. de Rosnay, and C. Maracke. 2010. *Intelligent multimedia. Managing creative works in a digital world.* Florence: European Press Academic Publishing.
Brank, J., M. Grobelnik, and D. Mladenic. 2005. *D.1.6.1 ontology evaluation*. SEKT IST-2003-506826 Deliverable 1.6.1, SEKT, EU-IST Project Jozef Stefan Institute.
Bratt, S. 2004. Spinning threads for the next generation of the web. In *Talk at the 16th IRIS Workshop*, Tucson, Arizona, USA: W3C (World Wide Web Consortium).
Bratt, S. 2008. Semantic Web, and other technologies to watch. In *Talk at SemTech 2008*. W3C (World Wide Web Consortium).
Breuker, J. 2003. Managing legal domains: In search of a core ontology for law. In *Proceedings of the Workshop on Knowledge Management and the Semantic Web at KCAP-2003*, ed. R. Dieng-Kuntz and F. Gandon. Sanibel, Florida, USA.

Breuker, J. 2004. Constructing a legal core ontology: LRI-Core. In *Proceedings of the Workshop on Ontologies and their Applications*, 115–126. Sao Luis, Maranhao – Brazil.

Breuker, J., P. Casanovas, M. Klein, and E. Francesconi. 2008. The flood, the channels and the dykes: Managing legal information in a globalized and digital world. In *Law, ontologies and the Semantic Web. Channelling the legal information flood*, ed. J. Breuker, P. Casanovas, M. Klein, and E. Francesconi, *Frontiers in artificial intelligence and applications*, Vol. 188. Amsterdam: IOS Press.

Breuker, J., P. Casanovas, M. C. A. Klein, and E. Francesconi, eds. 2009. *Law, ontologies and the Semantic Web – channelling the legal information flood. Frontiers in Artificial Intelligence and Applications*. Vol. 188. Amsterdam: IOS Press.

Breuker, J., A. Elhag, E. Petkov, and R. Winkels. 2002a. Ontologies for legal information serving and knowledge management. In *Legal knowledge and information systems. Jurix 2002: The Fifteenth Annual Conference*, ed. T. Bench-Capon, A. Daskalopulu, and R. Winkels, 73–82. Amsterdam: IOS Press.

Breuker, J., A. Elhag, E. Petkov, and R. Winkels. 2002b. IT support for the judiciary: Use of ontologies in the e-Court project. In *Proceedings of the ICCS Conference on Conceptual Graphs*, 17–26

Breuker, J., and R. Hoekstra. 2004a. Core concepts of law: Taking common-sense seriously. In *Proceedings of Formal Ontologies in Information Systems FOIS-2004*, 210–221. Amsterdam: IOS Press.

Breuker, J., and R. Hoekstra. 2004b. Epistemology and ontology in core ontologies: FOLaw and LRI-Core, two core ontologies for law. In *Proceedings of Workshop on Core Ontologies in Ontology Engineering in the 14th International Conference (EKAW'04)*, ed. A. Gangemi and S. Borgo, Whittlebury Hall, CEUR.

Breuker, J., R. Hoekstra, A. Boer, K. van den Berg, R. Rubino, G. Sartor, M. Palmirani, A. Wyner, and T. Bench-Capon. 2007. OWL ontology of basic legal concepts (LKIF-core). Deliverable 1.4 D.1.4, ESTRELLA project (IST-2004-027655).

Breuker, J., A. Valente, and R. Winkels. 2005. Use and reuse of legal ontologies in knowledge engineering and information management. In *Law and the Semantic Web. Legal ontologies, methodologies, legal information retrieval, and applications*, ed. V. R. Benjamins, P. Casanovas, J. Breuker, and A. Gangemi. *Lecture notes in computer science*, Vol. 3369, 35–64. Berlin/Heidelberg: Springer.

Breuker, J., and R. Winkels. 2003. Use and reuse of legal ontologies in knowledge engineering and information management. *Draft presentation paper at ICAIL 2003 Workshop on Legal Ontologies and Web based legal information management 28 June 2003, Edinburgh, Scotland, UK. Organised in conjunction with ICAIL 2003: Ninth International Conference on Artificial Intelligence and Law*, 24–28 June, 2003 Edinburgh, Scotland, UK.

Bromme, R., and H. Tillema. 1995. Fusing experience and theory: The structure of professional knowledge. *Learning and Instruction* 5:261–267.

Brooke, J. 1996. Sus: A 'quick and dirty' usability scale. In *Usability evaluation in industry*, ed. P. W. Jordan, B. Thomas, I. L. McClelland, and B. Weerdmeester. Chapter 21, 189–194. London: Taylor & Francis.

Brouwer, P. 1994. Legal knowledge representation in the perspective of legal theory. In *Legal knowledge based systems (JURIX'94) the foundation for legal knowledge systems: The relation with legal theory*, ed. H. Prakken, A. Muntjewerff, and A. Soeteman, 9–18. Lelystad: Koninklijke Vermande. ISBN 90 5458 190 5.

Buitelaar, P., P. Cimiano, M. Grobelnik, and M. Sintek. 2005a. Ontology learning from text. Tutorial at ECML/PKDD 2005, Porto, Portugal. In *Conjunction with the ECML/PKDD 2005 Workshop on: Knowledge Discovery and Ontologies (KDO-2005)*. Porto, Portugal 3–7 October. http://people.aifb.kit.edu/pci/OL_Tutorial_ECML_PKDD_05/.

Buitelaar, P., P. Cimiano, and B. Magnini. 2005b, July. Ontology learning from text: An overview. In *Ontology learning from text: Methods, evaluation and applications*, ed. P. Buitelaar, P. Cimiano, and B. Magnini, *Frontiers in artificial intelligence and applications series*, Vol. 123, 3–12. Amsterdam: IOS Press.

Buitelaar, P., D. Olejnik, and M. Sintek. 2004. A protégé plug-in for ontology extraction from text based on linguistic analysis. In *Proceedings of the 1st European Semantic Web Symposium (ESWS)*, Heraklion, May.

Burge, J. E. 1998. Knowledge elicitation tool classification. http://web.cs.wpi.edu/~jburge/thesis/kematrix.html

Bylander, T., and B. Chandrasekaran. 1987. Generic tasks for knowledge-based reasoning: The "right" level of abstraction for knowledge acquisition. *International Journal of Man-Machine Studies* 26(2):231–243.

Cabinet Office, e-Government Unit, T. P. T. 2006. e-government metadata standard. Standard 2006-08-29, Cabinet Office UK.

Cappelli, A., V. B. Lenzi, R. Sprugnoli, and C. Biagioli. 2007. Modelization of domain concepts extracted from the Italian privacy legislation. In *Proceedings of the Workshop on Computational Semantics (IWCS-7)*, Tilburg. http://www.ittig.cnr.it/Presentazione/OrganizzazioneLogistica/biagioli/Cappelli-et-al.pdf

Casanovas, P., N. Casellas, C. Tempich, D. Vrandečić, and R. Benjamins. 2007a, June. OPJK and DILIGENT: Ontology modeling in a distributed environment. *Artificial Intelligence and Law* 15(2):171–186. Presented at the ICAIL 2005 LOAIT Workshop.

Casanovas, P., N. Casellas, J.-Vallbé, M. Poblet, V. Benjamins, M. Blázquez, R. Peña-Ortiz, and J. Contreras. 2006. Semantic Web: A legal case study. In *Semantic Web technology: Trends and research in ontology-based systems*, ed. J. Davies, R. Studer, and P. Warren, Chapter 12, 259–280. Chichester/Hoboken: Wiley.

Casanovas, P., N. Casellas, J. Vallbé, M. Poblet, F. Ramos, J. Gorroñogointia, J. Contreras, M. Blázquez, and R. Benjamins. 2005a. Iuriservice II: Ontology development and architectural design. In *Proceedings of the Tenth International Conference on Artificial Intelligence and Law (ICAIL 2005)*, June 6–11, University of Bologna (Italy), 188–195. Bologna: ACM.

Casanovas, P., M. Poblet, N. Casellas, J. Contreras, R. Benjamins, and M. Blázquez. 2005b. Supporting newly-appointed judges: A legal knowledge management case study. *Journal of Knowledge Management* 9(5):7–27.

Casanovas, P., M. Poblet, N. Casellas, J. Vallbé, F. Ramos, R. Benjamins, M. Blázquez, L. Rodrigo, J. Contreras, and J. Gorroñogoitia-Cruz. 2004, December/January 2005. D10.2.1 legal case study: Legal scenario. Sekt ist-2003-506826 deliverable, SEKT, EU-IST Project IST-2003-506826, Intelligent Software Components S.A. and Universitat Autonoma de Barcelona.

Casanovas, P., M. Poblet, E. Teodoro, N. Casellas, N. Galera, E. Ferran, and J.-M. Lopez-Cobo. 2007b. Conceptualizing hearings in the Spanish civil courts: Knowledge acquisition methodology for legal multimedia applications. In *Workshop on Multimedia Ontologies and Artificial Intelligence Techniques in Law (MOAIL 2007) at JURIX 2007*, December 12th, Leiden. Organised by Xavier Binefa and Marie-Francine Moens and José-Manuel López-Cobo and Pompeu Casanovas.

Casellas, N. 2008, December. *Modelling legal knowledge through ontologies. OPJK: The Ontology of professional judicial knowledge*. Ph.D. thesis, Faculty of Law, Universitat Autònoma de Barcelona, Barcelona (Spain).

Casellas, N. 2009. Ontology evaluation through usability measures. An experiment with the sus scale in the legal domain. In *On the move to meaningful internet systems (OTM Conferences and Workshops). Lecture notes in computer science*, Vol. 5872, 594–603. Berlin/Heidelberg: Springer.

Casellas, N., M. Blázquez, A. Kiryakov, P. Casanovas, M. Poblet, and V. R. Benjamins. 2005. OPJK into PROTON: Legal domain ontology integration into an upper-level ontology. In *OTM Workshops, Lecture notes in computer science*, ed. R. Meersman, Z. Tari, P. Herrero, G. Méndez, L. Cavedon, D. Martin, A. Hinze, G. Buchanan, M. S. Pérez, V. Robles, J. Humble, A. Albani, J. L. G. Dietz, H. Panetto, M. Scannapieco, T. A. Halpin, P. Spyns, J. M. Zaha, E. Zimányi, E. Stefanakis, T. S. Dillon, L. Feng, M. Jarrar, J. Lehmann, A. de Moor, E. Duval, and L. Aroyo. *Lecture notes in computer science*, Vol. 3762, 846–855. Berlin/Heidelberg: Springer.

Casellas, N., P. Casanovas, J.-J. Vallbé, M. Poblet, M. Blázquez, J. Contreras, J. M. López-Cobo, and V. R. Benjamins. 2007. Semantic enhancement for legal information retrieval: Iuriservice performance. In *Proceedings of the Eleventh International Conference on Artificial Intelligence and Law. ICAIL 2007*, June 4–8, Stanford Law School, California, 49–57. New York: Association for Computing Machinery.

Casellas, N., J. E. Nieto, A. Meroño, A. Roig, S. Torralba, M. Reyes de los Mozos, and P. Casanovas. 2010. Ontological semantics for data privacy compliance: The neurona ontology. In *AAAI Spring Symposium Series Technical Reports SS-10-05 (Intelligent Information Privacy Management)*, Stanford, 23–25 March 2010, 34–38. California: AAAI Press.

Cevenini, C., G. Contissa, M. Laukyte, C. Information, R. Riveret, and R. Rubino. 2008. Development of the ALIS IP ontology: Merging legal and technical perspectives. In *Computer-aided innovation (CAI), IFIP International federation for information processing*, Vol. 277, 169–180. Boston: Springer.

Chandrasekaran, B. 1986, Fall. Generic tasks in knowledge-based reasoning: High-level building blocks for expert system design. *IEEE Expert* 1(3):23–30.

Chandrasekaran, B., J. Josephson, and R. Benjamins. 1998. The ontology of tasks and methods. In *Proceedings of the 11th Knowledge Acquisition Modeling and Management Workshop, KAW'98*, April. Banff: Voyager Inn. (Expanded version).

Chandrasekaran, B., J. R. Josephson, and V. R. Benjamins. 1999, Jan./Feb. What are ontologies, and why do we need them? *IEEE Intelligent Systems* 14(1):20–26.

Charalabidis, Y., and K. Metaxiotis. 2009. *Social and political implications of data mining: Knowledge management in e-Government. Ontology-based management of e-Government knowledge*, ed. H. Rahman, Chapter XIII, 221–234. February 2009, IGI Global, Hershey, USA.

Cimiano, P., and J. Völker. 2005. Text2Onto – a framework for ontology learning and data-driven change discovery. In *Proceedings of the 10th International Conference on Applications of Natural Language to Information Systems (NLDB)*, ed. A. Montoyo, R. Munoz, and E. Metais, *Lecture notes in computer science*, Vol. 3513, 227–238. Alicante: Springer.

Cimiano, P., J. Völker, and R. Studer. 2006. Ontologies on demand? a description of the state-of-the-art, applications, challenges and trends for ontology learning from text. *Information Wissenschaft und Praxis* 57(6–7):315–320.

Clancey, W. J. 1981, November. The epistemology of a rule-based expert system: A framework for explanation. Technical Report STAN-CS-81-896, Department of Computer Science, Stanford University, Stanford.

Connolly, D., F. van Harmelen, I. Horrocks, D. L. Mcguinness, L. A., and Stein. 2001, December. Daml+oil (march 2001) reference description. Technical report, World Wide Web Consortium (W3C).

Conrad, J. G., and F. Schilder. 2007. Opinion mining in legal blogs. In *Proceedings of the Eleventh International Conference on Artificial Intelligence and Law (ICAIL 2007)*, June 4–8, Palo Alto, 231–236. New York: ICAIL, ACM Press.

Consejo del Poder Judicial, G. 2007. Plan docente de formación inicial – 59ª promoción de la carrera judicial (curso 2007–2009). Available at the website of the Consejo General del Poder Judicial: http://www.poderjudicial.es

Corcho, O., M. Fernández, A. Gómez-Pérez, and A. López-Cima. 2005. Building legal ontologies with METHONTOLOGY and WebODE. In *Law and the Semantic Web. Legal ontologies, methodologies, legal information retrieval, and applications [outcome of the Workshop on Legal Ontologies and Web-Based Legal Information Management, June 28, 2003, Edinburgh, UK & International Seminar on Law and the Semantic Web, November 20–21, 2003, Barcelona, Spain]*, ed. V. R. Benjamins, P. Casanovas, J. Breuker, and A. Gangemi. *Lecture notes in computer science*, Vol. 3369, 142–157. Berlin/Heidelberg: Springer.

Corcho, O., M. Fernández-López, and A. Gómez-Pérez. 2001. Technical roadmap v.1.0. Ist-2000-29243 deliverable 1.1.1, OntoWeb: Ontology-based Information Exchange for Knowledge Management and Electronic Commerce IST EU Project.

Corcho, O., M. Fernández-López, and A. Gómez-Pérez. 2003. Methodologies, tools and languages for building ontologies: Where is their meeting point? *Data and Knowledge Engineering* 46(1):41–64.

Cortés-Domínguez, V., and V. Moreno-Catena. 2008a. *Derecho procesal civil. Parte especial.* 3ªrd ed. Tirant Lo Blanch.

Cortés-Domínguez, V., and V. Moreno-Catena. 2008b. *Derecho procesal civil. Parte general.* 3ªrd ed. Tirant Lo Blanch.

Costa, M., O. Sousa, and J. Neves. 1999. Managing legal precedents with case retrieval nets. In *Proceedings of Legal Knowledge Based Systems, JURIX 1999, The Twelfth Conference*, Nijmegen, ed. H. J. van den Herik, 13–22. Amsterdam: IOS Press.

Costilla, C., J. P. Palacios, J. Cremades, and J. Vila. 2005. e-government: A legislative ontology for the 'siap' parliamentary management system. In *Proceedings of TCGOV 2005*, ed. M. B. Böhlen, J. Gamper, W. Polasek, and M. A. Wimmer. *Lecture notes on artificial intelligence*, Vol. 3416, 134–146. IFIP International Federation for Information Processing. Heidelberg: Springer

Cunningham, H., D. Maynard, K. Bontcheva, and V. Tablan. 2002, July. GATE: A framework and graphical development environment for robust NLP tools and applications. In *Proceedings of the 40th Anniversary Meeting of the Association for Computational Linguistics (ACL'02)*, Philadelphia, 168–175.

Curtoni, P., L. Dini, V. di Tomaso, L. Mommers, W. Peters, P. Quaresma, E. Schweighofer, and D. Tiscornia. 2005. Semantic access to multilingual legal information. In *Proceedings of EU INFO Workshop "Free EU Information on the Web: The future beyond the new EUR-Lex" at JURIX 2005*, ed. E. Schweighofer, 1–11. Amsterdam: IOS Press.

da Rosa Alves, I. M., R. L. da Oliveira Chishman, and P. M. T. D. Quaresma. 2007. The construction of a juridical ontology. In *Proceedings of the Eleventh International Conference on Artificial Intelligence and Law (ICAIL 2007)*, June 4–8, Palo Alto, 93–94. New York: ACM Press.

d'Aquin, M., C. Baldassarre, L. Gridinoc, S. Angeletou, M. Sabou, and E. Motta. 2007. Characterizing knowledge on the Semantic Web with Watson. In *Proceedings of the 5th International Workshop on Evaluation of Ontologies and Ontology-based Tools, EON2007, Co-located with the ISWC2007*, Busan, November 11, ed. R. Garcia-Castro, D. Vrandečić, A. Gómez-Pérez, Y. Sure, and Z. Huang, *CEUR Workshop Proceedings*, Vol. 329, 1–10. CEUR-WS.org

Davies, R. 1999. Knowledge-based systems. In *The MIT Encyclopedia of the Cognitive Sciences*, ed. R. A. Wilson and F. C. Keil, 430–432. Cambridge: MIT Press.

Davies, J., R. Studer, and P. Warren, eds. 2006. *Semantic Web technology: Trends and research in ontology-based systems*. Chichester/Hoboken: Wiley.

de Bruijn, J., F. Martin-Recuerda, D. Manov, and M. Ehrig. 2004. D.4.2.1. state-of-the-art survey on ontology merging and aligning v1. SEKT IST-2003-506826 Deliverable 4.2.1, SEKT, EU-IST Project IST-2003-506826.

De Leenheer, P., and C. Debruyne. 2010. DOGMA-MESS: A tool for fact-oriented collaborative ontology evolution. In *On the move to meaningful internet systems: OTM 2008 Workshops*, ed. R. Meersman, Z. Tari, and P. Herrero, *Lecture notes in computer science*, Vol. 5333, 797–806. Berlin/Heidelberg: Springer.

de Moor, A., P. De Leenheer, and R. Meersman. 2006. DOGMA-MESS: A meaning evolution support system for interorganizational ontology engineering. In *Conceptual structures: Inspiration and application*, ed. H. Schärfe, P. Hitzler, and P. Øhrstrøm, *Lecture notes in computer science*, Vol. 4068, 189–202. Berlin/Heidelberg: Springer.

de Nicola, A., M. Missikoff, and R. Navigli. 2005. A proposal for a unified process for ontology building: UPON. In *Database and expert systems applications (DEXA)*, ed. K. V. Andersen, J. K. Debenham, and R. Wagner, *Lecture notes in computer science*, Vol. 3588, 655–664. Berlin/Heidelberg: Springer.

de Nicola, A., M. Missikoff, and R. Navigli. 2009. A software engineering approach to ontology building. *Information Systems* 34:258–275.

de Rosnay, M. D. 2003. Cognitive interfaces for legal expressions description – application to copyrighted works online sharing and transactions. In *Proceedings of the 16th Annual Conference on Legal Knowledge and Information Systems (JURIX'03)*, Utrecht, ed. D. Bourcier, 121–130. Amsterdam: IOS Press.

Dean, M., G. Schreiber, S. Bechhofer, F. van Harmelen, J. Hendler, I. Horrocks, D. L. McGuinness, P. F. Patel-Schneider, and L. A. Stein. 2004, February. OWL web ontology language reference. W3c recommendation 10 February 2004, World Wide Web Consortium (W3C). http://www.w3.org/TR/owl-ref/

Debruyne, C., P. De Leenheer, and R. Meersman. 2009. A method and tool for fact type reuse in the DOGMA ontology framework. In *On the move to meaningful internet systems: OTM 2009*, ed. R. Meersman, T. Dillon, and P. Herrero, *Lecture notes in computer science*, Vol. 5871, 1147–1164. Berlin/Heidelberg: Springer.

Delgado, J., I. Gallego, R. García, and R. Gil. 2002, June. An ontology for intellectual property rights: IPROnto. In *Collected Posters of the First International Semantic Web Conference (ISWC 2002)*, ed. R. Malyankar, Sardinia.

Delgado, J., I. Gallego, S. Llorente, and R. García. 2003. IPROnto: An ontology for digital rights management. In *Legal knowledge and information systems. Jurix 2003: The Sixteenth Annual Conference*, ed. D. Bourcier, 111–120. Amsterdam: IOS Press.

Dellschaft, K., H. Engelbrecht, J. Barreto, S. Rutenbeck, and S. Staab. 2008. Cicero: Tracking design rationale in collaborative ontology engineering. In *The Semantic Web: Research and applications*, ed. S. Bechhofer, M. Hauswirth, J. Hoffmann, and M. Koubarakis. *Lecture notes in computer science*, Vol. 5021, 782–786. Berlin/Heidelberg: Springer.

den Haan, N., and R. Winkels. 1994. The deep structure of law. In *Legal knowledge based systems (JURIX'94) The Foundation for legal knowledge systems: The relation with legal theory*, ed. H. Prakken, A. Muntjewerff, and A. Soeteman, 43–54. Lelystad: Koninklijke Vermande. ISBN 90 5458 190 5.

Denny, M. 2004, July. Ontology tools survey, revisited. Published on XML.com

Després, S., and B. Delforge. 2000. Designing medical law ontology from technical texts and core ontology. In *Proceedings of the Workshop on Ontologies and Text in the 12th European Workshop on Knowledge Acquisition, Modeling and Management (EKAW '00)*, Juan-Les-Pins, ed. N. Aussenac-Gilles and S. Szulman, (Application). Berlin: Springer.

Després, S., and S. Szulman. 2004. Construction of a legal ontology from a European community legislative text. In *Legal knowledge and information systems. Jurix 2004: The Seventeenth Annual Conference*, Amsterdam, ed. T. Gordon, 79–88. Amsterdam: IOS Press.

Després, S., and S. Szulman. 2006. TERMINAE method and integration process for legal ontology building. In *IEA/AIE*, ed. M. Ali and R. Dapoigny. *Lecture notes in computer science*, Vol. 4031, 1014–1023. Berlin/Heidelberg: Springer.

Després, S., and S. Szulman. 2007. Merging of legal micro-ontologies from European directives. *Artificial Intelligence and Law* 15:187–200.

Devedzić, V. 2002. Understanding ontological engineering. *Communication of the ACM* 45(4): 136–144.

Ding, L., and T. Finin. 2006. Characterizing the Semantic Web on the web. In *The Semantic Web – ISWC 2006, 5th International Semantic Web Conference, ISWC 2006*, Athens, GA, USA, November 5–9, 2006, Proceedings, ed. I.F. Cruz, S. Decker, D. Allemang, C. Preist, D. Schwabe, P. Mika, M. Uschold and L. Aroyo. *Lecture notes in computer science*, Vol. 4273, 242–257. Berlin/Heidelberg: Springer.

Ding, L., P. Kolari, Z. Ding, and S. Avancha. 2007. Using ontologies in the Semantic Web: A survey. In *Ontologies. A handbook of principles, concepts and applications in information systems*, ed. R. Sharman, R. Kishore, and R. Ramesh, *Integrated series in information systems*, Vol. 14, 70–113. New York: Springer.

Ding, L., P. Kolari, Z. Ding, S. Avancha, T. Finin, and A. Joshi. 2005, July. Using ontologies in the Semantic Web: A survey. e-Biquity TechReport TR-CS-05-07, UMBC eBiquity Research Group.

Dini, L., W. Peters, D. Liebwald, E. Schweighofer, L. Mommers, and W. Voermans. 2005. Cross-lingual legal information retrieval using a WordNet architecture. In *Proceedings of the Tenth International Conference on Artificial Intelligence and Law (ICAIL 2005)*, June 6th–11th, University of Bologna (Italy), 163–167. New York: ACM.

Domingue, J., L. Gutierrez, L. Cabral, M. Rowlatt, R. Davies, and S. Galizia. 2004, December. Wp 9: Case study egovernment. d9.3 e-government ontologye-government ontology. Dip project deliverable, Data, Information, and Process Integration with Semantic Web Services (DIP) Project.

Drumond, L., R. Girardi, and A. Leita. 2007. Architectural design of a multi-agent recommender system for the legal domain. In *Proceedings of the Eleventh International Conference on Artificial Intelligence and Law (ICAIL 2007)*, June 4–8, Palo Alto, 183–187. New York: ACM Press.

Drumond, L. R., R. Girardi, A. N. Lindoso, and B. L. Marinho. 2006a. A Semantic Web based recommender system for the legal domain. In *Proceedings of the 17th European Conference on Artificial Intelligence (ECAI 2006) Workshop on Recommender Systems*, Riva del Garda, ed. A. Felfernig and M. Zanker, 81–83. Amsterdam: IOS Press.

Drumond, L., A. Lindoso, and R. Girardi. 2006b, Dezembro. Infonorma: Um sistema de recomendação baseado em tecnologias da web semntica. *INFOCOMP – Jornal da Ciência da Computação* 5(4):93–102.

Dworkin, R. 1978. *Taking rights seriously*. London: Duckworth.

Dzbor, M., M. C. Suárez-Figueroa, E. Blomqvist, H. Lewen, M. Espinoza, A. Gómez-Pérez, and R. Palma. 2009, February. Experimentation and evaluation of the NeOn methodology. Deliverable D5.6.2, NeOn Project, http://www.neon-project.org

Epistemics. 2003, November. Knowledge acquisition. http://www.epistemics.co.uk/Notes/63-0-0.htm

Euzenat, J., T. L. Bach, J. Barrasa, and et al. 2004. State of the art on ontology alignment. Deliverable KWEB/2004/D2.2.3/v1.2, Knowledge Web.

Farquhar, A., R. Fikes, and J. Rice. 1997. Tools for assembling modular ontologies in Ontolingua. In *Proceedings of the Fourteenth National Conference on Artificial Intelligence and Ninth Innovative Applications of Artificial Intelligence Conference, AAAI 97, IAAI 97*, 27–31 July, 1997, Providence, Rhode Island. Vol. 14, 436–441. Wiley: AAAI Press/The MIT Press.

Feinerer, I. 2008, August. *A text mining framework in R and its applications*. Ph.D. thesis, Department of Statistics and Mathematics, Vienna University of Economics and Business Administration, Viena (Austria).

Fensel, D., A. Schönegge, R. Groenboom, and B. Wielinga. 1996. Specification and verification of knowledge-based systems. In *Proceedings of the 10th Banff Knowledge Acquisition for Knowledge-Based Systems Workshop (KAW'96)*, Banff, Vol. 1, 1–20.

Fernández-López, M. 1999, August. Overview of methodologies for building ontologies. In *Proceedings of the Workshop on Ontologies and Problem-Solving Methods in Conjunction with the Sixteenth International Joint Conference on Artificial Intelligence (IJCAI'99)*, Stockholm, 4.1–4.13.

Fernández-López, M., and A. Gómez-Pérez. 2002. Overview and analysis of methodologies for building ontologies. *Knowledge Engineering Review* 17(2):129–156.

Fernández-López, M., A. Gómez-Pérez, and N. Juristo. 1997. METHONTOLOGY: From ontological art towards ontological engineering. In *Ontological engineering: Papers from the 1997 Spring Symposium AAAI97*, ed. A. Farquhar and M. Gruninger, Volume Technical Report SS-97-06, Menlo Park, California, 33–40. Rhode Island: American Association for Artificial Intelligence.

Fortuna, B., M. Grobelnik, and D. Mladenic. 2007. OntoGen: Semi-automatic ontology editor. In *Proceedings of Human Interface and the Management of Information. Interacting in Information Environments, Symposium on Human Interface 2007, Held as Part of HCI International 2007*, Beijing, China, July 22–27, ed. M. J. Smith and G. Salvendy, *Lecture notes in computer science*, Vol. 4558, 309–318. Berlin/Heidelberg: Springer.

Francesconi, E., S. Montemagni, W. Peters, and D. Tiscornia. 2010a. Integrating a bottom-up and top-down methodology for building semantic resources for the multilingual legal domain. In *Semantic processing of legal texts: Where the language of law meets the law of language*, ed. E. Francesconi, S. Montemagni, W. Peters, and D. Tiscornia. *Lecture notes in computer science*. Vol. 6036, 95–121. Berlin/Heidelberg: Springer.

Francesconi, E., S. Montemagni, W. Peters, and D. Tiscornia, eds. 2010b. *Semantic processing of legal texts: Where the language of law meets the law of language. Lecture notes in computer science*. Vol. 6036. Berlin/Heidelberg: Springer.

Francesconi, E., and D. Tiscornia. 2008. Building semantic resources for legislative drafting: The dalos project. In *Computable models of the law*, ed. P. Casanovas, G. Sartor, N. Casellas, and R. Rubino, *Lecture notes in artificial intelligence*, Vol. 4884, 56–69. Berlin/Heidelberg: Springer.

Freitas, F., Z. Candeias, and H. Stuckenschmidt. 2010. A new usage for semantic technologies on egovernment: Checking official documents' consistency. In *Proceedings of the 10th European Conference on eGovernment, National Centre for Taxation Studies*, University of Limerick, Ireland, 17–18 June 2010.

Gaines, B. R., and M. L. Shaw. 1989. Comparing the conceptual systems of experts. In *Proceedings of the 11th International Joint Conference on Artificial Intelligence*, ed. N. S. Sridharan, 633–638. Detroit, MI, USA, August 1989. Morgan Kaufmann.

Galindo, F. 2007. Ontology and philosophy of the law: the reimdoc project. In *Trends in legal knowledge: The Semantic Web and the rebulaiton of electronic social systems. Papers form the B-4 Workshop on Artificial Intelligence and Law, May 25th–27th of the XXII World Congress of Philosophy of Law and Social Philosophy IVR'05*, Granada, ed. P. Casanovas, P. Noriega, D. Bourcière, and F. Galindo, 193–212. Florence: European Press Academic Publishing.

Gangemi, A. 2005. Ontology design patters for Semantic Web content. In *ISWC 2005*, ed. Y. Gil, et al., *Lecture notes in computer science*, Vol. 3729, 262–276. Berlin/Heidelberg: Springer.

Gangemi, A. 2007. Design patterns for legal ontology construction. In *Proceedings of the Workshop on Legal Ontologies and Artificial Intelligence Techniques (LOAIT 2007) at the International Conference on AI and Law (ICAIL'07)*, June 4, Stanford, ed. P. Casanovas, M. A. Biasiotti, and E. Francesconi, M. Teresa, T. Sagri, 65–85.

Gangemi, A. 2009. Introducing pattern-based design for legal ontologies. In *Law, ontologies and the Semantic Web – channelling the legal information flood*, ed. J. Breuker, P. Casanovas, M. C. A. Klein, and E. Francesconi. *Frontiers in artificial intelligence and applications*, Vol. 188, 53–71. Amsterdam: IOS Press.

Gangemi, A., C. Catenaccia, M. Ciaramita, and J. Lehmann. 2006, May. Qood grid: A metaontology-based framework for ontology evaluation and selection. In *Proceedings of the 4th International Workshop on Evaluation of Ontologies for the Web (EON2006) at the 15th International World Wide Web Conference (WWW 2006)*, ed. D. Vrandečić, M. del Carmen Suárez-Figueroa, A. Gangemi, and Y. Sure, Edinburgh, 8–15.

Gangemi, A., N. Guarino, C. Masolo, A. Oltramari, and L. Schneider. 2002. Sweetening ontologies with DOLCE. In *Knowledge engineering and knowledge management. Ontologies and the Semantic Web, 13th International Conference, EKAW 2002*, ed. A. Gómez-Pérez and V. Benjamins, 166–181. London: Springer.

Gangemi, A., D. M. Pisanelli, and G. Steve. 1999. An overview of the ONIONS project: Applying ontologies to the integration of medical terminologies. *Data and Knowledge Engineering* 31(2):183–220.

Gangemi, A., A. Prisco, M.-T. Sagri, G. Steve, and D. Tiscornia. 2003a. Some ontological tools to support legal regulatory compliance, with a case study. In *On the move to meaningful internet systems 2003: OTM 2003 Workshops, OTM Confederated International Workshops, HCI-SWWA,IPW, JTRES, WORM, WMS, and WRSM 2003*, November 3–7, Catania, ed. R. Meersman and Z. Tari. *Lecture notes in computer science*, Vol. 2889, 607–620. Berlin/Heidelberg: Springer.

Gangemi, A., M.-T. Sagri, and D. Tiscornia. 2003b, June. Metadata for content description in legal information. Draft presentation paper at ICAIL 2003 Workshop on Legal Ontologies and Web based legal information management 28 June 2003, Edinburgh. Organised in conjunction with ICAIL 2003: Ninth International Conference on Artificial Intelligence and Law.

Gangemi, A., M.-T. Sagri, and D. Tiscornia. 2003c. Metadata for content description in legal information. In *14th International Workshop on Database and Expert Systems Applications (DEXA'03)*, September 1–5, Prague, 745. Washington: IEEE Computer Society.

Gangemi, A., M.-T. Sagri, and D. Tiscornia. 2005. A constructive framework for legal ontologies. In *Law and the Semantic Web. Legal ontologies, methodologies, legal information retrieval, and applications [outcome of the Workshop on Legal Ontologies and Web-Based Legal Information Management, June 28, 2003, Edinburgh, UK & International Seminar on Law and the Semantic Web, November 20–21, 2003, Barcelona, Spain]*, ed. V. R. Benjamins, P. Casanovas, J. Breuker, and A. Gangemi. *Lecture notes in computer science*, Vol. 3369, 97–124. Berlin/Heidelberg: Springer.

Gangemi, A., G. Steve, and F. Giacomellli. 1996. ONIONS: An ontological methodology for taxonomic knowledge integration. In *Proceedings of the ECAI-96 Workshop on Ontological Engineering*, Budapest, 13 August, 1996.

García, R. 2006, November. *A Semantic Web approach to digital rights management*. Doctorate in computer science and digital communication, Department of Technologies, Universitat Pompeu Fabra, Barcelona.

García, R., I. Gallego, and J. Delgado. 2005. Formalising odrl semantics using web ontologies. In *Open Digital Rights Language Workshop (ODRL'05)*, ed. C. Serrão, R. Iannella, and S. Guth, 33–42. Porto: ADETTI.

García, R., and R. Gil. 2006. An OWL copyright ontology for semantic digital rights management. In *OTM Workshops 2006*, ed. R. Meersman, Z. Tari, and P. Herrero. *Lecture notes in computer science*, Vol. 4278, 1745–1754. Berlin/Heidelberg: Springer-Verlag.

García, R., and R. Gil. 2007. A web ontology for copyright contracts management. *International Journal of Electronic Commerce Special issue on "Contract Architectures and Languages"* 12(4):99–114.

García, R., and R. Gil. 2009. Copyright licenses reasoning an OWL-DL ontology. In *Law, ontologies and the Semantic Web – channelling the legal information flood*, ed. J. Breuker, P. Casanovas, M. C. A. Klein, and E. Francesconi. *Frontiers in artificial intelligence and applications*, Vol. 188, 145–162. Amsterdam: IOS Press.

García, R., and R. Gil. 2010. Content value chains modelling using a copyright ontology. *Information Systems* 35(4):483–495.

García, R., R. Gil, and J. Delgado. 2004. Intellectual property rights management using a semantic web information system. In *OTM Confederated International Conferences, CoopIS, DOA, and ODBASE 2004*, ed. R. Meersman and Z. Tari. *LNCS*, Vol. 3291, 689–704. Berlin/Heidelberg: Springer.

García-Castro, R., M. C. Suárez-Figueroa, M. Espinoza, M. Sini, H. Lewen, and E. Blomqvist. 2008, February. Experimentation with the NeOn methodologies and methods. Deliverable D5.6.1, NeOn Project, http://www.neon-project.org

Gazendam, H., and K. Liu. 2005. The evolution of organisational semiotics: A brief review of the contribution of Ronald Stamper. In *Studies in organisational semiotics*. ed. J. Filipe and K. Liu. Dordrecht: Kluwer Academic Publishers.

Geentjens, S., T. Rita, and P. K. en De Baer. 2006. Sociocognitive terminology and termontography. In *Proceedings of the Journées d'Etudes sur le Traitement Automatique de la Langue Arabe*, Rabat, 138–151.

Gelbart, D., and J. Smith. 1991. Beyond Boolean search: Flexicon, a legal text-based intelligent system. In *Proceedings of the 3rd International Conference on Artificial Intelligence and Law*, 225–234. New York: ACM.

Genesereth, M. R., and R. E. Fikes. 1992. Knowledge interchange format, version 3.0 reference manual. Technical Report Logic-92-1, Interlingua Working Group of the DARPA Knowledge Sharing Effort, Computer Science Department, Stanford University, Stanford.

Genesereth, M., R. Vogl, and M.-A. Williams, eds. 2010, March 22–24. *Intelligent information privacy management*, Number Technical Report SS-10-05 in AAAI Spring Symposium, Stanford.
Giereth, M., S. Koch, Y. Kompatsiaris, S. Papadopoulos, E. Pianta, L. Serafini, and L. Wanner. 2007. A modular framework for ontology-based representation of patent information. In *Legal knowledge and information systems. JURIX 2007: The Twentieth Annual Conference*, ed. A. R. Lodder and L. Mommers. *Frontiers in artificial intelligence and applications*, Vol. 165, 49–58. Amsterdam: IOS Press.
Golbreich, C., E. K. Wallace, and P. F. Patel-Schneider. 2009, October. OWL 2 web ontology language. New features and rationale. W3c recommendation 27 October 2009, W3C.
Gómez, J. M., C. B. Aranda, O. M. García, and W. Waterfeld. 2006, August. Requirements on NeOn architecture. Deliverable D6.1.1, NeOn Project, http://www.neon-project.org
Gómez-Pérez, A. 1994a, February. From knowledge based systems to knowledge sharing technology: Evaluation and assessment. Technical Reports KSL-94-73, Knowledge Systems Laboratory, Stanford University.
Gómez-Pérez, A. 1994b, October. Some ideas and examples to evaluate ontologies. Technical Reports KSL-94-65, Knowledge Systems Laboratory, Stanford University.
Gómez-Pérez, A. 1995, January. Criteria to verify knowledge sharing technology. Technical Reports KSL-95-10, Knowledge Systems Laboratory, Stanford University.
Gómez-Pérez, A. 1999, Autumn. Ontological engineering: A state of the art. *Expert Update. British Computer Society* 2(3):33–44.
Gómez-Pérez, A. 2001. Evaluation of ontologies. *International Journal of Intelligent Systems* 16(3):391–409.
Gómez-Pérez, A., and V. R. Benjamins. 1999, August. Overview of knowledge, sharing and reuse components: Ontologies and problem-solving methods. In *Proceedings of the Workshop on Ontologies and Problem-Solving Methods in conjunction with the Sixteenth International Joint Conference on Artificial Intelligence (IJCAI'99)*, Stockholm, 1.1–1.15.
Gómez-Pérez, A., M. C. S. de Figueroa Baonza, and B. Villazón. 2008. NeOn methodology for building ontology networks: Ontology specification. In *The Sixth Summer School on Ontological Engineering and the Semantic Web (SSSW'08)*, July 6, 2008–July 12, 2008, Cercedilla, Madrid, Spain.
Gómez-Pérez, A., M. Fernández-López, and O. Corcho. 2003. *Ontological engineering. With examples from the areas of knowledge management, e-commerce and the Semantic Web. Advanced information and knowledge processing*. London: Springer.
Gómez-Pérez, A., and D. Manzano-Macho. 2003. A survey of ontology learning methods and techniques. Ist-2000-29243 deliverable 1.5, OntoWeb: Ontology-based Information Exchange for Knowledge Management and Electronic Commerce IST EU Project.
Gómez-Pérez, A., and D. Manzano-Macho. 2004. An overview of methods and tools for ontology learning from texts. *Knowledge Engineering Review* 19(3):187–212.
Gómez-Pérez, A., F. Ortiz-Rodríguez, and B. Villazón-Terrazas. 2005. Legal ontologies for the Spanish e-government. In *Current topics in artificial intelligence, 11th Conference of the Spanish Association for Artificial Intelligence, CAEPIA 2005*, Santiago de Compostela, November 16–18, 2005, Revised Selected Papers, ed. R. Marín, E. Onaindia, A. Bugarín, and J. Santos. *Lecture notes in computer science*, Vol. 4177, 301–310. Berlin/Heidelberg: Springer.
Gómez-Pérez, A., F. Ortiz-Rodríguez, and B. Villazón-Terrazas. 2006. Ontology-based legal information retrieval to improve the information access in e-government. In *Proceedings of the 15th International Conference on World Wide Web, WWW 2006*, Edinburgh, May 23–26, 1007–1008.
Gómez-Pérez, A., and óscar Corcho. 2002, Jan/Feb. Ontology languages for the Semantic Web. *IEEE Intelligent Systems* 17(1):55–61.
Gómez-Pérez, A., and M. C. Suárez-Figueroa. 2009. Scenarios for building ontology networks within the NeOn methodology. In *K-CAP '09: Proceedings of the Fifth International Conference on Knowledge capture*, 183–184. New York: ACM.

Gordon, T. F. 1994. From jhering to alexy. using artificial intelligence models in jurisprudence. In *Legal knowledge based systems (JURIX'94) the foundation for legal knowledge systems: The relation with legal theory*, ed. H. Prakken, A. Muntjewerff, and A. Soeteman, 19–31. Lelystad: Koninklijke Vermande. ISBN 90 5458 190 5.

Gordon, T. F. 2007. 20 years of icail. Reflections on the field of ai and law. In Presentation (closing remarks) at the *Eleventh International Conference on Artificial Intelligence and Law (ICAIL 2007)*, June 4–8, Palo Alto.

Gracia, C., P. Casanovas, J. Carrabina, X. Binefa, E. Teodoro, M. Monton, N. Casellas, C. Montero, N. Galera, J. Serrano, and M. Poblet. 2007. Legal knowledge acquisition and multimedia applications. In *Proceedings of the Knowledge Acquisition from Multimedia Content Workshop (KAMC 2007) at the SAMT 2007 Conference*, December 5, 2007, Geneva.

Grau, B. C., I. Horrocks, B. Motik, B. Parsia, P. Patel-Schneider, and U. Sattler. 2008, November. OWL 2: The next step for OWL. *Web Semantic* 6:309–322.

Gray, P. N. 2007. The ontology of legal possibilities and legal potentialities. In *Proceedings of the Workshop on Legal Ontologies and Artificial Intelligence Techniques (LOAIT 2007) at the International Conference on AI and Law (ICAIL'07)*, Stanford, June 4, ed. P. Casanovas, M. A. Biasiotti, and E. Francesconi, M. T. Sagri, 7–23.

Gray, P. N., X. Gray, and J. Zeleznikow. 2007. Negotiating logic: For richer of poorer. In *Proceedings of the Eleventh International Conference on Artificial Intelligence and Law (ICAIL 2007)*, June 4–8, Palo Alto, 247–251. New York: ACM Press.

Greenleaf, G., A. Mowbray, and A. L. Tyree. 1987. Expert systems in law: The datalex project. In *Proceedings of the First International Conference on Artificial Intelligence and Law (ICAIL'87)*, May 27–29, 1987, Boston, 9–17. New York: ACM Press.

Greinke, A. 1994, December. Legal expert systems – a humanistic critique of mechanical legal inference. *E-Law. Murdoch University Electronic Journal of Law* 1(4), Available from: http://www.murdoch.edu.au/elaw/issues/v1n4/greinke14.html

Gries, S. T. 2009. *Quantitative corpus linguistics with R: A Practical Introduction*. New York/London: Routledge.

Groendijk, C., and M. Tragter. 1994. Legal theory and the design of milieu. In *Legal knowledge based systems JURIX 94: The foundation for legal knowledge systems*, ed. A. Soeteman, H. Prakken, and A. Muntjewerff, 105–114. Lelystad: Koninklijke Vermande.

Gruber, T. 2005. Ontology of folksonomy: A mash-up of apples and oranges. In *Invited paper/keynote to the First on-Line conference on Metadata and Semantics Research (MTSR'05)*, Palo Alto, October 29.

Gruber, T. 2006. Where the social web meets the Semantic Web. In *The Semantic Web – ISWC 2006, Proceedings of the 5th International Semantic Web Conference, ISWC 2006* , Athens, November 5–9 (Keynote Abstract), ed. I. F. Cruz, S. Decker, D. Allemang, C. Preist, D. Schwabe, P. Mika, M. Uschold, and L. Aroyo. *Lecture notes in computer science*, Vol. 4273, 994. Berlin/Heidelberg: Springer.

Gruber, T. R. 1991. The role of common ontology in achieving sharable, reusable knowledge bases. In *KR'91: Principles of knowledge representation and reasoning*, ed. J. F. Allen, R. Fikes, and E. Sandewall, 601–602. San Mateo: Morgan Kaufmann.

Gruber, T. R. 1992. Ontolingua: A mechanism to support portable ontologies. Technical report, Knowledge Systems Laboratory, Stanford University.

Gruber, T. R. 1993a. Toward principles for the design of ontologies used for knowledge sharing. Technical Report KSL 93-04, Knowledge Systems Laboratory, Stanford University.

Gruber, T. R. 1993b. A translation approach to portable ontology specifications. *Knowledge Acquisition* 5(2):199–220. Based on Technical Report KSL 92-71 (September 1992, revised April 1993), of the Knowledge Systems Laboratory, Computer Science Department, Stanford University.

Grüninger, M., and M. Fox. 1995. Methodology for the design and evaluation of ontologies. In *Proceedings of International Joint Conference on AI 1995, Workshop on Basic Ontological Issues in Knowledge Sharing*, Department of Industrial Engineering, University of Toronto.

Guarino, N. 1995. Formal ontology, conceptual analysis and knowledge representation. *International Journal of Human-Computer Studies* 43(5–6):625–640.

Guarino, N. 1997a. Semantic matching: Formal ontological distinctions for information organization, extraction, and integration. In *Information extraction: A multidisciplinary approach to an emerging information technology*, ed. M. T. Pazienza. *Lecture notes in computer science*, Vol. 1299, 139–170. New York: Springer

Guarino, N. 1997b. Understanding, building and using ontologies. *International Journal of Human-Computer Studies* 46(2–3):293–310. First appeared at *KAW'96, Proceedings of the 10th Banff Knowledge Acquisition for Knowledge-Based Systems Workshop (KAW'96)*, Banff.

Guarino, N. 1998. Formal ontology and information systems. In *Formal ontology in information systems. Proceedings of the International Conference on Formal Ontologies in Information Systemsof (FOIS'98)*, Trento, 6–8 June 1998, ed. N. Guarino, 3–15. Amsterdam: IOS Press.

Guarino, N., M. Carrara, and P. Giaretta. 1994a. Formalizing ontological commitments. In *AAAI '94: Proceedings of the twelfth national conference on Artificial intelligence (vol. 1)*, Seattle, ed. B. Hayes-Roth and R. Korf, 560–567. Menlo Park: American Association for Artificial Intelligence Press.

Guarino, N., M. Carrara, and P. Giaretta. 1994b. An ontology of meta-level categories. In *KR'94: Principles of knowledge representation and reasoning*, ed. J. Doyle, E. Sandewall, and P. Torasso, 270–280. San Francisco: Morgan Kaufmann.

Guarino, N., and P. Giaretta. 1995. Ontologies and knowledge bases: Towards a terminological clarification. In *Towards very large knowledge bases: Knowledge building and knowledge sharing*, ed. N. J. I. Mars, 25–32. Amsterdam: IOS Press.

Guarino, N., and C. Welty. 2002. Evaluating ontological decisions with OntoClean. *Communications of the ACM* 45(2):61–65.

Guarino, N., and C. Welty. 2004. An overview of OntoClean. In *Handbook on ontologies: International handbook on information systems*, ed. S. Staab and R. Studer, 151–171. Berlin: Springer.

Gugliotta, A., L. Cabral, J. Domingue, V. Roberto, M. Rowlatt, and R. Davies. 2005. A Semantic Web service-based architecture for the interoperability of e-government services. In *Proceedings of ICWE 2005 – 5th International Conference on web Engineering*, Sydney, 25–29 July.

Gugliotta, A., J. Domingue, L. Cabral, V. Tanasescu, S. Galizia, R. Davies, L. Gutiérrez-Villarías, M. Rowlatt, M. Richardson, and S. Stincic. 2008. Deploying Semantic Web services-based applications in the e-government domain. *Journal of Data Semantics* 10:96–132.

Haase, P., S. Rudolph, Y. Wang, S. Brockmans, R. Palma, J. Euzenat, and M. d'Aquin. 2006, November. Networked ontology model. Deliverable D1.1.1, NeOn Project, http://www.neon-project.org

Hafner, C. D. 1980. Representation of knowledge in a legal information retrieval system. In *SIGIR*, 139–153. Kent: Butterworth & Co.

Hage, J., and B. Verheij. 1999. The law as a dynamic interconnected system of states of affairs: A legal top ontology. *International Journal of Human-Computer Studies* 51(6):1043–1077.

Hart, H. 1961. *The concept of law. Clarendon law series*. Oxford: Oxford University Press.

Hartmann, J., P. Spyns, A. Gibboin, D. Maynard, R. Cuel, M. C. Suárez-Figueroa, and Y. Sure. 2005, January. D.1.2.3. methods for ontology evaluation. Deliverable IST-2004-507482 KWEB D.1.2.3., EU-IST Network of Excellence (NoE) Knowledge Web Consortium.

Hitzler, P., M. Krötzsch, B. Parsia, P. F. Patel-Schneider, and S. Rudolph. 2009. OWL 2 web ontology language: Primer. W3C Recommendation, 27 October 2009, W3C.

Hoekstra, R. 2001. Errors in modeling & representation. Master's thesis, Department of Computer Science and Law, University of Amsterdam.

Hoekstra, R. 2008. Use of OWL in the legal domain. Statement of interest. In *Fourth International Workshop OWLED 2008, OWL: Experiences and Directions*, 1–2 April 2008, Washington, (statement of interest).

Hoekstra, R. 2009a. BESTportal: Lessons learned in lightweight semantic access to court proceedings. In *Legal knowledge and information systems – JURIX 2009: The Twenty-Second Annual Conference on Legal Knowledge and Information Systems* , Rotterdam, 16–18 December 2009, ed. G. Governatori. *Frontiers in artificial intelligence and applications*. Vol. 205, 69–78. Amsterdam: IOS Press.

Hoekstra, R. 2009b. *Ontology representation. Design patterns and ontologies that make sense. Frontiers in artificial intelligence and applications*, Vol. 197. Amsterdam: IOS Press.

Hoekstra, R., and J. Breuker. 2008. Polishing diamonds in OWL 2. In *EKAW*, ed. A. Gangemi and J. Euzenat. *Lecture notes in computer science*, Vol. 5268, 64–73. Berlin/Heidelberg: Springer.

Hoekstra, R., J. Breuker, M. D. Bello, and A. Boer. 2007. The LKIF core ontology of basic legal concepts. In *Proceedings of the Workshop on Legal Ontologies and Artificial Intelligence Techniques (LOAIT 2007) at the International Conference on AI and Law (ICAIL'07)*, Stanford, June 4, ed. P. Casanovas, M. A. Biasiotti, E. Francesconi, and M. T. Sagri, 43–63.

Hoekstra, R., J. Breuker, M. D. Bello, and A. Boer. 2008. LKIF core: Principled ontology development for the legal domain. In *Law, ontologies and the Semantic Web. Channelling the legal information flood*, ed. J. Breuker, P. Casanovas, M. Klein, and E. Francesconi. *Frontiers in Artificial intelligence and applications*. Vol. 188. Amsterdam: IOS Press.

Hoekstra, R., J. Breuker, M. D. Bello, and A. Boer. 2009. LKIF core: Principled ontology development for the legal domain. In *Law, ontologies and the Semantic Web. Channelling the legal information flood*, ed. J. Breuker, P. Casanovas, M. C. A. Klein, and E. Francesconi. *Frontiers in artificial intelligence and applications*, Vol. 188, 21–52. Amsterdam: IOS Press.

Hoffman, R. R., N. R. Shadbolt, A. M. Burton, and G. Klein. 1995, May. Eliciting knowledge from experts: A methodological analysis. *Organizational Behavior and Human Decision Processes* 62(2):129–158.

Horrocks, I., B. Parsia, P. F. Patel-Schneider, and J. A. Hendler. 2005. Semantic Web architecture: Stack or two towers? In *PPSWR*, ed. F. Fages and S. Soliman. *Lecture notes in computer science*, Vol. 3703, 37–41. Berli/Heidelberg: Springer.

Horrocks, I., and P. F. Patel-Schneider. 2003. Three theses of representation in the Semantic Web. In *Proceedings of the WWW2003 Conference*, May 20–24, 2003, Budapest. New York: ACM.

Hughes, J.A., V. King, T. Rodden, and H. Andersen. 1994. Moving out from the control room: ethnography in system design. In *Computer supported cooperative work*, 429–439.

Hughes, J., J. O'Brien, T. Rodden, M. Rouncefield, and I. Sommerville. 1995. Presenting ethnography in the requirements process. In *RE '95: Proceedings of the Second IEEE International Symposium on Requirements Engineering*, 27. Washington: IEEE Computer Society.

IEEE. 1990, December. *Ieee standard glossary of software engineering terminology*. IEEE Standard 610.12-1990. New York: Institute of Electrical and Electronics Engineers.

IEEE. 1998, December. *Ieee standard for a software quality metrics methodology*. IEEE Standard 1061-1998. New York: Institute of Electrical and Electronics Engineers.

IEEE. 2004. *Ieee standard for software verification and validation*. IEEE Standard 1012-2004. New York: Institute of Electrical and Electronics Engineers.

IEEE. 2006, January. *Ieee standard for developing a software project life cycle process*. IEEE Standard 1074-2006. New York: Institute of Electrical and Electronics Engineers.

Ikeda, M., K. Seta, and R. Mizoguchi. 1997. Task ontology makes it easier to use authoring tools. In *Proceedings of the Fifteenth International Joint Conference on Artificial Intelligence (IJCAI'97)*, Nagoya, August 23–29, Vol. 1, 342–351. San Francisco: Morgan Kaufmann.

Jarrar, M. 2005, May. *Towards methodological principles for ontology engineering*. Doctor of Philosophy, Vrije Universiteit Brussel.

Jarrar, M. 2007, August. *Orm markup language, version 3*. Technical report, Vrije Universiteit Brussel, Brussels.

Jarrar, M. 2008. Towards effectiveness and transparency in e-business transactions, an ontology for customer complaint management. In *Semantic Web for Business: Cases and Applications*, ed. R. García, Hershey: IGI Global.

Jarrar, M., M. Keet, and P. Dongilli. 2006, February. *Multilingual verbalization of orm conceptual models and axiomatized ontologies*. Starlab technical report, STARLab, Vrije Universiteit Brussel.

Jarrar, M., and R. Meersman. 2002. Formal ontology engineering in the DOGMA approach. In *Proceedings of the International Conference on Ontologies, Databases and Applications of Semantics (ODBase 2002)*, ed. R. Meersman and Z. Tari. *Lecture notes in computer science*, Vol. 2519, 1238–1254. Berlin/New York: Springer.

Jarrar, M., and R. Meersman. 2007. Ontology engineering – the DOGMA approach. In *Advances in web semantic, A state-of-the Art Semantic Web advances in web semantics IFIP2.12.*, Vol. 1, Chapter 3. Berlin/Heidelberg: Springer-sbm.

Jarrar, M., R. Verlinden, and R. Meersman. 2003, November. Ontology-based customer complaint management. In *OTM 2003 Workshops, proceedings of the 1st International Workshop on Regulatory Ontologies and the Modeling of Complaint Regulations*, ed. R. Meersman and Z. Tari. *LNCS*, Vol. 2889, 594–606. Sicily: Springer.

Jedrzejek, C., M. Falkowski, and M. Smolenski. 2009. Link analysis of fuel laundering scams and implications of results for scheme understanding and prosecutor strategy. In *Proceeding of the 2009 conference on Legal Knowledge and Information Systems*, 79–88. Amsterdam: IOS Press.

Jones, J. M. 2009, Winter. Not just key numbers and keywords anymore: How user interface design affects legal research. *Law Library Journal* 101(1):7–30.

Jones, S., P. Mason, and R. Stamper. 1979, November. LEGOL 2.0: A relational specification language for complex rules. *Information Systems* 4(4):293–305.

Jouve, D., Y. Amghar, B. Chabbat, and J.-M. Pinon. 2003. Conceptual framework for document semantic modelling: An application to document and knowledge management in the legal domain. *Data & Knowledge Engineering* 46:345–375.

Kabilan, V. 2003. Using multi-tier contract ontology to model contract workflow models. Master's thesis, Department of Computer and System Sciences, Stockholm University and Royal Institute of Technology.

Kabilan, V., and P. Johannesson. 2003. Semantic representation of contract knowledge using multi tier ontology. In *First International Workshop on Semantic Web and Databases (SWDB'03)*, 395–414. Berlin.

Kabilan, V., J. Zdravkovic, and P. Johannesson. 2005. Using multi-tier contract ontology to deduce contract workflow model for enterprise interoperability. In *EMOI - INTEROP'05, Enterprise Modelling and Ontologies for Interoperability, Proceedings of the Open Interop Workshopon Enterprise Modelling and Ontologies for Interoperability, Co-located with CAiSE'05 Conference*, Porto, 13–14 June, ed. M. Missikoff and A. D. Nicola, CEUR-WS.org

Kalfoglou, Y., and M. Schorlemmer. 2005. Ontology mapping: The state of the art. In *Semantic interoperability and integration*, ed. Y. Kalfoglou, M. Schorlemmer, A. Sheth, S. Staab, and M. Uschold, Number 04391 in Dagstuhl Seminar Proceedings. Internationales Begegnungs- und Forschungszentrum fuer Informatik (IBFI), Schloss Dagstuhl, <http://drops.dagstuhl.de/opus/volltexte/2005/40> [date of citation: 1 January 2005].

Kayed, A. 2005. Building e-laws ontology: New approach. In *On the move to meaningful internet systems 2005: OTM Workshops*, ed. R. Meersman, Z. Tari, and P. Herrero. *Lecture notes in computer science*, Vol. 3762, 826–835. Berlin/Heidelberg: Springer.

Kehl, W. B., J. F. Horty, C. R. Bacon, and D. S. Mitchell. 1961. An information retrieval language for legal studies. *Communications of the ACM* 4(9):380–389.

Kelsen, H. 1991. *General theory of norms*. Oxford: Clarendon Press.

Kerremans, K., P. D. Baer, and R. Temmerman. 2007. Dealing with terminological variation in termontography: Examples from the PoCeHRMOM project. In *Proceedings of the LSP 2007 Conference*, August 27–31, Hamburg.

Kerremans, K., Y. Tang, and R. T. G. Zhao. 2005. Towards ontology-based e-mail fraud detection. In *Proceedings of EPIA 2005 BAOSW Workshop of 12th Portuguese conference on AI*, Covilha, ed. C. Bento, A. Cardoso, and G. Dias, 106–111. Piscataway, NJ: IEEE

Kerremans, K., R. Temmerman, and J. Tummers. 2003. Representing multilingual and culture-specific knowledge in a vat regulatory ontology: Support from the termontography methodology. In *OTM 2003 Workshops, Proceedings of the 1st International Workshop on Regulatory Ontologies and the Modeling of Complaint Regulations*, ed. R. Meersman and Z. Tari. *Lecture notes in computer science*, Vol. 2889, 662–674. Berlin/Heidelberg: Springer.

Kerremans, K., R. Temmerman, and J. Tummers. 2004. Discussion on the requirements for a workbench supporting termontography. In *Proceedings of the XI Euralex International Congress 2004* , 6–10 July, Lorient, 559–570.

Kerremans, K., R. Temmerman, and G. Zhao. 2005. Terminology and knowledge engineering in fraud detection. In *Proceedings of the International Conference on Terminology and Knowledge Engineering*, Copenhagen, 16–19 August 2005.

Kerremans, K., and G. Zhao. 2005, July. Topical ontology for vat. Deliverable of The FFPOIROT IP project (IST-2001-38248) Deliverable D2.3 (WP 2), STARLab VUB.

Khadraoui, A., W. Opprecht, C. Aïdonidis, and M. Léonard. 2008. Laws-based ontology for e-government services construction case study: The specification of services in relationship with the venture creation in Switzerland. In *PoEM*, ed. J. Stirna and A. Persson. *Lecture notes in business information processing*, Vol. 15, 197–209. Berlin/Heidelberg: Springer.

Kharbili, M., and P. Stolarski. 2009. Building-up a reference generic regulation ontology: A bottom-up approach. In *Business information systems workshops*, ed. W. Aalst, J. Mylopoulos, N. M. Sadeh, M. J. Shaw, C. Szyperski, W. Abramowicz, and D. Flejter. *Lecture notes in business information processing*, Vol. 37, 268–279. Berlin/Heidelberg: Springer.

Kingston, J., B. Schafer, and W. Vandenberghe. 2005. No model behaviour: Ontologies for fraud detection. In *Law and the Semantic Web. Legal ontologies, methodologies, legal information retrieval, and applications [outcome of the Workshop on Legal Ontologies and Web-Based Legal Information Management, June 28, 2003, Edinburgh, UK & International Seminar on Law and the Semantic Web, November 20–21, 2003, Barcelona, Spain]*, ed. V. R. Benjamins, P. Casanovas, J. Breuker, and A. Gangemi. *Lecture notes in computer science*, Vol. 3369, 33–247. Berlin/Heidelberg: Springer.

Kingston, J., and W. Vandenberghe. 2003. A comparison of a regulatory ontology with existing legal ontology frameworks. In *OTM 2003 Workshops, proceedings of the 1st International Workshop on Regulatory Ontologies and the Modeling of Complaint Regulations*, ed. R. Meersman and Z. Tari. *Lecture notes in computer science*, Vol. 2889, 648–661. New York: Springer.

Kingston, J., W. Vandenberghe, R. Leary, and J. Zeleznikow. 2003, June. User requirements analysis for ff poirot. Deliverable of The FFPOIROT IP project (IST-2001-38248) Deliverable D1.1 (WP 1), STARLab VUB.

Klein, M., W. van Steenbergen, E. Bruijntjes, F. van Harmelen, and A. R. Lodder. 2006. Supporting layman in finding relevant court decisions in the BEST-project. In *NWO TOKEN Symposium 2006*, Leiden, March 31.

Koepsell, D. R. 2000. *The Ontology of cyberspace. Philosophy, law, and the future of intellectual property*. La Salle: Open Court.

Kotis, K. 2004, December. Ontology engineering: Tools and methodologies for constructing and managing ontologies. Invited talk at the University of the Aegean, Department of I.C.S. Engineering.

Kotis, K. 2010. On supporting HCOME-3o ontology argumentation using semantic wiki technology. In *On the move to meaningful internet systems: OTM 2008 Workshops*, ed. R. Meersman, Z. Tari, and P. Herrero. *Lecture notes in computer science*, Vol. 5333, 193–199. Berlin/Heidelberg: Springer.

Kotis, K., and A. Vouros. 2006, July. Human-centered ontology engineering: The HCOME methodology. *Knowledge and Information Systems* 10(1):109–131.

Kotis, K., G. A. Vouros, and J. P. Alonso. 2005, August. HCOME: A tool-supported methodology for engineering living ontologies. In *Semantic web and databases. Second International Workshop – SWDB 2004*, ed. C. Bussler, V. Tannen, and I. Fundulaki. *LNCS*, Vol. 3372, 155–166. Berlin/Heidelberg: Springer.

Kowalski, R., and M. Sergot. 1990. The use of logical models in legal problem solving. *Ratio Juris* 3(2):201–218.

Kozaki, K., S. Endo, and R. Mizoguchi. 2008. Instance management problems in the role model of Hozo. In *PRICAI 2008: Trends in artificial intelligence*, ed. T.-B. Ho and Z.-H. Zhou. Vol. 5351, *Lecture notes in computer science*, 614–625. Berlin/Heidelberg: Springer.

Kozaki, K., E. Sunagawa, Y. Kitamura, and R. Mizoguchi. 2005. Hozo: An ontology development environment – treatment of "role concept" and dependency management – . In *Proceedings of Posters and Demos of the 4th International Semantic Web Conference (ISWC2005), PID-79*, Galway, November 6–10.

Kumazawa, T., O. Saito, K. Kozaki, T. Matsui, and R. Mizoguchi. 2009. Toward knowledge structuring of sustainability science based on ontology engineering. In *Proceedings of International Conference on Complex, Intelligent and Software Intensive Systems, 2009 (CISIS '09)*, ed. L. Barolli, F. Xhafa, and H.-H. Hsu, 1138–1143. Los Alamitos, CA: IEEE Computer Society

Kurematsu, M., M. Tada, and T. Yamaguchi. 1998a. Building up a legal ontology using a general ontology. http://www.google.com/url?sa=t&source=web&cd=1&sqi=2&ved=0CBgQFjAA&url=http%3A%2F%2Fciteseerx.ist.psu.edu%2Fviewdoc%2Fdownload%3Fdoi%3D10.1.1.39.1107%26rep%3Drep1%26type%3Dpdf&rct=j&q=%22Building%20up%20a%20legal%20ontology%20using%20a%20general%20ontology%22&ei=aRIXTqKONtOtgQftpMkC&usg=AFQjCNGcjgng6VM7xLzxn9T5-zSvokVS7Q&sig2=LmDIbxp6lgPu439TwnN8IA

Kurematsu, M., M. Tada, and T. Yamaguchi. 1998b. A legalontology refinement environment using a general ontology. http://citeseerx.ist.psu.edu/viewdoc/download?doi=10.1.1.46.5083&rep=rep1&type=pdf

Lame, G. 2000. Knowledge acquisition from texts towards an ontology of French law. In *Proceedings of the Workshop on Ontologies and Text in the 12th European Workshop on Knowledge Acquisition, Modeling and Management (EKAW '00)*, Juan-Les-Pins, ed. N. Aussenac-Gilles and S. Szulman (Application).

Lame, G. 2001. Constructing an ir-oriented legal ontology. In *Proceedings of the Second International Workshop on Legal Ontologies (LEGONT) in JURIX 2001*, Amsterdam, ed. R. Winkels, 31–36.

Lame, G. 2002, Décembre. *Construction d'ontologie a partie de textes. Une ontologie du droit dediée la recherche d'information sur le Web*. Ph.D. thesis, L'cole des Mines de Paris.

Lame, G. 2005. Using nlp techniques to identify legal ontology components: Concepts and relations. In *Law and the semantic web. Legal ontologies, methodologies, legal information retrieval, and applications*, ed. V. R. Benjamins, P. Casanovas, J. Breuker, and A. Gangemi. *Lecture notes in computer science*, Vol. 3369, 169–184. Berlin/Heidelberg: Springer.

Lame, G., and S. Desprès. 2005. Updating ontologies in the legal domain. In *Proceedings of the Tenth International Conference on Artificial Intelligence and Law (ICAIL 2005)*, June 6–11, University of Bologna, Vol. 155-162. New York: Association for Computing Machinery.

Lassila, O., and D. McGuinness. 2001, January. The role of frame-based representation on the Semantic Web. Technical Reports KSL-01-02, Knowledge Systems Laboratory, Stanford University.

Leary, R. M., W. Vandenberghe, and J. Zeleznikow. 2003. Towards a financial fraud ontology; a legal modelling approach. In *Proceedings of the ICAIL 2003 Workshop on Legal Ontologies and Web Based Legal Information Management*, Edinburgh.

Leenheer, P. D., A. de Moor, and R. Meersman. 2007. Context dependency management in ontology engineering: A formal approach. *Journal of Data Semantics* 8:26–56.

Lehmann, J., J. Breuker, and B. Brouwer. 2004. Causation in ai and law. *Artificial Intelligence and Law* 12(4):279–315.

Lehmann, J., J. Breuker, and B. Brouwer. 2005. CausatiONT: Modeling causation in ai&law. In *Law and the Semantic Web. Legal ontologies, methodologies, legal information retrieval, and applications [outcome of the Workshop on Legal Ontologies and Web-Based Legal Information Management, June 28, 2003, Edinburgh, UK & International Seminar on Law and the Semantic Web, November 20–21, 2003, Barcelona, Spain]*, ed. V. R. Benjamins, P. Casanovas, J. Breuker, and A. Gangemi. *Lecture notes in computer science*, Vol. 3369, 77–96. Berlin/Heidelberg: Springer.

Leith, P. 2010. The rise and fall of the legal expert system. In *A History of legal informatics*, ed. Paliwala, A. 2010. *A history of legal informatics. LEFIS series*, Vol. 9, LEFIS, Zaragoza: Prensas Universitarias de Zaragoza.

Lenat, D., M. Prakash, and M. Shepherd. 1985 Cyc: Using common sense knowledge to overcome brittleness and knowledge acquisition bottlenecks. *AI Magazine* 6(4):65–85.

Lenat, D. B. 1995, November. Cyc: A large-scale investment in knowledge infrastructure. *Communications of the ACM* 38(11):33–38.

Lenat, D. B., and R. V. Guha. 1990. *Building large knowledge-based systems: Representation and inference in the CYC project*. Reading: Addison-Wesley.

Lenci, A., S. Montemagni, V. Pirrelli, and G. Venturi. 2007. Nlp-based ontology learning from legal texts. A case study. In *LOAIT*, ed. P. Casanovas, M. A. Biasiotti, E. Francesconi, and M.-T. Sagri. *CEUR Workshop Proceedings*, Vol. 321, 113–129. CEUR-WS.org

Lenci, A., S. Montemagni, V. Pirrelli, and G. Venturi. 2009. Ontology learning from Italian legal texts. In *Law, ontologies and the Semantic Web – channelling the legal information flood*, ed. J. Breuker, P. Casanovas, M. C. A. Klein, and E. Francesconi. *Frontiers in artificial intelligence and applications*, Vol. 188, 75–94. Amsterdam: IOS Press.

Lenzi, V. B., C. Biagioli, A. Cappelli, R. Sprugnoli, and F. Turchi. 2009. The lme project: Legislative metadata based on semantic formal models. *International Journal of Metadata, Semantics and Ontologies* 4(3):154–164.

Li, Y., K. Bontcheva, and H. Cunningham. 2005. SVM based learning system for information extraction. In *Deterministic and statistical methods in machine learning*, ed. M. N. J. Winkler and N. Lawerence. *LNAI*, Vol. 3635, 319–339. Berlin/New York: Springer.

Liebwald, D. 2007. Semantic spaces and multilingualism in the law: The challenge of legal knowledge management. In *Proceedings of the Workshop on Legal Ontologies and Artificial Intelligence Techniques (LOAIT 2007) at the International Conference on AI and Law (ICAIL'07)*, Stanford, June 4, ed. P. Casanovas, M. A. Biasiotti, and E. Francesconi, M. T. Sagri, 131–146.

Liebwald, D. 2009. An ontology for the implementation of the eu services directive. In *Legal knowledge and information systems – JURIX 2009: The Twenty-Second Annual Conference on Legal Knowledge and Information Systems*, Rotterdam, 16–18 December 2009, ed. G. Governatori. *Frontiers in artificial intelligence and applications*. Vol. 205, 100–105. Amsterdam: IOS Press.

Linehan, M. H. 2007. Ontologies and rules in business models. *Enterprise Distributed Object Computing Conference Workshops, IEEE International* 0:149–156.

Liu, K. 2000. *Semiotics in information systems engineering*. New York: Cambridge University Press.

Liu, K., and L. Sun. 2000. Capturing temporality and intentionality in information systems. In *Proceedings of the Fifth International Workshop on the Language-Action Perspective on Communication Modelling (LAP 2000)*, Aachen, September 14–16, 2000, ed. M. Schoop and C. Quix, 77–93.

Loukis, E. 2007. An ontology for g2g collaboration in public policy making, implementation and evaluation. *Artificial Intelligence and Law* 15(1):19–48.

Lowe, W. 2006. Yoshikoder: An open source multilingual content analysis tool for social scientists. In *American political science association annual meeting*, Philadelphia, August 31–September 3. Washington: APSA

Lozano-Tello, A., A. Gómez-Pérez, and E. Sosa. 2003. Selection of ontologies for the semantic web. In *ICWE*, ed. J. M. C. Lovelle, B. M. G. Rodríguez, L. J. Aguilar, J. E. L. Gayo, and M. del Puerto Paule Ruíz. *Lecture notes in computer science*, Vol. 2722, 413–416. Berlin/New York: Springer.

Luz Clara, B., A. H. Di Iorio, and R. G. Lerena. 2010. Ontologies, icts and law. The international ontojuris project. In *LOAIT 2010 Legal Ontologies and Artificial Intelligence Techniques, Proceedings of the 4th Workshop on Legal Ontologies and Artificial Intelligence Techniques*, European University Institute, Florence, July 7th, 2010, ed. E. Francesconi, S. Montemagni, P. Rossi, and D. Tiscornia, 95–102.

Maedche, A., and S. Staab. 2001. Ontology learning for the Semantic Web. *IEEE Intelligent Systems* 16(2):72–79.

Maedche, A., and S. Staab. 2004. Ontology learning. In *Handbook on ontologies. International handbooks on information systems*, 173–190. Berlin/Heidelberg: Springer.

Marcus, S. L. 1999. Knowledge acquisition. In *The MIT encyclopedia of the cognitive sciences*, ed. R. A. Wilson and F. C. Keil, 428–430. Cambridge: MIT Press.

Mariani, P., D. Tiscornia, and F. Turchi. 1992. The formalization of retrieval and advisory systems. In *Proceedings of the Legal Knowledge Based Systems JURIX 92: Information Technology and Law*, ed. C. Grütters, J. Breuker, H. van der Herik, A. Schmidt, and C. de Vey Mestdagh, 71–80. Lelystad: Koninklijke Vermande.

Masolo, C., S. Borgo, A. Gangemi, N. Guarino, and A. Oltramari. 2003, December. Ontology library (final). Technical Report D.18, IST Project 2001-33052 WonderWeb: Ontology Infrastructure for the Semantic Web.

Masolo, C., S. Borgo, A. Gangemi, N. Guarino, A. Oltramari, and L. Schneider. 2002. WonderWeb deliverable D17. The WonderWeb library of foundational ontologies and the DOLCE ontology. Technical report, National Research Council, Institute of Cognitive Sciences and Technology (ISTC-CNR).

McCarty, L. T. 1980. Some requirements for a computer-based legal consultant. In *AAAI-80 Proceedings*, 298–300. Los Altos: Kaufmann.

McCarty, L. T. 1989. A language for legal discourse i. basic features. In *ICAIL '89: Proceedings of the 2nd International Conference on Artificial Intelligence and Law*, 180–189. New York: ACM Press.

McCarty, L. T. 1991. On the role of prototypes in appellate legal argument (abstract). In *Proceedings of the International Conference in Artificial Intelligence and Law (ICAIL'91)*, 185–190. Oxford: ACM

McClure, J. 2007. The legal-RDF ontology. a generic model for legal documents. In *Proceedings of the Workshop on Legal Ontologies and Artificial Intelligence Techniques (LOAIT 2007) at the International Conference on AI and Law (ICAIL'07)*, Stanford, June 4, ed. P. Casanovas, M. A. Biasiotti, E. Francesconi, and M. T. Sagri, 25–42.

McGuinness, D. L. 2003. Ontologies come of age. In *Spinning the Semantic Web: Bringing the world wide web to its full potential*, ed. D. Fensel, J. A. Hendler, H. Lieberman, and W. Wahlster, 171–194. Cambridge: MIT Press.

McGuinness, D. L., R. Fikes, J. Rice, and S. Wilder. 2000. The chimaera ontology environment. In *Proceedings of the Seventeenth National Conference on Artificial Intelligence (AAAI 2000)*, Austin, July 30–August 3.

McGuinness, D. L., and F. van Harmelen. 2003, March. OWL web ontology language: Overview. W3c recommendation 10 February 2004, World Wide Web Consortium.

Melz, E., and A. Valente. 2004. Modeling the tax code. In *OTM Workshops 2004*, ed. R. Meersman, et al. *Lecture notes in computer science*, Vol. 3292, 652–661. Berlin/Heidelberg: Springer.

Meroño-Peñuela, A., N. Casellas, S. Torralba, M. R. de los Mozos, and P. Casanovas. 2010. Legal compliance in an ontology-based information system (poster). In *EKAW 2010 – Knowledge Engineering and Knowledge Management by the Masses*, 11 October–15 October, 2010, Lisbon.

Miller, G. A. 1995. WordNet: A lexical database for English. *Communications of the ACM* 38(11): 39–41.

Milton, N. 2007. *Knowledge acquisition in practice. A step-by-step guide. Decision engineering*. London: Springer.

Minsky, M. 1970. Form and content in computer science (1970 acm turing lecture). *Journal of the ACM* 17(2):197–215.

Missikof, M., R. Navigli, and P. Velardi. 2002, November. Integrated approach to web ontology learning and engineering. *Computer* 35(11):54–57.

Mitre, H. A., A. I. G-T. Ferreres, B. Ramos, and A. Ribagorda. 2006. A legal ontology to support privacy preservation in location-based services. In *OTM Workshops (2)*, ed. R. Meersman, Z. Tari, and P. Herrero. *Lecture notes in computer science*, Vol. 4278, 1755–1764. Berlin/Heidelberg: Springer.

Mizoguchi, R., and K. Kozaki. 2009. Ontology engineering environments. In *Handbook on ontologies*, ed. S. Staab and R. Studer, 2nd ed. *International handbooks information system*, 315–336. Berlin/Heidelberg: Springer.

Mizoguchi, R., Y. Tijerino, and M. Ikeda. 1995. Task analysis interview based on task ontology. *Expert Systems with Applications* 9(1):15–25.

Mizoguchi, R., J. Vanwelkenhuysen, and M. Ikeda. 1995. Task ontology for reuse of problem solving knowledge. In *Towards very large knowledge bases: Knowledge building and knowledge sharing (KBKS'95)*, ed. N. Mars, 45–59. Amsterdam: IOS Press.

Moens, M.-F. 2001. Innovative techniques for legal text retrieval. *Artificial Intelligence and Law* 9:29–57.

Moens, M.-F., C. Uyttendaele, and J. Dumortier. 1997. Abstracting of legal cases: The Salomon experience. In *ICAIL '97: Proceedings of the 6th International Conference on Artificial Intelligence and Law*, 114–122. New York: ACM.

Moles, R. N. 1992. Expert systems, the need for theory. In *Legal knowledge based systems JURIX 92: Information Technology and Law, the Foundation for Legal Knowledge Systems*, ed. C. Grütters, J. Breuker, H. V. den Herik, A. Schmidt, and C. de Vey Mestdagh, 113–121. Lelystad: Koninklijke Vermande.

Moles, R. N. 2008. Ronald Stamper and norm based systems. Legal Theory Lecture published at Networked Knowledge web site. Retrieved October 22, 2008, from http://netk.net.au/LegalTheory.asp

Moliner, M. 2000. Diccionario de Uso del Español. Gredos.

Mommers, L. 1998. On the ontological status and representation of legal concepts. In *Proceedings of the Eleventh Conference of Legal Knowledge-Based Systems (JURIX'98)*, ed. J. Hage, T. Bench-Capon, A. Koers, C. de Vey Mestdagh, and C. Grütters, 45–58. Nijmegen: Gerard Noodt Instituut.

Mommers, L. 2001. A knowledge-based ontology of the legal domain. In *Proceedings of the Second International Workshop on Legal Ontologies (LEGONT) in JURIX 2001*, Amsterdam, ed. R. Winkels, 1–7.

Mommers, L. 2002. *Applied legal epistemology. Building a knowledge-based ontology of the legal domain*. Ph.D. thesis, Leiden University.

Mommers, L. 2003. Applications of a knowledge-based ontology of the legal domain in collaborative workspaces. In *Proceedings of the International Conference on Artificial Intelligence and Law (ICAIL)*, 70–108. New York: ACM.

Montero-Aroca, J., J. Gómez-Colomer, A. Montón-Redondo, and S. Barona-Vilar. 2005a. *Derecho jurisdiccional I. Parte general*. 14th ed. Valencia: Tirant Lo Blanch.

Montero-Aroca, J., J. Gómez-Colomer, A. Montón-Redondo, and S. Barona-Vilar. 2005b. *Derecho jurisdiccional II. Proceso civil*. 14th ed. Valencia: Tirant Lo Blanch.

Montero-Aroca, J., J. Gómez-Colomer, A. Montón-Redondo, and S. Barona-Vilar. 2005c. *Derecho jurisdiccional III. Proceso penal*. 14th ed. Valencia: Tirant Lo Blanch.

Montero-Aroca, J., J. Gómez-Colomer, A. Montón-Redondo, and S. Barona-Vilar. 2007. *Derecho jurisdiccional III. Proceso penal*. 15th ed. Valencia: Tirant Lo Blanch.

Montero-Aroca, J., J. Gómez-Colomer, A. Montón-Redondo, and S. Barona-Vilar. 2008. *Derecho jurisdiccional I. Parte general*. 16th ed. Valencia: Tirant Lo Blanch.

Moor, A. D. 2002. Language/action meets organisational semiotics: Situating conversations with norms. *Information Systems Frontiers* 4(3):257–272.

Moreno-Catena, V., and V. Cortés-Domínguez. 2008. *Derecho procesal penal*. 3ª ed. Valencia: Tirant lo Blanch.

Morita, T., N. Fukuta, N. Izumi, and T. Yamaguchi. 2006. DODDLE-OWL: A domain ontology construction tool with OWL. In *The Semantic Web, ASWC 2006*, ed. R. Mizoguchi, Z. Shi, and F. Giunchiglia. *Lecture notes in computer science*, Vol. 4185, 537–551. Berlin/Heidelberg: Springer.

Morita, T., N. Izumi, and T. Yamaguchi. 2008. Integrating a domain ontology development environment and an ontology search engine. In *Proceeding of the 2008 Conference on Knowledge-Based Software Engineering*, 263–272. Amsterdam: IOS Press.

Motik, B., B. C. Grau, I. Horrocks, Z. Wu, A. Fokoue, C. Lutz, D. Calvanese, J. Carroll, G. D. Giacomo, J. Hendler, I. Herman, B. Parsia, P. F. Patel-Schneider, A. Ruttenberg, U. Sattler, and M. Schneider. 2009, October. OWL 2 web ontology language. profiles. W3c recommendation 27 October 2009, W3C.

Mulder, R. D., K. van Noortwijk, and L. Combrink-Kuiters. 2010. Chapter Jurimetrics please!. In *A history of legal informatics*, ed. Paliwala, A. 2010. *A history of legal informatics. LEFIS series*, Vol. 9, LEFIS, Zaragoza: Prensas Universitarias de Zaragoza.

Muller, M. 2001. Legal RDF dictionary. In *Proceedings of the Second International Workshop on Legal Ontologies (LEGONT) in JURIX 2001*, Amsterdam, ed. R. Winkels, 20–21.

Musen, M. A. 1992. Dimensions of knowledge sharing and reuse. *Computers and Biomedical Research* 25:435–467.

Musen, M. A. 1993. An overview of knowledge acquisition. In *Second generation expert systems*. ed. J.-M. David, J.-P. Krivine, and R. Simmons, 405–427. Berlin: Springer-Verlag New York. http://portal.acm.org/citation.cfm?id=167940&CFID=31371873&CFTOKEN=85315380

Nadah, N., M. D. de Rosnay, and B. Bachimont. 2007. Licensing digital content with a generic ontology: Escaping from the jungle of rights expression languages. In *Proceedings of the Eleventh International Conference on Artificial Intelligence and Law (ICAIL 2007)*, June 4–8, Palo Alto, 65–69. New York: ACM Press.

Navigli, R., and P. Velardi. 2004. Learning domain ontologies from document warehouses and dedicated web sites. *Computational Linguistics* 30(2):151–179.

Navigli, R., P. Velardi, A. Cucchiarelli, and F. Neri. 2004. Automatic ontology learning: Supporting a per-concept evaluation by domain experts. In *Proceedings of the ECAI-2004 Workshop on Ontology Learning and Population*, Sevilla.

Nebel, B. 1999. Frame-based systems. In *The MIT Encyclopedia of the Cognitive Sciences*, ed. R. A. Wilson and F. C. Keil, 324–326. Cambridge: MIT Press.

Neches, R., R. Fikes, T. Finin, T. Gruber, R. Patil, T. Senator, and W. R. Swartout. 1991. Enabling technology for knowledge sharing. *AI Magazine* 12(3):36–56.

Newell, A. 1981, Summer. The knowledge level (presidential address American association for artificial intelligence aaai80, Stanford university 19 august 1980). *AI Magazine* 2(2):1–20, 33.

Nielsen, J. 1994a. *Usability engineering*. San Francisco: Morgan Kaufmann.

Nielsen, J. 1994b. Usability inspection methods. In *CHI '94: Conference Companion on Human Factors in Computing Systems*, 413–414. New York: ACM.

Nielsen, J. 2005. How to conduct a heuristic evaluation. Web. (Available at 01-10-2008).

Niles, I., and A. Pease. 2001. Towards a standard upper ontology. In *Proceedings of FOIS'01*, October 17–19, Ogunquit.

Noy, N. F., and C. D. Hafner. 1997. The state of the art in ontology design: A survey and comparative review. *AI Magazine* 18(3):53–74.

Noy, N. F., and D. L. McGuinness. 2001. Ontology development 101: A guide to creating your first ontology. Technical Report SMI-2001-0880, Stanford University School of Medicine.

Oberle, D., A. Ankolekar, P. Hitzler, P. Cimiano, M. Sintek, M. Kiesel, B. Mougouie, S. Vembu, S. Baumann, M. Romanelli, P. Buitelaar, R. Engel, D. Sonntag, N. Reithinger, B. Loos, R. Porzel, H.-P. Zorn, V. Micelli, C. Schmidt, M. Weiten, F. Burkhardt, and J. Zhou. 2007, September. DOLCE ergo SUMO: On foundational and domain models in swinto (smartweb integrated ontology). *Web Semantics: Science, Services and Agents on the World Wide Web* 5(3):156–174.

Ortiz-Rodríguez, F. 2007. Egodo and applications: Sharing, retrieving and exchanging legal documentation across e-government. In *Proceedings of the Workshop on Semantic Web technology for Law (SW4Law) at the International Conference on AI and Law (ICAIL'07)*, Stanford, June 8, ed. M. Klein, P. Quaresma, and N. Casellas, 21–26.

Ortiz-Rodríguez, F., R. Palma, and B. Villazón-Terrazas. 2006. Aplicaciones para gobierno electrónico semántico en méxico: Una aproximación para el desarrollo municipal. In *Proceedings of the IV Encuentro Internacional de Estudios Municipales: Políticas y Gestión Pblica para el Desarrollo Municipal: análisis y perspectivas*, 18 al 20 de Octubre, Tamaulipas.

Ortiz-Rodríguez, F., and B. Villazón-Terrazas. 2006. Ego ontology model: Law and regulation approach for egovernment. In *Proceeding of the Workshop on Semantic Web for eGovernment 2006 Workshop at the 3rd European Semantic Web Conference*, 12 June 2006, Budva, ed. A. Abecker and G. M. L. Stojanovic, 13–24.

Osborn, J., and L. Sterling. 1999a. Automated concept identification within legal cases. *The Journal of Information, Law and Technology (JILT)* 1. http://www2.warwick.ac.uk/fac/soc/law/elj/jilt/1999_1/osborn

Osborn, J., and L. Sterling. 1999b. Justice: A judicial search tool using intelligent concept extraction. In *ICAIL '99: Proceedings of the 7th International Conference on Artificial Intelligence and Law*, 173–181. New York: ACM.

Paschke, A., M. Bichler, and J. Dietrich. 2005. Contractlog: An approach to rule based monitoring and execution of service level agreements. In *Rules and rule markup languages for the semantic web*, ed. A. Adi, S. Stoutenburg, and S. Tabet. *Lecture notes in computer science*, Vol. 3791, 209–217. Berlin/Heidelberg: Springer.

Paslaru, E., and C. Tempich. 2006, November. Ontology engineering: A reality check. In *The 5th International Conference on Ontologies, DataBases, and Applications of Semantics (ODBASE2006)*, ed. R. Meersman, Z. Tari, et al. *Lecture notes in computer science (LNCS)*, Montpellier, Vol. 4275, 836–854. Berlin/New York: Springer.

Pazienza, M. T., N. Scarpato, and A. Stellato. 2009. Stia: Experience of semantic annotation in jurisprudence domain. In *Legal knowledge and information systems – JURIX 2009: The Twenty-Second Annual Conference on Legal Knowledge and Information Systems* , Rotterdam, 16–18 December 2009, ed. G. Governatori. *Frontiers in artificial intelligence and applications*. Vol. 205, 156–161. Amsterdam: IOS Press.

Peek, N. 1997. Representing law in partial information structures. *Artificial Intelligence and Law* 5:263–290.

Perakath, B., C. P. Menzel, R. J. Mayer, F. Fillion, M. T. Futrell, P. S. DeWitte, and M. Lingineni. 1994, October. Ontology capture method (IDEF5). Interim technical rept. mar 92-sep 94, Knowledge Based Systems, Inc.

Peters, W. 2004. The LOIS project. In *GWC 2006, Proceedings*, ed. P. Sojka, K.-S. Choi, and C. F. P. Vossen, 331–332. Masaryk University, Brno.

Peters, W. 2009. Text-based legal ontology enrichment. In *3rd Workshop on Legal Ontologies and Artificial Intelligence Techniques Joint with 2nd Workshop on Semantic Processing of Legal Text (LOAIT 2009), Co-located with the 12th International Conference on Artificial Intelligence and Law (ICAIL 2009)*, ed. N. Casellas, E. Francesconi, R. Hoekstra, and S. Montemagni. *IDT series*, Vol. 2, 55–65. Barcelona: IDT/Huygens Editorial.

Peters, W., M.-T. Sagri, and D. Tiscornia. 2007. The structuring of legal knowledge in LOIS. *Artificial Intelligence and Law* 15(2):117–135.

Pinto, H. S., C. Tempich, and S. Staab. 2004. DILIGENT: Towards a fine-grained methodology for distributed, loosely-controlled and evolving engineering of ontologies. In *Proceedings of the 16th European Conference on Artificial Intelligence (ECAI 2004)*, August 22–27 Valencia, ed. R. L. de Mantaras and L. Saitta, 393–397. Amsterdam: IOS Press.

Pinto, H. S., C. Tempich, S. Staab, and Y. Sure. 2005. Distributed engineering of ontologies (DILIGENT). In *Semantic Web and peer-to-peer*, ed. S. Stuckenschmidt and S. Staab, 301–320. Berlin: Springer.

Poblet, M., N. Casellas, S. Torralba, and P. Casanovas. 2009. Modeling expert knowledge in the mediation domain: A mediation core ontology. In *3rd Workshop on Legal Ontologies and Arificial Intelligence Techniques joint with 2nd Workshop on Semantic Processing of Legal Text (LOAIT 2009), Co-located with the 12th International Conference on Artificial Intelligence and Law (ICAIL 2009)*, ed. N. Casellas, E. Francesconi, R. Hoekstra, and S. Montemagni. *IDT series*, Vol. 2, 19–28. Barcelona: IDT/Huygens Editorial.

Polo, L., J. M. Alvarez, and E. R. Azcona. 2008. Promoting government controlled vocabularies to the Semantic Web: EUROVOC thesaurus and cpv product classification scheme. In *Proceedings of the Semantic Interoperability in the European Digital Library workshop (SIEDL2008), co-located with 5th European Semantic Web Conference (ESWC2008)*, Tenerife, June 2, 2008, 111–122.

Presutti, V., A. Gangemi, S. David, G. A. de Cea, M. C. Suárez-Figueroa, E. Montiel-Ponsoda, and M. Poveda. 2008, February. A library of ontology design patterns: Reusable solutions for collaborative design of networked ontologies. Deliverable D2.5.1, NeOn Project, http://www.neon-project.org

Quaresma, P., and I. P. Rodrigues. 2005. A question-answering system for Portuguese juridical documents. In *Proceedings of the Tenth International Conference on Artificial Intelligence and Law (ICAIL 2005)*, June 6–11, University of Bologna, 256–257. New York: ACM.

Rahmouni, H. B., T. Solomonides, M. C. Mont, and S. Shiu. 2009. Privacy compliance in European healthgrid domains: An ontology-based approach. In *Proceedings of the 22nd IEEE International Symposium on Computer-Based Medical Systems, 2009* (CBMS 2009), 1–8. Piscataway, NJ: IEEE.

Ramos-Méndez, F. 1997a. *Enjuiciamiento civil*. Vol. Tomo I, Barcelona: J.M. Bosch Editor.

Ramos-Méndez, F. 1997b. *Enjuiciamiento civil*. Vol. Tomo II, Barcelona: J.M. Bosch Editor.

Ramos-Méndez, F. 2006. *Enjuiciamiento criminal. Octava lectura constitucional*. 8th ed. Barcelona: Atelier.

Rational. 2001. Rational unified process. Best practices for software development teams. White Paper TP026B, Rev 11/01, Rational. The Software Development Company.

Rector, A., N. Drummond, M. Horridge, J. Rogers, H. Knublauch, R. Stevens, H. Wang, and C. Wroe. 2004. OWL pizzas: Practical experience of teaching OWL-DL: Common errors & common patterns. In *Proceedings of the 14th International Conference on Knowledge Engineering and Knowledge Management EKAW'04* , 5–8 October, Whittlebury Hall, Northamptonshire.

Reinert, M. 2003. Le rôle de la répétition dans la représentation de sens et son approche statistique par la méthode alceste. *Semiotica* 147(164):389–420.

Rissland, E. L. 1985. Ai and legal reasoning. In *Proceedings of the International Joint Conference in Artificial Intelligence (IJCAI85)*, 681–687, Los Angeles.

Rissland, E. L., K. D. Ashley, and R. Loui. 2003. Ai and law: A fruitful synergy. *Artificial Intelligence* 250:1–15.

Rodríguez-Aguilar, J.-A. 2001, Maig. *On the design and construction of agent-mediated institutions*. Doctor enginyer en informtica, Facultat de Ciències, Secció d'Enginyeria Informtica, Universitat Autònoma de Barcelona, Bellaterra (Barcelona).

Ross, A. 1957. T-t. *Harvard Law Review* 70(5):812–825.

Ross, A. 1958. *On law and justice*. Berkeley and Los Angeles: University of California Press.

Ross, A. 1968. *Directives and norms*. New York: Humanities Press.

Rubino, R., A. Rotolo, and G. Sartor. 2006. An OWL ontology of fundamental legal concepts. In *Legal knowledge and information systems. JURIX 2006: The Nineteenth Annual Conference*, ed. T. van Engers. *Frontiers of artificial intelligence and applications*. Vol. 152, Amsterdam: IOS Press.

Rubino, R., A. Rotolo, and G. Sartor. 2007. An OWL ontology of norms and normative judgements. In *Proceedings of the V Legislative XML Workshop*, 14–16 June, 2006, ed. E. F. Carlo Biagioli and G. Sartor, 173–188. Florence: European Press Academic Publishing.

Ryan, H., P. Spyns, P. De Leenheer, and R. Leary. 2003. Ontology-based platform for trusted regulatory compliance services. In *On the move to meaningful internet systems 2003: OTM 2003 Workshops. Lecture notes in computer science*, Vol. 2889, 675–689. Berlin/Heidelberg: Springer.

Sagri, M. T., D. Tiscornia, and F. Bertagna. 2004. Jur-WordNet. In *GWC 2004, Proceedings*, ed. P. Sojka, K. Pala, P. Smrz, C. Fellbaum, and P. Vossen, 305–310. Brno: Masaryk University.

Saias, J., and P. Quaresma. 2002. Semantic enrichment of a web legal information retrieval system. In *Legal knowledge and information systems. JURIX 2002: The Fifteenth Annual Conference*, ed. T. Bench-Capon, A. Daskalopulu, and R. Winkels. *Frontiers in artificial intelligence and applications*, 11–19. Amsterdam: IOS Press.

Saias, J., and P. Quaresma. 2003a. A methodology to create ontology-based information retrieval systems. In *Progress in Artificial Intelligence, 11th Portuguese Conference on Artificial Intelligence, EPIA 2003, Proceedings*, Beja, December 4–7, 2003, ed. F. Moura-Pires and S. Abreu. *Lecture notes in computer science*, Vol. 2902, 424–434. Springer.

Saias, J., and P. Quaresma. 2003b. Using nlp techniques to create legal ontologies in a logic programming based web information retrieval system. In *Proceedings of the ICAIL 2003 Workshop on Legal Ontologies and Web Based Legal Information Management)*, Edinburgh, June 24–28.

Saias, J., and P. Quaresma. 2005. A methodology to create legal ontologies in a logic programming information retrieval system. In *Law and the Semantic Web. Legal ontologies, methodologies, legal information retrieval, and applications [outcome of the Workshop on Legal Ontologies and Web-Based Legal Information Management, June 28, 2003, Edinburgh, UK & International Seminar on Law and the Semantic Web, November 20–21, 2003, Barcelona, Spain]*, ed. V. R. Benjamins, P. Casanovas, J. Breuker, and A. Gangemi. *Lecture notes in computer science*, Vol. 3369, 185–200. Berlin/Heidelberg: Springer.

Sánchez-Ruenes, D. 2007. *Domain ontology learning from the web.* Tesi doctoral programa de doctorat en intelligència artificial, Departament de Llenguatges i Sistemes Informtics, Universitat Politècnica de Catalunya.

Saravanan, M., B. Ravindran, and S. Raman. 2007. Using legal ontology for query enhancement in generating a document summary. In *Legal knowledge and information systems. JURIX 2007: The Twentieth Annual Conference*, ed. A. R. Lodder and L. Mommers. *Frontiers in artificial intelligence and applications*, Vol. 165, 171–172. Amsterdam: IOS Press.

Sartor, G. 2006. Fundamental legal concepts: A formal and teleological characterisation. EUI Working Papers Law 11, European University Institute.

Sartor, G., P. Casanovas, M. Biasiotti, and M. Fernández-Barrera. 2011. *Approaches to legal ontologies. Theories, domains and methodologies. Number 1 in law, governance and technology series.* New York/Heidelberg: Springer.

Savvas, I., and N. Bassiliades. 2008. A process-oriented ontology-based knowledge management system for facilitating operational procedures in public administration. *Expert Systems with Applications* [to appear]. Available online 13 May 2008.

Schneider, L. 2003. Foundational ontologies and the realist bias. In *KI Workshop on Reference Ontologies and Application Ontologies*, Hamburg, September 16.

Schneider, L., and J. Cunningham. 2003. Ontological foundations of natural language communication in multiagent systems. In *Knowledge-Based Intelligent Information and Engineering Systems, 7th International Conference, KES 2003*, September 3–5, 2003, Proceedings, Part I. Oxford, UK, ed. V. Palade, R. J. Howlett, and L. C. Jain. *Lecture notes in computer science*, Vol. 2773, 1403–1410. Springer.

Schreiber, G., H. Akkermans, A. Anjewierden, R. de Hoog, N. Shadbolt, W. V. de Velde, and B. Wielinga. 1999. *Knowledge engineering and management. The commonKADS methodology.* Cambridge: A Bradford Book. MIT Press.

Schweighofer, E., and D. Liebwald. 2007. Advanced lexical ontologies and hybrid knowledge based systems: First steps to a dynamic legal electronic commentary. *Artificial Intelligence and Law* 15:103–115.

Sclano, F., and P. Velardi. 2007. Termextractor: A web application to learn the common terminology of interest groups and research communities. In *Proceedings of the 9th Conference on Terminology and Artificial Intelligence (TIA'07)*, Sophia Antinopolis, October.

Segaran, T., C. Evans, and J. Taylor. 2009. *Programming the Semantic Web.* Sebastopol: O'Reilly.

Sergot, M. J., F. Sadri, R. A. Kowalski, F. Kriwaczek, P. Hammond, and H. T. Cory. 1986. The British nationality act as a logic program. *Communications of the ACM* 29(5):370–386.

Sevcenko, M. 2003. Online presentation of an upper ontology. In *Proceedings of Znalosti 2003*, Ostrava, February 19–21.

Shaheed, J., A. Yip, and J. Cunningham. 2005, May. A top-level language-biased legal ontology. In *LOAIT, Workshop on Legal Ontologies and Artificial Intelligence Techniques at ICAIL 2005*, ed. J. Lehmann, M. A. Biasiotti, E. Francesconi, and M. T. Sagri. *IAAIL workshop series*, Vol. 4. Bologna: Wolf Legal Publishers.

Shen, Y., R. Steele, and J. Murphy. 2008. Building a semantically rich legal case repository in OWL. In *Proceedings of AusWeb08, the Fourteenth Australasian World Wide Web Conference*, Ballina Beach Resort, 5–9 April.

Shin, I., T. Kawamura, H. Nakagawa, K. Nakayama, Y. Tahara, and A. Ohsuga. 2009. Ontomo: Development of ontology building service. In *Principles of practice in multi-agent systems*, ed. J.-J. Yang, M. Yokoo, T. Ito, Z. Jin, and P. Scerri. *Lecture notes in computer science*, Vol. 5925, 143–158. Berlin/Heidelberg: Springer.

Singh, M. P. 1999. An ontology for commitments in multiagent systems: Toward a unification of normative concepts. *Artificial Intelligence and Law* 7:97–113.

Smith, B. 2003. Ontology. In *Blackwell guide to the philosophy of computing and information*, ed. L. Floridi, 155–166. Oxford: Blackwell.

Smith, M. K., C. Welty, and D. L. McGuinness. 2004, February. OWL ontology web language guide. Recomendation, World Wide Web Consortium (W3C).

Sommerville, I. 2004, May. Making ethnography accessible. In *Procceedings Workshop on Software Engineering/HCI*, 36–40. Edinburgh: Institute of Electrical Engineers.

Sommerville, I., T. Rodden, P. Sawyer, and R. Bentley. 1993. Sociologists can be surprisingly useful in interactive systems design. In *HCI'92: Proceedings of the conference on people and computers VII*, 342–354. New York: Cambridge University Press.

Sonntag, M. 2009. Generating cases for e-learning. In *Legal knowledge and information systems – JURIX 2009: The Twenty-Second Annual Conference on Legal Knowledge and Information Systems*, Rotterdam, 16–18 December 2009, ed. G. Governatori. *Frontiers in artificial intelligence and applications*. Vol. 205, 172–181. Amsterdam: IOS Press.

Sowa, J. F. 1976. Conceptual graphs for a data base interface. *IBM Journal of Research and Development* 20(4):336–357.

Sowa, J. F. 1980. A conceptual schema for knowledge-based systems. In *Workshop on data abstraction, databases and conceptual modelling*, ed. M. L. Brodie and S. N. Zilles, Vol. 11, 193–195. New York: ACM Press.

Sowa, J. F. 1995. Top-level ontological categories. *International Journal of Human-Computer Studies* 43(5–6):669–685.

Sowa, J. F. 2000. *Knowledge representation: Logical, philosophical, and computational foundations*. Pacific Grove: Brooks Cole Publishing Co.

Spinosa, P., G. Giardiello, M. Cherubini, S. Marchi, G. Venturi, and S. Montemagni. 2009. Nlp-based metadata extraction for legal text consolidation. In *ICAIL '09: Proceedings of the 12th International Conference on Artificial Intelligence and Law*, 40–49. New York: ACM.

Spyns, P., and A. Lisovoy. 2003, July. The DOGMA modeller manual. EuroLan 2003 tutorial material STAR-2003-11, STAR Lab, Vrije Universiteit Brussel.

Spyns, P., R. Meersman, and M. Jarrar. 2002. Data modelling versus ontology engineering. *ACM SIGMOD Record* 31(4):12–17.

Spyns, P., Y. Tang, and R. Meersman. 2008. An ontology engineering methodology for DOGMA. *Applied Ontology* 3(1–2):13–39.

Stadlhofer, B., P. Salhofer, and G. Tretter. 2009. Ontology driven e-government. In *ICONS*, ed. R. K. Ege, W. Quattrociocchi, D. Dragomirescu, and O. Dini, 251–255. Washington: IEEE Computer Society.

Stamper, R. 1976, May. The LEGOL project: A survey. Technical Report 0081, IBM United Kingdom Scientific Center.

Stamper, R. 1994. Social norms in requirements analysis: An outline of measur. In *Requirements engineering: Social and technical issues*, ed. M. Jirotka and J. A. Goguen, 107–139. San Diego: Academic Press Professional, Inc.

Stamper, R. K. 1977, May. The LEGOL 1 prototype system and language. *The Computer Journal* 20(2):102–108.

Standard, I. 1998. Ergonomic requirements for office work with visual display terminals (vdts) – part 11: Guidance on usability. ISO Standard 9241-11:1998, International Organization for Standardization.

Standard, I. 1999a. Human-centred design processes for interactive systems. ISO Standard 13407:1999, International Organization for Standardization.

Standard, I. 1999b. Information technology – measurement and rating of performance of computer-based software systems. ISO Standard 14756:1999, ISO/IEC.

Standard, I. 1999c. Information technology – software product evaluation – part 1: General overview. ISO Standard 14598-1:1999, ISO/IEC.
Standard, I. 2001. Software engineering – product quality – part 1: Quality model. ISO Standard 9126-1:2001, ISO/IEC.
Standard, I. 2002. Ergonomics of human-system interaction – usability methods supporting human-centred design. ISO Standard TR 16982:2002, International Organization for Standardization.
Standard, I. 2003a. Software engineering – product quality – part 2: External metrics. ISO Standard TR 9126-2:2003, ISO/IEC.
Standard, I. 2003b. Software engineering – product quality – part 3: Internal metrics. ISO Standard TR 9126-3:2003, ISO/IEC.
Standard, I. 2004a. Information technology – process assessment – part 1: Concepts and vocabulary. ISO Standard 15504-1:2004, ISO/IEC.
Standard, I. 2004b. Software and system engineering – guidelines for the design and preparation of user documentation for application software. ISO Standard 18019:2004, ISO/IEC.
Standard, I. 2004c. Software engineering – product quality – part 4: Quality in use metrics. ISO Standard TR 9126-4:2004, ISO/IEC.
Standard, I. 2005. Software engineering – software product quality requirements and evaluation (square) – guide to square. ISO Standard 25000:2005, ISO/IEC.
Standard, I. 2006a. Ease of operation of everyday products – part 1: Design requirements for context of use and user characteristics. ISO Standard 20282-1:2006, ISO/IEC.
Standard, I. 2006b. Software engineering – software life cycle processes – maintenance. ISO Standard 14764:2006, ISO/IEC.
Standard, I. 2006c. Systems and software engineering – content of systems and software life cycle process information products (documentation). ISO/IEC 13407:1999, International Organization for Standardization.
Standard, I. 2007a. Software engineering – software product quality requirements and evaluation (square) – planning and management. ISO Standard 25001:2007, ISO/IEC.
Standard, I. 2007b. Software engineering – software product quality requirements and evaluation (square) – quality requirements. ISO Standard 25030:2007, ISO/IEC.
Standard, I. 2008a. Systems and software engineering – software life cycle processes. ISO Standard 12207:2008, ISO/IEC.
Standard, I. 2008b. Systems and software engineering – system life cycle processes. ISO Standard 15288:2008, ISO/IEC.
Steels, L. 1990. Components of expertise. *AI Magazine* 11(2):28–49.
Steve, G., A. Gangemi, and D. Pisanelli. 1997. Integrating medical terminologies with ONIONS methodology. In *Information modelling and knowledge bases VIII*, ed. H. Kangassalo and J. Charrel, Amsterdam: IOS Press.
Studer, R., V. R. Benjamins, and D. Fensel. 1998. Knowledge engineering: Principles and methods. *Data Knowledge Engineering* 25(1–2):161–197.
Suárez-Figueroa, M. C., E. Blomqvist, M. D'Aquin, M. Espinoza, A. Gómez-Pérez, H. Lewen, I. Mozetic, R. Palma, M. Poveda, M. Sini, B. Villazón-Terrazas, F. Zablith, and M. Dzbor. 2009a, February. Revision and extension of the NeOn methodology for building contextualized ontology networks. Deliverable D5.4.2, NeOn Project, http://www.neon-project.org
Suárez-Figueroa, M., A. Gómez-Pérez, and B. Villazón-Terrazas. 2009b. How to write and use the ontology requirements specification document. In *On the move to meaningful internet systems: OTM 2009*, ed. R. Meersman, T. Dillon, and P. Herrero. *Lecture notes in computer science*, Vol. 5871, 966–982. Berlin/Heidelberg: Springer.
Suárez-Figueroa, M. C., G. A. de Cea, C. Buil, C. Caracciolo, M. Dzbor, A. Gómez-Pérez, G. Herrrero, H. Lewen, E. Montiel-Ponsoda, and V. Presutti. 2007, August. NeOn development process and ontology life cycle. Deliverable D5.3.1, NeOn Project, http://www.neon-project.org

Suárez-Figueroa, M. C., K. Dellschaft, E. Montiel-Ponsoda, B. Villazón-Terrazas, Z. Yufei, G. A. de Cea, A. García, M. Fernández-López, A. Gómez-Pérez, M. Espinoza, and M. Sabou. 2008a, February. NeOn methodology for building contextualized ontology networks. Deliverable D5.4.1, NeOn Project, http://www.neon-project.org

Suárez-Figueroa, M. C., M. Fernández-López, A. Gómez-Pérez, K. Dellschaft, H. Lewen, and M. Dzbor. 2008b, November. Revision and extension of the NeOn development process and ontology life cycle. Deliverable D5.3.2, NeOn Project, http://www.neon-project.org

Sugiura, N., N. Izumi, and T. Yamaguchi. 2004. A support environment for domain ontology development with general ontologies and text corpus. *IEEE Intelligent Informatics Bulletin* 3(1):25–30.

Sugiura, N., M. Kurematsu, N. Fukuta, N. Izumi, and T. Yamaguchi. 2003. A domain ontology engineering tool with general ontologies and text corpus. In *EON2003, Evaluation of Ontology-based Tools, Proceedings of the 2nd International Workshop on Evaluation of Ontology-Based Tools held at the 2nd International Semantic Web Conference ISWC 2003, 20th October 2003 (Workshop day)*, Sundial Resort, Sanibel, ed. Y. Sure and óscar Corcho. *CEUR Workshop Proceedings*, Vol. 87, CEUR-WS.org

Sure, Y. 1993. A tool-supported methodology for ontology-based knowledge management. In *Ontology and Modeling of Real Estate Transactions in European Juristictions*, ed. E. Stubkjaer. *International land management series, 2002*. Ashgate, Hampshire, UK.

Sure, Y. 2003. *Methodology, tools and case studies for ontology based knowledge management*. Ph.D. thesis, Fakultät für Wirschaftwissenschaften der Universität Fridericiana zu Karlsruhe.

Sure, Y., S. Staab, and R. Studer. 2002. Methodology for development and employment of ontology based knowledge management applications. *ACM SIGMOD Record* 31(Special Issue)(4):18–23.

Sure, Y., S. Staab, and R. Studer. 2004. On-To-Knowledge methodology (OTKM). In *Handbook on ontologies*, ed. S. Staab and R. Studer. *International handbooks on information systems*, 117–132. Berlin: Springer.

Sure, Y., and R. Studer. 2002, September. On-To-Knowledge methodology – final version. Project Deliverable D. 18, EU IST-1999-10132 On-To-Knowledge (Institute AIFB, University of Karlsruhe).

Sure, Y., and R. Studer. 2003. A methodology for ontology-based knowledge management. In *Towards the Semantic Web. Ontology-driven knowledge management*, ed. J. Davies, D. Fensel, and F. van Harmelen, 33–46. Chichester: Wiley.

Sure, Y., C. Tempich, and D. Vrandečić. 2006. Ontology engineering methodologies. In *Semantic web technology: Trends and research in ontology-based systems*, ed. J. Davies, R. Studer, and P. Warren, Chapter 9, 171–190. Chichester/Hoboken: Wiley.

Sure, Y., C. Tempich, D. Vrandečić, and H. S. Pinto. 2004, December. D.7.1.1 sekt methodology: Survey and initial framework. SEKT IST-2003-506826 Deliverable 7.1.1, SEKT, EU-IST Project IST-2003-506826, Institute AIFB, University of Karlsruhe.

Susskind, R. 1987. *Expert systems in law: A jurisprudential inquiry*. New York: Oxford University Press.

Susskind, R. 2010. Chapter Legal Informatics – a personal appraisal of context and progress. *European Journal of Law and Technology* 1(1):119–145.

Tang, Y., and D. Trog. 2010. Model ontological commitments using orm+ in t-lex. In *On the move to meaningful internet systems: OTM 2008 Workshops*, ed. R. Meersman, Z. Tari, and P. Herrero. *Lecture notes in computer science*, Vol. 5333, 787–796. Berlin/Heidelberg: Springer.

Tartir, S., I. B. Arpinar, M. Moore, A. P. Sheth, and B. Aleman-Meza. 2005. OntoQA: Metric-based ontology quality analysis. In *Proceedings of IEEE Workshop on Knowledge Acquisition from Distributed, Autonomous, Semantically Heterogeneous Data and Knowledge Sources*, Houston, November 27.

Temmerman, R., and K. Kerremans. 2003. Termontography: Ontology building and the sociocognitive approach to terminology description. In *Proceedings of CIL17, MFF UK (CD-ROM)*, ed. E. Hajicová, A. Kotešovcová, and J. Mírovský. Prague: Matfyz Press.

Tempich, C., H. S. Pinto, Y. Sure, D. Vrandečić, N. Casellas, and P. Casanovas. 2007. Ontology engineering with DILIGENT. A legal case study. In *Trends in legal knowledge: The Semantic Web and the rebulaiton of electronic social systems. Papers form the B-4 Workshop on Artificial Intelligence and Law, May 25th–27th of the XXII World Congress of Philosophy of Law and Social Philosophy IVR'05*, Granadam, ed. P. Casanovas, P. Noriega, D. Bourcière, and F. Galindo, 269–277. Florence: European Press Academic Publishing.

Terziev, I., A. Kiryakov, and D. Manov. 2005. D1.8.1 base upper-level ontology (bulo) guidance. SEKT IST-2003-506826 Deliverable 1.8.1, SEKT, EU-IST Project IST-2003-506826, Ontotext Lab, Sirma Group (Bulgaria).

Tiscornia, D. 2007. The LOIS project: Lexical ontologies for legal information sharing. In *Proceedings of the V Legislative XML Workshop*, ed. C. Biagioli, E. Francesconi, and G. Sartor, 189–204. Firenze: European Press Academic Publishing.

Toharia, J. J., and J. J. García. 2005. *La Justicia ante el espejo: 25 años de estudios de opinión del CGPJ*. Madrid: Consejo General del Poder Judicial.

Trog, D., Y. Tang, and R. Meersman. 2007. Towards ontological commitments with omega-ridl markup language. In *Advances in rule interchange and applications*, ed. A. Paschke and Y. Biletskiy. *Lecture notes in computer science*, Vol. 4824, 92–106. Berlin/Heidelberg: Springer.

Trog, D., J. Vereecken, S. Christiaens, P. De Leenheer, and R. Meersman. 2006. T-lex: A role-based ontology engineering tool. In *On the move to meaningful internet systems 2006: OTM 2006 Workshops*, ed. R. Meersman, Z. Tari, and P. Herrero. *Lecture notes in computer science*, Vol. 4278, 1191–1200. Berlin/Heidelberg: Springer.

Tudorache, T., N. Noy, S. Tu, and M. Musen. 2010. Supporting collaborative ontology development in protégé. In *The Semantic Web – ISWC 2008*, ed, A. Sheth, S. Staab, M. Dean, M. Paolucci, D. Maynard, T. Finin, and K. Thirunarayan. *Lecture notes in computer science*, Vol. 5318, 17–32. Berlin/Heidelberg: Springer.

Tullis, T. S., and J. N. Stetson. 2004. A comparison of questionnaires for assessing website usability. In *UPA 2004: Connecting communities*, Minneapolis, June 7–11, 2004.

Uijttenbroek, E. M., M. C. Klein, A. R. Lodder, and F. van Harmelen. 2007. Case law retrieval by concept search and visualization. In *Proceedings of the Eleventh International Conference on Artificial Intelligence and Law (ICAIL 2007)*, June 4–8, Palo Alto, 95–96. New York: ACM Press.

Uijttenbroek, E. M., M. C. Klein, A. R. Lodder, F. van Harmelen, and P. E. Huygen. 2007. Semantic case law retrieval – findings and challenges. In *Proceedings of the Workshop on Semantic Web Technology for Law (SW4Law) at the International Conference on AI and Law (ICAIL'07)*, Stanford, June 8, ed. M. Klein, P. Quaresma, and N. Casellas, 33–39.

Uijttenbroek, E. M., A. R. Lodder, M. C. Klein, G. R. Wildeboer, W. V. Steenbergen, R. L. Sie, P. E. Huygen, and F. van Harmelen. 2008. Retrieval of case law to provide layman with information about liability: Preliminary results of the BEST-project. In *Computable models of the law*, ed. P. Casanovas, G. Sartor, N. Casellas, and R. Rubino. *Lecture notes in artificial intelligence*, Vol. 4884, 291–311. Berlin/Heidelberg: Springer.

Uschold, M. 1996, September. Building ontologies: Towards a unified methodology. In *Technical Report AIAI-TR-197, and in Proceedings of Expert Systems 1996, the 16th Annual Conference of the British Computer Society Specialist Group on Expert Systems*. Cambridge: The University of Edinburgh.

Uschold, M. 2003, Fall. Where are the semantics in the Semantic Web? *AI Magazine* 24(3):25–36.

Uschold, M., and M. Grüninger. 1996a, February. Ontologies: Principles, methods and applications. Technical Report AIAI-TR-191, University of Edimburgh.

Uschold, M., and M. Grüninger. 1996b. Ontologies: Principles, methods, and applications. *Knowledge Engineering Review* 11(2):93–155.

Uschold, M., and R. Jasper. 1999. A framework for understanding and classifying ontology applications. In *IJCAI-99 Workshop on Ontologies and Problem-Solving Methods (KRR5)*, ed. V. R. Benjamins, Stockholm.

Uschold, M., and M. King. 1995. Towards a methodology for building ontologies. In *Proceedings of the Workshop on Basic Ontological Issues in Knowledge Sharing at IJCAI'95*, ed. D. Skuce, Montreal.

Uszok, A., J. M. Bradshaw, M. Johnson, R. Jeffers, A. Tate, J. Dalton, and S. Aitken. 2004, July. Kaos policy management for Semantic Web services. *IEEE Intelligent Systems* 19:32–41.

Valente, A. 1995. *Legal knowledge engineering; a modelling approach*. Amsterdam: IOS Press.

Valente, A. 2005. Types and roles of legal ontologies. In *Law and the Semantic Web. Legal ontologies, methodologies, legal information retrieval, and applications [outcome of the Workshop on Legal Ontologies and Web-Based Legal Information Management, June 28, 2003, Edinburgh, UK & International Seminar on Law and the Semantic Web, November 20–21, 2003, Barcelona, Spain]*, ed. V. R. Benjamins, P. Casanovas, J. Breuker, and A. Gangemi. *Lecture notes in computer science*, Vol. 3369, 65–76. Berlin/Heidelberg: Springer.

Valente, A., and J. Breuker. 1992. A model-based approach to legal knowledge engineering. In *Legal knowledge based systems JURIX 92: Information technology and law, the foundation for legal knowledge systems*, ed. C. Grütters, J. Breuker, H. V. den Herik, A. Schmidt, and C. de Vey Mestdagh, 123–133. Lelystad: Koninklijke Vermande.

Valente, A., and J. Breuker. 1994a. A commonsense theory of normative systems. In *Proceedings of the ECAI'94 Workshop on Artificial Normative Systems*, ed. J. Breuker, 56–69. ECCAI.

Valente, A., and J. Breuker. 1994b. A functional ontology of law. In *Towards a global expert system in law*. ed. G. Bargellini and S. Binazzi. Padua: Cedam Publishers.

Valente, A., and J. Breuker. 1994c. Ontologies: The missing link between legal theory and ai /& law. In *Legal knowledge based systems (JURIX'94) the foundation for legal knowledge systems: The relation with legal theory*, ed. H. Prakken, A. Muntjewerff, and A. Soeteman, 138–150. Lelystad: Koninklijke Vermande. ISBN 90 5458 190 5.

Valente, A., and J. Breuker. 1995. On-line: An architecture for modelling legal information. In *Proceedings of the Fifth International Conference on Artificial Intelligence and Law (ICAIL'95)*, ed. T. Bench-Capon, 307–315. New York: ACM Press.

Valente, A., and J. Breuker. 1996. Towards principled core ontologies. In *Proceedings of the 10th Banff Knowledge Acquisition for Knowledge-Based Systems Workshop (KAW'96)*, Banff.

Valente, A., and J. Breuker. 1999. Legal modeling and automated reasoning with on-line. *International Journal of Human-Computer Studies* 51(6):1079–1125.

Vallbé, J.-J. 2009, July. *Facing uncertainty: Institutional and cognitive constraints in Spanish junior judges decision-making*. Ph.D. thesis, Department of Constitutional Law and Political Science, Universitat de Barcelona, Barcelona.

Vallbé, J.-J., M. A. Martí, B. Fortuna, A. Jakulin, D. Mladenič, and P. Casanovas. 2007. Stemming and lemmatisation: Improving knowledge management through language processing techniques. In *Trends in legal knowledge: The Semantic Web and the rebulaiton of electronic social systems. Papers form the B-4 Workshop on Artificial Intelligence and Law, May 25th–27th of the XXII World Congress of Philosophy of Law and Social Philosophy IVR'05*, Granada, ed. P. Casanovas, P. Noriega, D. Bourcière, and F. Galindo, 227–242. Florence: European Press Academic Publishing.

van de Ven, S., R. Hoekstra, J. Breuker, L. Wortel, and A. El-Ali. 2008. Judging amy: Automated legal assessment using OWL 2. In *OWLED*, ed. C. Dolbear, A. Ruttenberg, and U. Sattler. *CEUR Workshop Proceedings*. Vol. 432, CEUR-WS.org

van der Lieth Gardner, A. 1987. *An artificial intelligence approach to legal reasoning*. Cambridge: MIT Press.

van Engers, T. 2004. Legal engineering: A knowledge engineering approach to improving legal quality. In *eGovernment and eDemocracy: Progress and challenges*, ed. J. Padget, R. Neira, and J. D. León, 189–206. Instituto Politéchnico Nacional Centro de Investigacion en Computación. ISBN 970-36-0152-9.

van Engers, T., L. van Driel, and M. Boekenoogen. 2002. The effect of formal representation formats on the quality of legal decision-making. In *Legal knowledge and information systems. Jurix 2002: The Fifteenth Annual Conference*, ed. T. Bench-Capon, A. Daskalopulu, and R. Winkels. *Frontiers in artificial intelligence and applications*, 63–71. Amsterdam: IOS Press.

van Engers, T. M. 2001. *Knowledge management. The role of mental models in business systems design*. Number 2001-11 in SIKS Dissertation Series. Belastingdienst.

van Engers, T. M., and E. Glassée. 2001, January/February. Facilitating the legislation process using a shared conceptual model. *IEEE Intelligent Systems* 16:50–58.

van Engers, T. M., P. Kordelaar, J. D. Hartog, and E. Glassée. 2000. Power: Programme for an ontology based working environment for modeling and use of regulations and legislation. In *In Proceedings of the 11th Workshop on Databases and Expert Systems Applications (IEEE)*, ed. A. M. Tjoa, R. R. Wagner, A. Al-Zobaidie, Greenwich, 327–334. ISBN: 0-7695-0680-1.

van Engers, T. M., P. J. Kordelaar, and S. A. ter Horst. 2001. Power to the e-government. In *Knowledge management in e-Government KMGov-2001*. IFIP.

van Engers, T. M. and R. A. W. Vanlerberghe. 2002. The power-light version: Improving legal quality under time pressure. In *Proceedings of the First International Conference on Electronic Government (EGOV'02)*, ed. K. Lenk and R. Traunmüller. *Lecture notes in computer science*, Vol. 2456, 75–83. Berlin/Heidelberg: Springer.

van Heijst, G. 1995, May. *The role of ontologies in knowledge engineering*. Ph.D. thesis, Social Science Informatics, University of Amsterdam.

van Heijst, G., S. Falasconi, A. Abu-Hanna, G. Schreiber, and M. Stefanelli. 1995 A case study in ontology library construction. *Artificial Intelligence in Medicine* 7(3):227–255.

van Heijst, G., A. T. Schreiber, and B. J. Wielinga. 1997a. Roles are not classes: A reply to Nicola Guarino. *International Journal of Human-Computer Studies* 46(2):311–318.

van Heijst, G., A. T. Schreiber, and B. J. Wielinga. 1997b. Using explicit ontologies in KBS development. *International Journal of Human-Computer Studies* 46(2):183–292.

van Kralingen, R. W. 1995. *Frame-based conceptual models of statute law*. Hague: Kluwer Law International.

van Kralingen, R. W. 1997. A conceptual frame-based ontology for the law. In *Proceedings of the First International Workshop on Legal Ontologies (LEGONT'97)*, Melbourne, ed. P. Visser and R. Winkels, 15–22.

van Kralingen, R. W., E. Oskamp, and E. Reurings. 1993. Norm frames in the representation of laws. In *Legal knowledge based systems JURIX 93: Intelligent Tools for Drafting Legislation, Computer-Supported Comparison of Law*, ed. J. Svensson, J. Wassink, and B. van Buggenhout, 11–22. Lelystad: Koninklijke Vermande.

van Kralingen, R. W., P. R. Visser, T. J. Bench-Capon, and H. J. V. D. Herik. 1999. A principled approach to developing legal knowledge systems. *International Journal of Human-Computer Studies* 51(6):1127–1154.

van Laarschot, R. 2005, August. Ontology-based knowledge modelling in Dutch law. Master's thesis, Department of Artificial Intelligence, Vrije Universiteit Amsterdam.

van Laarschot, R., W. van Steenbergen, H. Stuckenschmidt, A. R. Lodder, and F. van Harmelen. 2005. The legal concepts and the layman's terms. In *Legal knowledge and information systems. JURIX 2005: The 18th Annual Conference*, ed. M. Moens and P. Spyns. *Frontiers in artificial intelligence and applications*. Vol. 134, Amsterdam: IOS Press.

Vázquez-Salceda, J., V. Dignum, and F. Dignum. 2005. Organizing multi-agent systems. *Autonomous Agents and Multi-Agent Systems* 11:307–360.

Vega, J. C. A. 2003, December. *WebODE User's Manual* (Draft version 0.1 ed.). Laboratory of Artificial Intelligence, School of Computer Science, Technical University of Madrid (UPM). http://www.oeg-upm.net/

Velardi, P., R. Navigli, A. Cucchiarelli, and F. Neri. 2005, July. Evaluation of OntoLearn, a methodology for automatic population of domain ontologies. In *Ontology learning from text: Methods, evaluation and applications*, ed. P. Buitelaar, P. Cimiano, and B. Magnini. *Frontiers in artificial intelligence and applications series*, Vol. 123. Amsterdam: IOS Press.

Venturi, G. 2010. Legal language and legal knowledge management applications. In *Semantic processing of legal texts: Where the language of law meets the law of language*, ed. E. Francesconi, S. Montemagni, W. Peters, and D. Tiscornia. *Lecture notes in computer science*. Vol. 6036, 3–26. Berlin/Heidelberg: Springer.

Verheij, B., and J. Hage. 1997. States of affairs, events, and rules: An abstractmodel of the law. In *JURIX'97*, ed. A. Oskamp, R. V. De Mulder, C. van Noortwijk, C. A. F. M. Grütters, K. Ashley and T. Gordon, 3–20. The Foundation for Legal Knowledge Systems, Nijmegen.

VillaGómez, M., V. Guzmán, R. Castillejo, I. Flores, E. de Llera, L. Martín, and A. Arnaiz. 2003. *Manual de organización judicial*. Valencia: Tirant Lo Blanc.

Visser, P., and T. Bench-Capon. 1996a. The formal specification of a legal ontology. In *Proceedings of JURIX'96, Legal knowledge based systems (Foundations of legal knowledge systems)*, ed. R. van Kralingen, H. van den Herik, J. Prins, M. Sergot, and J. Zeleznikow, 15–24. Tilburg: Tilburg University Press.

Visser, P., and T. Bench-Capon. 1997. A comparison of two legal ontologies. In *Proceedings of the First International Workshop on Legal Ontologies (LEGONT'97)*, ed. P. Visser and R. Winkels, Melbourne, 37–45. University of Melbourne.

Visser, P., and T. Bench-Capon. 1998a. Ontologies in the design of legal information systems; towards a library of legal domain ontologies. In *Proceedings of the Conference on Applied Ontology*, Buffalo University, 76–85.

Visser, P. R. 1998. Implicit assumptions in legal knowledge systems. In *Proceedings of the 13th BILETA Conference: The Changing Jurisdiction, Trinity College, Dublin March, 27th–28th*, Dublin. BILETA, British and Irish Legal Education Technology Association.

Visser, P. R. S. 1995. Framer: Source code of a legal knowledge system that performs assessment and planning. Reports on Technical Research in Law Vol. 2, No. 1, University of Leiden, Leiden.

Visser, P. R. S., and T. J. M. Bench-Capon. 1996b. On the reusability of ontologies in knowledge system design. In *Proceedings of the Seventh International Workshop on Database and Expert Systems Applications (DEXA '96)*, Zurich, September 9–10, ed. R. Wagner and H. Thoma, 256–261. Washington: IEEE-CS Press.

Visser, P. R. S., and T. J. M. Bench-Capon. 1998b. A comparison of four ontologies for the design of legal knowledge systems. *Artificial Intelligence and Law* 6:27–57.

Visser, P. R. S., R. W. van Kralingen, and T. J. M. Bench-Capon. 1997. A method for the development of legal knowledge systems. In *Proceedings of the International Conference on Artificial Intelligence and Law (ICAIL'97)*, ed. J. Zeleznikow, D. Hunter, and L. K. Branting, Melbourne, 151–160. New York: ACM Press.

Völker, J., D. Vrandečić, and Y. Sure. 2005, November. Automatic evaluation of ontologies (aeon). In *Proceedings of the 4th International Semantic Web Conference (ISWC2005)*, ed. Y. Gil, E. Motta, V. R. Benjamins, and M. A. Musen, *Lecture notes in computer science*, Vol. 3729, 716–731. Berlin/Heidelberg: Springer.

von Wright, G. 1963. *Norm and action: A logical enquiry. International library of philosophy and scientific method*. London: Routledge & Kegan Paul.

von Wright, G. 1983. *Practical reason. Philosophical papers of Georg Henrik von Wright*. Vol. 1. Oxford: Basil Blackwell.

Vrandečić, D., and A. Gangemi. 2006, October. Unit tests for ontologies. In *Proceedings of the 1st International Workshop on Ontology Content and Evaluation in Enterprise (OntoContent)*, ed. M. Jarrar, C. Ostyn, W. Ceusters, and A. Persidis. *LNCS*, Montpellier, Berlin/Heidelberg: Springer.

Vrandečić, D., and Y. Sure. 2007. How to design better ontology metrics. In *The Semantic Web: Research and applications – Proceedings of the 4th European Semantic Web Conference (ESWC 2007)*, June 3–7, 2007, Innsbruck, ed. E. Franconi, M. Kifer, and W. May. *Lecture notes in computer science*, Vol. 4519, 311–325. Berlin/Heidelberg: Springer.

Wahlgren, P. 1994. A general theory of artificial intelligence and law. In *Legal knowledge based systems (JURIX'94) the foundation for legal knowledge systems: The relation with legal theory*, ed. H. Prakken, A. Muntjewerff, and A. Soeteman, 79–91. Lelystad: Koninklijke Vermande. ISBN 90 5458 190 5.

Walter, A., and G. Nagypál. 2010. Imagenotion: Methodology, tool support and evaluation. In *On the move to meaningful internet systems 2007: CoopIS, DOA, ODBASE, GADA, and IS*, ed. R. Meersman and Z. Tari. *Lecture notes in computer science*, Vol. 4803, 1007–1024. Berlin/Heidelberg: Springer.

Wang, T., B. Parsia, and J. Hendler. 2006. A survey of the web ontology landscape. In *Proceedings of the International Semantic Web Conference (ISWC'06)*, Athens, November 5, 158–171.

Warren, P., R. Studer, and J. Davies. 2006. Introduction. In *Semantic web technology: Trends and research in ontology-based systems*, ed. J. Davies, R. Studer, and P. Warren, Chapter 1, 1–8. Chichester/Hoboken: Wiley.

Weiten, M. 2009. OntoSTUDIO® as a ontology engineering environment. In *Semantic Knowledge Management*, ed. J. Davies, M. Grobelnik, and D. Mladenic. *Lecture notes in computer science*, 51–60. Berlin/Heidelberg: Springer.

Westlaw, T. 2003. The west key number system. Quick reference guide, Thomson Westlaw.

Wielinga, B., and A. T. Schreiber. 1993. Reusable and shareable knowledge bases: A European perspective. In *Proceedings of the International Conference on Building and Sharing of Very Large-Scale Knowledge Bases Proceedings (KB&KS'93)*, December 1–4, ed. K. Fuchi, Tokyo, 103–115.

Wildeboer, G. R., M. C. Klein, and E. Uijttenbroek. 2007. Explaining the relevance of court decisions to laymen. In *Legal knowledge and information systems. JURIX 2007: The Twentieth Annual Conference*, ed. A. R. Lodder and L. Mommers. *Frontiers in artificial intelligence and applications*, Vol. 165, 129–138. Amsterdam: IOS Press.

Winkels, R., A. Boer, and R. Hoekstra. 2002. CLIME: Lessons learned in legal information serving. In *Proceedings of the 15th European Conference on Artificial Intelligence (ECAI 2002)*, Lyon, 230–234. Amsterdam: IOS Press.

Winkels, R., A. Boer, and R. Hoekstra. 2003. Metalex: An XML standard for legal documents. In *Proceedings of the XML Europe Conference: Powering the Information Society*, London.

Winkels, R., A. Boer, and E. Hupkes. 2007. Legal atlas: Access to legal sources through maps. In *Proceedings of the Eleventh International Conference on Artificial Intelligence and Law (ICAIL 2007)*, June 4–8, Palo Alto, 27–36. New York: ACM Press.

Winkels, R., A. W. Boer, J. A. Breuker, and D. J. Bosscher. 1998. Assessment based legal information serving and cooperative dialogue in CLIME. In *Proceedings of the Eleventh Conference of Legal Knowledge-based Systems (JURIX'98)*, ed. J. Hage, T. Bench-Capon, A. Koers, C. de Vey Mestdagh, and C. Grütters, 131–146. Gerard Noodt Instituut (GNI), Nijmegen.

Winkels, R., D. Bosscher, A. Boer, and R. Hoekstra. 2000. Extended conceptual retrieval. In *Legal knowledge and information systems (JURIX-2000)*, ed. J. Breuker, R. Leenes, and R. Winkels, 85–98. Amsterdam: IOS Press.

Winkels, R., D. J. B. Bosscher, A. W. F. Boer, and J. A. Breuker. 1999. Generating exception structures for legal information serving. In *Proceedings of the Seventh International Conference on Artificial Intelligence and Law (ICAIL-99)*, 182–195. New York: ACM.

Wooldridge, M. 2008/2005/1966. Chapter communication. In *An introduction to multiagent systems*, 163–187. Number 8. Chichester: Wiley.

Wyner, A. 2007. An ontology in OWL for legal case-based reasoning. In *Proceedings of the Workshop on Modelling Legal Cases (JURIX'07)*, ed. K. Atkinson, Barcelona.

Wyner, A. 2008. An ontology in OWL for legal case-based reasoning. *Artificial Intelligence and Law* 16:361–387. doi:10.1007/s10506-008-9070-8.

Wyner, A. 2009. An OWL ontology for legal cases with an instantiation of Popov v. Hayashi. In *Modelling legal cases. Proceedings of the Workshop Co-located with the 12th International Conference on Artificial Intelligence and Law.*, ed. K. Atkinson. *IDT series*, Vol. 5, 21–40. IDT/Huygens Editorial.

Wyner, A., and T. Bench-Capon. 2007. Argument schemes for legal case-based reasoning. In *Legal knowledge and information systems. JURIX 2007: The Twentieth Annual Conference*, ed. A. R. Lodder and L. Mommers. *Frontiers in artificial intelligence and applications*, Vol. 165, 139–149. Amsterdam: IOS Press.

Wyner, A., and R. Hoekstra. 2010. A legal case OWL ontology with an instantiation of Popov v. Hayashi. *The Knowledge Engineering Review* 14(2):1–24.

Yamaguchi, T., and M. Kurematsu. 1998. A legal ontology rapid development environment using a machine readable dictionary. In *Proceedings of First International Workshop on Legal Ontologies (LEGONT)* 1997, ed. P. Visser and R. Winkels, 69–73, Melbourne, Australia. http://citeseerx.ist.psu.edu/viewdoc/download?doi=10.1.1.39.5525&rep=rep1&type=pdf

Yan, Y., J. Zhang, and M. Yan. 2006. Ontology modeling for contract: Using OWL to express semantic relations. In *EDOC*, 409–412. Washington: IEEE Computer Society.

Yehia-Dahab, M., H. A. Hasan, and A. Rafea. 2008. TextOntoEx: Automatic ontology construction from natural English text. *Expert Systems with Applications* 34:1474–1480.

Zablith, F. 2009. Evolva: A comprehensive approach to ontology evolution. In *The Semantic Web: Research and applications*, ed. L. Aroyo, P. Traverso, F. Ciravegna, P. Cimiano, T. Heath, E. Hyvönen, R. Mizoguchi, E. Oren, M. Sabou, and E. Simperl. *Lecture notes in computer science*, Vol. 5554, 944–948. Berlin/Heidelberg: Springer.

Zablith, F., M. Sabou, M. d'Aquin, and E. Motta. 2009. Ontology evolution with evolva. In *The Semantic Web: Research and applications*, ed. L. Aroyo, P. Traverso, F. Ciravegna, P. Cimiano, T. Heath, E. Hyvönen, R. Mizoguchi, E. Oren, M. Sabou, and E. Simperl. *Lecture notes in computer science*, Vol. 5554, 908–912. Berlin/Heidelberg: Springer.

Zeleznikow, J., and A. Stranieri. 2001. An ontology for the construction of legal decision support systems. In *Proceedings of the 2nd International Workshop of Legal Ontologies in Conjunction with the 14th Annual International Conference on Legal Knowledge and Information Systems (JURIX'01)*, University of Amsterdam.

Zhao, G., and R. Leary. 2005a, August. AKEM: An ontology engineering methodology in ff poirot. Deliverable of The FFPOIROT IP project (IST-2001-38248) Deliverable D6.8 (WP 6), STARLab VUB.

Zhao, G., and R. Leary. 2005b, August. Topical ontology of fraud. Deliverable of The FFPOIROT IP project (IST-2001-38248) Deliverable D2.3 (WP 2), STARLab VUB.

Zurek, T., and E. Kruk. 2009. Legal advisory system for the agricultural tax law. In *Business information systems workshops*, ed. W. Aalst, J. Mylopoulos, N. M. Sadeh, M. J. Shaw, C. Szyperski, W. Abramowicz, and D. Flejter. *Lecture notes in business information processing*, Vol. 37, 304–309. Berlin/Heidelberg: Springer.

Index

N. Casellas, *Legal Ontology Engineering: Methodologies, Modelling Trends, and the Ontology of Professional Judicial Knowledge*, Law, Governance and Technology Series 3, DOI 10.1007/978-94-007-1497-7,

MIX
Papier aus verantwortungsvollen Quellen
Paper from responsible sources
FSC® C105338

If you have any concerns about our products,
you can contact us on
ProductSafety@springernature.com

In case Publisher is established outside the EU,
the EU authorized representative is:
Springer Nature Customer Service Center GmbH
Europaplatz 3, 69115 Heidelberg, Germany

Printed by Libri Plureos GmbH
in Hamburg, Germany